Basic Research in Parapsychology

SECOND EDITION

Basic Research in Parapsychology

Compiled and Edited by
K. Ramakrishna Rao

SECOND EDITION

McFarland & Company, Inc., Publishers
Jefferson, North Carolina, and London

Library of Congress Cataloguing-in-Publication Data

Basic research in parapsychology / compiled and edited by
   K. Ramakrishna Rao—2nd ed.
       p.   cm.
     Earlier ed. published under title: The basic experiments in
parapsychology.
     Includes bibliographical references and index. ∞
     ISBN 0-7864-1008-6 (softcover : 50# alkaline paper)
     1. Parapsychology.   I. Rao, K. Ramakrishna.   II. Basic
experiments in parapsychology.
BF1029.B38   2001
133.8'07'2—dc21   2001030250

British Library cataloguing data are available

Manufactured in the United States of America

*McFarland & Company, Inc., Publishers
  Box 611, Jefferson, North Carolina 28640
  www.mcfarlandpub.com*

To our grandchildren
Silpa and Kavya
Vivek and Sunila
Mira and Tarun
wishing them the very best
of both worlds, East and West

Contents

Preface

This book is an expanded and revised edition of the 1984 work, slightly mistitled by the publisher, *The Basic Experiments in Parapsychology*. It is offered in response to continued demand for *The Basic Experiments*, which is now out of print. The new edition has undergone extensive revisions. In the first edition we had fourteen experimental reports. Of these eight are retained. Five other reports of experimental studies are added. In addition, seven review articles involving meta-analysis and assessment of evidence in specific areas of psi research are included. I deleted very reluctantly the six experimental reports, which were in the first edition, primarily to include articles containing more recent research and assessment of the overall data base without greatly increasing the size of the book. The feedback I received from those who used *The Basic Experiments* suggested the need to include articles that presented cumulative evidence that showed the replicability of the results of individual experiments.

Considering the fact that the present edition includes an addition to experimental reports, several articles that cumulatively evaluate different areas of psi research we substituted, in the title the word *research* for *experiments*. Thus the present volume is on the one hand decidedly different from the previous edition and on the other hand essentially its continuation with much expanded coverage.

Any selection reflects the editor's bias. The present one is no exception. Many important experiments and research reports that I personally value could not be included in this collection. What we have in these pages are representative samples of a vast literature in this controversial field. In making the selections my concern was to present a relatively few basic experiments that illustrate diverse procedures and broadly reflect the major trends of psi research. As before, this book is addressed to those who wish to get to know the state of the art in experimental parapsychology

1

and who desire to carry out an experiment on their own and are looking for viable experimental procedures and promising areas of research. Also, I believe, this book would be helpful to those seeking to consult original research reports for their own assessment of the degree of validity of psi research results and the viability of the field as a scientific enterprise.

As a partial remedy to the significant omissions in the selection, I have attempted in the introductory chapter to present an overall survey of the field from J.B. Rhine to the present, guiding the reader to the various sources with extensive referencing. The references are given in the section on Bibliography. Some readers may find the omission of skeptical review articles somewhat glaring. No apologies are offered for not including them in this collection. There is no dearth of books containing such articles. They are readily available in numerous publications. Prometheus Books, for example, has over a dozen books in its published list, which are primarily directed at debunking psychical research. I have referred, however, to several critical evaluations of psi research in the introduction.

I gratefully acknowledge the courtesy of authors, editors, and publishers for granting me permission to include in this volume the papers first printed elsewhere. I specially acknowledge my appreciation and thanks to Robert Franklin, the president of McFarland. Robbie is not merely my publisher; he is a true friend whose personal support and professional counsel have meant much for me. Thanks to Stanley Krippner and John Palmer for their helpful feedback and suggestions. My thanks are also to Mr. N.V.V.S.S. Markandeyulu who cheerfully offered his secretarial services.

K. Ramakrishna Rao
35 Dasapalla Hills
Visakhapatnam
March 2001

CHAPTER 1

Introduction: Reality, Replicability, and Lawfulness of Psi

What are parapsychological phenomena? Are they real? Can they be investigated scientifically, i.e., by observation and experiment? Answers to these questions have profound implications for our understanding of who we are and what our place in nature is.

The general public often confuses parapsychology with spiritualism, ufology, astrological, palm- and tarot-card readings, hypnotic regression to "past lives," and a host of other occult practices. In contradistinction to these practices, however, parapsychology is concerned with "psychic" abilities that can be studied by observation and experimentation under controlled conditions. The Parapsychological Association (1989), an international body of professionals engaged in the study and research of parapsychological phenomena, defines parapsychology as the discipline which studies "apparent anomalies of behavior and experience that exist apart from currently known explanatory mechanisms that account for organism-environment and organism-organism information and influence flow" (pp. 394–395). The abilities that lend themselves to this scrutiny are broadly referred to as psi. Basically, two forms of psi are distinguished: extrasensory perception (ESP) and psychokinesis (PK). ESP is the ability to acquire information that is shielded from the senses; PK is the ability to influence external systems that are outside the sphere of one's motor activity. ESP is differentiated into telepathy (ESP of another's thoughts) and clairvoyance (ESP of external objects and events). Precognition and retrocognition refer to ESP of future and past events respectively. Even though parapsychologists have developed specific methods to test for each

3

of these types of psi, it is now increasingly recognized that all of them stem from the same source.

Surveys show that a significant majority of people, even in the Western societies, believes in ESP and related phenomena. Further, many people who responded attest to their occurrence in their own lives. For example, a *Newsweek* poll (November 3–4, 1994) revealed that about 60% of Americans felt the need to experience spiritual growth and that one third of them thought that they had mystical/religious experiences. In another survey, 51% of Charlottesville, VA, residents and 55% of University of Virginia students reported to have experienced some form of ESP (Palmer, 1979). Whereas many scientists outside of parapsychology remain skeptical of the paranormal claims, the consensus among the scientists who are actually involved in psi research is that there is compelling evidence in support of ESP and PK. Why does this divide exist between evidence and scientific acceptance, between popular belief and skepticism on the part of academic establishment? Is the evidence really compelling? This volume attempts to answer that question by bringing together some of the credible reports for the existence of psi.

Background

The evidence for psi is of two kinds. First is the body of reported cases of paranormal experience. The second kind of evidence comes from laboratory experiments. Consider, for example, the case noted by the renowned German philosopher Immanuel Kant. Emanuel Swedenborg, a versatile scholar, visiting a friend in Stockholm, had a sudden "vision" of the raging fire at that very moment in the city of Gothenburg about 300 miles away. Swedenborg described in great detail the fire and how it was extinguished "third door" from his house to about fifteen people gathered at his friend's house. A messenger arrived much later from Gothenburg and, as Kant notes, in the letters he brought with him "the conflagration was described as Swedenborg had stated it" (quoted in Inglis, 1977, p. 132). There was apparently no way Swedenborg could have known about the fire in any normal way. Edmund Gurney and colleagues published in 1886 many cases of apparent telepathy in their book *Phantasms of the Living*. Since then there have been several other surveys of spontaneous ESP experiences, prominent among them being a collection of several thousand cases by L.E. Rhine which is now deposited in the Duke University archives.

Not only belief in but also the practice of "psychic" phenomena can be found throughout recorded history. An interesting account of psychic cases in antiquity is given by Dodds (1971), and Brian Inglis (1977) provides an excellent history of the paranormal prior to World War I in his book *Natural and Supernatural*. However, attempts to investigate "psychic" abilities in a systematic way are fairly recent. In England, the Society for Psychical Research (S.P.R.) was established in 1882, with the express purpose of investigating "without prejudice or prepossession and in a scientific spirit those faculties of man, real or supposed, which appear to be inexplicable on any generally recognized hypothesis." Early experimental work at the S.P.R. was in the area of telepathy. For example, Henry and Eleanor Sidgwick and G.A. Smith (1889) carried out interesting experiments aimed at testing the possibility of telepathy under hypnosis. ESP under hypnosis was also the subject of investigation in France by Pierre Janet (1886) and in the erstwhile U.S.S.R. by the physiologist L.L. Vasiliev (1963). Also in France, Charles Richet (1975/1923) carried out ESP tests with playing cards and attempted to apply the calculus of probability to evaluate the significance of the results.

Among the first to experimentally study ESP in the U.S. was J.E. Coover (1975/1917) at Stanford University. His studies were followed by the experiments of Leonard Troland (1976/1917) and G.H. Estabrooks (1961/1927) at Harvard University. About the same time, a group of psychologists in Germany carried out an ESP experiment, reported by H.J.F.W. Brugmans (1922), which is still cited as an important evidential experiment (Beloff, 1980).

It was not, however, until J.B. Rhine's arrival at Duke University that parapsychology as an experimental science was born. The scientific stage of parapsychology began, as Brian Mackenzie (1977) has noted, with the founding of the Parapsychology Laboratory at Duke University in 1927, or perhaps with the first major output of this laboratory, Rhine's *Extra-Sensory Perception* (1973/1934). By 1940, when another major work entitled *Extrasensory Perception After Sixty Years* (Pratt et al., 1966/1940) was published, 145 experimental studies of ESP had been carried out.

Since then, there has been a significant increase in the number and sophistication of psi experiments. A large body of experimental data has accumulated which is strongly supportive of the reality of psi; and with this support, the attention of research scientists in parapsychology has shifted. The attention that was once directed toward proving the existence of psi in its various forms is now turned towards understanding its nature. By exploring the attitudes, moods, personality factors and states of mind of persons who participate in psi experiments, researchers hope to see the psi process revealed. Also being studied for this purpose are cognitive processes such as memory and subliminal perception, as well as sex differences and the effects of motivation, feedback, distance, and target differences. The discovery of psi-missing, the tendency to significantly miss the target when attempting to hit it, has further led to a variety of research strategies and interesting results.

Clearly, it would be impractical to include in one volume all the major experimental reports, which run into several hundreds. Since a few selected ones are unlikely to enable a discerning reader to have a reasonable understanding and insight into the strength of the evidence, and what it means, I have included in this collection not only a representative sample of experimental reports but also a few review articles containing cumulative analysis and evaluation of existing databases. Together, I believe, they convey a sense of the state of psi research today.

The Conclusive Experiment

Since the publication of Rhine's monograph *Extra-Sensory Perception* in 1934, there have been numerous experimental reports that provided evidence for ESP and PK. There were also various kinds of criticism against the evidential value of Rhine's results, but Rhine held his ground. He stoutly maintained that none of the criticisms invalidated the evidential value of the results barring a presumption of fraud on the part of the investigators, an unlikely possibility (see Rao, 1982). There were also some successful replications of Rhine's experiments. However, there were a few others who were unable to replicate successfully Rhine's results. This led to demands for a "conclusive experiment," a completely "foolproof" study that would control for all conceivable error, including experimenter fraud. I find the demand for an error-proof experiment an impossible goal, at best a tempting mirage, because in retrospect one can always speculate on a possible source of error. If, however, by "conclusive" we make a more modest claim, viz., that it is highly improbable that the results of a successful experiment are due to some possible artifact, then, a good case can be made for more than one such experiment in parapsychology.

John Beloff (1980) listed seven experiments which, according to him, provide "an overwhelming case for accepting the reality of psi phenomena" (p. 94). Beloff based his selection on the following criteria:

(a) the chief experimenter must be someone of good standing and long experience who is well known to the international parapsychological community; (b) the report of the experiment must have appeared in a reputable scientific journal; (c) the overall scores must reach a level where the odds against chance are so high that any suspicion of selective reporting or optional stopping can be discounted; (d) conditions must be such as to rule out effectively the possibility of sensory cueing or of cheating by the subject; (e) the scoring rate should, if possible, be at a level which would exclude any counter-explanation in terms of some subtle artifact; (f) other things being equal an experimental finding which has been confirmed many times is to be preferred to one which is unique or has seldom been replicated; (g) the list should represent a variety of methods and effects [1980, p. 92].

Indeed, parapsychology can boast of a number of well controlled experiments which have provided strong evidence that ESP occurs in a variety of forms such as telepathy, clairvoyance and precognition, and that PK acts on diverse systems, including quantum physical processes and explicit and implicit mental events. The first experiment that comes as close as one could get to a conclusive experiment is the Pearce-Pratt series by Rhine and Pratt (Chapter 2).

Rhine's continued work at Duke University for about one half of a century gave the field "a shared language, methods, and problems" (McVaugh & Mauskopf 1976), provided "radical innovation and a high potential for elaboration" (Allison 1973, p. 34) and, in short, turned psychical research, an amateur endeavor, into parapsychology, a professional scientific study of anomalous psychological phenomena. Rhine's experimental procedure was simple and easy to repeat. He asked his subjects to guess the randomized order of the cards in a deck of twenty-five consisting of five each of five symbols: circle, cross, wavy lines, square, and star. His testing procedures were such that the subjects were well shielded from the target cards so as to rule out the possibility of their gaining any sensory access to the symbols or enabling them to make correct calls by logical inferences. By August 1, 1933, he collected 85,724 trials with an average score of 7.1 correct guesses per 25 guesses. The probability that such a result could occur by chance is extremely small indeed (Rhine 1973/1934).

The Pearce-Pratt series is a methodological culmination of the early attempts to obtain laboratory evidence for ESP. This series, which had special precautions to exclude all possibilities of error, including two experimenter controls, independent records and several hundred yards of distance between the target cards and the subject, gave highly significant results supporting the ESP hypothesis.

C.E.M. Hansel published a brief critique of this series in 1961 and an expanded version of it later (Hansel, 1966, 1980). Hansel does not fault the analyses of the data or the significance of the results. He accepts that "something other than chance obviously was operating in each of the four subseries" (1980, p. 112). Hansel argues, however, that the subject, Pearce, could have cheated to obtain the high scores. There is of course no evidence of cheating by the subject. Hansel goes on to describe imaginary scenarios, such as drilling a hole in a trap door located in the ceiling and later filling in the hole without being observed, that would have permitted the subject or his accomplice to obtain sensory information about the targets. Rhine and Pratt (1961) pointed out how implausible the above argument was.

In his book of 1966 and its subsequent editions, Hansel (1980, 1989) expands on his criticism and makes the following points to discredit the Pearce-Pratt experiment: (1) it was not reported in adequate detail at the time it was carried out; (2) there were discrepancies in its different published versions; and (3) the experimental conditions were such that the subject, Pearce, could have cheated in a number of possible ways.

Let us consider the fraud issue first. Neither Hansel, nor anyone else for that matter, presented any evidence or circumstances that suggest even remotely that Pearce did cheat. The best Hansel (1980) was able to say was his concluding statement in the book, "A further unsatisfactory feature lies in the fact that a statement has not been made by the central figure, Hubert Pearce. The experimenters state that trickery was impossible, but what would Pearce have said? Perhaps one day he will give his own account of the experiment" (p. 123). This statement does not tally with the facts. Contrary to Hansel's expectations, Pearce did make a statement in which he unequivocally asserted that he did not cheat (Stevenson, 1967).

The implausible scenario imaginatively described by Hansel, that Pearce could have sneaked out of the library and peered through the transom at the top of the door to Pratt's room to obtain target information, based in part on a distorted architectural plan (Stevenson, 1967), highlights the fact that a determined skeptic can always call attention to certain features of the experiment to make it look less than definitive. In the case of the Pearce-Pratt experiment, for example, Hansel's exercise is one of arguing that Pearce's whereabouts during the experiment were not completely monitored, leaving the possibility that he could have cheated, however improbable that may seem to be. Even if we assume that the conditions of the Pearce-Pratt experiment were such that the subject could not have possibly cheated, it could still be argued that the subject and the experimenters conspired to falsely obtain the results. In the final analysis, it can be seen that fraud can never be completely eliminated. Consequently, the fraud hypothesis becomes essentially nonfalisifiable in the sense that we cannot absolutely rule out fraud in any given experiment. A specific hypothesis of fraud can be subjected to a test of falsification, but fraud as such can never be completely ruled out. Inasmuch as one can always imagine after the fact some hypothetical fraud scenario, any attempt to completely eliminate fraud will catch us in an infinite regress, carrying out experiment after experiment without ever rejecting absolutely the possibility of fraud.

Conceding that "it is difficult to see how either Rhine or Pratt, unaided, could have cheated to bring about the result," Hansel goes on to raise questions about the competence of Rhine and Pratt as experimenters. He makes much of two observations: (1) that the original report of the Pearce-Pratt experiment did not give all the details of procedure and experimental conditions that may be considered necessary now, and (2) that there are some discrepancies between the various published reports of the experiment. Even some parapsychologists have accused Rhine, somewhat unfairly I believe, of inadequately reporting the results of the Pearce-Pratt experiment first. Stevenson (1967), for example writes, "Rhine had already published informal reports [of the Pearce-Pratt experiment] in two of his popular books and it is doubtful procedure in science to announce one's result first to the general public and then (in this case many years later) present a detailed report for scientists" (p. 259).

It is not the case that Rhine announced his results first to the public. The results of the Pearce-Pratt experiment were first published in *The Journal of Abnormal and Social Psychology* (Rhine, 1936) and were only subsequently mentioned in his popular books. (The first of these, *New Frontiers of the Mind,* appeared in 1938.) *The Journal of Abnormal and Social Psychology* is a respected journal in mainstream psychology and Rhine had no editorial control over it. Does this not clearly imply that the additional details that we now consider necessary were not considered so then by the psychologists who refereed his paper and the editor who published it? If the *Journal of Parapsychology* was in existence at that time and Rhine had published his report in it with inadequate details, we might have had some reason to blame him for not giving all the details. The truth of the matter is that details of the sort that we now require of parapsychological reports were simply not found necessary then. When it became increasingly clear that further details of the experimental procedure were called for, Rhine and Pratt published a more detailed report in 1954.

Finally, the discrepancies between various published accounts of the experiment pointed out by Hansel are trivial and clerical, and none is sufficient to call into question the veracity of the experiment or the credibility of the experimenters. Interestingly, Hansel makes more errors in his very brief review of the experiment than do the authors in their report (see Rao, 1981, 1992).

There were of course other critics of Rhine's experiments (cf., Pratt et al., 1940; Rao, 1982). Some of the criticisms were constructive. They enabled Rhine and others who attempted to replicate his early experiments to improve the methods of collecting data and their analyses.

The next selection in this collection represents the important experiments of Helmut Schmidt. His research comes as close as one can get to a definitive experiment in such controversial areas as parapsychology. His first psi experiments (Schmidt, 1969) were conducted when he was a physicist at Boeing Scientific Laboratories. Schmidt's experiments were carried out with specially built machines that controlled against artifacts such as recording errors, sensory leakage, subject cheating, and improper analysis of the data. The Schmidt machine, as it has come to be known, randomly selected the targets and automatically recorded both the target selections and subject's responses. The subject's task was to select which of the four lamps in the panel would light up and then press the corresponding button to indicate the selection. Random lighting of the lamps was achieved by a sophisticated random event generator (REG) with a weak radioactive source, strontium 90. After extensive testing in control trials, it was determined that the output of the REG did not deviate significantly from chance. The results of each of the three experimental series gave highly significant results suggesting ESP on the part of the subjects tested.

Schmidt published several experimental reports in which REGs were used to test for ESP and PK. Chapter 3 is a reprint of his 1973 report. In this experiment he tested the PK mode of psi. In these tests the source of randomness is electronic noise and not radioactive decay. The importance of Schmidt's work is many-fold. First, it represents one of the major experimental paradigms in contemporary psi research. Second, his results are regarded by most parapsychologists as solid evidence for psi. Third, Schmidt used fully-automated equipment to record the targets as well as subjects' responses, which rules out the possibility of unintended errors. In fact, his experimental set up was far superior to the VERITAC machine designed by W.R. Smith et al. (1963), which was hailed by Hansel (1966) as "admirably designed." Fourth, in some of his studies Schmidt had attempted through a multi-experimenter design to control against his own competence and reliability as an experimenter. For example, in one of Schmidt's PK experiments (Schmidt, Morris & Rudolph, 1986) the experimenter himself was supervised by observes in another laboratory in order that negligence and even fraud by the experimenter could be ruled out. Interestingly, the results of this experiment also provided significant evidence for psi. Fifth, the REG experiments were extensively replicated by other investigators such as Robert Jahn and associates at Princeton University (Jahn, 1982). Finally, Schmidt's experiments withstood detailed scrutiny by critics. Hansel (1981) attempted to show the "weakness" of Schmidt's experiments under three headings: (1) experimental design, (2) unsatisfactory features of the equipment, and (3) inability to confirm the findings. Each of these criticisms was shown to be inadequate and unsubstantiated. (For a point by point discussion of Hansel's criticism of Schmidt's experiments see Rao & Palmer, 1987).

Replication

Whereas a call for a conclusive and completely error-proof experiment seems to be somewhat misconstrued, the emphasis on the need for replication, especially when controversial empirical claims are made, is well founded. If parapsychological phenomena are not replicable, though genuine, they would hardly excite any scientific interest. Isolated findings and unique events ordinarily hold little interest to scientists, unless they lead to or are capable of leading to some kind of general law. ESP as a laboratory effect must be repeatedly observed with reasonable ease in order that it can be studied and understood as a natural phenomenon. Also, the necessity of a foolproof experiment recedes into the background as the phenomenon becomes increasingly replicable.

As mentioned, others have replicated Rhine's ESP experiments. By 1940 there were numerous experimental reports confirming Rhine's results (see Pratt, et al., 1940). Likewise, the Schmidt's REG experiments were also successfully carried out independently by several other investigators. The most prominent of these came from the laboratory of Robert Jahn at Princeton University (Jahn, 1982; Nelson, et al., 1984). In the experiments by Jahn and colleagues, REGs based on a commercial noise source were used. The subject's task in these experiments was to influence the device mentally to produce an excess of hits on predesignated PK+ trials and an excess of misses on PK-trials. The hits were displayed on the instrument panel and were permanently recorded on a strip printer and stored in a computer file. Jahn and colleagues utilized a variety of experimental strategies, equipment and modes of feedback to the subjects. For example, in some experiments a large scale mechanical device called "Random Mechanical Cascade" was used. In this device polystyrene spheres trickle downward through a five-chute array and are scattered into 19 collection bins. The subject's task is to shift by volition the mean bin population to the right or the left. In another experiment the REG units are used to drive two competing scenes to dominate on the computer screen. The subject attempts to cause mentally a pre-selected scene to dominate over the other.

Jahn and associates carried out more than 1000 experimental series during a twelve-year period. The report reprinted in this volume (Chapter 4) is a summary review of the results with some 100 subjects. Although the absolute effect sizes are very small, the huge databases provide strong evidence for psi ($p=3.5 \times 10^{-13}$). Other interesting findings include differences in the scores of male and female subjects and serial position effects. It was also observed that the effects obtained with REGs could not be obtained when fully deterministic pseudo random sources were used.

The Princeton laboratory is one of several that have successfully replicated the REG-PK experiments. Parapsychologists have extensively utilized a statistical technique known as meta-analysis to judge cumulatively the reality and strength of an effect by examining a group of conceptually or methodologically related studies. In fact, as early as 1940 Rhine and associates (Pratt et al., 1940/1966) attempted such an analysis, albeit in a preliminary fashion. Now, the parapsychological literature contains several reports of sophisticated meta-analyses. Some of these are reprinted in this volume. Radin, May and Thomson (1986) made a survey of all the binary REG experiments published between 1969 and 1984, i.e., between the time Schmidt first published the results of his psi experiments and the time of their report. This review, which included 332 individual experiments carried out by 30 principal investigators, showed that 71 of them gave statistically significant results in favor of the existence of psi. The combined binomial probability of all the studies is shown to be so small ($p = 5.4 \times 10^{-43}$) that it is virtually impossible that the reported results could be attributable to chance coincidence.

Chapter 5 is a report by R.D. Nelson and D.I. Radin (1989) which contains a meta-analysis of more than 800 REG experiments by some 68 investigators. Again, the results show a statistically robust effect which suggests the replicability of REG PK experiments, like Rhine's early card experiments.

Free-Response ESP Testing in Natural Settings

J.B. Rhine and associates used forced-choice tests almost exclusively in their ESP card experiments. The REG experiments, though very different from card tests, also utilize forced-choice procedures in which the subject is aware of the possible target alternatives, e.g., the five symbols in ESP cards, or the four lights in Schmidt's machine. Unlike forced-choice experiments, in free-response experiments the target pool is unknown to the subject. In the early stages of psychical research free-response tests were extensively used. They were, however, overshadowed by the success of Rhine's forced-choice experiments, which appeared to be simple and easy to evaluate for statistical significance. With the emergence of suitable statistical techniques to evaluate free-response data with the same ease as forced-choice experiments, the use of free-response targets has become more common. Now, many experimenters regard free-response tests as capable of eliciting rich and more meaningful responses than the card experiments. Moreover, free-response experiments appear to mimic life situations and to be better suited for administering during naturally occurring states of the mind believed to be conducive to psi. For example, remote viewing experiments are modeled after such "psychic" practices as locating missing persons and "divining" hidden or lost objects. Similarly, dream-ESP experiments utilize the state of dreaming to test for psi. Free-response targets are generally employed in all these test situations.

Remote Viewing Studies

At Stanford Research Institute, Russell Targ and Harold Puthoff successfully carried out remote viewing experiments. The remote viewing protocol simply consists of having an experimenter (the outbound experimenter) visit a randomly selected target site and asking the subject, who is sensorially unaware of the location, to describe to a second experimenter the place which the outbound experimenter is visiting at the time. A judge later attempts to match the subject's description to a predetermined pool of target cites. The results of the Targ-Puthoff experiments were published in their book *Mind Reach* (1977). A more technical version of it may be found in Puthoff and Targ (1976). Attempts to replicate Targ-Puthoff experiments include those by J. Bisaha and B.J. Dunne (1979) and Robert Jahn and Brenda Dunne(1987).

Some of the remote viewing experiments were severely criticized with some justification. D. Marks and R. Kammann (1978, 1980) criticized the Targ-Puthoff experiments on the ground that the subjects' transcripts, which were used to match with the target locations, may have contained clues relating to the order of the trials. These clues could have been helpful to the judges in successfully matching the target locations with the subjects' descriptions. Targ and Puthoff attempted to counter this criticism by conducting new judging and fresh analysis after the presumed clues were edited out (Tart, Puthoff, & Targ, 1980). Marks and Scott (1986), however, were not satisfied with the adequacy of the editing, which did not really matter because the target sequence was also randomized. In the Bisha-Dunne experiments the judges were provided with pictures of the target location. It is argued that the pictures may have contained cues as to weather and seasonal variations that might have provided for an artificial match of the target location and the transcript (Marks, 1986). Again, some experiments by Jahn and Dunne were criticized on the grounds of nonrandom target selection (Hansel, Utts, & Markwick (1994), but this was disputed by Dobyns, Dunne, Jahn & Nelson (1994).

Chapter 6 is a report of a remote viewing experiment carried out by Marilyn Schlitz and Elmar Gruber. The subject was in Detroit, Michigan while the experimenter visited sites in Rome, Italy. This experiment is also not completely free from possible artifacts. In this case, the judges had access to the impressions of the agent. Like the photographs in the Bisaha-Dunne experiments it is suggested that they may provide cues that could bias the judge's matching. Allowing for the possibility of such artifacts, (though they consider such a possibility quite remote), Schlitz and Gruber (1981) arranged for rejudging by new judges, without providing them the agents impressions (Appendix, Chapter 6). The results of rejudging also showed statistically significant evidence for psi. Some critics are not satisfied. Ray Hyman (1986) argued that since Gruber, who acted as the agent, was associated with the translation of the subject's transcript into Italian for presentation to the judges he may have biased the translation so that the judge's matching would still be successful.

The remote viewing experiments, as mentioned, were first designed and carried out by Targ and Puthoff at Stanford Research Institute. They were funded for several years by US government agencies. Federal government support continued for this line of research at SRI International and later (1992–94) at Science Applications International Corporation (SAIC). Edwin May and associates at SAIC conducted several ESP studies, which they prefer to call anomalous cognition experiments. These experiments are somewhat procedurally different from the original remote viewing studies and are more like traditional ESP tests with distance intervening between the targets and the subject. For example, in the study by Lantz, Luke, and May (1994) there was no sender. The main finding of this study is that free-response ESP studies can be conducted successfully without a sender in clairvoyance type of experiments.

As a member of the panel to review the Federal Government's program in remote viewing and related areas, statistician Jessica Utts reviewed the relevant work within the broad framework of contemporary psi research. Utilizing eight methodological criteria, Utts found significant evidence for the existence of psi. Chapter 7 contains Utts' assessment of the evidence. Ray Hyman (1996) another member of the panel, also found little to criticize in the SAIC experiments. His main concern, however, was that in these experiments, the main investigator, Ed May, served as the judge. May, however, was completely blind to the targets when he performed the judging. Therefore, it is difficult to see how he could have biased the results. Hyman prefers, however, to withhold his judgment on the significance of these results as evidence for psi because, in his view, they may contain hidden biases and subtle errors that may come to surface in due course. Thus, it would seem, as Douglas Stokes (1998) pointed out, " Hyman and other critics are starting to absolve themselves of the need to point to possible flaws in an experiment when they fail to find any. It is now evidently sufficient merely to state that there may be undetected flaws" (p. 166). More recently, Richard Wiseman and Julie Milton (1998) pointed out some possible pathways for information leakage and weakness in the conduct of some of these experiments. May (1998), however, questioned the possible leakage hypothesis of Wiseman and Milton and argued that they simply ignored contradictory evidence in their criticism of the Lantz, Luke, and May (1994) experiments.

ESP in Dreams

According to some estimates (L.E. Rhine, 1962), 65 percent of spontaneous psychic experiences occur in dreams. A number of psychoanalysts have reported what appear to be paranormal dreams in the therapeutic setting (Devereux, 1953). Therefore, it is only natural to consider the dream state as psi-conducive. According to Van de Castle (1977), the earliest experimental effort to paranormally influence a dream was reported by H.M. Weserman in 1819.

With the advent of dream-monitoring techniques made possible by the discovery of such physiological correlates of the dream state as rapid eye movements (REMs), the opportunity has come about to study ESP dreams in laboratory settings. Montague Ullman and associates were quick to avail themselves of it. The full account of a decade-long study of ESP and dreams at the Maimonides Medical Center in Brooklyn, N.Y., is to be found in the book by Ullman, Krippner, and Vaughan (1973). The paper that is reprinted in this volume (Chapter 8) is one of several publications from the Maimonides group. Other studies by the group include Ullman, Krippner, & Feldstein (1966), Krippner (1969), Ullman, & Krippner (1970), Honorton, Krippner, & Ullman (1971), Krippner et al. (1971), Krippner, Honorton, & Ullman (1972), and Krippner, Honorton, & Ullman (1973).

Among the attempts to replicate the Maimonides dream studies is the one carried out by E. Belvedere and D. Foulkes (1971) at the University of Wyoming, which did not give significant ESP results. A comprehensive review of ESP and dreams is to be found in a chapter by Robert Van de Castle (1977) in Wolman's *Handbook of Parapsychology*. The review, in Vande Castle's words, "offers very encouraging evidence that telepathic incorporation of stimuli into dreams can be demonstrated under good experimental conditions" (p. 494). Michael Persinger and Stanley Krippner (1989) reported that in the Maimonides dream studies, the 24-hour periods in which the most accurate telepathic dreams occurred had significantly quiter geometric activity than the days before or after.

In chapter 9 we have the more recent review by Yale psychologist Irvin Child (1985), who attempts to answer the question of ESP in dreams. After a careful review of the Maimonides research by Ullman and colleagues and the attempted replications of it, Child examines incisively the manner in which the Maimonides research is represented in books by psychologists. Pointing out numerous distortions and misrepresentations of ESP research in these books, Child argues that "psychologists are ill served by the apparently scholarly books that seem to convey information about the dream experiments." In Child's view the Maimonides dream-ESP experiments "clearly merit careful attention from psychologists who, for whatever reason, are interested in the question of ESP."

Experimenter Effects in Psi Research

In contrast to research in the physical sciences and to a degree in the biological sciences, the experimenter is an important factor in studies of humans. In psychological studies the occurrence of experimenter expectancy effects (Rosenthal, 1966; Rosenthal & Rubin, 1978) is widely acknowledged. It has been observed from the early days of scientific research into psi that the experimenter is a relevant variable. It is now well known that some researchers are more successful than others in obtaining significant psi scores. This is sometimes construed by those who take a skeptical stance regarding psi phenomena as a weakness in psi research. A strong case can be made, however, that experimenter effects observed in parapsychological research are genuine psi effects and not artifactual outcomes of experimenter incompetence or unreliability. The main problem with parapsychological experimenter effects is that their range and modus operandi are still unclear. This is hardly surprising, because the nature of psi itself is little understood.

The very first volume of the *Journal of Parapsychology* contains a paper by V. Sharp and C.C. Clark (1937) which reports results that suggest "some observers ... may be unable to secure positive results, while other observers are better able to secure good results" (p. 142). For example, it is observed that the same subjects averaged 4.30 hits per a run of 25 trials with one experimenter and 5.38 hits per run with another experimenter. The difference in the average run scores obtained by the two experimenters is statistically significant, suggesting possible influence by the experimenter on the performance of the subjects. Sharp and Clark speculated that the difference between the two experimenters was due to the way they acted in administering the tests, the negative scores resulting from the manifest distractions caused by one experimenter's behavior. Honorton, Ramsey, and Cabibbo (1975) carried out an experimental study to test the hypothesis that the way the experimenter interacts with the subjects has an effect on their ESP scores. They administered ESP tests to two groups of subjects. With one group the experimenter acted in a friendly and supportive way and the subjects in this group obtained significant positive scores. The other group, with which the experimenter interacted in an abrupt, formal, and unfriendly manner, showed psi-missing. There are several other studies in the early literature, which suggest that the performance of ESP subjects can be influenced by the experimenter (Pratt, & Price 1938; Osis, & Dean, 1964).

If the ESP performance of a subject is influenced by the way the experimenter deals with the subject, it is hardly surprising. There is, however, more to the influence of the experimenter on the performance of ESP subjects than the usual psychological variables like interest, expectation, motivation and handling of the subjects. Consider, for example, a study reported by D.J. West and G.W. Fisk (1953). In this study, 20 subjects attempted to guess the hour a concealed clock card was showing (the target cards were printed like the face of a clock and were concealed in an envelope). Unknown to the subjects, half of these concealed packs of cards were prepared by Fisk and the other half by West. All the target decks were mailed to the subjects by Fisk. The results showed that the subjects obtained highly significant ESP scores on the decks prepared by Fisk and only chance scores on those prepared by West. Assuming that the packs prepared by Fisk were as secure as those provided by West, we have here an instance of a parapsychological (or psi) experimenter effect, which, if genuine, can account for the differences in the success rate of even well motivated experimenters. That success in psi experiments is partially dependent on the psi abilities of the experimenters has several ramifications. First, it gives a handle to those who question experimenter competence and reliability. Second, even for those convinced of the reality of psi, the psi experimenter effect becomes a confounding variable that may contaminate the data and make it difficult to investigate specific hypotheses. Therefore, it is important to obtain unequivocal evidence for psi experimenter effects and see if any genuine limit can be set to the extent to which an experimenter may influence the ESP performance of a subject. At the present time, the evidence for the existence of psi experimenter effects appears strong, as the reviews indicate (Kennedy & Taddonio, 1976; White, 1976, 1977), even though their range and magnitude are still unclear.

Chapter 10 is a combined report by two experimenters, one who is known to be successful in eliciting psi effects, and the other who has a record of failures. This study, which addresses the question of experimenter effects in psi research, is built around the commonly experienced phenomenon of being started at. A feeling of being stared at when no one is directly looking at you, is reported by a vast majority of the population. In some surveys the percentage of those reporting such experiences is as high as 80% (Sheldrake, 1994) and 94% (Braud, Shafer, & Andrews, 1990). Attempts to test experimentally the genuineness of this as a psi effect date back to 1913 when J.C. Coover at Stanford University unsuccessfully tested 10 subjects. Subsequently, J.J. Poortman (1959) and D.M. Peterson (1978) reported results which showed that the subjects reported more often that they were being stared at when someone was covertly staring at them (i.e., unnoticed by the subjects) than during control periods when no one was staring at them.

William Braud, Shafer, and Andrews (1990) designed a more sophisticated study in which they attempted to utilize autonomic nervous system activity as an indication of the subject's detection of covert staring, in place of conscious guessing by the subject. The reason behind this move is the belief that the detection may take place at the level of the unconscious and that it may manifest more readily in the form of spontaneous behavioral and body changes than in overt recognition. In fact, people often report tingling of the skin when they are stared at. Accordingly, the experimenters monitored the electrodermal activity of the subjects during periods of covert staring and nonstaring, which were randomly dispersed.

The results revealed that the electrodermal properties of the subjects correlated to a statistically significant degree with the intense attention of the staring person.

In an attempt to replicate the above experiment of Braud et al. (1990), Schlitz and LaBerge (1997) tested 39 subjects in a total of 48 sessions. The subjects were randomly assigned to experimental and control periods and during these periods their phasic skin conductance responses were sampled once a second for the 30 second period of recording. During the experimental sessions, unknown to the subject, an observer situated in a different room from the subject stared intently at the television image of the subject. During the control periods, the observer spent the time reading a book and tried "to shift his or her attention from the subject." The results confirmed the hypothesis of greater skin conductance activity during periods of covert observation than during control periods.

Marilyn Schlitz has a long track record of being a successful psi experimenter. She has been successful, as we have noted, in the remote staring experiments as well. Richard Wiseman is a skeptic about the claims of parapsychology and his attempts to replicate the remote staring experiments were unsuccessful in the past (Wiseman & Smith, 1994; Wiseman et al., 1995). Now the two, the skeptic and the proponent of psi, joined together to replicate the remote staring phenomena. Each carried out a separate experiment; but they conducted them in the same location and used the same equipment. The subjects were drawn from the same pool. The results are, however, different. Schlitz's series shows statistically significant evidence of a psi effect, whereas Wiseman's data are at chance.

It is interesting to note that the Wiseman-Schlitz study is a replication in two important senses. First, the Schlitz part is a successful replication of her earlier work, which in turn was a replication of Braud's work. Second, the Wiseman part is a replication of his failure to obtain evidence for this kind of psi effect. Thus we are led to confront the reality of psi experimenter effects. However inconvenient they may be for interpreting experimental results, and whatever may be the difficulties they may pose for designing psi experiments, experimenter effects have come to stay in parapsychology, and future researchers must attempt to address the range, magnitude and the process of these effects.

Some Other Aspects of Parapsychological Phenomena

Parapsychological research has gone well beyond the question of the existence of psi. As mentioned earlier, there has been experimental demonstration of various forms of psi such as ESP (Chapter 2) and PK (Chapter 4). Attempts are underway to discover lawful regularities between psi and other psychological and physical variables. There are indeed several significant process oriented research results such as the finding that ESP is apparently unconstrained, unlike any other abilities, by space/time variables or the complexity of the task. We could not include in this volume, for reasons of space limitations, many of the important reports containing these results. To make up for this, we review in this section some of the major findings that relate psi to other variables.

Space, Time, and the Complexity of Psi Task

Quite early in his experimental investigations, J.B. Rhine found that the distance between the subject and the target in ESP experiments made no significant difference in the success rate of his subjects (Rhine, 1934). Similarly, Russian physiologist L.L. Vasiliev (1963) reported that he was able to hypnotize his subject telepathically during randomly determined periods of time from a distance of about 1,700 kilometers. He found also that his attempts to shield any possible electromagnetic wave transmission between the hypnotist and the subject by placing them in separate Farady cages did not diminish the success rate of the telepathic induction of hypnosis. Marilyn Schlitz and Elmar Gruber (Chapter 7) successfully carried out transcontinental remote viewing experiments in which the subject, totally unaware of it sensorially, attempted to describe a randomly selected location in another continent being visited by an experimenter.

There is also experimental evidence to support the precognition hypothesis. As in spontaneous cases in which people have reported their experiences of having information about future events apparently without any other means of knowing them, experimental studies have also shown that it is possible to have information about a target that does not exist now but will come into being at a time in the future. For example, it was found in some remote viewing experiments that the subjects were able to successfully describe the location where the experimenter will be at a predetermined future time (Jahn, 1982). Earlier, J.B. Rhine (1938) had reported significant results suggesting that his subjects were able to guess correctly the target order in a deck of ESP cards randomized after the subjects made their calls. In a meta-analysis of forced-choice experiments comparing clairvoyance, and precognition, F. Steinkamp, J. Milton, and R.L. Morris (1998) found no significant difference in the success rate in precognition and clairvoyance studies, even though the cumulative overall effect is significant in both clairvoyance and precognition studies.

Another significant aspect of psi appears to be the relative ineffectiveness of task complexity in constraining it. Rex Stanford (1977) has reviewed the relevant literature and concluded that the efficiency of PK function is not reduced by an increase in the complexity of the target system. Thus, psi, which is believed to involve no sensory mediation, is also found not to be constrained by the variables of space and time nor by the physical properties of the items of information. There is nothing to indicate from the research results available to date that any energy patterns emanating from the target objects reach the subject in ESP tests. It would seem that somehow the subject has access to information under conditions that simply do not permit any known physical energy transmission from the target. Such a possibility raises serious questions about the subject-object distinctions in cognitive processes and the representational theory of knowledge in general.

For example, if it is the case that a subject (S) in a telepathy experiment is able to know what an agent(A) is thinking at a particular time, what then is the cause of S's knowledge? One would normally assume that the cause of S's knowledge is the act of A's thinking. We know, however, that A's act of thinking cannot cause telepathy in S, because not only are we unable to discover any causal sequences connecting his act of thinking and S's extrasensory knowledge of his thoughts, but we also know that S could do the same thing if A were not actually thinking at that time but were to do so at some time in the future.

It would seem that C.G. Jung had a better insight into this problem than his critics when he described ESP in terms of synchronicity or acausal relationships (Jung & Pauli, 1953). Similarly, Polanyi's (1958) concept of tacit knowing appears to be more appropriate than conventional perceptual models to conceptualize paranormal awareness. Tacit knowing, according to Polanyi, consists in the "capacity of attending from one thing to another"—that is, from a *proximal* term to the *distal* term. The perceptual process, for example, consists in the tacit integration of perceptual clues into feelings. The way we see an object is mainly determined by our awareness of certain events inside our bodies, which are not observable in themselves. In a perceptual process, then, we are attending from the internal processes to the qualities of things outside.

Now, if the tacit integration or structuring of perceptual clues that results in meaningful experiences is fundamental for perceptual knowledge, there is then no good sense in which we can say that the perceptual experiences are produced primarily by the action of material things on our senses. While the perceptual clues may be necessary, on occasion, to have veridical perceptions, they may not be sufficient. It is important to note that the clues of the steps involved in tacit knowing need not be identifiable and in some instances may not even be discernible. As Polanyi puts it, "Tacit knowing will tend to reach conclusions in ignorance of the steps involved."

Likewise, ESP seems to involve a sort of tacit knowing in ignorance of the clues involved. In an ESP experience we are not merely ignorant of the clues involved, but the clues themselves do not appear to have any sensory basis. It is more like the stage I processing speculated by L.E. Rhine, which is believed to be unlike other cognitive processes. At this stage, the individual psyche resembles a microcosm, potentially capable of acquiring all the information in the cosmos. "ESP" as L.E. Rhine (1967) put it, "is not limited by inherent unavailability, but by the person, the individual himself, through whose psychological structure it must be filtered into consciousness" (p. 264).

Subliminal Perception and ESP

There are interesting similarities between ESP and subliminal perception (SP) that encourage us to consider them as two species of covert awareness. In fact, a number of researchers were sufficiently impressed by these similarities to undertake research relating SP and ESP (Rao & Rao, 1982; Kreitler & Kreitler, 1973). The French philosopher Henri Bergson (1921) pointed out the relevance of implicit awareness to psychical research. J.B. Rhine (1977) also observed: "It is here in the common unconscious function of both sensorimotor and extrasensorimotor (or psi) character, that parapsychology comes closest to psychology." He added that it would therefore "be advisable to keep our attention on all the psychological research on unconscious mental activities, watching for similarities and differences" (p. 171).

Norman Dixon (1979) identified several areas of contact between subliminal perception and parapsychology. He pointed out that a number of variables, such as motivation, memory, altered states of consciousness, e.g., relaxation and dreams, right-hemispheric modes of functioning, etc., have similar influence on both SP and ESP. Gertrude Schmeidler (1971) also remarked that "whatever psychological laws apply to the processing of ambiguous sensory material will apply also to the processing of ESP information" (p. 137). Another psi researcher, Charles Honorton (1976) wrote: "Both subliminal and psi influences are facilitated by internal-attention states, both are subject to subtle experimenter effects and situational factors, and both involve the transformation and mediation of stimulus influence through ongoing mentation processes" (pp. 215–216).

So far, the results of the experimental studies of ESP and SP have not been clear cut. Stanford (1974), in analyzing the data of an experiment by Eisenbud (1965), found a significant positive correlation between SP and ESP scores. Rao and Puri (1978), however, reported a significant negative correlation. But in a study by Rao and Rao (1982), a significantly positive correlation was found to exist between the SP and ESP scores of subjects who practiced transcendental meditation immediately before the testing. The possibility of interaction between ESP and SP is explored in a series of investigations by Kreitler and Kreitler (1972, 1973, 1974a, 1974b) and by Lubke and Rohr (1975).

Influence of Beliefs and Attitudes on ESP Scores

Gertrude Schmeidler, then a professor of psychology at the City College of New York, asked her subjects if they believed ESP to be possible under the conditions of the experiment. On the basis of their replies, she labeled them as "sheep," those who believed in the possibility of ESP, and "goats," those who rejected such a possibility. She found that sheep generally tended to obtain more hits than goats did. The sheep-goat effect, as it is now known, is one of the more widely researched topics in parapsychology. Her first report was published in the July 1943 issue of *The Journal of American Society for Psychical Research*, and a comprehensive account of sheep-goat experiments is available in the book by Schmeidler and McConnell (1958). One of the strong independent confirmations of the sheep-goat effect may be found in the report of Bhadra (1966). John Palmer's (1971, 1972) review of sheep-goat studies has shown that, of the 17 experiments that used standard methods and analyses, the sheep obtained better scores in 13 of the experiments, with 6 of these achieving statistical significance. Also suggestive was that none of the four experiments giving results in the opposite direction were significant.

As Palmer (1978) points out, the effect of belief on ESP scoring is more complex than it appears. In contrast with Schmeidler's sheep-goat classification, which was based on the subject's belief or disbelief that ESP would occur specifically in the testing situation, some other investigators classified their subjects on the basis of their belief in ESP in the abstract. The latter classification generally tended to be less successful in separating the sheep and the goats in terms of significant differences in their ESP scores. Results further suggest that the sheep-goat effect may interact with other variables. Again, manipulation of belief and expectancy factors seems to produce predictable effects (Taddonio, 1976; Lovitts, 1981). A more recent meta-analysis of sheep-goat studies is found in Tony Lawrence (1993).

Inspired by the work Dutch parapsychologist J.G. Van Busschbach (1958, 1955, 1956, 1959, 1961), American researchers Margaret Anderson and Rhea White carried out a series of experiments with children. They used a clairvoyance technique for group testing and attempted to explore interpersonal dynamics between the experimenters who administered the test and the subjects. Anderson and White (1956, 1957, 1958) reported results suggesting a significant relation between teacher-pupil attitudes and the clairvoyance scores of the pupil subjects. In these studies, the teachers gave the tests to their students. By means of questionnaires, the attitudes of pupils to their teachers and those of teachers to their pupils were ascertained. Anderson and White found that significantly positive scores were associated with a positive attitude on the part of the teacher towards the students and negative scoring was associated with a negative attitude. When the teacher and pupil attitudes were combined, it was found that mutually positive attitudes on the part of both teacher and pupils were associated with highly significant positive results and mutually negative attitudes with significant negative results.

The results of these studies are extremely interesting because they point to an important dimension of the experimenter-subject relationship. It is likely that mutually agreeable relationships and favorable attitudes between the teacher and the pupils help to create the experimental context necessary for the successful manifestation of psi and that a contrary situation favors psi-missing.

ESP and Personality Variables

In the search for those characteristics associated with hitting and missing in psi tests, researchers have also explored the subjects' moods (Nielsen, 1956; Humphrey, 1946a, 1946b; McMahan, 1946), interests (Stuart, 1946), and a variety of personality measures. Neuroticism, defined as a tendency "toward maladaptive behavior caused either by anxiety or by defense mechanisms against anxiety" (Palmer, 1978), is an area that has received considerable attention. Parapsychologists have used inventories such as Taylor's Manifest Anxiety Scale (Rao, 1965c; Freeman & Nielsen, 1964; Honorton, 1965) and Cattell's 16PF or the HSPQ (Kanthamani & Rao, 1973a; Kramer & Terry, 1973) as measures of anxiety/neuroticism and have attempted to correlate these scores with ESP scores. After listing a large number of these studies, Palmer (1978) observed that "there is a clear trend" for subjects with relatively good emotional adjustment to score better on ESP tests than their counterparts do.

The Defense Mechanism Test (DMT) is a projective test developed in Sweden by Ulf Kragh and his associates (Kragh & Smith, 1970). An early experiment by Johnson and Kanthamani (1967) found, as one would expect, a negative relationship between DMT scores and ESP scores. Since the publication of this report, as Haraldsson (1978) has pointed out, there have been seven series of experiments, all but one of which have given statistically significant results in support of a negative relationship. Considering the specialized training required to administer and score the DMT, training that only a few in parapsychology have had, one can be reasonably confident that Haraldson's review covered all the studies up to that time. DMT-ESP studies thus seem to show a fairly stable, replicable effect, suggesting that less defensive subjects tend to obtain better ESP scores. A more recent review of DMT-ESP studies may be found in Johnson and Haraldsson (1984), which also shows their significant replicability, even though there appears to be a gradual decline in the success rate over time.

Psi in Animals

That some animals may possess extraordinary psi abilities is suggested by numerous anecdotes of psi-trailing cases in which pets apparently have traveled long distances to find their masters. An excellent review of these cases is found in Rhine and Feather (1957).

Karlis Osis (1952) and Osis and Foster (1953), among others, have systematically studied psi in animals (anpsi). Other anpsi experiments of considerable interest are those carried out by P. Duval and E. Montredon (1968a, 1968b), S.A. Schouten (1972), and R.L. Morris (1978). Although W.J. Levy reported the most extensive series of experiments with animal subjects, his work has been completely discredited on the grounds of possible tampering with the data (Rhine, 1974). Robert Morris (1970) and James Davis (1979) have published very useful reviews of anpsi literature.

I must point out, however, that even though some experimental studies have given results suggestive of psi in animals, in no case has the possibility that psi on the part of the experimenter or someone else associated with the experiment is responsible for the observed effect been ruled out. The possibility of a psi experimenter effect looms large in this area. The inability to control for this is an important impediment to further anpsi research.

Physiological Studies of Psi

Biofeedback studies in the sixties and seventies have raised the hope that a number of internal responses that are normally considered to be beyond the range of voluntary control can be brought under such control. By receiving instant information about heart rate, blood pressure, muscle tension, brain activity, and the like, human subjects, as well as some animals, learn to regulate these internal responses (Miller et al., 1974). Joe Kamiya (1969) and Barbara Brown (1970), among others, have successfully trained subjects to regulate their own brain-wave patterns through biofeedback. Kamiya's subjects, when trained to produce high levels of alpha activity, reported feelings of relaxation and passivity. Also, studies of yogins (Anand, Chhina, & Singh, 1961) and Zen meditators (Kasamatsu & Hirai, 1969) have shown that yogic and meditative states produce EEG patterns characterized by alpha abundance. Traditionally the yogins are credited with psychic abilities, and there is experimental evidence to suggest that relaxation as well as meditation facilitates ESP manifestation (see Honorton, 1977; Rao et al., 1978; and White (1964), for a review of these studies). It is, therefore, reasonable to suppose that there may be a positive relation between alpha activity of the brain and ESP scores. If such a relation should exist, the ability to self-regulate brain wave activity opens up the possibility of achieving greater predictability, if not control, of ESP performance.

Among the EEG-ESP studies of interest are those by Honorton (1969); Honorton, Davidson, & Bindler (1971); Stanford & Stanford (1969); Stanford (1971); Stanford & Stevenson (1972); Stanford & Palmer (1973); Morris, Roll, Klein & Wheeler (1972); and Rao & Feola (1979). Even though the results of these studies are not uniformly significant, the bulk of the evidence is suggestive of a positive relationship between ESP and alpha activity. A review of the earlier work on the physiological correlates of psi is found in Beloff (1974).

There have been a number of attempts to use physiological indices as indicators of psi. S. Figar (1959) and Douglas Dean (1962), among others, utilized plethysmographic recordings as ESP indicators. Soji Otani (1965) and K. Tenny (1962) employed skin resistance measures to monitor psi. As we have seen, William Braud and others examined autonomic detection of the phenomenon of "being stared at" using electrodermal response.

More recently, Norman Don, Bruce McDonough and Charles Warren have attempted to study event-related potentials (ERPs) as indicators of psi. ERPs are minute fluctuations in the voltage of EEG recordings from the scalp following sensory stimulation. In one study with the psychic Malcolm Bessent, Warren, McDonough, and Don (1992a) recorded ERPs elicited by target and nontarget stimuli in forced-choice ESP tests. They observed that P100, a positive spike at about 100ms after the onset of the stimulus, and NSW (a negative slow wave 400–500 ms after the stimulus is applied) were significantly larger in response to target stimuli than to nontarget stimuli. In an attempted replication of the above with the same subject (Warren, McDonough, & Don, 1992b), the P100 effect did not occur, but there was evidence of the NSW effect. In a more recent study Don, McDonough, & Warren (1998) attempted to test the NSW effect at the 400–500 ms range as well as at the 150–400 ms range. The subjects in this study were unselected volunteers. The results confirmed the NSW effect in the 150–400 ms range. For the NSW at 400–500 ms range the results fell short of significance (p=.085). The authors interpreted the results as evidence of unconscious psi.

Memory and ESP

There are a number of interesting similarities between ESP and some cognitive processes, such as memory. Memory, like ESP, involves representations of objects and events with which the organism is not directly in sensory contact. We know something about the way memory representations are stored and retrieved, as well as their biochemical and physiological bases. However, our knowledge of ESP does not provide any evidence that psi representations have a cortical basis. Further, much of our memory material is accessible for introspection, whereas most ESP phenomena, being unconscious, are unavailable for any introspective analysis. These important differences not withstanding, memory and ESP seem to have a good deal in common as psychological processes, and the understanding of one may aid the understanding of the other. Therefore, it is not surprising that, from the time of F.W.H. Myers (1915/1903) to that of J.B. Rhine, a role for memory in ESP was anticipated. J.B. Rhine wrote in *Extra-sensory Perception* (1973/34): "It [ESP] is simple cognition ... but it uses memory, visual or other imagination ... in its functioning" (p. 191).

Hermann Ebbinghaus (1964/1885), who pioneered quantitative studies of memory, wondered, as have most experimental psychologists since, how to control "the bewildering mass of causal conditions which, insofar as they are of mental nature, almost completely elude our control, and which, moreover, are subject to endless and incessant change." The challenge for him was how to "measure numerically the mental processes which flit by so quickly and which on introspection are so hard to analyze" (pp. 7–8). He attempted to solve the problem by inventing nonsense syllables which the subject may learn and recall under controlled conditions, a tradition which is strikingly similar to the one heralded by early ESP testers who used forced-choice card-guessing methods.

Considerable similarity is also found in the topics for research chosen for study by memory researchers and parapsychologists. Just as memory researchers are concerned with the effect on recall of differences in the material to be remembered, so are parapsychologists concerned with the effect of target differences on subjects' ESP scores. Individual differences are as extensively investigated in studies of memory as they are in studies of psi. The search for states favorable to improved ESP scoring bears similarity to the research into the conditions for optimal memory. Whereas the classical card-guessing tests are like the methods used by Ebbinghaus and those who followed him, the open-ended, free-response studies of psi remind us of the Bartlett (1932) tradition in memory research. Again, the position effects, such as the tendency to score higher on the first and the last trials of a test run, the differential effect, and psi-missing seem to have their analogs in memory, e.g., U curves in serial learning, retroactive inhibition, and parapraxes. If both memory and ESP involve information-processing mechanisms, as some hold, memory psychologists and parapsychologists may find common points of theoretical interest. For example, the "retrieve-edit" model of William James (1890) or its later development in Underwood's (1969) notion of retrieval and discrimination attributes may be applied to the ESP process for a better understanding of the nature of psi. Also, some of the concepts found in memory literature such as short-term and long-term memory, episodic and semantic memory, and productive and reproductive memory may be relevant not only in suggesting new lines of ESP research but also in clarifying some of the questions already raised. The memory psychologist also has much to gain by reflecting on such concepts as psi-missing and the methodological advances parapsychology has made in recent years.

The first significant attempt to relate memory scores with ESP scores was made by Sara Feather (1967). In two series of preliminary tests the subject was first shown a list of ESP symbols or digits for 15 or 20 seconds, then was given a card-calling ESP test, and finally was asked to recall the symbols or numbers seen initially. The results showed that the subjects whose recall was better also performed better in the ESP test than did those whose recall was poorer. In a confirmatory experiment consisting of three series, she again obtained significant positive correlations between memory and ESP scores. Other studies that explored the memory-ESP relation include those by Stanford (1970; 1973), Kanthamani and Rao (1974), Rao, Morrison and Davis (1977), and Rao, Morrison, Davis, and Freeman (1977).

Psi-Missing and the Differential Effect

Another significant area that is not represented in this collection of articles is psi-missing and the effects associated with it. Psi-missing is the tendency to miss a target when attempting to hit it. Even though systematic study of psi-missing is a recent development, the phenomenon of psi-missing was encountered quite early in experimental parapsychology. We find in the 1927 experiment of George Estabrooks (1961), for example, that in the series of tests in which distance was introduced as a variable, his subjects averaged 4.06 hits per run of 25 trials, where the mean chance expectation is 5.00. The negative deviation in this series is statistically significant. Rhine (1952) himself found that some of his outstanding subjects (e.g., Linzmayer and Pearce) produced strong negative deviations when they were inadvertently kept overtime, or when they were exposed to unpleasant experimental conditions. As L.E. Rhine (1965) noted, the early investigators considered psi-missing to be "a kind of nemesis which could catch up with an ESP experimenter and trip him unawares" (p. 263).

It was J.B. Rhine who first recognized the importance of psi-missing and the need to study it systematically. In two of his articles (Rhine, 1952, 1969) he discussed at length the question of psi-missing, described the different situations in which psi-missing is likely to occur, and suggested two hypotheses to account for it. Extensive discussions of psi-missing appear also in articles by K.R. Rao (1965a, 1965b) and J.C. Carpenter (1977).

In much of the process-oriented research, psi-missing occurs in one form or another. In the attitude-ESP studies, for example, the goats tended to significantly psi-miss. In the personality studies, the subjects with high scores on neuroticism and introversion also gave significant negative scores. It would seem that a successful experimental strategy for obtaining reliable evidence of psi, especially among unselected subjects, is one that separates hitters and missers.

One of the more frequently observed psi effects is the tendency of subjects to score differentially when tested under two contrasting conditions, such as two sets of targets or two kinds of response modes. This tendency is what I called the differential effect (Rao, 1965a, 1965b). My unpublished survey of the literature bearing on this question revealed 124 series of experiments involving differential conditions. Sixty-five percent of them showed differential scoring when it would be expected by chance to be just one half. More striking was that over a third of the studies provided statistically significant evidence for the differential effect. For experimental reports on the differential effect, see Rao (1962, 1963a, 1963b, 1963c, 1964a), Sailaja and Rao (1973), Sanders (1962), Freeman (1969), Kanthamani (1965), and Carpenter (1971).

Geomagnetic Activity and Psi

In recent years a number of studies have attempted to explore the relationship between the occurrence of psi and geomagnetic activity in the atmosphere. Investigators reported significant positive correlations between the frequency of spontaneous ESP experiences and quiet geomagnetic activity (Persinger, 1985, 1989), and between successful psi tests and low levels of geomagnetic activity, at the time the tests were conducted (Berger & Persinger, 1991; Persinger & Krippner, 1989). These correlations are interpreted as evidence in support of the ELF hypothesis. The ELF hypothesis assumes that extremely low frequency (ELF) waves are involved in psi communication and that ESP is a primitive communication system, consisting of electromagnetic field effects which may function more effectively during periods of less turbulent geomagnetic activity (Becker, 1992).

Psi and Sensory Noise Reduction

ESP is considered by some to be "an ancient and primitive form of perception" (Eysenck, 1967). Therefore, it is suggested that conditions of high cortical arousal may inhibit ESP, whereas a state of relaxation and reduced sensory input may facilitate its occurrence. British psychologist H.J. Eysenck (1967) surveyed a surprisingly large number of studies that have bearing on this. Pointing out that introverts are habitually in a state of greater cortical arousal than extraverts, Eysenck hypothesized that extraverts would do better in ESP tests than introverts. Indeed, there is much evidence in support of this hypothesis. For over fifty years, extraversion-introversion was one of the most widely explored dimensions of personality in relation to ESP. Carl Sargent (1981) reviewed all the English-language reports bearing on the extraversion-ESP hypothesis and found that significant confirmations of a positive relationship between ESP and extraversion occur at over six times the chance error.

Chapter 11 is a report of one of the major investigations of the relationship between ESP and personality factors. This report, which is the third of a five-part series, presents results obtained in four experiments. In all the experiments, the extraverts obtained higher ESP scores than the introverts, and in three of them the differences are statistically significant. It may be mentioned that in the fourth experiment (Experiment C), Kanthamani (the main investigator) did not administer the ESP tests. She administered the personality test before the subjects took the ESP tests by another experimenter. Consequently, the subjects had no knowledge of their ESP scores at the time they took the personality test. The difference in the ESP scores of extraverts and introverts is significant in this experiment as well.

Chapter 12 reports a comprehensive meta-analysis of 60 independent studies of ESP-extraversion relationship involving 2,963 subjects. The overall weighted mean correlation for all the studies is significant. Honorton, Ferrari, and Bem (1998) report, however, that, when the order of presentation of the ESP test is taken into consideration, only the free-response studies showed significant overall correlation between extraversion and ESP scores when the personality tests were administered first and the subjects did not have any knowledge of their ESP scores before they took the personality test. This observation leads them to conclude that the significant correlations observed in forced-choice studies may be an artifact of the subjects' knowledge of their ESP scores. The report also contains the results of a new confirmation of ESP/extraversion relationship in a free-response study.

In Chapter 13, John Palmer and James Carpenter (1998) question the conclusion of Honorton, Ferrari, and Bem that the extraversion/ESP relationship is limited to free-response studies. They point out that (a) personality scales are not generally susceptible to situational biases and that (b) additional analyses show that the extraversion-ESP relationship for forced-choice tests is a genuine psi effect. Extraversion-ESP studies used in the meta-analysis include both group testing and individual testing for ESP. Most of the free-response studies employed individual testing whereas many of the forced-choice studies were done in groups. This is more likely to be the confounding variable rather than testing by forced-choice or free-response methods. Palmer and Carpenter show that significant relationship between ESP and extraversion scores is present in the data of individual tests and not in the group test data. When group testing studies are removed from the analysis, the extraversion-ESP relationship is found to be of comparable magnitude for forced-choice and free-response ESP tests. Palmer and Carpenter refer also to Experiment C of Kanthamani-Rao study (chapter 11) in which the subjects did not have knowledge of their ESP scores at the time they took the personality test. Moreover, a study by Krishna and Rao (1991) showed that feedback of ESP scores did not bias the responses of the subjects to a personality questionnaire, as the hypothesis of Honorton et al., assumes.

There are a number of other studies, which shed direct light on the hypothesis of ESP facilitation via sensory noise reduction. There is substantial evidence to suggest that the occurrence of ESP may be enhanced by procedures that result in the reduction of meaningful sensory stimuli and proprioceptive input to the organism. In fact many of the traditional psychic development techniques such as yoga appear to employ sensory noise reduction procedures. So do a variety of relaxation exercises and altered state of consciousness. Psi researchers have explored some of them.

Relaxation and ESP

Several subjects who have done well on psi tests have claimed that they did their best when they were physically relaxed and their minds were in a "blank" state. Mary Sinclair, whom her husband novelist Upton Sinclair found to be an outstanding subject, gave the following advice: "You first give yourself a 'suggestion' to the effect that you will relax your mind and your body, making the body insensitive and the mind a blank" (Sinclair, 1930, p. 180). Rhea White (1964), who reviewed the early literature on this topic, also concluded that attempts "to still the body and mind" are common among the techniques used by successful subjects.

There are 33 ESP studies in which progressive relaxation procedures have been used. Seventeen of these gave significant results. The most extensive work in this area was carried out by William Braud and associates. Chapter 14 is a report of two experiments carried out by Lendell and William Braud. In the first experiment there were 16 subjects and the subjects self-rated their degree of relaxation. Braud and Braud report that those who performed well in the ESP tests rated themselves as more relaxed than the poor psi performers. The second experiment consisted of 20 volunteer subjects who were assigned randomly to "relaxation" or "tension" conditions. Those in the relaxation condition went through a taped, progressive-relaxation procedure (an adaptation of Jacobson's) before taking an ESP test, which was to guess the picture being "transmitted" by an agent in another room. The subjects in the other group were given taped, tension-inducing instructions before they did the same ESP test. Each subject's level of relaxation was assessed through electromyographic recordings. The EMG results showed a significant decrease in the EMG activity among the subjects in the "relaxation" group and significant increase among those in the "tension" group. As predicted, the ESP scores of the subjects in the relaxation group were significantly better than the scores of the subjects in the tension group.

Other reports of interest are Braud and Braud (1973), Braud (1975), Altom and Braud (1976). Confirmation of Braud's results may be found in Stanford and Mayer (1974). Honorton's (1977) summary of studies on relaxation and psi shows a 77% success rate. Ten of the 13 studies he reviewed involving induced relaxation achieved statistical significance at the 5% level in support of psi.

Psi in Hypnotic States

The idea that the hypnotic state may be psi-conducive is as old as scientific parapsychology. A French physician, E. Azam, observed that one of his patients in a hypnotic state responded to an unspoken thought. Pierre Janet was reportedly successful in inducing a somnambulistic trance state 16 out of 20 times by mere mental suggestion (Podmore, 1894). Eleanor Sidgwick (Sidgwick et al., 1889), at the Society for Psychical Research in England, experimented with hypnotized subjects by using two-digit numbers and colors as targets. The Russian physiologist Vasiliev (1963) was highly successful in inducing hypnotic trance by telepathy from a distance. Within the card-calling paradigm, the first ESP experiment with hypnosis was reported by J.J. Grela (1945).

Jarl Fahler (1957) carried out experiments in Finland which gave significant results when the subjects were under hypnosis. Chapter 15 is an account of his experiments carried out at Duke University in collaboration with Remi Cadoret. Important work in the area of hypnosis and psi was also reported by L. Casler (1962, 1964). Casler went a step further than Fahler by giving explicit suggestions to the subjects for improvements in their ESP scoring. Milan Ryzl (Ryzl & Ryzlova, 1962) claimed that the outstanding subject Pavel Stepanek was trained by him with the help of hypnosis. Charles Honorton's (1977) review lists 42 psi studies using hypnosis, 22 of which gave significant evidence of psi.

In Chapter 16 we have a review and meta-analysis of the experimental studies of ESP and hypnosis by Ephraim Schechter (1984). The analysis confirms the hypothesis that subjects tend to obtain higher ESP scores in the hypnotic state than in a controlled waking state. That the hypnotic state is psi conducive fits well with the observation that people who report spontaneous psychic experiences tend to have dissociative tendencies (Pekala, Kumar, & Marcano, 1995). Hypnotic susceptibility, like psychological absorption, is a dimension of dissociative processes.

A more recent meta-analysis of ESP studies involving hypnosis and contrasting conditions is reported by Rex Stanford and Adam Stein (1994). Included in the analysis are 25 studies by 12 chief investigators. Claiming that their attempt was to extend and refine Schechter's work, Stanford and Stein also report cumulative ESP-test scores significant for hypnosis. They, however, caution that we may not draw any substantive conclusions from the current database, because the difference in ESP scores between hypnosis and contrast conditions is significant only when the comparison condition preceded hypnosis. They point out also that there is significant psi-missing in the contrasting condition.

Meditation and Psi

The practice of yoga, it is said, enables one to develop psychic abilities. In the third century before Christ, Patanjali wrote a treatise on Raja Yoga (Woods, 1927) detailing the processes and procedures involved and the varieties of supernormal abilities one may obtain by practicing this discipline. Meditation is the most important feature of yoga. It is pointed out that the practice of intensely focusing attention on a single object and following this by meditation enables the practitioner to hold his focus for an extended period of time, which results in a standstill state of the mind (*samadhi*). The *samadhi* state is the one in which psychic abilities are believed to manifest. Unfortunately, there are no systematic studies of yogins to test for their psi, even though there is a vast amount of anecdotal material concerning their extraordinary psychic claims. However, several exploratory studies, in which some kind of meditation procedure was used, seem to suggest a positive relationship between meditation and ESP.

Chapter 17 is a report of a series of experiments conducted by a team of researchers at Andhra University in India to explore the possibility of enhancing one's psi abilities through practice of yoga. In this study, 59 subjects who had various degrees of proficiency in meditation took ESP tests before and immediately after they had meditated for half an hour or more. The ESP tests involved matching cards with ESP symbols and guessing concealed pictures. Both the tests yielded results that showed that the subjects obtained significantly better ESP scores in the post-meditation sessions than in the pre-meditation sessions. Other meditation-psi studies include those by Schmeidler (1970), Osis and Bokert (1971), and Schmidt and Pantas (1972). Honorton (1977) reports a survey that shows 9 out of 16 experimental series involving meditation to have given significant psi results.

ESP in the Ganzfeld

Finally, a number of well designed studies looked at the effects of reduced external stimulation on subject's ESP scoring by utilizing the ganzfeld. Ganzfeld is a homogeneous visual field produced, for instance, by taping two halves of a ping-pong ball over the eyes and focussing on them a uniform red light from about two feet. The subject may also be given "pink" noise through attached earphones. After being in the ganzfeld for about one half hour, subjects typically report being immersed in a sea of light. Some subjects report total "black out," complete absence of visual experience. Continuous uniform and unpatterned stimulation in the ganzfeld, it is believed, produces a state that, in the absence of meaningful external stimulation, enhances the possibility of attention to internal states, which in turn facilitates the detection of ESP signals.

In a typical ganzfeld-ESP experiment, the subject while in the ganzfeld for about 30 minutes, is asked to report whatever is going on in his/her mind at that time. The subject's mentation is monitored and recorded by an experimenter in another room via a microphone link. A second experimenter or subject, acting as an agent, located in a different room isolated from the subject and the experimenter monitoring the subject, looks at a picture for about 15 minutes, attempting to "transmit" it to the subject in the ganzfeld. At the end of the ganzfeld period, the monitoring experimenter gives the subject four pictures with a request to rank them 1 through 4 on the basis of their correspondence to the subject's mental images and impressions during the ganzfeld. The monitoring experimenter of course does not have any knowledge as to which of the four pictures is the one looked at by the agent. After all the four pictures are ranked, the subject is shown the target picture. The rank the subject gives to that picture provides the score for a statistical analysis of the matching of the subject's mentation with the target. Sometimes, the ranking is done by a judge in addition to or in the place of the subject.

Honorton and Harper (1974) reported the first ganzfeld-ESP experiment, which provided evidence that the subjects' mentation during the ganzfeld matched significantly with the target picture. Between 1974 and 1981 there were in all 42 published ganzfeld-ESP experiments of which 19 gave significant evidence for psi; it seemed that psi in the ganzfeld is a highly replicable effect. However, at the joint conference of the Society for Psychical Research and the Parapsychological Association held at Cambridge University during August 1982 psychologist Ray Hyman made a presentation raising serious questions about the replicability of the ganzfeld psi experiment. Subsequently, a comprehensive critical appraisal of ganzfeld ESP experiments was published in the *Journal of Parapsychology* (Hyman, 1985). In this paper Hyman (1) challenged the claimed success rate of replication, (2) argued that possible flaws involving inadequate randomization and insufficient documentation vitiate experiments reporting significant psi effects, and (3) concluded that the ganzfeld-ESP data base is "too weak to support any assertions about the existence of psi."

Chapter 18 is a response to Hyman's critique by Charles Honorton. Honorton points to examples of inconsistent or inappropriate assignment of flaw ratings in Hyman's analysis. He presents his own meta-analysis that eliminates multiple analysis and other problems mentioned by Hyman and argues that neither selective reporting nor alleged procedural flaws account for significant psi effects reported in the ESP-ganzfeld studies.

Subsequently, Hyman and Honorton (1986) issued a "joint communiqué" on the psi ganzfeld debate. In it they agree that the overall significance of the effect cannot be reasonably explained away by such considerations as selective reporting or multiple analyses. They disagree, however, on the degree to which the effect constitutes evidence for psi, because of remaining differences over the impact of alleged flaws. More important, however, are the recommendations they make for conducting future experiments in this area.

The final chapter in this volume is a report of a replication of psi ganzfeld effect by Cornell psychologist Daryl Bem and parapsychologist Charles Honorton (1994) published in the mainstream psychology journal, *Psychological Bulletin*. This study, consisting of 11 experiments, utilized computer control of the experimental protocol. It complied with all the guidelines Hyman and Honorton recommended in their joint communiqué. The new setup is called autoganzfeld. Interestingly, the results of the autoganzfeld studies strongly support the existence of a psi effect in the data, and they replicate the ESP ganzfeld effect meeting the "stringent standards" requirement as recommended by Hyman and Honorton in their joint communiqué.

Julie Milton and Richard Wiseman (1999) published a follow-up meta-analysis of 30 more ganzfeld ESP studies conducted between 1983 and 1997. Their analysis did not provide significant cumulative evidence for the ganzfeld effect. Bem, Palmer and Broughton (2001) further updated the ESP ganzfeld database by adding ten more studies published after 1997 and not included in the meta-analysis by Milton and Wiseman. When these 10 additional studies are included, the meta-analysis yields a mean effect size that is again statistically significant, though smaller than the one observed in the earlier studies. Bem et al. observed, however, that some of the experiments included in the new database appeared to deviate significantly from the standard protocol of the ganzfeld experiment. Therefore, they arranged for three independent raters unfamiliar with the studies involved to rate the degree to which each of the 40 studies in the new database deviated from the standard protocol. As expected they found that "the effect size achieved by a replication is significantly correlated with the degree to which it adhered to the standard protocol." They point out: "Standard replications yield significant effect sizes comparable to those obtained in the past." As it stands now, we have a broad range of replications covering over a period of 25 years, involving over 90 experiments by a wide range of investigators. They show a fairly robust effect comparable across studies that adhere to the standard ganzfeld protocol.

Correlational studies have shown more psi when subjects say the ganzfeld produced an altered state of consciousness in them. The results from ESP studies involving meditation, relaxation, hypnosis, and ganzfeld thus meaningfully converge to suggest that a reduction of ongoing sensorimotor activity may facilitate the manifestation of ESP in laboratory tests. Whatever may be the mechanism involved in ESP, it is reasonable to assume that ESP is a weak signal that must compete for the information processing resources of the organism. In this process, any reduction of ongoing sensory activity should improve the chances of detecting and registering the ESP signal. It would therefore seem reasonable to conclude from our review of psi research bearing on the sensory noise reduction model that (a) psi exists; (b) that psi effects are replicable, and (c) that sensory noise reduction through such procedures as ganzfeld is psi conducive.

Parapsychology has traveled far since J.B. Rhine conducted the Pearce-Pratt experiment. It has crossed many milestones, overcoming many hurdles, and accumulated massive evidence. It has survived savage attacks from some of the most vociferous critics science has ever known. Researchers in this field have attempted to answer all reasonable questions. In response to criticisms they have modified their experimental protocols, revised their analyses, and introduced additional safeguards. Yet in terms of achieving a broad consensus among scientists on the question of the existence or otherwise of psi we have come no further than when Rhine published his early ESP test results. Optimism that the two camps could carve out a common ground for communication and for evaluating psi research generated by the dialogue between parapsychological researchers and their critics culminating in the Hyman-Honorton joint statement has been eroded. The proponents and opponents of psi continue to live in two separate universes. Therefore, it remains for each of us to make up our own minds. One can do this in a rational way by becoming familiar with the available evidence. This volume is offered as a useful resource for that endeavor.

References for this Introduction may be found in the Bibliography at the end of the book.

CHAPTER 2

A Review of the Pearce-Pratt Distance Series of ESP Tests

J.B. Rhine *and* J.G. Pratt

A number of considerations have contributed to our decision to present the original and subsequent work identified with what has come to be known as the Pearce-Pratt Distance Series of ESP tests, carried out in 1933-34 at the Parapsychology Laboratory at Duke University. One reason for the review is the need expressed by some students of the subject for a more complete and detailed account of the original experiment than is to be found in any one publication. The first part of the series, what is known as Subseries A, was published in the monograph *Extrasensory Perception* written in 1934 by J.B.R. (Rhine, 1934). This section was all that was completed at the time the monograph was written. In 1936 a brief account of the series and its total results was given in an article by J.B.R. in the *Journal of Abnormal and Social Psychology* (Rhine, 1936), and in 1937 a condensed version of this article was included in the first number of the *Journal of Parapsychology* (Rhine, 1937).

Another reason for the present undertaking is the fact that almost immediately upon publication the Pearce-Pratt Series received special attention. It represented a methodological advance over earlier experimental work in parapsychology; and both for the laboratory group associated with the experiment and for those who were attempting to appraise and criticize the evidence for extrasensory perception, the series had to be considered. Moreover, as new questions were raised about the series,

Reprinted with permission from *Journal of Parapsychology*, 1954, **18**, 165–177.

further analyses of the data resulted. Most of these analyses were reported as they were completed, but to the student of today it would be a difficult undertaking to run them all down.

There is the further point that it is now possible to appraise the experiment and its results in the light of the developments of the intervening twenty years, the most productive period of parapsychology. It was considered an advantage to older students as well as new, therefore, for the authors to assemble for re-examination the factual matter that has accumulated around this single experimental series.

Something should be said regarding the general background of the research. First, there is the all-important aspect of personnel. It should not be forgotten that without Prof. William McDougall's appreciation of the problem and his tolerant and courageous interest in seeing it investigated under good conditions in a psychology laboratory, the experiment would not have been possible. J.B.R. was at the time an assistant professor in the department of which Professor McDougall was head; it was generally understood in those days that research in parapsychology was approved by the Department. J.G.P. was a graduate student in psychology, specially employed as research assistant to J.B.R. From the viewpoint of objectivity, it should be noted that J.G.P. had not at that time shown special interest in the problems of parapsychology, and in fact worked on other problems for his graduate researches. It was not until some years later that he decided to devote his energy to parapsychology.

The subject, Hubert E. Pearce, Jr., was at the time a student in the Divinity School at Duke. He had introduced himself to J.B.R. approximately eighteen months earlier and had stated that he believed he had inherited his mother's clairvoyant powers. In ESP card tests given by J.G.P. and J.B.R. during the intervening period he had exceeded the average score to be expected from chance in practically every experimental session under a wide variety of conditions. During that period he had participated in tests involving nearly 700 runs through the standard deck of ESP cards, averaging approximately 32% successes as compared with the mean chance expectation of 20%. Nothing like this prolonged series of tests had ever been made up to that time, and H.E.P.'s performance was recognized even then as highly exceptional.

The Distance Series was the first step involving different buildings in the separation of H.E.P. from the target card he was attempting to identify. The move was not so much a strictly necessary requirement for the exclusion of visual cues as it was a matter of providing a conspicuously wide margin of safety against the possibility of such cues. The use of different buildings, incidentally, was convenient for the independent recording of the subject's responses and the card sequences. It became easily possible at the same time to provide for duplicate recording and independent checking.

To those of us who had participated in the long series of earlier tests with H.E.P. under gradually improving conditions of test and observation, this further advance in experimental conditions was hardly required. The essential safeguards had already been approximated. There is, however, a tendency of the mind, when confronted with so incredible a hypothesis as that of ESP, to exaggerate the possibility of alternative factors such as visual cues, recording errors, the loss of records, and the like. The revolutionary character of the ESP hypothesis, then, made necessary a range of precautions that were not normally considered a part of the routine of experimental psychology. This atmosphere of critical apprehension concerning the adequacy of the design needs to be taken into account, for it was a part of the actual situation in which the experiment was conducted.

Some idea of the state of mind prevailing at the time can be gained from the circumstances leading to the planning of Subseries D. Subseries A, B, and C had been designed on the assumption that no error was possible that could favor the ESP hypothesis—not unless the two men, J.G.P. and H.E.P., were deliberately to conspire to produce a fraudulent set of results. Wisely (and accurately) anticipating that there would be those who would find it easier to suspect collusion than to accept ESP as established, Professor McDougall recommended that J.B.R. identify himself with the actual performance of at least a short subseries of the distance tests in order that a theory of collusion would have to involve all three of the participants in the experiment. On the basis of this plan Subseries D was conducted with J.B.R. actively officiating with J.G.P.

Actually the primary research objective in the experiment was to compare the effect of short and long distance on the results. In the planning of the test series, this concern with the role of distance was the essentially novel feature of the experimental design. In most of the tests in which H.E.P. took part during the preceding period, the target cards had been within a yard of him. It was considered a sufficient first step to introduce a distance of at least a hundred times that unit as one that should reveal any effect of distance on any possible radiant energy that conceivably intermediated in the operation of ESP. Later in the series this distance was increased still farther. While, then, for the general public and the critic especially, the Pearce-Pratt Series came into focus as a conclusive demonstration of the *occurrence* of ESP, to the workers in the Parapsychology Laboratory it became the first definite step in the testing of the hypothesis of the *non-physical nature* of psi, the hypothesis suggested by earlier experimental work as well as by the study of spontaneous psi experiences.

Procedure

A single subject, H.E.P., was tested for his ability to identify ESP test cards manipulated by the experimental assistant, J.G.P., in another building, part of the time at a distance of 100 yards and part of the time at a distance of more than 250 yards from the location of the subject. The experiment was designed to test for the clairvoyant type of ESP; and J.G.P., accordingly, did not know the card order in the test.

Aside from planning the experiment, J.B.R. participated only in the independent checking of results, except for Series D in which he participated with J.G.P. as the witness to the operation of the test.

There were, in all, four subseries, A, B, C, and D, totaling 74 runs through the pack of 25 cards; and the series extended from August, 1933, into March, 1934. The testing days were not consecutive, though within a given subseries they were more or less so. They were selected, however, at the mutual convenience of H.E.P. and J.G.P. Subseries C was begun in October, 1933, and four runs were added to it in March, 1934, with Subseries D following thereafter. Specific dates may be found in Table 1. Subseries A was done with the 100 yards distance, Subseries B at 250 yards, and the other two subseries back at 100 yards. The 74 runs represent all the ESP tests made with H.E.P. during this experiment under the condition of working with the subject and target cards in different buildings. It was, in fact, the only distance test involving different buildings done at the Duke Laboratory at the time.

Series A was set up with an advance commitment on termination point. It was agreed that 300 trials were to be given H.E.P. The following Subseries, B, was intended to be a duplication with only the additional distance involved, but the experimenters were interested in the big shift of scoring level from day to day which was shown at the longer distance. It was decided to allow H.E.P. to continue further so as to see what would happen. Subseries C was intended to be a repetition of Subseries A consisting of 300 trials designed to discover whether the lower scoring rate of Subseries B at the longer distance was a result of the altered situation or whether H.E.P. had declined in scoring ability. Subseries D, as has been stated, was intended as introducing a check on J.G.P., and its length was agreed upon in advance (150 trials, or six runs).

In actual operation the experiment proceeded as follows, regardless of which subseries was involved: At the time agreed upon, H.E.P. visited J.G.P. in his research room on the top floor of what is now the Social Science Building on the main Duke campus. The two men synchronized their watches and set an exact time for starting the test, allowing enough time for H.E.P. to cross the quadrangle to the Duke Library where he occupied a cubicle in the stacks at the back of the building. From his window J.G.P. could see H.E.P. enter the Library.

J.G.P. then selected a pack of ESP cards from several packs always available in the room. He gave this pack of cards a number of dovetail shuffles and a final cut, keeping them face-down throughout. He then placed the pack on the right-hand side of the table at which he was sitting. In the center of the table was a closed book on which it had been agreed with H.E.P. that the card for each trial would be placed. At the minute set for starting the test, J.G.P. lifted the top card from the inverted deck, placed it face-down on the book, and allowed it to remain there for approximately a full minute. At the beginning of the next minute this card was picked up with the left hand and laid, still face-down, on the left-hand side of the table, while with the right hand J.G.P. picked up the next card and put it on the book. At the end of the second minute, this card was placed on top of the one on the left and the next one was put on the book. In this way, at the rate of one card per minute, the entire pack of 25 cards went through the process of being isolated, one card at a time, on the book in the center of the table, where it was the target or stimulus object for that ESP trial.

In his cubicle in the Library, H.E.P. attempted to identify the target cards, minute by minute, and recorded his responses in pencil. At the end of the run, there was on most test days a rest period of five minutes before a second run followed in exactly the same way. H.E.P. made a duplicate of his call record, signed one copy, and sealed it in an envelope for J.B.R. Over in his room J.G.P. recorded the card order for the two decks used in the test as soon as the second run was finished. This record, too, was in duplicate, one copy of which was signed and sealed in an envelope for J.B.R. The two sealed records were delivered personally to J.B.R., most of the time before J.G.P. and H.E.P. compared their records and scored the number of successes. On the few occasions when J.G.P. and H.E.P. met and compared their unsealed duplicates before both of them had delivered their sealed records to J.B.R., the data could not have been changed without collusion, as J.G.P. kept the results from the unsealed records and any discrepancy between them and J.B.R.'s results would have been noticed. In Subseries D, J.B.R. was on hand to receive the duplicates as the two other men met immediately after each session for the checkup.

Thus, from day to day as the experiment proceeded, H.E.P. was kept informed, as he had been in all his earlier experiments, as to the rate of success achieved. The practice of expressing enthusiastic congratulations should be mentioned as a part of the procedure. If, as rarely happened, the scoring rate was low, favorable emphasis was placed on the overall performance, the general average maintained, and the high standing of the subject in the comparative scale of ESP subjects. Throughout the series the paramount objective of high-order performance was held before the subject with all the vigor and expectation that could be communicated.

Results

Table 1
Pearce-Pratt Distance Series: General Results

Subseries	Dates Start	End	Runs	Dev.	SD	CR	P
A	8/25/33	9/1/33	12	+59	7.07	8.35	$<10^{-14}$
B	9/2/33	9/30/33	44	+75	13.54	5.54	$<10^{-6}$
C	10/18/33	3/10/34	12	+28	7.07	3.96	.000075
D	3/12/34	3/13/34	6	+26	5.00	5.20	$<10^{-6}$
Total	8/25/33	3/13/34	74	+188	17.57	10.70	$<10^{-22}$

General Evaluation

Since they were one series of tests carried out under essentially the same conditions, the four subseries (totaling 74 runs, or 1850 trials) may be pooled. Mean chance expectation is 20%, or 370 hits. The total number of successes actually scored for the series is 558, which is better than 30%. The theoretical standard deviation derived on a conservative basis is 17.57. This total of 558 hits is 188 above the theoretical expectation and it gives a critical ratio of 10.70. The probability that a critical ratio so large as this would occur on the basis of random sampling is less than 10^{-22}. In the determination of the critical ratio given above, allowance is made for the slight correction applicable when, as in this experiment, the balanced ESP deck is used; that is, when there are five of each symbol in each pack. The variance of scores obtained with the 5×5 ESP deck depends upon the frequency with which the subject calls the different symbols. The largest variance results when the subject always calls exactly five of each symbol, and the SD of 17.57 was obtained on this assumption (Greenwood, 1938). However, the subject rarely called five of each symbol in a run, and the exact SD would therefore be smaller than the one used here, which makes the estimate of statistical significance a conservative one.

Each of the four subseries is independently significant, as may be seen by reference to Table 1. The table shows for each subseries the date, number of runs, deviation, standard deviation, critical ratio, and the associated probability.* A complete record of the card order and calls for the series has been furnished from time to time to qualified workers who wish to make some special study of the material. This practice will continue.

Results of Further Studies and Analyses

Since this series was first reported, the data have been used by a number of research workers at the Parapsychology Laboratory for additional analyses. Some of the analyses bear upon the general question of whether the target order was sufficiently random to justify the assumptions underlying the statistical methods used in the evaluation of the results. Other analyses were aimed at trying to discover further psychological information relevant to questions of how ESP operates. The following review includes most of these analyses, though it does not cover all of the critical reviews and discussions.

TESTS OF ASSUMPTIONS UNDERLYING STATISTICAL METHODS

Greenwood and Stuart (1937) did a cross-check in which the subject's calls were arbitrarily matched against the cards of the third run following, the calls for the first run being checked against the card sequence of the third run, the calls of the second against the cards of the fourth, etc. To make the cross-check series the same length as the experimental series, the calls of the last two runs were checked against the cards of the first and second runs respectively. The 74 cross-check runs give a total of 387 hits, a deviation of 17 above mean chance expectation, which is less

*In the two reports, mentioned above, in which the run scores of the series were published, the scores of Subseries B and C were not given consecutively, and there were two other minor errors. It seems worth while, therefore, to list the complete run scores in chronological order here. The division between days or sessions is indicated by the use of semicolons.

Subseries A: 3; 8, 5; 9, 10; 12, 11; 11, 12; 13, 13, 12.

Subseries B: 1, 4; 4, 4; 7, 6; 5, 0; 6, 3; 11, 9; 0, 6; 8, 6; 9, 4; 10, 6; 11, 9; 5, 12; 7, 7; 12, 10; 6, 3; 10, 10; 6, 12; 2, 6; 12, 12; 4, 4; 3, 0; 13, 10.

Subseries C: 9, 8; 4, 9; 11, 9; 5, 4; 9, 11; 2, 7.

Subseries D: 12, 3; 10, 11; 10, 10.

than one standard deviation.* The empirical variance of the cross-check run score distribution is 4.772, which is a close approximation to the expected value when the size of the sample is taken into account. Greenwood (1938) also obtained the variance of the series by an exact method which takes into account the actual frequency with which the subject called the different symbols in each run. The average variance per run by this method was found to be 4.116, which is slightly greater than the theoretical variance of 4 for the binomial hypothesis which applies to the open deck or random order of cards and the value of 4.167 for the matching case based upon comparing two adequately shuffled closed decks. All four variances agree so closely in value that it makes no difference in the conclusions drawn from the data which of the four is used to compute the critical ratio. Stuart (1935) calculated the empirical variance from the run scores and found a value of 12.83. The extreme range of the scores, from 0 to 13, with the tendency for scoring to be below chance on many runs in Subseries B, contributed to the large empirical variance; but even so, the Pearce-Pratt Series is highly significant when evaluated by the empirical SD (CR=6.10, P <10^{-8}).

ANALYSES FOR SECONDARY ESP EFFECTS

The data of this experiment were checked for displacement by Russell (1943), who compared each call with the targets in the run for as many places away as the position of the call permitted. In the usual terminology this means that for backward displacement the data were checked for -1 through -24 displacement; and for forward displacement, for +1 through +24. No evidence of displacement was found.

The Pearce-Pratt Series was included by Pratt (1947) among a number of high-scoring experiments, the results of which were studied to see whether the hits were clustered or whether, conversely, they were distributed as if they were in a random series. There was no evidence of grouping of hits in the Pearce-Pratt Series not in any of the other ESP and PK data analyzed.

This experiment was also included among those surveyed by Pratt (1949) in his analysis of ESP data to determine if there was any evidence that the subject interrupted or changed his habitual sequence of calling after making a hit. The Pearce-Pratt Series did not yield any evidence of

The cross-check score as originally reported was 385 hits. In the present paper the practice followed has been to report the corrected figure when any analysis previously published has been found to have an error. All of these corrections are trivial and none affects any interpretation of the findings. The student who notices any such discrepancies should give this review precedence over the earlier publications.

change-of-call; that is, there was no difference between the frequency with which the subject followed a response that make a hit by the different ones of the five symbols in his next call and the frequency with which one of his calls that made a miss was followed by the various symbols.

Also, without giving the detailed figures, we can report here that there was no evidence that could be detected by a chi-square analysis to indicate that the subject interrupted his habitual sequences of symbol association at the point of making a hit. This is a question that needs to be examined in longer series of high-scoring subjects where a weak effect would more likely be revealed by the statistical measures applied. If it is true that subject scores well above the level attributable to chance without deviating from whatever habitual sequence preferences he may have, this fact might provide an important clue regarding the manner in which ESP impressions are brought to conscious expression.

In still another analysis of this series, Cadoret and Pratt (1950) examined the misses in the subject's trials to see if there was any evidence of consistent wrong associations between responses and target symbols. No evidence of consistent missing in the Pearce-Pratt Series was found, though evidence in the results of other experiments led to the tentative conclusion that consistent missing was a genuine secondary effect.

All in all, the results of the analyses for secondary effects that have been made with the Pearce-Pratt data add up to a strong indication that H.E.P. was successful in achieving what he was attempting to do; namely, to direct his ESP calling upon the target for that trial, the card that was on the book at the moment the call was made. The single exception to this rule is one that was apparent while the series was still being done. That was the tendency in Subseries B for the subject to score below chance in some runs. That subseries produced a remarkable number of low scores, too many to be attributed to random fluctuation, though the above-chance scores still predominated to such an extent that the total score of the 44 runs of Subseries B is significantly above chance expectation.

Discussion

Viewed twenty years later, the results of the Pearce-Pratt Series still appear to allow no interpretation except that they were due to extrasensory perception. So far as the extra chance character of the series has been re-examined, it has led only to confirmation of the fact that the statistical significance of the results cannot be challenged. Moreover, no tenable sensory interpretation has even been proposed to explain the data. The recording-error hypothesis has presented no reasonable claim for support, and the additional studies of the card distribution in the series have shown no peculiarities of patterning that could in any way alter the conclusions. Even the collusion hypothesis would have to involve all three of the participants in a deliberate conspiracy. And finally, the scores were high enough and consistent enough over the series that common sense without benefit of involved mathematics would assure us that the series was not mere chance.

If, then, as the Warner survey revealed (1952), these results, along with all the other researches on extrasensory perception, failed to establish a convincing case for ESP for the majority of the members of the American Psychological Association responding to Warner's questionnaire, it can safely be said that the issue is not a matter of scientific evidence. The series contributed all that an experiment can do toward establishing the ESP hypothesis. The rest is a question of receptivity on the part of the professional group.

It is true, the conclusions are circumscribed. Only one subject was involved and from this no generalization can be made regarding other subjects. Only a short span of time in a lifetime of the individual subject, H.E.P., was involved, and from this one study it would not be possible to make a general statement beyond those limits. This particular study could not claim to have brought out what enabled Pearce at this time to score at this percentage rate or to enable a prediction that he could, under definable circumstances, repeat this performance. None of these things, however, has been claimed for the Pearce-Pratt Series. It was enough to say that under the circumstances, within the limits, and at the time, an extra chance performance did take place that could not be ascribed to anything but the operation of extrasensory perception, whatever that is and however it is to be explained. But to have reached this point with the degree of reliability and unequivocality represented was sufficient to constitute a turning-point in the thought and experimental plans of the laboratory concerned. From that point on, another problem, another stage in the investigation of ESP was in order.

While incidentally intended to provide improved test conditions, the Pearce-Pratt Series introduced a comparison of distances. In the 30 runs of tests made at the distance of 100 yards in Subseries A, C, and D, the average per run was 8.8 hits. The average for all of H.E.P.'s 690 runs made up to the time the series began was 7.9 per 25. The comparison of the results indicated, then, that this order of distance could not be considered a limiting condition. In this experiment, at least, the subject's scoring could not be said to have been lowered by the introduction of distance at the 100-yard stage.

With the longer distance, 250 yards, introduced in Subseries B, the 44 runs averaged 6.7 hits per 25. This might, on the basis of averages, raise the question of a possible effect of the longer distance. A closer look, however, at the chronological score distribution on page 171 discourages that type of interpretation. The score distribution suggests, rather, some other factor, something that apparently raised or lowered the scoring for a given day's work. Whatever the factor was, it was not one of mere distance between the subject and the pack of cards. At least, so the reasoning went at the time, and the experimental results were taken to suggest, though not conclusively to prove, that distance of this order was not a factor related in any essential way to the operation of ESP. Since the distances were comparatively short, the results suggested the importance of tests with longer distances. And the suggested absence of a relationship between ESP and distance logically raised the question of the relationship of ESP to time. This experiment thus had much to do with precipitating the experimental investigation of precognition, which was begun with the same subject, H.E.P.

Nothing stands out now in retrospect more strongly than the shift of importance of different features of such an experimental research as this one. During the intervening decades the Pearce-Pratt Series came to have its greatest value because of the character of the experimental conditions under which it was done. Its principal contribution to the understanding of the nature of ESP—its bearing on the question of distance—was hardly noticed, and it may still be some time before it is. However, it did accomplish its purpose in turning the attention of the workers immediately concerned to problems that logically followed acceptance of the results as showing no effect of the distance involved.

Today, however, for the experimenters who are confronted with the more urgent problems of the field and who look back at this series, the paramount feature is the exceptionally high scoring produced and held for so long a time by this individual subject, H.E.P. There had been in his earlier work ample evidence that H.E.P. worked up to a crescendo of enthusiasm and ambition in his tests and that in general his scoring rate followed the rise and fall of his motivation.

As already indicated, he actually rose above his earlier scoring when introduced, in the first subseries, to the distance test conditions. It was as if this was a special challenge to him, something of a climax, as indeed it was. In the general intellectual atmosphere which he breathed, the conquest of distance was a climatic undertaking. The eye falls, too, on the striking shiftiness of scoring introduced when the distance was increased to 250 yards. It was shortly after this series was over, a matter of months, that H.E.P. suddenly lost his capacity to score significantly in the card tests under any of the conditions or in any of the types of tests in which he had performed so steadily and brilliantly for about two years. This special series may have a point of relevance to the primary problem of parapsychology today, the problem of acquiring control over psi performance.

References

Cadoret, R., and Pratt, J.G. The consistent missing effect in ESP. *Journal of Parapsychology*, 1950, 14, 244-56.

Greenwood, J.A. Variance of the ESP call series. *Journal of Parapsychology.*, 1938, 2, 60-65.

Greenwood, J.A., and Stuart, C.E. Mathematical techniques used in ESP research. *Journal of Parapsychology*, 1937, 1206-26.

Pratt, J.G. Change of call in ESP tests. *Journal of Parapsychology.* 1949, 13, 225-46.

_____. Trial-by-trial grouping of success and failure in psi tests. *Journal of Parapsychology*, 1947, 11, 254-68.

Rhine, J.B. *Extrasensory Perception*. Boston: Boston Society for Psychic Research, 1934.

_____. Some basic experiments in extrasensory perception—a background. *Journal of Parapsychology*, 1937, 1, 70-80.

_____. Some selected experiments in extrasensory perception. *Journal of Abnormal and Social Psychology*, 1936, 31, 216-28.

Russell, W. Examination of ESP records for displacement effects. *Journal of Parapsychology*, 1943, 7, 104-17.

Stuart, C.E. In reply to the Willoughby "critique." *Journal of Abnormal and Social Psychology*, 1935, 30, 384-88.

Warner, L. A second survey of psychological opinion on ESP. *Journal of Parapsychology*, 1952, 16, 284-95.

CHAPTER 3

PK Tests with a High-Speed Random Number Generator

Helmut Schmidt

One of the main goals of parapsychology at its present stage is to find means for producing psi effects more efficiently. This increase in efficiency would be of importance not only with regard to applications but also with regard to basic research, which makes slow progress largely because so much effort is required to obtain significant psi effects.

For increasing efficiency the use of high-speed test machines might have a two-fold advantage: the efficiency with respect to the time invested might be higher simply because more trials would be made in a given time; and in addition, the more realistic feedback on the subject's temporary performance might help the subject to detect states of optimal psi performance and to cultivate these states.

With the help of modern electronics it is easy to build high-speed random number generators. These generators are particularly suited for PK tests because the subjects do not have to make motor responses which limit the operation rate. PK tests at extremely high generation rates are possible if we use an integrating feedback which continuously displays to the subject his average scoring rate over, say, the last $\frac{1}{5}$ second. But even if we want to inform the subject of the outcome of each individual random event, operation rates of several tens per second are possible.

The main purpose of the present experiment was to explore and confirm the practical usefulness of a fast generator for observing PK

Reprinted with permission from *Journal of Parapsychology*, 1973, 37, 105–119.

effects. A mathematical measure for this practical usefulness is given by the psi efficiency with respect to the invested test time:

$$PQ \text{ (sec)} = 1000 \ CR^2/T,$$

where CR is the obtained critical ratio and T is the actual test time in seconds. The definition of PQ (sec) is analogous to the definition of the efficiency with respect to the number N of trials, defined previously (Schmidt, 1970b):

$$PQ = 1000 \ CR^2/N.$$

An attempt to compare the PK performance under two conditions in an objective way leads to typical difficulties because the result of a psi experiment depends not only on physiologically and psychologically controllable variables, but also on other more subtle factors like subconscious preferences of the subject for one or the other test situation and even on the mood and perhaps the expectation of the experimenter. Thus, in comparing the efficiencies obtained in the reported PK tests at different speeds, we cannot conclusively distinguish whether observed differences are due to the variations in speed per se, to subconscious or conscious preferences of the subjects for one test situation, or to differences in the experimenter's attitude toward the respective tests.

For a study of how the speed per se affects the scoring rate, one might use a sensorially balanced feedback such that from the display the subjects cannot distinguish between two compared operating speeds. Such an arrangement was used in part of the tests. It has, however, some theoretical and practical shortcomings. From the theorist's viewpoint we have to consider that a conscious or unconscious bias in the experimenter or an unconscious bias in the subject might lead to a scoring difference. The possibility that the subject may distinguish clairvoyantly between two test situations which are sensorially equivalent is by no means a purely academic one (West & Fisk, 1953).

From the viewpoint of the application-oriented experimenter who is interested in developing means for more efficient PK demonstration, sensorially equivalent test conditions might seem unfavorably restrictive; he would rather search for types of displays which are specifically suited for the used speed.

Since the reported experiments were primarily aimed at the development of practically useful methods for more efficient PK testing, sensorially equivalent conditions were not used throughout. Furthermore, the subjects were tested only under conditions they liked. In particular, in order to avoid unpleasant or frustrating associations with the tests, they were not forced to operate under all of the four different test conditions under study. In order to obtain statistically meaningful results concerning the existence of PK in the data, the total number of trials under each test condition was prespecified, but it was left open how much each subject should contribute to the test. This arrangement would correspond to what might appear the most efficient procedure in future applications of psi: one would select a number of promising subjects in pretests and then use each subject when and as long as he seemed to be in a particularly favorable state for high scoring.

Test Equipment

Random Number Generator

The random generator used in the tests can produce sequences of binary random numbers of specified length at speeds of up to 1,000 binary numbers per second. In each test run the cumulative numbers of produced +1's and -1's are continuously displayed by bright readout tubes. Two output channels provide short electric pulses with each generated +1 or -1, respectively, for driving external feedback or recording devices. The generator operates similarly to the one described earlier (Schmidt, 1970c) with the main difference that the basic random element is an electronic noise rather than radioactive decay. This change was made only for the practical reason that no sufficiently strong radioactive source was available to provide the desired high counting rate.

Recording

In the exploratory tests the readings of the two display counters (which much add up to the present length of the sequence of 100 or 1,000, respectively) were manually recorded. In all of the confirmatory tests, in addition to manual recording, one of the following two automatic recording methods was used:

1. Automatic printout of the scores with the help of a ten-pen event recorder. The difference (hits minus misses) was expressed as a binary number and the digits of this number were recorded by the on or off positions of the pens. This somewhat awkward recording method was chosen only because this equipment was most easily available.

2. Detailed recording of the sequence of generated +1's and -1's on an ordinary stereo tape recorder. By a replay of the tapes the scores were rechecked. This type of detailed recording will be particularly interesting for further work since a computer can be used to check for nonrandom patterns in the generated sequence.

Display

Before each test session the experimenter specified the subject's "abstract goal," the mental enforcement of an increased generation rate of +1's or -1's, respectively. Each of these two abstract goals was used equally often in the experiments. The purpose of the display was to translate this abstract goal into an apparent and psychologically desirable goal. Depending on whether the experimenter had set the +1 or the -1 as the goal, this number was shown by the display as a "hit" and the other number as a "miss." The subject could choose how he wanted his hits and misses displayed, i.e., for what apparent goal he wanted to strive.

The electronic test equipment permits a large variety of visual and/or auditory feedback displays. In the experiments to be reported the following two types of display were used:

1. A very simple feedback was provided with a pair of headphones which presented each hit as a click in one ear (the target ear selected by the subject) and each miss as a click in the other ear. The subject's apparent goal was to obtain an increased frequency of clicks in the target ear.

The tests were run at two different generation speeds of 30 per second and 300 per second, respectively. At the lower speed the subjects could clearly distinguish the individual clicks and had a fair judgment of how well they were scoring momentarily. At the higher speeds they could no longer hear the single clicks, but they could notice the statistical fluctuations in the noise volume between the right and left ears, and they could aim for a high noise volume in the target ear.

2. A visual display of the current cumulative score as well as the momentary scoring rate was provided by a pen chart recorder. With the help of a binary up-down counter and a simple digital-to-analog converter the recorder was connected to the random number generation in such a way that the deflection of the pen from the center line of the chart toward the apparent target side was always proportional to the difference (generated hits minus generated misses). During a test run the subject tried to move the pen mentally as far as possible from the center line toward the target side, corresponding to an increased generation rate of hits. Thus

the subject could clearly judge his present cumulative score (total deflection of the pen from the center toward the target side) as well as his momentary scoring rate, indicated by the momentary movement of the pen.

With the auditory feedback the subjects could well distinguish between the two different operating speeds (30 or 300 per second) and they usually displayed a strong preference for one particular speed. With the visual feedback, on the other hand, the inertia of the pen smoothed out the contributions of the individual events and the subjects could not estimate the generation speed. This opened the possibility of comparing the PK performance at different generation speeds under visually identical conditions. For this purpose the pen sensitivity for the fast tests (300 per second) was reduced by a factor $1/\sqrt{10}$ in comparison to the slow tests (30 per second) such that the random fluctuations of the pen after a given time had the same magnitude in both cases.

Machine Randomness Tests

For the purpose of randomness tests, the generator was left operating unattended for long periods of time, usually overnight. In these tests, the numbers of generated +1's and -1's as well as the number of "flips" (i.e., events where +1 follows a -1 or a -1 follows a +1) was counted. These tests established the randomness of the generated numbers with higher precision than required for the following PK tests. (See Appendix.)

Table 1
Results of the Exploratory PK Tests

Display	Subject No.	Random Events	Dev.	Rate (%)	CR	PQ	PQ (sec.)	Runs N+	Runs N-	Rate± (%)	R±
Visual	1	5,000	49	51.0	1.39	.38	11.4	26	18	59.1	1.21
Visual	3	3,000	61	52.0	2.23	1.65	49.5	16	13	55.2	0.56
Total		8,000	110	51.4	2.48	.77	23.1	42	31	57.7	1.29
Auditory	4	9,000	108	51.2	2.28	.58	17.4	51	31	62.2	2.21
Auditory	6	3,000	67	52.2	2.45	2.00	60.0	22	6	78.6	3.02
Total		12,000	175	51.5	3.20	.85	25.5	73	37	66.4	3.43
Grand total		20,000	285	51.4	4.03	.81	24.4	115	68	62.8	3.47

Rate=scoring rate in %. *CR* =corresponding *CR*. *PQ*=1000 *CR²/N*. *PQ* (sec.)=1000 *CR²/T*, where *T* is the total actual test time (3 sec per run) measured in seconds. *N⁺,N⁻*= number of runs with above or below chance score, respectively. Rate±=*N⁺/(N⁺+N⁻)*. *CR*±=corresponding *CR*.

Exploratory Tests

Before systematic testing was begun, a number of test situations differing in the type of display and the lengths of test runs were tried. The highest scores appeared under the two feedback conditions mentioned, when the length of each test run was kept rather short, approximately three seconds. It was therefore decided to perform a well-controlled exploratory test under these conditions.

It was planned to complete, in the exploratory tests, a total of 200 runs, each run containing 100 binary numbers generated at the rate of 30 per second, and to let the preselected subjects choose between the two mentioned types of display.

Four subjects were selected from an initial population of approximately 20, because they seemed to be highly interested and seemed to perform well at a rather stable rate. Subjects 1 and 3 had already obtained high scores in several previous tests, partly with other experimenters. Subject 4 was the author, and subject 6, a 14-year-old boy. Of the four participating subjects, two chose the auditory and two the visual display. Table 1 summarizes the results. It is seem that the average scoring rates with visual and auditory display (Rate %) happened to be nearly equal and that this scoring rate of approximately 51.4% led to a significant total result with $CR=4.03$; $P<.0001$.

Considering next the run (consisting of 100 trials made within three seconds) as the basic unit, we can designate a run as a hit or a miss ($p=\frac{1}{2}$) depending on whether its score is above or below chance expectancy, omitting the runs which come out even. Table 1 (Rate ± %) shows that 62.8% of these runs are hits.

The subjects' goal was to obtain a high scoring rate on the individual events. Assuming as a simple model the situation that the subjects did change the hit probability for the individual events uniformly to 51.4%, a simple calculation shows that approximately 61% of the runs (of 100 trials) should be hit runs.* This is reasonably close to the observed 62.8%.

In further accord with the simple model is the finding that the CR values for the total experiment, $CR=4.03$ and $CR\pm=3.47$ (see Table 1) are not significantly different.

*The exact value is given by the expression

$$\sum_{n=51}^{100} p^n q^{N-n} \binom{N}{n} \left/ \left(\sum_{n=0}^{49} + \sum_{51}^{100} \right) p^n q^{N-n} \binom{N}{n} \right.$$

with $N = 100$. The mentioned approximate value was obtained by replacing the binomial by a normal distribution.

Confirmation and Further Studies

Test Conditions

The confirmatory test was done partly under the same conditions as the previous one, at a generation speed of 30 per second with visual or auditory display. For the other part of the test the generation speed was increased to 300 per second. In order to make the test conditions externally similar, the test runs at the higher speed contained 1,000 generated numbers instead of the 100 numbers per run at the lower speed. Thus both types of runs lasted an equal time, approximately three seconds.

With auditory feedback the hits and misses were displayed as clicks in one or the other ear, respectively, as before. The sound volume was kept rather low, equal in both ears. The subjects were told that the goal was to obtain an increased number of clicks in the target ear, and it was suggested that they remain relaxed and just listen attentively to the clicks in this ear as one would listen to a distant low-level conversation one might want to overhear.

In the tests with the visual feedback the subjects had the apparent goal of moving the pen of the recorder as far as possible in the specified direction. It was left to the subjects whether they wanted to approach the task aggressively or in a relaxed, meditative way.

Whereas with the auditory feedback the subjects could clearly hear a difference between the two speeds, the two speeds could not sensorially be distinguished in the visual display, as mentioned before. Since the participants in the tests with visual feedback were experienced test subjects, however, no attempt was made to conceal the fact that two speeds were being compared or to refuse information on the current speed. Generally the subjects showed no interest in the speed; they were concerned only with influencing the display pen.

One test session usually contained between 10 and 40 runs (of three seconds duration each). The runs were generally separated by breaks of 5 to 40 seconds. After each run the subject was informed of the score. For the subjects who worked under two different test conditions, sessions with one or the other condition were alternated such that any scoring differences could not be ascribed to a decline effect.

Statistical Specifications and Subject Selection

It was decided in advance to complete a total of 200 runs under each of the four mentioned conditions and to evaluate primarily the frequency of hits among the individual random events as well as the percentage of above-chance runs.

The subjects who contributed to the test were selected by informal pretests and their momentary efficiency was frequently rechecked in warm-up runs before they were allowed to contribute a test session to the confirmatory series. It was attempted to use each subject only under test conditions which appealed to him. Most subjects showed a strong preference either for the auditory or the visual feedback.

As subjects for the tests with visual display, there happened to be available three persons who had performed outstandingly well in previous psi tests, partly conducted by other experimenters. Since with the visual display there was no sensory difference between the tests with fast and slow number generation, each of these three subjects operated under both conditions. Seven other subjects who had expressed a preference for the auditory feedback situation participated in this part of the experiment. Here, however, the fast and the slow tests were psychologically so different that the subjects were allowed to choose one speed, since a sensorially unbiased comparison between the two speeds could not be guaranteed anyway.

Table 2
Test Results for the Individual Subjects Under the Four Different Test Conditions

Display Speed	Subject No.	Random Events	Dev.	Rate (%)	Runs N⁺	N⁻	Rate± (%)
Visual Slow	1	12,000	199	51.7	76	36	68
	2	3,000	68	52.3	19	10	66
	3	5,000	106	52.1	34	13	72
Auditory Slow	4	10,000	89	50.9	51	41	55
	5	5,000	132	52.6	38	10	79
	6	5,000	55	51.1	29	16	64
Visual Fast	1	100,000	218	50.22	53	42	56
	2	60,000	381	50.64	39	18	68
	3	40,000	116	50.29	20	19	51
Auditory Fast	4	50,000	222	50.44	29	21	58
	7	50,000	191	50.38	32	16	67
	8	60,000	299	50.50	39	21	65
	9	30,000	97	50.32	18	12	60
	10	10,000	-35	49.65	4	6	40

Table 2 gives the test results for the individual subjects. Subjects number 1, 3, 4, and 6 had already contributed to the previous tests (Table 1). It is seen that their scores in the slow tests are similar to their previous scores. Table 3 gives the total results under each of the four different test conditions.

Scoring Rate and Speed

Table 3 shows that significant scores were obtained under all four test conditions.

The scoring rates of 51.9% and 51.4% in the slow tests are not significantly different. Similarly the scoring rates of 50.36% and 50.39% in the two fast tests do not differ significantly. But there is a significant different in the average scoring rates of the fast and slow tests (Cr_d=4.75). The lower efficiency of the fast test with respect to the number of trials is also reflected by the lower PQ values for the fast tests. Considering, however, the efficiency with respect to the time spent on the test, measured by PQ (sec) (Schmidt, 1970b), we observe only a slight (i.e., statistically not significant) drop in efficiency from the slow to the fast tests.

A similar, slight decrease in efficiency is found by considering each three-second run as a binary trial. Disregarding the runs which happened to come out even, it is seen that for the slow and fast tests 66.2% and 60.1%, respectively, of the runs produced an above-chance score. The difference between these two scoring rates is not statistically significant (Cr_d=1.66).

It was to be expected that the fraction of runs (Rate±) with an above-chance score would be higher than the scoring rate on the individual events (Rate). Assuming, as before, the simple model where we have, during the

Table 3
Total Results Under Four Different Conditions

Display Speed	Random Events	Dev.	Rate (%)	CR	PQ	PQ (sec)	Runs N⁺	Runs N⁻	Rate± (%)	CR±
Visual Slow	20,000	373	51.9	5.28	1.4	42	129	59	68.6	5.11
Auditory Slow	20,000	276	51.4	3.90	0.76	23	118	67	63.8	3.75
Slow Total	40,000	649	51.6	6.49	1.05	32	247	126	66.2	6.27
Visual Fast	200,000	715	50.36	3.20	0.051	15	112	79	58.6	2.39
Auditory Fast	200,000	774	50.39	3.46	0.060	18	122	76	61.6	3.27
Fast Total	400,000	1,489	50.37	4.71	0.055	16	234	155	60.1	4.01

Table 4

Efficiencies PQ and PQ (sec) Obtained in the Previously Published Precognition and PK Tests as Compared with the Efficiencies Observed with the High-Speed Generator

Type of Test	Speed (Events per sec)	p	No. of Trials	CR	PQ	PQ (sec)	Reference
Precognition	1	¼	63,000	6.4	.65	.65	Schmidt, 1969
	1	¼	20,000	6.6	.33	.33	Schmidt, 1969
	1	¼	10,000	n.s.	n.s.	n.s.	Unpublished
	$1/60$	¼	1,000	4.7	22.10	.37	Schmidt & Pantas, 1972
PK	1	½	32,768	3.3	.33	.33	Schmidt, 1970a
	1	½	6,400	3.6	2.00	2.0	Schmidt, 1971
	1	½	6,400	3.9	2.40	2.4	Schmidt, 1971
	30	½	40,000	6.5	1.05	32.0	Present study
	300	½	400,000	4.7	.055	16.0	Present study

experiment, simply an increased scoring rate on the individual events, 51.6% in the slow and 50.37% in the fast tests, the expected scoring rates R± become 62.5% and 59.9%, which are not significantly different from the observed values of 66.2% and 60.1%. Also, in accordance with the simple model, the values of *CR* and *CR*± are very similar for each of the four test conditions individually.

It is interesting to compare the scoring rates and efficiencies in the reported tests with the scoring rates and efficiencies obtained by the same experimenter in PK and precognition tests performed previously at an average speed of one trial per second or less. It must be stressed that such a comparison can have only suggestive value, since factors other than speed per se might have contributed to the results, subject differences in particular.

Table 4 gives the writer's previously published precognition and PK tests with individual subjects, in comparison with the results of the present report. The indicated speed of one per second for the precognition experiments is an upper limit for the actual speed. In some of the tests the subjects, who determined the operating speed by their rate of guessing, worked more slowly. Thus also the *PQ* (sec) values in the precognition tests are upper limits.

Visual and Auditory Feedback

The similar scoring rates obtained in the tests with visual and auditory display suggest that both possibilities should be pursued further.

Experiments in which both types of feedback are given simultaneously are in preparation.

Discussion

The availability of fast generators with the associated fast feedback which can display to the subject his momentary performance might encourage researchers to attack anew the old question of whether states which are favorable for PK performance can be cultivated. Under the described experimental conditions the subject might actively search for the mental state which leads to the highest scoring rate, and the feedback would immediately indicate the success of his effort. Furthermore, because of the high number of random events evaluated per second, one could discover possible "bursts" of psychic activity even if they lasted only a fraction of a second. Whether this type of feedback could be used for the training of psi performance in analogy to the training of other "involuntary" body functions recently achieved by "biofeedback" methods remains to be seen.

A further interesting aspect of these high-speed PK tests may be their possible relationship to PK effects on quasi static targets. Consider, for example, a feather suspended by a string in air, and assume that a subject could mentally move this feather under rigorously controlled conditions. Such an effect on a seemingly static object might be considered as a statistical PK effect since the feather would be subject to the very frequent impacts (approximately 10^{24} per second) by the air molecules. If the subject could mentally achieve just a very slight unbalancing of these collisions in the sense that the fraction of molecules hitting the feather from the right was just minutely larger than the fraction of molecules hitting the feather from the left, then a macroscopic response of the feather could result. A suspended feather might thus even appear to provide the most natural high-speed random generator, and by changing the air pressure surrounding the feather one could even experiment at different generation speeds (impact rates of the air molecules on the feather). The main advantage of the electronic fast generator over the suspended feather is that with the electronic generator we can count each individual event, whereas the numbers of molecules hitting the feather from the right or left respectively is not directly measurable and we have to depend on rather crude macroscopic measurements which reduce the sensitivity of this PK detector.

Appendix
Randomness Tests with the Fast Generator in the Absence of Human Subjects

For the purpose of randomness tests in the absence of human subjects, the generator was operated automatically during a total of twenty nights. In these runs, which were done partly before, partly between, and partly after the PK experiments, the numbers of generated +1's, -1's and the number of "flips" (i.e., events where a +1 is followed by a -1 or vice versa) were recorded (Schmidt, 1970c).

In each of ten nights 10^6 numbers were generated at the rate of 30 per second, and in each of the remaining ten nights 10^7 numbers were generated at the rate of 300 per second, in correspondence with the two speeds used in the PK tests. Table 5 gives explicitly the deviations from chance expectancy for the number of generated +1's and for the number of flips.

Table 5
Results of the Machine Randomness Tests

	$n-\bar{n}$	CR	$F-\bar{n}$	CR
$N = 10^6$	−259	.518	1,050	2.100
	−824	1.648	58	0.116
	567	1.134	−556	1.112
	−223	0.446	−108	0.216
	183	0.366	−307	0.614
	−886	1.772	378	0.756
	41	0.082	−445	0.890
	592	1.184	−79	0.158
	320	0.640	955	1.910
	426	0.854	1,066	2.132
	+63	x^2=10.29	2,012	x^2=15.67
	CR=0.03		CR=1.3	P=.1
$N=10^7$	−932	0.589	1,984	1.255
	−1,402	0.887	628	.397
	1,034	0.654	1,124	.711
	2,194	1.388	−632	.400
	−2,775	1.755	−3,425	2.166
	−740	0.468	421	.266
	1,954	1.236	1,090	.689
	1,144	0.724	−518	.328
	2,001	1.265	−1,938	1.226
	215	0.136	−527	.333
	+2,693	x^2=10.48	−1,793	x^2=9.36
	CR=1.2		CR=0.8	

n=number of hits; F=number of flips

The total chance deviations and the chi-square values are well within the chance limits consistent with ideal randomness.

The scoring rates obtained in the slow and fast machine tests, respectively, are $(50.00063 \pm 0.032)\%$ for the lower speed, and $(50.0027 \pm 0.01)\%$ for the higher speed.

Considering the possibility of a time constant bias of the generator we can conclude with 95% confidence that the true scoring rate lies within the given confidence intervals ($\pm 2\sigma$). The deviations observed in the reported PK tests lie far outside these intervals.

References

Schmidt, H. Precognition of a quantum process. *Journal of Parapsychology*, 1969, 33, 99–108.

Schmidt, H. A PK test with electronic equipment. *Journal of Parapsychology*, 1970, 34, 175–81. (a)

Schmidt, H. The psi quotient: An efficiency measure for psi tests. *Journal of Parapsychology*, 1970, 34, 210–14. (b)

Schmidt, H. A quantum mechanical random number generator for psi tests. *Journal of Parapsychology*, 1970, 34, 219–24. (c)

Schmidt, H. Mental influence on random events. *New Scientist* and *Science Journal*, June 24, 1971, 757–58.

Schmidt, H., & Pantas, L. Psi tests with internally different machines. *Journal of Parapsychology*, 1972, 36, 222–32.

West, D.J., & Fisk, G.W. A dual ESP experiment with clock cards. *Journal of the Society for Psychical Research*, 1953, 37, 185–89.

CHAPTER 4

Correlations of Random Binary Sequences with Pre-Stated Operator Intention: A Review of a 12-Year Program

R.G. Jahn, B.J. Dunne, R.D. Nelson, Y.H. Dobyns *and* G.J. Bradish

I. Background

The role of human consciousness in the establishment of physical reality has been debated in many contexts and formats throughout every era of scientific history. The issue was central to ancient Egyptian and Greek philosophy, and to the enduring Hermetic tradition from which classical empirical science emerged. Even well into the period of scientific enlightenment, scholars of the stature of Francis Bacon (Walker, 1972), Robert Hooke (1976), Robert Boyle (1962), and Isaac Newton (Kubrin, 1981) addressed many of their empirical investigations to "the mystery by which mind could control matter" (p. 113). Although the maturing scientific establishment of the following two centuries came largely to dismiss such possibility, a number of distinguished physicists, including J.J. Thompson, William Crookes, Lord Rayleigh, and Marie and Pierre Curie continued to regard this topic as relevant to their scholarship, and were

Reprinted with permission from *Journal of Scientific Exploration*, 1997, **11**, 345–367.

active participants in the Society for Psychical Research (Beloff, 1977). A subtler form of the question arose in the early "observational" interpretations of quantum mechanics which were construed by a number of the patriarchs of modern physics, including Planck (1932), Bohr (1961), Schrödinger (1967), de Broglie (1955), Heisenberg (1962), Pauli (1994), Einstein (Schilpp, 1949), Jeans (1943), Eddington (1978), Wigner (1967), Jordan (1960), and von Weisäcker (1980), to raise important questions of the implicit or explicit role of human consciousness in the collapse of the wave function. Although they vigorously debated such possibilities from both scientific and philosophical perspectives, little consensus was reached, other than the need for better direct experimental data.

The enigma of consciousness continues to interest some contemporary physicists in such contexts as the non-locality/EPR paradox/Bell's theorem debates (Kafatos, 1989), single photon interference (Clausor, 1974), causality violations in thermodynamics (Donald and Martin, 1976), neurophysics (Shear, 1996), complexity and chaos theory (Atmanspacher and Dalenoort, 1994), and numerous other aspects of quantum epistemology and measurement (Hiley and Peat, 1987; Schommers, 1989), once again without much resolution. Indeed, although a myriad of theoretical and empirical attempts have been made to define the elusive concept of consciousness itself, curiously little agreement on its origins, substance, characteristics, or functions has yet been achieved. Some of these efforts relegate consciousness to a complex of emergent phenomena of the human brain, and thus to an ensemble of neurochemical and neuroelectrical processes (Scott, 1995; Borstner and Shawe-Taylor, 1995). Others attempt to invoke quantum indeterminacy in explication of brain function (Stapp, 1993). While many philosophers of science maintain that the concept of consciousness is so intrinsically subjective that it must be excluded from scientific attention, others plead that scientific scholarship cannot indefinitely ignore such dimensions.

Earlier in this century, attempts to codify the psychological dimensions of the problem were undertaken by a community of "parapsychologists" rooted in the pioneering research of J.B. and Louisa Rhine (Rhine et al. 1965). In most such studies, the consciousness aspect hypothesized to correlate with the behavior of physical systems entailed some form of volition, intention, or desire, a presumption consistent with the premises of most religions, mystical traditions, personal superstitious practices, and the innate human propensity to hope or to wish. Portions of this early work attracted the attention of Pauli (1994) and other quantum physicists. Einstein reports on a conversation he held with "an important theoretical physicist" regarding the relevance of Rhine's research to the EPR paradox:

He: I am inclined to believe in telepathy.
I: This has probably more to do with physics than with psychology.
He: Yes.—[Schilpp, 1949, p. 683].

Notwithstanding this interest, much of the subsequent research of this genre proved vulnerable to technical criticism and unpersuasive to the scientific mainstream.

Most recently, the more sophisticated information processing technology that has advanced our understanding of the physical world over the last half century has also provided tools for addressing this class of anomalous phenomena with a methodological rigor unimaginable in the earlier parapsychological research. For example, over the period 1959 to 1987, some 832 experimental studies conducted by 68 investigators directly addressed the influence of human intention on the performance of a broad variety of random event generators. Meta-analytical assessment of these results yields strong statistical evidence for small but consistent anomalous effects that correlate with the intentions or desires of their operators (Radin and Nelson, 1989), raising possible implications for experimental and theoretical study of many other probabilistic physical events, and for their technological applications. At the least, these findings should motivate performance and contemplation of yet more precise and extensive empirical studies.

The purpose of this article is to present a major body of new data that bears on this issue, acquired over twelve years of experimental study of anomalous human/machine interactions, conducted in an engineering laboratory context. Specifically, these studies have searched for possible correlations between the output data distributions of various random binary processes and the pre-stated intentions of attendant human operators. The history of this laboratory program, details of its instrumentation, protocols, data reduction and interpretation techniques, its attempts to model the observed effects, and the possible implications of the results for various regimes of basic science and technical applications have been described elsewhere (Jahn and Dunne, 1988; Jahn, 1982; Jahn, Dunne and Nelson, 1987; Jahn and Dunne, 1986; Jahn, 1988). Here we shall focus only on the empirical results and their individual and collective statistical merit.

II. Equipment and Protocol

The machine employed in the "benchmark" experiments of this program is a microelectronic random event generator (REG) driven by a commercial noise board (Elgenco #3602A–15124), involving a reverse-biased semi-conductor junction, precision preamplifiers, and filters. The output spectrum of this noise source, essentially constant (± 1 db) from 50 Hz to 20Khz, is clipped and further amplified to provide a randomly alternating flat-topped wave form of ± 10 volt amplitude with 0.5 μsec rise and fall times which is gate-sampled at selectable regular intervals to yield a randomly alternating sequence of positive and negative pulses. A set number of these are then counted against a regularly alternating +, −, +, −, ... template, thereby differentially eliminating any distortion of randomicity due to ground reference drift. The immediate and cumulative results are displayed via LEDs on the machine face and graphically on a computer screen, and transmitted on-line to a data management system. The balance of the device entails a variety of voltage and thermal monitors, redundant counters, and other fail-safe features that ensure its nominal operation and preclude tampering, and other security features are incorporated in the operational software. The machine is extensively and frequently calibrated in unattended operation, and is invariably found to reproduce the theoretical binomial combinatorial distributions having the appropriate means and standard deviations, with all higher moments and sequential correlations negligible, to statistical confidence more than adequate to support the claimed experimental correlations. A block diagram of this REG is shown in Figure 1; further technical details are available upon request.

For the benchmark experiments, this REG is set to generate *trials* of 200 binary samples each, which are counted at a rate of 1000 per second. The protocol requires individual human operators, seated in front of the machine but having no physical contact with it, to accumulate prescribed equal size blocks of data under three interspersed states of intention: to achieve a higher number of bit counts than the theoretical mean (HI); to achieve a lower number of bit counts than the theoretical mean (LO); or not to influence the output, *i.e.* to establish a baseline (BL). Data are collected in *runs* of 50, 100, or 1000 trials, depending on operator preference and protocol variations, and compounded over some number of experimental *sessions* into predefined data *series* of a specified number of trials, ranging from 1000 to 5000 per intention. Data processing is performed at the level of these individual series, which are regarded as the basic experimental units for interpretation and replication of any results. The essential criteria for anomalous correlations are statistically significant departures of the HI and/or LO series mean scores from the theoretical chance expectation and, most indicatively, the separation of the high- and low-intention data (HI-LO).

The order of the operator intentions is established either by their own

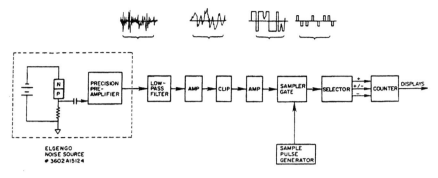

FUNCTIONAL DIAGRAM OF REG

Fig. 1. Functional diagram of electronic Random Event Generator (REG) used in benchmark experiments. A commercial noise source based on a reverse-biased semiconductor junction is processed to yield a randomly alternating sequence of positive and negative pulses, which are compared with a regularly alternating binary template. The number of coincidences from a specified number of samples are displayed immediately and cumulatively on the machine face and graphically on a computer screen, and are transmitted on-line to a data management system.

choice (volitional protocol) or by random assignment (instructed protocol), and is unalterably recorded in the database manager before the REG is activated by a remote switch. All subsequent data are automatically recorded on-line, printed simultaneously on a permanent strip recorder, and summarized by the operators in a dedicated logbook. Any discrepancy among these redundant records, or any fail-safe indication from the REG or its supporting equipment (both extraordinarily rare), invoke preestablished contingency procedures that preclude inclusion of any fouled data or any possible means of favorable data selection.

III. Primary Results

A. Collective Mean Shifts

Over a 12-year period of experimentation, 91 individual operators, all anonymous, uncompensated adults, none of whom claimed unusual abilities, accumulated a total of 2,497,200 trials distributed over 522 tripolar series in this benchmark experiment. Table 1 lists the overall results for the three categories of intention, HI, LO, and BL, and for the HI-LO separations, for comparison with the concomitant calibration data and the theoretical chance expectations. With reference to the symbol list below the table, the salient indicators are the mean shifts from the theoretical expectation, σ_μ, the corresponding z-scores, z_μ, and the one-tail probabilities of chance occurrence of these or larger deviations, p_μ. Also listed are the proportions of the 522 series yielding results in the intended directions, S.I.D., and the preparations of operators achieving results in the intended directions, O.I.D. (Note that as defined, d_μ is expressed in units of bits/trial. We could equally well represent the effect size in absolute units of bits/bit processed, *i.e.* $\varepsilon_\mu = \delta_\mu/2\mu_0$, which in turn differs by a factor of two from the common statistical effect size, $z_\mu/N_b = \delta_\mu/\mu_0$, where N_b denotes the total number of bits processed. We shall henceforth use δ_μ and ε_μ more or less interchangeably, as befits the context).

The measures tabulated in Table 1 individually and collectively define the scale and character of the primary anomaly addressed in these studies, i.e. the statistically significant correlations of the output of this microelectronic random binary process with the pre-recorded intentions of a large pool of unselected human operators. Specifically to be noted is the

Table 1

Statistical data from benchmark REG experiments, listed for passive calibrations (CAL); Operator high intentions (HI), Low intentions (LO), and null intentions (BL); and HI-LO separations.

Parameter	CAL	HI	LO	BL	HI-LO
N_t	5,803,354	839,800	836,650	820,750	1,676,450
μ	99.998	100.026	99.984	100.013	
s_t	7.075	7.070	7.069	7.074	
σ_s	0.002	0.006	0.006	0.006	
δ_μ	-0.002	0.026	-0.016	0.013	0.042
σ_μ	0.003	0.008	0.008	0.008	0.011
z_μ	-0.826	3.369	-2.016	1.713	3.809
p_μ	0.409*	3.77×10^{-4}	0.0219	0.0867*	6.99×10^{-5}
S.I.D.		0.523	0.536	0.502†	0.569
O.I.D.		0.623	0.473	0.593†	0.516

Key

N_t: Number of trials (200 binary samples each). μ: Mean of trial score distribution. s_t: Standard deviation of trial score distribution. σ_s: Measurement uncertainty (statistical) in the observed value of s_t; $\sigma_s \equiv \sigma_0/\sqrt{2N_t}$ where $\sigma_0 = \sqrt{50}$ is the theoretical trial standard deviation. σ_μ: Difference of mean from theoretical chance expectation; $\delta_\mu \equiv \mu - \mu_0$ for HI and LO; δ_μ(HI-LO) $\equiv \mu$(HI)$-\mu$(LO) $\equiv \delta_\mu$(HI)$-\delta_\mu$(LO). σ_μ: Measurement uncertainty (statistical) in the observed value of δ_μ; $\sigma_\mu = \sigma_0/\sqrt{N_t}$ for HI and LO; σ_μ(HI-LO) $= \sigma_0\sqrt{1/N_t(HI)+1/N_t(LO)}$. z_μ: z-score of mean shift; $z_\mu \equiv \delta_\mu/\sigma_\mu$ (calculated with full precision from raw data values, not from the rounded values presented above in the table.) p_μ: One-tail probability of z_μ (CAL, BL two-tail). S.I.D.: Proportion of series having z_μ in the intended direction. O.I.D.: Proportion of operators with overall results in the intended direction.

*p-values for CAL and BL are two-tailed due to lack of intention.
†BL is treated as in intended direction when positive.

overall scale of the effect, $O(10^{-4})$ bits inverted per bit processed; the somewhat higher deviation in the HI results compared to the LO; the slight departure of the BL results from both the theoretical chance expectation and the calibration value, and the negligible alterations in the variances of the score distributions. The overall figure of merit for the HI-LO separation, which is the postulated primary indicator, is $z_\mu = 3.81$ ($p_\mu = 7 \times 10^{-5}$).

The anomalous correlations also manifest in the fraction of experimental series in which the terminal results confirm the intended directions. For example, 57% of the series display HI-LO score separations in the intended direction ($z_s = 3.15$, $p_s = 8 \times 10^{-4}$). In contrast, the anomaly is not statistically evident in the 52% of individual operators producing databases in the intended directions ($z_0 = 0.31$, $p_0 = 0.38$), a feature having possible structural implications, as discussed below.

B. Cumulative Deviations

An instructive alternative display of these results is in the form of cumulative deviation graphs, wherein are plotted the accumulating total departures from the chance mean sequentially compounded by this group of operators in their HI, LO, and BL efforts over the long history of the experiment (Figure 2). The superimposed parabolic envelopes indicate the increasing width of one-tailed 95% confidence intervals about the theoretical mean as the database evolves. In this format, the deviate trends in the HI and LO performances appear as essentially random walks about shifted mean values, leading to steadily increasing departures from expectation. Consistent with the terminal values listed in Table 1, the average slopes of these two patterns of achievement, in units of bits deviation per bit processed, are roughly 1.3×10^{-4} and -7.8×10^{-5} respectively. Although local segments reflective of individual operators or particular periods of operation may differ somewhat from these overall effect sizes, as described below, this 10^{-4} order of magnitude tends to characterize virtually all of the anomalous correlations achieved in these experiments.

C. Count Distributions

Any structural details of the trial count distributions that compound to the observed anomalous mean shifts may hold useful implications for modeling such correlations. While no statistically significant departures of the variance, skew, kurtosis, or higher moments from the appropriate chance values appear in the overall data, regular patterns of certain finer scale features can be discerned. For example, deviations of the trial count populations,

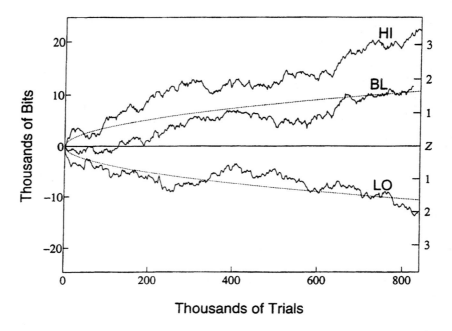

Fig 2. Cumulative deviation graphs of benchmark REG results for HI, LO, and BL operator intentions. Parabolic envelopes are one-tail 95% confidence intervals about the theoretical chance mean. The scale on the right ordinate refers to the terminal z-scores.

n_i, from their theoretical chance values, n_{io}, conform to statistical linear regressions of the form $\Delta n_i / n_{io} = 4\varepsilon_\mu (\chi_i - \mu_0)$ where χ_i denotes the given trial count (e.g. 100, 102, 94, etc.), μ_0 is the theoretical chance mean of the full distribution (100), and $4\varepsilon_\mu$ is the slope of the linear regression fit. Figure 3 depicts this effect graphically for the database of Table 1 and Figure 2. Such functional behavior is consistent with a simple displacement of the chance Gaussian distribution to the observed mean value or, equivalently, to a shift in the elementary binomial probability from the exact theoretical value of 0.5 to $(0.5 + \varepsilon_\mu)$ (Jahn, Dobryns and Dunne, 1991). Given the consistency of all other features of the distributions with chance expectation, this suggests that the most parsimonious model of the anomalous correlation is between operator intention and the binary probability intrinsic to the experiment.

D. Individual Operator Effects

Given the correlation of operator intentions with the anomalous mean shifts, it is reasonable to search the data for operator-specific features that

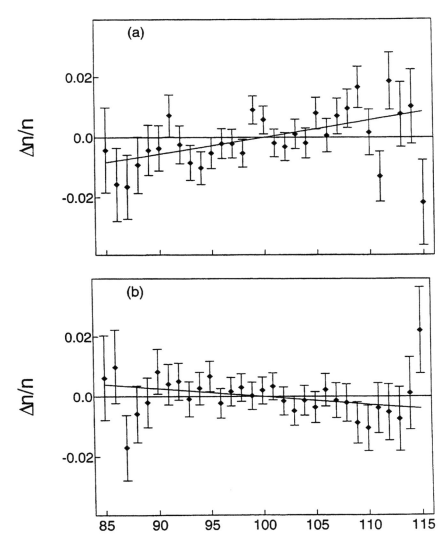

Fig. 3. Normalized deviations of benchmark REG individual count populations from chance expectations: (a) HI intention data: linear fit, $z_1 = 3.27$; quadratic correction, $z_2 = 0.69$; (b) LO intention data: linear fit, $z_1 = 1.55$; quadratic correction, $z_2 = 0.48$.

might establish some pattern of individual operator contributions to the overall results. Unfortunately, quantitative statistical assessment of these is complicated by the unavoidably wide disparity among the operator database sizes, and by the small signal-to-noise ratio of the raw data, leaving

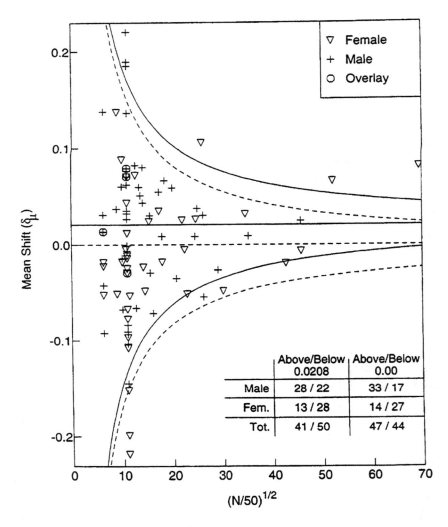

Fig. 4. Deployment of 91 individual operator HI-LO mean shift separations achieved in the benchmark REG experiments, as a function of their database sizes. The inset table highlights the imbalances in male and female operator performance with respect to the empirical and theoretical chance mean-shift values.

graphical and analytical representations of the distribution of individual operator effects only marginally enlightening. For example, Figure 4 deploys the 91 individual operator HI-LO mean shift separations as a function of their various data base sizes. Superimposed are the theoretical mean value, the mean value of the composite data, and the 1.64σ

(p_μ=0.05) deviation loci with respect to these two means. Of interest here are the ratios of positive and negative points about the theoretical and empirical means, their dependence on data base size and on operator gender, and the positions and genders of the outliers.

The limited number of operator data points make density plots of these mean shift data sensitive to the bin sizes and locations selected, but Figure 5 compares one such display with appropriate theoretical distributions centered on the chance and empirical mean values. The attached *chi*-squared values indicate some preference of the latter model, but for these data the direct z_μ calculation underlying Table 1 is a far more accurate indicator of the anomalous mean shift. Attempts to interpret the operator distribution of z-scores, rather than mean shifts, suffer from the same limitations of available data points, and are similarly inconclusive.

Given the specification of the experimental series as the pre-established unit for data interpretation, and the significantly larger fraction of series having HI-LO differences in the intended directions (Table 1), it is also reasonable to search for indications of data structure in the distribution of series scores achieved by all operators. Since a total of 522 such data units are available, the resolution of mean shift and z-score distributions is considerably better here, but as shown in Figure 6, beyond more clearly confirming the overall shifts of the mean, further identification of structural detail remains speculative. This situation is further confused by the obvious operator gender disparity in the data, as highlighted in the inset table on Figure 4, and discussed below.

IV. Secondary Correlations

Possible secondary correlations of effect sizes with a host of technical, psychological, and environmental factors e.g., the type of random source; the distance of the operator from the machine; operator gender; two or more operators attempting the task together; feedback modes; the rate of bit generation; the number of bits sampled per trial; the number of trials comprising a run or series; the volitional/instructed protocol options; the degree of operator experience; and others have been explored to various extents within the course of these experiments, and in many other related studies not discussed here. Very briefly, qualitative inspection of these data, along with a comprehensive analysis of variance (Nelson, Dobyns, Dunne, and Jahn, 1991) indicate that most of these factors do not consistently alter the character or scale of the combined operator effects from those outlined above, although some may be important in

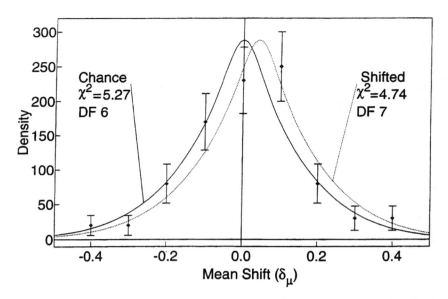

Fig. 5. *Density plot of 91 individual operator HI-LO mean shifts achieved on benchmark REG experiments, superimposed on theoretical distributions centered on the chance and empirical mean-shift values. These two comparison curves are constructed as the sums of 91 operator normal distributions, each of observation error $\sigma_i \propto 1/N_i$ where N_i is the individual database size. The "chance" curve assumes all individual effect sizes are zero; the "shifted" curve assumes all are the same as the composite effect size. The latter assumption yields a better χ^2 fit.*

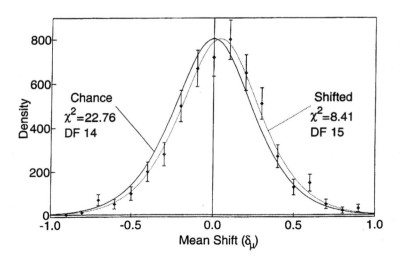

Fig. 6. *Density plot of 522 series HI-LO mean shifts achieved on benchmark experiments, superimposed on theoretical distributions centered on the chance and empirical mean-shift values (constructed as in Fig. 5).*

certain individual operator performance patterns. The few potentially important exceptions to this generalization that have been identified are described in the following paragraphs.

A. Gender-Related Effects

Segregation of the total REG database described above into male and female operator components reveals several striking disparities. As evident in Figure 4, although three of the female operators have produced the largest individual z-scores, the overall correlations of mean shifts with intention are much weaker for the females than for the males. In fact, while a majority of the males succeed in both directions of effort, most of the females' low intention results are opposite to intention. Specifically, some 66% of the male operators succeed in separating their overall HI and LO scores in the intended direction, compared to only 34% of the females. In other words, there is some indication that the total operator performance distribution has three components: a) three outstanding female datasets; b) 38 female datasets indistinguishable from a chance distribution; and c) 50 well-distributed male datasets compounding to significant positive performance. Many other aspects of the gender-related disparities are detailed in Dunne (1995).

B. Device Dependence

The sensitivity of the anomalous correlations to the particular random source employed or to its form of implementation into an experimental device has been extensively explored via a variety of machines and protocols (Jahn, Dunne and Nelson, 1988; Nelson, Dobyns, Dunne, and Jahn, 1991; Dunne, 1995). In the simplest variants, the commercial microelectronic noise diode in the benchmark configuration was replaced by identical and similar units, with no detectable changes in the character of the results. In a more substantial and, as it turned out, more critical set of modifications, the physical noise source was replaced by three distinctly different pseudorandom sources:

1) A pseudorandom-number generating algorithm included in the Borland Turbo Basic programming package was implemented on an IBM AT-286 computer to provide binary strings that could be counted and displayed in the same formats as the benchmark experiments. More specifically, the floating-point numbers provided by the Borland function, which distribute uniformly over the interval 0 to 1, were converted into bits by assigning 1 to all values above 0.5, and 0 to all values below.

The initiating seeds were obtained by starting a microsecond clock when the operator prompts first appeared on the screen, and stopping it when the operators responded by pressing a key. The accumulated values were then added to the number of seconds since midnight to compound the seeds. In performing these experiments, the operators had the options of digital, digital cumulative, or graphical cumulative deviation displays on the monitor, akin to those available on the benchmark version.

2) The benchmark equipment was modified to allow replacement of the Elgenco noise source by a hard-wired electronic shift register containing 31 flip-flops comprising a sequence length of over 2×10^6 steps. This generator produced strictly deterministic sequences from the same initial seed that, at a sampling rate of 1000 Hz, recycled roughly every 60 hours, far exceeding the length of any signal experimental session. From the operator's perspective, all other aspects of the protocol, machine operation, and feedback display were identical to those of the benchmark experiments.

3) A random element was overlaid on the pseudorandom processor just described by introducing an asynchronous shift frequency for the register, driven by an analog element that swept from a few kHz to a few tens of kHz over a period of several minutes. This unpredictable component of the sampling imbued the device with a complex combination of random and pseudorandom characteristics.

As discussed further below, when source #3, which retains some physically random features, is utilized, statistically significant correlations of results with operator intention, comparable to those seen in the benchmark experiments, continue to appear. For the strictly deterministic sources #1 and #2, however, no such correlations are observed.

A more substantial extension of the experimental concept employs a large scale mechanical device called a "Random Mechanical Cascade" (RMC), in which 9000 × ¾" dia. polystyrene spheres trickle downward through a quincunx array of 330 × ¾" dia. nylon pegs, whereby they are scattered into 19 collection bins in a close approximation to a Gaussian population distribution. In this experiment, operators endeavor to shift the mean bin population to the right or left, or to exert no intention in randomly interspersed trials. The large databases from this experiment display a similar size and character of anomalous correlations to those of the smaller scale random source experiments, and similar count population and other structural details (Dunne, Nelson and Jahn, 1990).

C. Series Position Effects

While it might be reasonable to expect that operators' proficiency at these experimental tasks would improve with increasing experience, no systematic learning tendencies are evident in the data. Rather, the progression of the anomalous effect sizes as a function of the number of series completed by the operators is found to take the somewhat unanticipated form shown in Figure 7. Namely, when the mean shifts obtained by all operators on their respective first, second, third, ... series are plotted against that series ordinal position, a peak of initial success is followed by sharp reduction on the second and third series, where after the effect gradually recovers to an asymptotic intermediate value over the higher series numbers (Dunne, Dobyns, Jahn, and Nelson, 1994). This pattern obtains, with minor disparities, for the overall HI, LO, and HI-LO data, but not for the baselines. It also appears in a majority of the individual operator databases having five or more series. The interpretation of this pattern on psychological or physical grounds can only be speculative at this point, but its ubiquitous appearance clearly complicates any consistency or replicability criteria.

D. Distance and Time Dependence

The dependence of the effect sizes on the distance of the operator from the machine could also be an important indicator of fundamental mechanism. Actually, no such dependence has been found over the dimensions available in the laboratory itself. More remarkably, these operator/machine

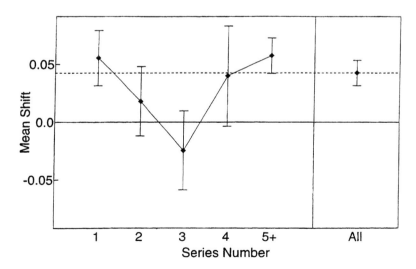

Fig. 7. Benchmark REG HI-LO mean separations achieved by all 91 operators on their first, second, third ... experimental series. The value at 5+ subsumes all series beyond the fourth. The value at "all" is the grand average of all data.

aberrations continue to manifest in a substantial body of experiments wherein operators are physically separated from the devices by distances of up to several thousand miles, again with no statistically detectable dependence of the effect sizes on the degree of separation. Rather, the results of some 396,000 trials per intention conducted under this "remote" protocol, wherein the device is run unobserved at prearranged times by staff members who remain blind to the operators' intentions, are very similar in character to those of the local experiments, including the scale of effect, and the relatively larger results under HI intentions compared to LO (Dunne and Jahn, 1992).

In a subset of this remote database, comprising some 87,000 trials per intention, the operators address their attention to the machine's operation at times other than those at which the data are actually generated. Such "off-time" experiments have ranged from 73 hours before to 336 hours after machine operator, and display a scale and character of anomalous results similar to those of the locally generated data, including gender effects and count population distortions. In fact, the overall mean shift in the high-intention efforts in these "off-time" remote experiments is twice as large as that in the "on-time" remote data, although this difference is not statistically significant, given the smaller size off-time database. As with the distance separations, no dependence of the yield on the magnitude of the temporal separations is observed over the range tested. Comparable remote and off-time results are found in the RMC experiment, as well.

E. Operator Strategy and Psychological Correlates

Although no systematic assessment of any of the multitude of potentially relevant psychological parameters characterizing the operators has been attempted, on the basis of informal discussions, casual observations of their styles, occasional remarks they record in the experimental logbooks, and our own experiences as operators, it is clear that individual strategies vary widely. Most operators simply attend to the task in a quiet, straightforward manner. A few use meditation or visualization techniques or attempt to identify with the device or process in some transpersonal manner; others employ more assertive or competitive strategies. Some concentrate intently on the process; others are more passive, maintaining only diffuse attention to the machine and diverting their immediate focus to some other activity, such as glancing through a magazine, or listening to music. We find little pattern of correlation of such strategies with achievement. Rather, the effectiveness of any particular operational style seems to be operator-specific and transitory; what seems to help one operator does not appeal to another, and what seems to help on one occasion may fail on the next. If there is any commonality to be found in this diversity of strategy, it would be that the most effective operators tend to speak of the devices in frankly anthropomorphic terms, and to associate successful performance with the establishment of some form of bond or resonance with the device, akin to that one might feel for one's car, tools, musical instruments, or sports equipment.

V. Combined Results

A summary of the results from all of the experimental excursions noted above, along with a few others not specifically mentioned, is presented in Table 2. Listed here are the number of complete experimental series, N_s; the number of binary samples processed, N_b; the z-scores based on the difference of the HI-LO means, z_μ; the statistical effect sizes per bit, here reconstructed from ε_μ, *i.e.* $\varepsilon_\mu = z_\mu/2\sqrt{N_b}$, as discussed in Section III-A; and the one-tail probabilities associated with z_μ, p_μ. Note that the table segregates those experiments having truly random sources from those whose sources are deterministic pseudorandom. Of the former, only the two with the smallest data sets fail to contribute positively to the overall HI-LO separation; in fact, all but three independently achieve significance by the $p_\mu < .05$ criterion. In contrast, none of the deterministic experiments show any correlations with operator intention, despite their identical protocols and data processing, and their similar operator pools.

Combination of data from all of these experiments into an overall statistical figure of merit is complicated by the major disparities in the various database sizes, some distinctions in the protocols and measurable, the absence of theoretical expectations in the RMC experiments, the pervasive gender disparities and the HI *vs.* LO asymmetries associated with them, and the ambiguities associated with the interplay of series position effects with individual operator database sizes. However, a number of meta-analytic techniques can be invoked to provide composite estimates for the overall likelihood of the entire collection of anomalous mean shifts. For example, one could simply compound the values of z_μ listed in Table 2 into an unweighed composite value. Alternatively, one could weight the individual experiment z_μ values by the numbers of series in the databases, or by the numbers of binary samples each contains. Finally, one could combine results at the level of p_μ values, rather than z_μ, using a method proposed by Rosenthal (1984). In a separate paper, we have presented

Table 2

HI-LO mean shift statistics for all REG-class experiments, as defined in Key below.

Expt.	N_s	N_b	z_μ	ε_μ ($\times 10^5$)	P_μ
		Random Experiments			
D_L	522	3.35×10^8	3.809	20.8±5.5	6.99×10^{-5}
D_R	212	1.83×10^8	2.214	16.4±7.4	0.0134
PR_{LR}	46	4.94×10^7	2.765	39.3±14.3	0.00284
D_C	45	3.62×10^7	1.635	27.2±16.6	0.0510
D_{2K}	44*	3.25×10^8	2.718	15.1±5.6	0.00328
D_{20}	20	1.64×10^6	-0.956	-74.7±78.1	0.830
MC_L	87	4.07×10^8	3.891	19.3±5.0	4.99×10^{-5}
MC_R	26	9.32×10^7	2.139	22.2±10.4	0.0162
MC_C	12	4.32×10^7	-0.040	-0.6±15.2	0.513
		Deterministic Experiments			
PD_{LR}	23	9.20×10^6	-1.390	-45.8±33.0	0.918
AP_L	396	1.58×10^8	-06.46	-5.1±7.9	0.741
AP_R	86	3.44×10^7	0.335	5.7±17.0	0.369
AP_C	8	3.20×10^6	0.427	23.9±55.9	0.335

Key

N_s: Number of series. N_b: Number of binary samples. z_μ: z-score of mean shift. ε_μ: Statistical effect size per bit; $\varepsilon_\mu \equiv z_\mu/\sqrt{N_b}$. (See text.) P_μ: One-tail probability of z_μ. D_L: Diode REG, local. D_R: Diode REG, remote (includes off-time data). PR_{LR}: Pseudorandom REG (hardwired with random element), local and remote. D_C: Diode REG, co-operator data. D_{2K}: Diode REG, 2000-sample trials. D_{20}: Diode REG, 20-sample trials. MC_L: Random Mechanical Cascade, local. MC_R: Random Mechanical Cascade, remote (includes off-time data). MC_C: Random Mechanical Cascade, co-operator. PD_{LR}: Pseudorandom REG (hardwired, no random element), local and remote AP_L: Algorithmic pseudorandom REG, local. AP_R: Algorithmic pseudorandom REG, remote (includes off-time data). AP_C: Algorithmic pseudorandom REG, co-operator data.

*This dataset includes 7 series by 2 operators that used the PR source rather than the D source. Since there is no detectable difference between the two subsets, they are combined as a single table entry.

detailed arguments for preference of the sample-weighted recipe for this type of data combination (Dobyns, 1996) although, as displayed in Table 3, the quantitative disparities among all of these methods are insufficient to obscure the magnitude of the bottom-line results. Again note that by any of the recipes the ensemble of experiments utilizing physically random sources compound to overwhelming statistical likelihood, while the deterministic group lies well within chance expectation.

A similar sharp discrimination appears in both the composite series success rate and operator success rate criteria. In the former, 58.4% of the total of 1014 random source experimental series show a positive HI-LO separation (z_s = 5.339, p_s = 4.68 x 10^{-8}), compared to 49.7% for the deterministic group ($z_s = 0.132$, $p_s = 0.55$). In the latter, 57.3% of the 199 operators of the random source experiments succeed in splitting their HI and LO results in the intended direction ($z_0 = 2.056$, $p_0 = 0.0199$), compared to 45.7% of the 46 operators of the deterministic group ($z_0 = -0.590$, $p_0 = 0.722$). By either criterion, the success rates are broadly distributed over the various random source experiments, with eight of the nine contributing positively to both the series and operator composites.

The strong distinction between the results using random and deterministic sources may help discriminate among various theoretical models that have been proposed for effects of this genre. For example, the "Decision Augmentation Theory" proposed by May *et al.* (1995), which predicts that the nature of the source should be irrelevant to the presence or scale of the effect, is clearly incompatible with this observed difference in performance. (A more detailed and quantitative review of the implications of this database for the "D.A.T." model can be found in reference (Dobyns and Nelson, 1997).

Table 3

Combined HI-LO z-scores of all REG-class experiments computed by four methods described in the text references, (with associated one-tail probabilities of chance occurrence in parentheses).

Method	Random Expts.	Determ. Expts.	Both
Unweighted	6.058 (6.88×10^{-10})	-0.637 (0.738)	4.687 (1.38×10^{-6})
Series Weighted	6.588 (2.22×10^{-11})	-0.671 (0.749)	4.980 (3.18×10^{-7})
Data Weighted	7.180 (3.50×10^{-13})	-0.671 (0.749)	6.492 (4.24×10^{-11})
Rosenthal	6.445 (5.80×10^{-11})	-0.714 (0.762)	5.812 (3.09×10^{-9})

VI. Replicability Requirements

From time to time, the experiments reported here have been assessed, both formally and informally, by a number of critical observers, who have generally agreed that the equipment, protocols, and data processing are sound (National Research Council, 1988). Frequently, however, the caveat is added that such results must be "replicated" before they can be fully accepted, with the replication criteria variously defined to require strict preservation of all technical and procedural details, or to allow more flexible similarities in equipment and protocols. It is our opinion that for experiments of this sort, involving as they clearly do substantial psychological factors and therefore both individual and collective statistical behaviors, to require that any given operator, on any given day, should produce identical results, or that any given operator group should quantitatively replicate the results of any other, is clearly unreasonable. Rather more apt would be such criteria as might be applied to controlled experiments in human creativity, perception, learning, or athletic achievement, where broad statistical ranges of individual and collective performance must be anticipated, and results therefore interpreted in statistically generic terms.

By such criteria, the experiments outlined here can be claimed both to show internal consistency, and to replicate results of similar experiments in many other laboratories. For example, the statistical consistency of individual operator performances across multiple experimental series that compound to their particular positions on Figure 4 defines one level of internal replicability. The systematic accumulation of intention-correlated effects across many operators, as displayed in Table 1, defines a second level. The consistently similar results of the same group of operators on the various extensions of the basic REG experiment to other protocols, noise sources, and categorically different random physical devices, shown in Table 3, establishes a third, inter-experiment level of replicability.

With respect to inter-laboratory reproducibility, it should first be noted that the experiments reported here were originally undertaken as an attempt to replicate previous studies by Schmidt (1973) and others (Puthoff and Targ, 1975), albeit with modifications in design and equipment that would respond to various criticisms and allow more rapid accumulation of very large quantities of data. Our results indeed reinforce this earlier work in confirming the existence, scale, and character of anomalous correlations with pre-stated operator intentions. On a broader front, the previously mentioned quantitative review of 30 years of research of this genre, covering more than 800 experiments reported by 68 principal investigators, including ourselves, concludes that despite the historical improvement in experimental quality, a statistically constant anomalous effect size has pervaded most of the results (Radin and Nelson, 1989).

VII. Theoretical Modeling

Any attempts to model phenomena like those reported here must be immensely complicated by the evidence that human volition is the primary correlate of the observed anomalous physical effects, and thus that some proactive role for consciousness must somehow be represented. This challenge is compounded by the absence of clear-cut psychological or physiological indicators, and by the lack of demonstrable space and time dependence. While a variety of attempts to combine conventional psychological and neurophysiological concepts with established physical and mathematical formalisms, such as electromagnetic theory, statistical thermodynamics, quantum mechanics, geophysical mechanics, and hyperspace formalisms have been proposed (Schmidt, 1973), few of these propositions seem competent to accommodate the salient features of the empirical data, let alone to survive critical scientific and epistemological criteria.

Rather, a more comprehensive approach to formulation of the interaction of consciousness with the physical world seems requisite. Over the past two decades, a growing number of theoretical physicists and philosophers of science have addressed the problem of consciousness from this broader perspective, and have offered an assortment of more sophisticated models which may eventually prove effective for dialogue with the empirical results. Some of these apply quantum physical concepts and formalisms to neurological processes and functions (Stapp, 1993; *Consciousness Research* Abstracts, 1996). Others employ non-linear systems concepts underlying information science, chaos, and complexity theories to provide degrees of freedom to accommodate the intervention of consciousness into physical processes (Atmanspacher, 1994). Still others propose a holistic complementarity between the epistemology of human experience and the ontology of the physical world (Jahn and Dunne, 1986). While each of these approaches at least acknowledges the problem, the chasm between the role of consciousness and self-consistent physical theory is far from bridged and, given its troublesome empirical and conceptual aspects, will require much more visionary work from both the experimental and theoretical sides.

VIII. Extended Experiments

Since completion of the databases described above, a number of new experiments involving substantially different physical processes, modes of feedback, and protocols have been deployed in the hope of better identification of the most critical physical and psychological properties bearing on the anomalous phenomena. For example, similar but more compact REG units are being used to drive an "ArtREG" experiment, wherein two competing scenes are superimposed on a computer screen with relative illumination determined by the accumulating balance of binary events from the noise source. The task of the operator is to cause one pre-selected scene to dominate over the other, without current knowledge of the binary balance. In another experiment, a compact REG drives a large musical drum to produce a random alternation of equally spaced loud and soft beats or, in another variant, a random alternation of long and short intervals of equal amplitude. The goal of the operator in either version is to impose some regularity of pattern on the audible beat stream. Analysis programs compute the overall entropy of the bit stream and search for repetitive sub-patterns indicative of an imposed cadence. Other devices, such as classical single and boule slit diffraction equipment, and REGs that alternate digital and analog data sampling, or that compare two grossly different bit-sampling rates, help search for further physical correlates. In a complementary effort to access the importance of operator feedback modalities, various aesthetically engaging systems, such as a large linear pendulum or an upward bubbling water fountain, have been employed, along with a mobile robot driven in random motion by an onboard REG. Although the databases from these new experiments are not yet sufficient to provide robust quantitative results, various anomalous effects correlated with operator intention are apparent in the structural details of their data distributions, of comparable scales to those seen in the direct REG interactions.

IX. Summary

The extensive databases described above, comprising more than 1500 complete experimental series generated over a period of 12 years in rigid tripolar protocols by over 100 unselected human operators using several random digital processors, display the following salient features:

1) Strong statistical correlations between the means of the output distributions and the pre-recorded intentions of the operators appear in virtually all of the experiments using random sources.

2) Such correlations are not found in those experiments using deterministic pseudo-random sources.

3) The overall scale of the anomalous mean shifts are of the order of 10^{-4} bits per bit processed which, over the full composite database, compounds to a statistical deviation of more than 7σ ($p = 3.5 \times 10^{-13}$).

4) While characteristic distinctions among individual operator performances are difficult to confirm analytically, a number of significant differences between female and male operator performance are demonstrable.

5) The series score distributions and the count population distributions in both the collective and individual operator data are consistent with chance distributions based on slightly altered binary probabilities.

6) Oscillatory series position patterns in collective and individual operator performance appear in much of the data, complicating the replication criteria.

7) Experiments performed by operators far removed from the devices, or exerting their intentions at times other than that of device operation, yield results of comparable scale and character to those of the local, on-time experiments. Such remote, off-time results have been demonstrated on all of the random sources.

8) Appropriate internal consistency, and inter-experiment and inter-laboratory replicability of the generic features of these anomalous results have been established.

9) A much broader range of random-source experiments currently in progress display a similar scale and character of anomalous results.

Acknowledgments

The authors are deeply indebted to the many anonymous and uncompensated operators who have unselfishly contributed immense time and effort to generation of the data on which this study is based. We also appreciate the suggestions of many professional colleagues, both supportive and critical, that have helped us refine and solidify these complex experiments.

References

Atmanspacher, H. & Dalenoort, G.J. (Eds.) (1994). *Inside Versus Outside: Endo- and Exo-Concepts of Observation and Knowledge in Physics, Philosophy and Cognitive Science*. Berlin: Springer-Verlag.

Atmanspacher, H. (1994). Complexity and meaning as a bridge across the Cartesian cut. *Jnl. Consciousness Studies*, 1, 2, 168.

Beloff, J. (1977). "Historical Overview." In B.B. Wolman, Ed., *Handbook of Parapsychology*. New York: Van Nostrand Reinhold Co.

Bohr, N. (1961). *Atomic Theory and the Description of Nature*, Cambridge: University Press.

Borstner, B. & Shawe-Taylor, J. (1995). "Consciousness at the Crossroads of Philosophy and Cognitive Science" and "Consciousness Research Abstracts: 'Towards a Scientific Basis for Consciousness'." Thorverton, U.K.: Imprint Academic.

Clauser, J.F. (1974). Experimental distinction between the quantum and classical field-theoretic predictions for the photoelectric effect. *Phys. Rev. D*, 9, 4, 853.

Consciousness Research Abstracts (1996). "Tuscon IL: Toward a Science of Consciousness 1996." Tucson, AZ, April 8-13, 1996. Thorverton, UK: Imprint Academic.
de Broglie, L. (1955). *Physics and Microphysics* (Trans. M. Davidson). New York: Pantheon Books.
Dobyns, Y.H. & Nelson, R.D. (1997). "Empirical Evidence Regarding Decision Augmentation Theory." Technical Report PEAR 97001, Princeton Engineering Anomalies Research, School of Engineering/Applied Sciences, Princeton University.
Dobyns, Y.H. (1996). "Drawing Conclusions from Multiple Experiments." Technical Report PEAR 96002, Princeton Engineering Anomalies Research, School of Engineering/Applied Sciences, Princeton University.
Donald, J.A. & Martin, B. (1976). Time-symmetric thermodynamics and causality violation. *European Jnl. Parapsych.*, 1, 3, 17.
Dunne, B.J. & Jahn, R.G. (1992). Experiments in remote human/machine interaction. *Journal of Scientific Exploration*, 6, 4, 311.
Dunne, B.J. (1995). "Gender Differences in Human-Machine Anomalies Experiments." Technical Report PEAR 95006, Princeton Engineering Anomalies Research, School of Engineering/Applied Sciences, Princeton University.
Dunne, B.J., Dobyns, Y.H., Jahn, R.G., and Nelson, R.D. (1994). Series position effects in random event generator experiments; With an Appendix by A.M. Thompson, "Serial position effects in the psychological literature." *Journal of Scientific Exploration*, 8, 2, 197.
Dunne, B.J., Nelson, R.D., and Jahn, R.G. (1990). Operator-related anomalies in a random mechanical cascade. *Journal of Scientific Exploration*, 2, 2, 155.
Eddington, A. (1978). *The Nature of the Physical World*. Ann Arbor, MI: University of Michigan Press.
Heisenberg, W. (1962). *Physics and Philosophy: The Revolution in Modern Science*. New York: Harper and Row (Harper Torchbooks).
Hiley, B.J. & Peat, F.D. (Eds.) (1987). *Quantum Implications: Essays in Honour of David Bohm*. London and New York: Routledge & Kegan Paul.
Hooke, R. (1976). In R. Waller, Ed., *The Posthumous Works of Robert Hooke, M.D., S.R.S., Containing his Cutlerian Lectures and Other Discourses, Read at the Meetings of the Illustrious Royal Society*. London: Smith and Walford (Printers to the Royal Society), 1705. (Quoted in B.R. Singer, "Robert Hooke on Memory, Association, and Time Perception," in R.V. Jones and W.D.M. Paton, Eds., *Notes and Records of the Royal Society of London*, 31, 1).
Ibid., p. 113.
Jahn, R.G. & Dunne, B.J. (1986). On the quantum mechanics of consciousness, with application to anomalous phenomena. *Fndns. Physics*, 16, 8, 721.
Jahn, R.G. & Dunne, B.J. (1988). *Margins of Reality: The Role of Consciousness in the Physical World*. New York, San Diego: Harcourt Brace Jovanovich.
Jahn, R.G. (1982). The persistent paradox of psychic phenomena: An engineering perspective. *Proc. IEEE*, 70, 2, 136.
Jahn, R.G. (1988). Physical aspects of psychic phenomena. *Phys. Bulletin*, 9, 235.
Jahn, R.G. (Ed.) (1981). *The Role of Consciousness in the Physical World*: AAAS Selected Symposium 57, Boulder, CO: Westview Press, Inc.
Jahn, R.G., Dobyns, Y.H., and Dunne, B.J. (1991). Count population profiles in engineering anomalies experiments. *Journal of Scientific Exploration*, 5, 2, 205.

Jahn, R.G., Dunne, B.J., and Nelson, R.D. (1987). Engineering anomalies research. *Journal of Scientific Exploration*, 1, 1, 21.

Jeans, J. (1943). *Physics and Philosophy*. Cambridge: University Press.

Jordan, P. (1960). Parapsychological implications of research in atomic physics. *International Journal of Parapsychology*, 2, 4, 5.

Kafatos, M. (Ed.) (1989). *Bell's Theorem, Quantum Theory and Conception of the Universe*. Heidelberg: Klewer Academic Press.

Kubrin, D. (1981). "Newton's Inside Out! Magic, Class Struggle, and the Rise of Mechanism in the West." In H. Woolf, Ed., *The Analytical Spirit: Essays in the History of Science*. Ithaca and London: Cornell University Press.

May, E.C. Utts, J.M., and Spottiswoode, S.J.P. (1995). Decision augmentation theory: Applications to the random number generator database. *Journal of Scientific Exploration*, 9, 4, 453.

National Research Council (1988). *Enhancing Human Performance: Issues, Theories, and Techniques*. Report of the Committee on Techniques for the Enhancement of Human Performance, Commission on the Behavioral and Social Sciences and Education. Washington, DC: National Academy Press.

Nelson, R.D., Dobyns, Y.H., Dunne, B.J. and Jahn, R.G. (1991). "Analysis of Variance of REG Experiments: Operator Intention, Secondary Parameters, Database Structure." Technical Report PEAR 91004, Princeton Engineering Anomalies Research, School of Engineering/Applied Sciences, Princeton University.

Oteri, L. (Ed.) (1975). *Quantum Physics and Parapsychology:* Proceedings of an International Conference held in Geneva, Switzerland, August 26-27, 1974. New York: Parapsychology Foundation, Inc.

Pauli, W. (1994). "Ideas of the Unconscious." In C.P. Enz and K. von Meyenn, Eds., *Wolfgang Pauli: Writings on Physics and Philosophy* (Trans. R. Schlapp). Berlin, Heidelberg: Springer-Verlag.

Pauli, W. (1994). "Ideas of the Unconscious." In C.P. Enz and K. von Meyenn, Eds., *Wolfgang Pauli: Writings on Physics and Philosophy* (Trans. R. Schlapp). Berlin, Heidelberg: Springer-Verlag, p. 149-164.

Planck, M. (1932). *Where Is Science Going?* (Trans. J. Murphy). New York: W. Norton & Co.

Puthoff, H. & Targ, R. (1975). "Physics, Entropy, and Psychokinesis." In L. Oteri, Ed., *Quantum Physics and Parapsychology:* Proceedings of an International Conference held in Geneva, Switzerland, August 26-27, 1974. New York: Parapsychology Foundation, Inc.

R. Boyle (1962). *Works*, Vol. 1, p. CXXX. (Quoted in L.T. Moore, *Newton: A Biography*, New York: Dover Publications.

Radin, D.I. & Nelson, R.D. (1989). Evidence for consciousness-related anomalies in random physical systems. *Fndns. Physics*, 19, 12, 1499.

Rhine, J.B. *et. al.* (1965). *Parapsychology from Duke to FRNM*. Durham, NC: The Parapsychology Press.

Rosenthal, R. (1984). *Meta-Analytic Procedures for Social Research*. Beverly Hills, CA: SAGE Publications, Inc.

Schilpp, P.A. (Ed.) (1949). *Albert Einstein: Philosopher-Scientist*. Evanston, IL: The Library of Living Philosophers, Inc. (George Banta Publishing Co., Menasha, W.I.).

Schilpp, P.A. (Ed.) (1949). *Albert Einstein: Philosopher-Scientist*. Evanston, IL:

The Library of Living Philosophers, Inc. (George Banta Publishing Co., Menasha, W.I.), p. 683.

Schmidt, H. (1973). PK tests with a high-speed random number generator. *Jnl. Parapsych.*, 37, 105.

Schommers, W. (Ed.) (1989). *Quantum Theory and Pictures of Reality: Foundations, Interpretations, and New Aspects.* Berlin, Heidelberg: Springer-Verlag.

Schrödinger, E. (1967). *What is Life? and Mind and Matter.* Cambridge: University Press.

Scott, A. (1995). *Stairway to the Mind: The Controversial New Science of Consciousness.* New York: Springer-Verlag (Copernicus).

Shear, J. (Ed.) (1996). Controversies in science and the humanities: Exploring consciousness—the "Hard Problem." *Jnl. Consciousness Studies*, Special Issue, Part II, 3, 1.

Stapp, H.P. (1993). *Mind, Matter, and Quantum Mechanics.* Berlin: Springer-Verlag.

von Weizsäcker, C.F. (1980). *The Unity of Nature* (Trans. F.J. Zucker). New York: Fauar, Straus, Giroux, Inc.

Walker, D.P. (1972). "Francis Bacon and Spiritus," In A.G. Debus, Ed., Science, Medicine and Society in the Renaissance. New York: Neale Watson Academic Publications, Inc., Science History Publications.

Wigner, E.P. (1967). *Symmetries and Reflections.* Bloomington and London: Indiana University Press.

CHAPTER 5

Statistically Robust Anomalous Effects: Replication in Random Event Generator Experiments

Roger D. Nelson *and* Dean I. Radin

A large experimental database linking human intention to anomalous effects in statistical distributions has been accumulating during the last 30 years. Some 68 investigators have performed and reported results from more than 800 independent studies using random event generators (REGs). These experiments all address the same fundamental question: Is there evidence of an anomalous correspondence of the statistical output of the REG with an observer's intention to shift parameters (usually the mean) of the output distribution?

This large database contains both weak and strong replications, and beginning with a circumscription ensuring that the primary hypothesis is represented in all the studies, the techniques of meta-analysis are used for a quantitative assessment. The meta-analytic procedures, enhanced by a standardized quality rating, allow the combination of results from many independent reports into a single concatenation from which it is possible to draw several strong conclusions about this class of experiments.

Reprinted with permission from *Research in Parapsychology*, 1988, 23–27.

Procedure

A bibliographic search located 152 reports, beginning in 1959, of experiments meeting the circumscription constraints. Most reports contained a number of separable experimental units defined as pilot, control, or experimental data, with the latter frequently divided into conditions (e.g., high aim or low aim). The full database, broken into such units of analysis, contains 235 control studies and 597 experimental studies. Each study was represented by a z score reflecting the deviation of results in the direction of intention, and an effect size was computed by normalizing the z score by the square root of the number of probabilistic events (usually binaries) in the experimental unit. A weight was assigned to the study based on 16 quality criteria.

Results

The distribution of 235 z scores for control studies is centered about z = 0, as expected from theory, but the variance of the empirical distribution is much smaller than expected (F = 1.29, p < .01). This suggests that the nominal specification of a control condition may be questionable and that the role of baseline controls may be less obvious than usually assumed, at least in experiments of this sort. In a large subset of data from the Princeton Engineering Anomalies Research (PEAR) laboratory, which is known to be fully reported, the same effect appears.

The 597 experimental studies include both high-aim and low-aim conditions, which are combined by inverting the sign of the low-aim studies; thus a positive z score represents success in the direction of effort. The mean of the experimental score distribution is shifted, and in contrast to the control studies, the variance is increased (F = 2.62, p < .00001). This distribution is skewed, with a disproportionate number of large z scores, and the skew coefficient is significant (at about 4 sigma).

As the database has grown, the mean z score for experimental studies has settled at about z = 0.8 or 0.9, whereas the estimate for control studies is close to zero. Because of the enormous size of the combined database, the average z score for experiments is extremely unlikely, representing a 15 sigma deviation from chance expectation.

Quality

Of major concern in interpreting the results of REG experiments is their quality. Indeed, critics have specifically suggested that the effects are smaller in high quality studies, implying that as controls are made even more rigorous the effect must regress to zero. A quality assessment using 16 criteria embodying a variety of points made by critics as well as the accumulated experience of researchers in the field was applied to the REG database. A weight was assigned to each study by counting the number of these criteria satisfied, according to the description in the report. The procedure adopted is a "worst case" approach, and although it yields a standardized measure suitable for the correlation analyses intended, the quality weights do not necessarily measure absolute quality. To assess the degree of objectivity achieved with this procedure, a comparison was made of ratings by the two authors. The independent ratings are highly correlated, and a Spearman-Brown effective reliability coefficient of .89 indicates that two other raters using the procedure would generate a very similar picture.

A regression of the assigned quality weights on the number of studies shows a positive trend. The slope is significant, with t = 3.275, for the literature excluding the PEAR database, demonstrating that quality has increased over time. This effect is much stronger with the disproportionate contribution of the PEAR data. Investigators in this field have obviously learned from experience.

Given an effective measure of the relative quality of experiments, it becomes possible to address definitively the critics' hypothesis of effects regressing to zero. The regression slope of the mean z score per investigator as a function of quality weight is nonsignificantly positive (t = 0.476). A similar test using effect size also shows no decline associated with quality (t = -0.047). Thus the hypothesis that effect size will regress to zero as quality increases is demonstrably incorrect.

Effect Size

The entire 30-year database may be used to estimate the overall effect of intention to shift the distribution mean and to see what the influence is of factors such as experiment quality and heterogeneous experimental results. The effect size estimate for control studies definitely includes zero effect size, whereas the estimate for experimental studies separately or grouped by investigator is on the order of six standard deviation units from zero.

Using a procedure applied in physical and social sciences to produce homogeneous distributions, potential outliers are iteratively removed from the distribution until it becomes statistically homogeneous. For the REG database, this procedure tests whether the effect is attributable to a few extreme scores that might derive from spurious sources. (There is no evidence of problems with these studies; they simply have large scores.) The process requires exclusion of 17% of experiments and 13% of investigators, and although nearly all the excluded data are positive contributions, the overall effect remains robust.

When the effect size is weighted for quality, in either the original or the homogeneous distribution, it remains robust.

Filedrawer

Finally, a potential serious problem in estimating the size of effects from experimental data of this nature arises because not all studies are reported. This is referred to as the "filedrawer" effect, and it is hypothesized that most unreported studies show weak or null results and hence that their inclusion would weaken or, if sufficiently numerous, nullify apparent effects. An even greater distortion of effect size estimates would be introduced by failures to report significant negative results. Although no argument can be made that all negative effects are reported, this database contains 37 z scores in the negative tail, where only 30 would be expected by chance.

The filedrawer hypothesis implicitly maintains that all significant positive results would be reported. Modeling based on this assumption can be implemented as a fit to data in the positive distribution tail. This procedure indicates that there is a substantial filedrawer and that the total database may comprise on the order of 1,000 studies. However, explicitly incorporating as many as 1,500 surrogate studies with a net null contribution does not eliminate the anomalous effect, and it is instructive to determine how many filedrawer studies with average null results would be required to reduce the effect to nonsignificance. This quantity, which Rosenthal calls a failsafe, is 54,000; it is approximately 90 times the number of studies actually reported. Again, the fully reported PEAR experimental database shows virtually the same distribution characteristics as the literature, with shifted mean and increased variance, suggesting from another perspective that the filedrawer effect cannot explain the anomalous results.

Conclusions

The REG database contains unequivocal evidence for a replicable statistical effect in a variety of specific protocols, all designed to assess an anomalous correlation of distribution parameters with the intentions of human observers. The effect is robust, and it is not significantly diluted by incorporated adjustments for experiment quality and for inhomo-geneity, nor is it eliminated by incorporating an estimated filedrawer of unreported nonsignificant studies.

CHAPTER 6

Transcontinental
Remote Viewing

Marilyn Schlitz *and* Elmar Gruber

Introduction

Experimental parapsychology basically utilizes two forms of ESP testing: forced-choice, in which the range of target/responses is restricted, and free-response, which allows for a vast scope of target/response possibilities. The forced-choice paradigm has been highly influential in establishing parapsychology within the scientific framework. This is largely due to the ease with which statistical methods are applied to it. The early free-response work by such researches as Thaw (1892), Sinclair (1930), and Warcollier (1938), however, provided great quantities of rich qualitative materials. Although these early studies are devoid of any true form of statistical assessment, the available protocols are provocative, to say the least. Recognizing the usefulness of free response, investigators such as Carington (1940), Stuart (1942), and Marsh (reported in Fisk, 1960) attempted to incorporate quantitative approaches within their designs. Unfortunately, these initiatives were limited by the cumbersome methods of evaluation available at that time. Today we are equipped with simpler, more refined methods of quantitative analysis, which allow us to go further in exploring the potential advantages of free response without sacrificing scientific rigor.

Reprinted with permission from *Journal of Parapsychology*, 1980, 44, 305–317; 1981, 45, 234–237.

From the authors' point of view, there are a number of possible advantages to the free-response method. One such advantage lies in the richness and complexity of the targets. Participants in free-response studies are able to freely express a wide variety of impressions, feelings, and hunches. As pointed out by Carington (1940), the difference between free response and forced choice becomes more a question of what, rather than which, for a given subject.

In this way, free response has strong ties with reported psi events in daily life. For one, spontaneous manifestations generally do not occur in a forced-choice, decision-making context, but result from a broad range of stimuli. Child and Levi (1979) caution that generalizations to most of everyday life from the classical forced-choice methods, which restrict the possibilities to a task so clear as guessing a card, is somewhat risky. As noted by Haight (1979), a gap has existed between spontaneous cases of psi and those which occur under controlled, quantitatively assessable conditions. The resurgence of interest in free response may well serve to bridge this gap. As stated by Burdick and Kelly (1977):

> Many investigators have felt that something vital was lost in the transportation of psi from its natural setting into the forced-choice paradigm and have sought ways of extending quantitative techniques back into situations which more nearly resemble the conditions of spontaneous psi occurrences [p. 109].

Another feature of the free-response procedures is the great investment of time. Although this can be thought of as a disadvantage, it has several advantages as well. For instance, it requires a great deal of involvement on the part of the experimenters, which possibly serves to enhance the subject's feeling for the importance of individual trials.

Perhaps the most powerful asset of free-response methods lies in the subjective realm of personal evaluation. For many people, a strong qualitative "hit" is more impressive than a successful outcome based totally on statistical probability. There are also dangers in this approach, of course; for, as noted by Child (1980), one must use caution when jumping to conclusions based on single selected cases:

> This error is paralleled in [the] study of spontaneous cases by the danger of concluding merely from very obvious similarity between a person's imagery and a distant event that the coincidence must be an instance of psi [p. 177].

We are now, however, in a position to explore the best of both worlds, with free response giving us rich qualitative data as well as statistically quantitative evidence for psi.

Although there are several free-response procedures in use today, the present study was designed as an attempted replication of the remote-viewing work developed by Puthoff and Targ (1975). Within this controlled laboratory design, the percipient is asked to describe the whereabouts of an outside experimenter (the agent) whose exact location at the time is unknown to the percipient.

Despite recent acceptance of the term *remote viewing*, it is interesting to note that the implied phenomenon has been discussed in a broad range of literature throughout the years. As pointed out by Targ and Puthoff (1977):

> The basic phenomenon appears to cover a range of subjective experience variously referred to in the literature as astral projection (occult); simple clairvoyance, traveling clairvoyance, or out-of-body experiences (parapsychological); exteriorization (psychological); or autoscopy (medical) [p. 5].

Remote viewing was chosen then as a descriptive term, free of past prejudice and occult assumptions. It is often a matter of taste to favor a specific term and henceforth a slightly different concept. This same discussion may be applied to other areas of psi research as well; for example, the distinction between precognition and backward causation.

Conditions for remote viewing have been diverse. Although studies have involved real-time situations, whereby the design required simultaneous viewing of a target location by the agent and descriptions by the percipient (Puthoff & Targ, 1975; Puthoff et al., 1979; Schlitz & Deacon, 1980), some studies have also explored the possibilities of precognition* (Dunne & Bisaha, 1978, 1979) as well as the effects of distance on the remote-viewing process (Puthoff & Targ, 1976).

In exploring the remote-viewing design, it was decided to attempt a replication of the long-distance work. Throughout the history of parapsychology, there has been evidence, although usually informal, that distance has no effect on the psi process. As stated by Warcollier (1938):

> We sought telepathically to transmit drawings from one room to another, from one quarter of Paris to another, from one city to another, and from one country to another. Distance never seemed to affect the results [p. 5].

---

*In any discussion of precognition, alternative explanations such as psychokinetic effects on the random number generator must be considered.

In a different light, Rao (1966) noted:

> Several of the spontaneous cases of psi experiences in which the sub-
> jects and the ostensible target objects were widely separated by long dis-
> tances not only suggested the relative independence of psi and distance,
> but this observation led to the strengthening of the conviction that psi
> is extrasensory [p. 63].

Procedure

In conducting the present experiment, carried out in November 1979, the percipient, E_1 (M. S.), remained in Detroit, Michigan, while the agent, E_2 (E. R. G.), visited the target sites in Rome, Italy. The experimenters acted as percipient and agent in order to provide the opportunity of observing a remote-viewing experience first-hand. It was felt that this might lead to greater insights which could be of some help in the design of future studies of the remote-viewing type.

Target Pool and Target Selection

E_2, together with a colleague in Italy, A.M. Turi, selected 40 target sites in Rome. The target pool was carefully constructed to contain several targets of given types (i.e., fountains, churches, parks, etc.). It was furthermore decided to include indoor as well as outdoor targets within the pool. Indoor targets included rooms, churches, sports halls, museum exhibits, and so on.

On each experimental day at 2:00 P.M. central European time (CET) corresponding to 8:00 A.M. eastern standard time (EST), the target for the day was randomly selected from the pool, without replacement, by means of a random number generator. No attempt was made to avoid similar targets within the pool. It was originally decided to perform 12 trials on 12 consecutive days (November 3-14). However, due to external problems on the part of the subject, only 10 protocols were generated and 10 trials completed. The 10 target sites finally chosen were: the view from the roof of St. Peter's cathedral; the Spanish Steps; the interior of an apartment in the Via Vittoria; a room in the Academia Tiberina; view from a hill outside the Rome International Airport; the ruins of the Cara-calla baths; the park of the Villa Borghese; a room filled with paintings in the Vatican museum; and an overlook from the Sports Palace in Rome-Eur.

Outbound Experimenter Behavior

E_2 arrived at the target location by 5:00 P.M. (CET), 11:00 A.M. Detroit time. At the target site, E_2 was free to walk around or sit, observing the surroundings. He carried a tape recorder with him and recorded thoughts, impressions of the scene, or specific street scenes and situations at the site. This was done for a period of 15 minutes. E_2 visited all target locations alone except the flat in Via Vittoria (November 6).

Following the experimental period, E_2 sent the final target order, as well as transcripts of his impressions, to two colleagues, both of whom were blind to the nature of the experiment.

Inbound Experimenter Behavior

At 11:00 A.M. (EST) on each of 10 consecutive days, E_1 sat in a dimly lit room and attempted to describe the whereabouts of the distant agent. Although she was in a calm state throughout the series, no formal relaxation procedure was utilized. When making a response, M.S. made an effort to think constantly about the target/agent—trying not to allow other thoughts, such as those concerning daily activities, to intrude. The impressions were recorded on paper, with both sketches and thoughts being written out as the protocol for a given trial.

Following completion of the 10 trials, E_1 prepared two photocopies of the protocols. One set was sent to E.R.G., who was then in Austria, for judging preparation, and the other to Hans Bender in Germany for safekeeping. No trial-by-trial feedback was given in this study, and, in fact, no feedback was available to the percipient for several months following the series.

Judging Preparation

After receiving the transcripts from E_1, E.R.G. and another person, blind to the correct targets, translated the transcripts into Italian. The translators then checked the transcripts for phrases from which one might infer temporal order of the transcript target sequence (see criticisms by Marks & Kammann, 1978; discussion by Puthoff, Targ, & May, 1979), although no editing was found to be necessary. The lack of trial-by-trial feedback to the percipient and agent also served to control for such a criticism. As E.R.G. was not blind to the correct target sites while aiding in the translation of the transcripts into Italian, the translation was reexamined for accuracy by a professional translator, P. Giovetti, in Modena,

Italy. During this time, she was blind to the correct target sites. In the course of her double-checking, several small changes were made, although nothing of major significance.

The Italian transcripts were typed, each on a separate sheet. E_2 then cut out photocopies of the sketches and attached them to the respective transcripts. The translated transcripts, together with the drawings, were finally photocopied and given to a set of judges.

As a follow-up of a previous work (Schlitz & Deacon, 1980), it was decided to use several judges. For this study, each of five judges scored all protocols against all target sites visited during the experimental period. In this way, the free-response procedure adopted a forced-choice judging process where all the target possibilities were known to the judges. In so doing, judges were asked to rank each transcript to each target site on a scale of 1 to 10. In addition, judges rated the degree of correspondence between protocol and site by making a slash along a line, with one end designating zero correspondence and the other end representing total correspondence. Protocols were presented to each judge in random order, this order being different for each judge. This was done to avoid any potential stacking effect. Judges visited the target locations independently and in the order of their choice. For each target site, judges were also provided with the impressions E_2, the agent, had recorded while visiting the target sites during the control period.

After receiving the judges' responses, E_2 sent the materials to E_1 at the FRNM for statistical evaluation.

Quantitative Assessment

After receiving the judges' responses, E_1 prepared the ratings and rankings for analysis. To do this, she first measured the lines for ratings and then summed the ratings for all judges for each transcript target. The same procedure of summing the judges' responses was used for rankings, with both sets of scores being double-checked by two independent assistants. Following this, E_1 arranged the scores into two 10 x 10 matrices, one for ratings and one for rankings. In this way all of the five judges' responses were added together to represent one score in the matrix (see Table 1).

In deriving an appropriate statistical evaluation for this "closed deck" series, we assumed nonindependence of target protocols (Kennedy, 1979a). We then utilized the direct-count-of-permutations method to assess the statistical significance of the given matrices (Burdick & Kelly, 1977;

Table 1
Combined Judges' Rankings and Ratings on Protocols

Rankings

(42)	62	56	88	42	24	66	68	50	56
34	(30)	61	67	81	66	50	58	70	45
67	54	(10)	36	69	69	32	69	77	67
68	65	27	(20)	70	82	42	71	62	47
81	51	64	62	(10)	43	93	56	52	38
24	77	81	77	46	(34)	91	34	40	48
74	44	30	34	76	76	(12)	78	71	62
54	60	64	80	62	28	70	(36)	50	44
68	76	81	66	42	54	68	22	(44)	29
36	78	68	68	64	56	76	58	32	(16)

$$p = 5.8 \times 10^{-6}$$

Ratings

(288)	192	181	68	260	367	164	174	269	209
398	(343)	182	162	96	174	258	195	157	297
148	262	(498)	355	135	153	368	143	93	122
136	171	373	(426)	125	61	304	134	157	266
84	203	162	179	(500)	277	37	190	160	282
378	105	76	92	264	(317)	40	319	293	215
156	248	380	333	92	136	(458)	112	132	207
242	141	152	89	147	369	140	(308)	223	237
166	118	110	164	298	227	192	369	(290)	340
313	87	141	119	149	213	86	184	352	(422)

$$p = 4.7 \times 10^{-6}$$

Puthoff et al., 1979; Scott, 1972). This statistic computed an exact p by scoring and counting all possible permutations of targets while keeping the response matrix fixed. The permutations method yielded a p of 5.8 x 10^{-6} for rankings and 4.7 x 10^{-6} for ratings.*

In addition to the combined judging, we also looked at each judge's scoring separately. This was done in an attempt to observe the degree of consistency within judges. Since four out of five judges showed significant scoring based on the permutations method for both rankings and ratings, we must conclude that there appears to be a general consistency between judges (see Table 2). It is interesting to note, however, that one judge produced non-significant results over-all, indicating the importance of multiple judges.

---

*While the permutations of rankings and ratings were the planned method of analysis, we also looked at the number of direct matches on the diagonal (see Puthoff et al., 1979). It is interesting to note that this method was, as expected, less sensitive than the permutations method, although it was still significant, with 6 direct hits out of 10, yielding a p of 6×10^{-4}.

Table 2
Results of Judges Taken Individually

	Ranking	Rating
Judge 1	9.4×10^{-6}	3.6×10^{-6}
Judge 2	1.2×10^{-4}	1.8×10^{-3}
Judge 3	5.4×10^{-7}	1.8×10^{-6}
Judge 4	.22	.83
Judge 5	1.7×10^{-3}	1.7×10^{-3}

Discussion

In view of the highly successful results of the present study, we might again stress the value of free-response remote viewing as a psi-conducive procedure, which is seemingly unaffected by distance. However, since both experimenters have obtained significant results in previous psi experiments (Gruber, 1979; Schlitz & Deacon, 1980), it may well be that the results are not necessarily due to a psi-conducive procedure but to the subjects/experimenters themselves, who, moreover, are the most highly motivated persons to want a positive outcome from the experiment. This is in line with observations made by Puthoff et al. (1979) where they stress that the seriousness of purpose on the part of the subjects may be one factor serving to enhance success in remote viewing.

Another issue which is in question with relation to the present study is the importance of immediate trial-by-trial feedback, since delayed feedback seemed in no way to impair the psi process. It was even noted (Morris, Robblee, Neville, & Bailey, 1978) that trial-by-trial feedback, both positive and negative, had a detrimental effect on the participants. Work by Puthoff et al. (1979), however, seems to show no such apparent problem. Therefore we suggest that a direct comparison be made to gain greater insight into the role of feedback in the experimental setting.

A potential area of controversy should also be pointed out in regard to the present study. This involves the inclusion of the agent's subjective impressions in the judges' descriptions of the target sites. While the authors feel that any criticism based on this point is ill-founded in the present work, the argument goes as follows: A certain amount of shared experience can be expected between two persons with similar interests. This would therefore allow for a potential non-psi factor to contribute to the results. Such a criticism might be especially applicable if reference to weather or news events were included. However, given the great distances in the present study and the fact that neither experimenter was noting weather or news events in the distant location, the number of contributory factors would seem to have been greatly reduced.

It was the authors' feeling that elimination of the agent's impressions from the information received by the judges narrows the role of telepathy in the experimental design. If the agent is important, then it would make sense that his impressions of the site, as well as activities going on at the location during the trial period, would influence the impressions gained by the distant percipient. It is for this reason that the agent's impressions were included. However, since the issue can be seen as potentially controversial, we are now planning to have the transcripts rejudged without inclusion of the agent's responses. It is our firm conviction that the correspondences between the percipient's protocols and the geographical target sites is clear enough that the results will not be influenced to any noticeable degree.

In the future, the authors would like to see a greater concern in experimental reporting for the "method of response." Perhaps we should take stock of the earlier work in free response, in which we are able to observe such an interest. Upton Sinclair (1930), for instance, devoted an entire chapter to describing the ways in which Mrs. Sinclair formulated her impressions about an ESP target. Carlson (see White, 1964) reported her impressions in the following way:

> At first ... very dark shadowy lines could be perceived which, when the drawing was opened, proved to be fragments of the drawing—and, later on, the complete drawing. The lines were often very faint and there was a certain strain experienced in trying to see [p. 38].

Thaw (1892) reported quite differently:

> For myself, I cannot describe my sensation as a visualization of any kind. It seemed rather to be by some wholly subjective process that I knew what the agents were looking at [p. 430].

By *subjective*, we would assume that he was referring to an intuitive sort of reasoning when making his responses.

Although no formal attempt to describe such an area was undertaken within the present study, a brief discussion will be given to E_1's method of response throughout the session. It should be noted that 11:00 A.M. was usually not a good time for E_1 and she would often sit down for the session at the very last minute, taking no time to induce any form of relaxation. In some ways, M.S. has noted that her strategy was very similar to that of Mrs. Sinclair, who used a focal image of a rose to begin each session. In the present case, E_1 used the face of E.R.G. as a starting point with which to focus her attention. She would then use a game-type strategy, asking over and over in her mind: "Where is he?". It should be noted that this effort may be considered as something of a state-altering procedure although the remote-viewing design does not require a formal manipulation of one's state of consciousness.

Impressions developed in several ways. Often it was as Carlson described her impressions—the appearance of faint lines frequently followed by a more complete picture. On several occasions, impressions triggered a distinct memory, which was then recounted as the response. It was tempting, in such case, to avoid an analytical response to the impressions, as the images appeared to be too complete. This was in line with Targ and Puthoff's (1977) warning to avoid an analysis of information. As an example, we have included the verbal description of the transcript from November 8, 1979, which reads as follows:

> Flight path? Red lights. Strong depth of field. Elmar seems detached, cold. A hole in the ground. A candle-shaped thing. Flower—maybe not real. Maybe painted. Outdoors. See sky dark. Windy and cold. Something shooting upward.

After the 15-minute period, the percipient expanded further on her impression:

> [For some reason a boat comes to mind.] The impressions that I had were of outdoors and Elmar was at some type of—I don't know if institution is the right word—but some place. Not a private home or anything like that—something—a public facility. He was standing away from the main structure, although he could see it. He might have been in a parking lot or field connected to the structure that identifies the place. I want to say an airport but that just seems too specific. There was activity and people but no one real close to Elmar.

In this example, M.S. obtained a clear picture of an airport drawing she had seen several months earlier. In fact, the target site was the Rome International Airport, where the outbound experimenter had been standing on a little hill aside from the structure. Near the hill were holes in the ground, where clandestine diggers searched for Roman coins. Although this is a striking protocol, many of the transcripts contained equally provoking content, as is reflected in the statistical analysis.

In order to further our investigation into individual methods of response, we suggest that a phenomenological approach might prove useful. A possible means of incorporating this approach into the experimental design would be an inventory, aimed at an understanding of how the experience of each participant (whether percipient, agent, or experimenter) is organized. That is, it should attempt to establish a foundation for describing the basic structures of consciousness involved in the remote-viewing experience.

A final point should be made in relation to the present work. Although the protocols from this series indicate strong evidence for ESP, we cannot neglect the hypothesis that PK may have played a role in the experimental outcome. As pointed out by Stanford (1981), an experimenter influence on the RNG used to generate the targets on each experimental day cannot be eliminated from consideration. This would be especially true if psi is, in fact, goal-oriented—detached, as it were, from the complexity of the task (Kennedy, 1978, 1979b). Therefore, any conclusion about the fruitfulness of the free-response remote-viewing procedure must take this factor into account.

In conclusion: the study provides further evidence for the existence of psi. The results are strong and certainly warrant further investigations into the remote-viewing procedure. Perhaps this design may offer a productive avenue into more process-oriented investigations. The authors are therefore looking forward to a follow-up of the present ideas.

References

Burdick, D.S., & Kelly, E.F. Statistical methods in parapsychological research. In B.B. Wolman (Ed.), *Handbook of parapsychology*. New York: Van Nostrand Reinhold, 1977.

Carington, W.W. Experiments on the paranormal cognition of drawings. *Journal of Parapsychology*, 1940, 4, 1-129.

Child, I.L. The use of judges' ratings to test hypotheses about psi processes. *Journal of the American Society for Psychical Research*, 1980, 74, 171-181.

Child, I.L., & Levi, A. Psi-missing in free-response settings. *Journal of the American Society for Psychical Research*, 1979, 73, 273-289.

Dunne, B.J., & Bisaha, J.P. Multiple channels in precognitive remote viewing. In W.G. Roll (Ed.), *Research in parapsychology*, 1977. Metuchen, N.J.: Scarecrow Press, 1978.

Dunne, B.J., & Bisaha, J.P. Precognitive viewing the Chicago area: A replication of the Stanford experiment. *Journal of Parapsychology*, 1979, 43, 17-30.

Fisk, G.W. Review of M.C. Marsh "The Rhodes Experiment: Linkage in Extrasensory Perception." *Journal of the Society for Psychical Research*, 1960, 40, 219-239.

Gruber, E.R. Conformance behavior involving animal and human subjects. *European Journal of Parapsychology*, 1979, 3, 167-175.

Haight, J.M. Spontaneous psi cases: A survey and preliminary study of ESP, attitude, and personality relationships. *Journal of Parapsychology*, 1979, 43, 179-204.

Kennedy, J.E. The role of psi complexity in PK: A review. *Journal of Parapsychology*, 1978, 42, 89-122.

Kennedy, J.E. Methodological problems in free-response ESP experiments. *Journal of the American Society for Psychical Research*, 1979, 73, 1-15. (a)

Kennedy, J.E. Redundancy in psi information. *Journal of Parapsychology*, 1979, 43, 290-314. (b)

Marks, D., & Kammann, R. Information transmission in remote viewing experiments. *Nature*, August 17, 1978, pp. 680-681.

Morris, R.L.; Robblee, P.; Neville, R.; & Bailey, K. Free-response ESP training with feedback to agent and receiver. In W.G. Roll (Ed.), *Research in parapsychology*, 1977. Metuchen, N.J.: Scarecrow Press, 1978.

Puthoff, H.E., & Targ, R. Remote viewing of natural targets. In J.D. Morris, W.G. Roll, & R.L. Morris (Eds.), *Research in parapsychology*, 1974. Metuchen, N.J.: Scarecrow Press, 1975.

Puthoff, H.E., & Targ, R. A perceptual channel for information transfer over kilometer distances: Historical perspective and recent research. *Proceedings of the IEEE*, 1976, 64 (3), 329-354.

Puthoff, H.E., Targ, R., & May, E.C. Experimental psi research: Implications for physics. Menlo Park, Cal.: SRI International, 1979.

Rao, K.R. *Experimental parapsychology*. Springfield, Ill.: Charles C. Thomas, 1966.

Schlitz, M., & Deacon, S. Remote viewing: A conceptual replication of Targ and Puthoff. In W.G. Roll (Ed.). *Research in parapsychology*, 1979. Metuchen, N.J.: Scarecrow Press, 1980.

Scott, C. On the evaluation of verbal material in parapsychology: A discussion of Dr. Pratt's monograph. *Journal of the American Society for Psychical Research*, 1972, 46, 79-90.

Sinclair, U. *Mental radio*. Monrovia, Cal.: Upton Sinclair, 1930.

Stanford, R.G. Are we shamans or scientists? *Journal of the American Society for Psychical Research*, 1981, 75, 61-70.

Stuart, C.E. An ESP test with drawings. *Journal of Parapsychology*, 1942, 6, 20-43.

Targ, R., & Puthoff, H.E. *Mind reach*. New York: Delacorte Press/Eleanor Friede, 1977.

Thaw, A.B. Some experiments in thought transference. *Proceedings of the Society for Psychical Research*, 1892, 8, 422-435.

Warcollier, R. *Experimental telepathy*. Boston: Boston Society for Psychical Research, 1938.

White, R. A comparison of old and new methods of response to targets in ESP experiments. *Journal of the American Society for Psychical Research*, 1964, 58, 21-56.

*Appendix**

Procedure

The procedure followed in the rejudging of the "Transcontinental Remote Viewing" study departed from the initial protocol in three main

The appendix is from a subsequent paper by Schlitz, M. and Gruber, E. (1981). Journal of Parapsychology, 45, 233–237.

ways: exclusion of the agent E_2's impressions of the target sites; the use of two judges instead of five; and changes in the appearance of several of the target sites, when the new judges witnessed them, as a result of a year's duration between the first judging and the second.

Judging Procedure

The judges, two students enrolled in a philosophy of science course at the University of Rome, were given copies of those materials presented to the initial set of judges. These included: photocopies of the subject E_1's impressions of the distant target sites, a list of the 10 geographical target sites as well as directions to the sites, a response sheet on which the judges were to record their judgments, and, finally, some brief instructions.

As in the initial series, the judges were asked to rank each transcript to each target site on a scale of 1 to 10, a 1 being given to the closest match, 2 to the next, and so on. In addition, judges rated the degree of correspondence between the actual site and the subject's impressions of the site by making a slash along a line, with one end designating zero correspondence and the other end representing total correspondence. Following completion of this task, they were asked to return the materials to their instructor, who then mailed these judgments to E_2 in Freiburg, Germany. After receiving the judges' responses, E_2 sent the materials to E_1 at the FRNM for statistical evaluation.

Quantitative Assessment

After receiving the judges' responses, E_1 followed the same procedure as used in the initial evaluation. To do so, she arranged the scores in two 10×10 matrices, one for ratings and one for rankings. Both judges' responses were added together to represent one score in the matrix. The direct count-of-permutations method was then used, this statistic computing an exact p by scoring and counting all possible permutations of targets while keeping the response matrix fixed. The permutations method yielded a p of .0016 for both the ranking and rating. Thus the reanalysis verifies the presence of psi in the experiment although the result is less significant than the probability of 10^{-6} in the first judging.

Given the magnitude of the difference between the overall probabilities, the question arises: Are the results of the two judgings significantly different from each other? To address this question, we employed the randomization test (Siegal, 1956, p. 152), using as data items the probability values from the permutation analysis of the matrix of rankings for each of the judges (*i.e.*, values of 9.4×10^{-6}; 1.2×10^{-4}; 5.4×10^{-7}; .22; and 1.7×10^{-3} for the first group, and 1.3×10^{-3} and 1.7×10^{-2} for the second). Given the presence of ESP in the data, this test evaluates whether the two sets of judgings follow different distributions. Similarly, the test evaluates whether the differences between groups is greater than would be expected given the variability within groups. The result of the randomization test did not reach even a suggestive level of significance $p > .1$. The same was true of a Mann-Whitney U test (which is a randomization test applied to the ranks of the data items rather than to the raw data).

It should be noted that the rejudging was intended to evaluate the presence of ESP and was not designed with the comparison between judgings in mind. As a result, the comparison is both post hoc and of very low power—the most significant result possible with groups of five and two is 1 in 21. Further, if a significant difference had been found, it would have been uninterpretable. Factors that could have contributed to a less significant result in the second judging include: (1) sensory cues in the first judging, (2) the loss of information due to changes in the target sites, (3) the fact that, assuming the same level of ESP information, the pooled results of five judges might be expected to be more significant than that of two judges, due to the larger amount of redundancy, and (4) as discussed below, additional ESP information contributed by the presence of the agent's impressions.

Discussion

Given the results of the present exercise, we conclude that the results of "Transcontinental Remote Viewing" are due to psi and not to some subtle sensory cueing in the data.

What seems of relevance here is a discussion of the weakness in the general design of restrictive ESP experiments, be they remote viewing or other forms of psi testing. As was mentioned in the earlier work (Schlitz & Gruber, 1980), elimination of the agent's impressions from information received by the judges narrows the role of telepathy in the experimental design. It seems quite likely that telepathic impressions, not only of the target site, but also of inner states, might play an important role in psi experiments. It appears also that our experimental procedures do not allow for things that are "natural" to the dreamlike structure of ESP. For example, consider a session in the Maimonides dream series (see Bender, 1971, pp. 44-45), where Ullman was acting as the agent but was faced with difficulty when concentrating on the target. He noted in his protocol that he had a severe stomach ache and was having difficulty focusing. He also noted that he thought he would have to undergo a stomach operation and that he would need a blood transfusion. At the same time, the percipient dreamed that she was in a clinic. The doctor in this dream told her that she was being prepared for stomach surgery and that she would need a blood transfusion. Of course the judges would not note any correspondence between the subjects' dream and the target picture if they were not informed of the additional impressions of the agent.

Granted, this material might cause methodological problems for the experiment per se; but on the other hand, it yields much more information about the structure of ESP than does the more restrictive free-response methodology. What is needed is a procedure which allows for the dreamlike quality of psi, or other qualities which are as yet unnoted, while maintaining a strong basis of scientific rigor.

Just how one does this is not quite clear. A phenomenological approach may help to shed light on the contextual features of the elicitation process although this still does not address our problem of sensory cuing. Douglas Stokes* has suggested a possible compromise between inclusion of the agent's impressions and the need for total security in the experimental procedure. Here he suggests that multiple agents could be sent to each of five different sites in a target pool. After the agents record their impressions and the percipient has recorded his/her impressions, the target could be determined by a random number generator. Although this is a worthy suggestion, it is somewhat troublesome on two counts: first, it is a precognitive approach to remote viewing, not allowing for real-time design; and second, it still seems to include the potential possibility—although less so—of sensory cuing due to the increased randomness when selecting out which of the agents' impressions would be included in the judging process.

Further thought must certainly be given to the problem. An easy answer may not be forthcoming. In fact, it may be that current scientific methods may be inadequate for our insight into the nature of psi (see Gruber, 1980, 1981). Whatever resolution comes of the problem, we must be very clear that we are not, as White (1980) put it, "throwing the baby out with the bath water."

References

Bender, H. *Unser sechster Sinn [Our sixth sense]*. Stuttgart: Deutsche-Verlags-Anstalt, 1971.

Private correspondence, 1981.

Gruber, E.R. Der Parapsychologe vor dem Fremden. Skizzen uber die skandalose Unordnung des Paranormalen [Parapsychologists in the face of the foreign. Sketches about the scandalous disorder of the paranormal.] In H.P. Dueer (Ed.), *Der Wissenschaftler und das Irrationale [The scientist and the irrational].* Frankfurt: Syndikat, 1981.

Gruber, E.R. Psi, methodology and the social context. In W.G. Roll (Ed.), *Research in parapsychology,* 1979. Metuchen, N.J.: Scarecrow Press, 1980.

Rhine, J.B.; Pratt, J.G.: Smith, B.M.; Stuart, C.E.; & Greenwood, J.A. *Extra-sensory perception after sixty years.* Boston: Bruce Humphries, 1940.

Schlitz, M., & Gruber, E. Transcontinental remote viewing. *Journal of Parapsychology,* 1980, 44, 305–317.

Siegel, S. *Nonparametric statistics for the behavioral sciences.* New York: McGraw-Hill, 1956.

White, R. On the genesis of research hypotheses in parapsychology. *Parapsychology Review,* 11 (1), 1980, 6–9.

CHAPTER 7

An Assessment of the Evidence for Psychic Functioning

Jessica Utts

1. Introduction

This paper was written for the American Institutes of Research, which had been commissioned by the CIA, at the request of Congress, to evaluate the government program in remote viewing and related areas. We were asked to limit our investigation to the government work. Therefore, this report is not intended to be an overall assessment of the field of parapsychology, or even of all of the work in remote viewing or anomalous cognition. A report written for a more general audience, rather than specifically requested by the CIA and Congress, would have rightfully had a broader focus than the one we were directed to use here. My conclusions in this report are substantiated by the limited review provided, but are firmly supported by broader reviews previously published by myself and others.

The purpose of this report is to examine a body of evidence collected over the past few decades in an attempt to determine whether or not psychic functioning is possible. Secondary questions include whether or not such functioning can be used productively for government purposes, and whether or not the research to date provides any explanation for how it works.

There is no reason to treat this area differently from any other area

Reprinted with permission from *Journal of Scientific Exploration*, 1996, **10**, 3–30.

of science that relies on statistical methods. Any discussion based on belief should be limited to questions that are not data-driven, such as whether or not there are any methodological problems that could substantially alter the results. It is too often the case that people on both sides of the question debate the existence of psychic functioning on the basis of their personal belief systems rather than on an examination of the scientific data.

One objective of this report is to provide a brief overview of recent data as well as the scientific tools necessary for a careful reader to reach his or her own conclusions based on that data. The tools consist of a rudimentary overview of how statistical evidence is typically evaluated, and a listing of methodological concerns particular to experiments of this type.

Government-sponsored research in psychic functioning dates back to the early 1970s when a program was initiated at what was then the Stanford Research Institute, now called SRI International. That program was in existence until 1989. The following year, government sponsorship moved to a program at Science Applications International Corporation (SAIC) under the direction of Dr. Edwin May, who had been employed in the SRI program since the mid 1970s and had been Project Director from 1986 until the close of the program.

This report will focus most closely on the most recent work, done by SAIC. Section 2 describes the basic statistical and methodological issues required to understand this work; Section 3 discusses the program at SRI; Section 4 covers the SAIC work (with some of the details in an Appendix); Section 5 is concerned with external validation by exploring related results from other laboratories; Section 6 includes a discussion of the usefulness of this capability for government purposes and Section 7 provides conclusions and recommendations.

2. Science Notes

2.1 Definitions and Research Procedures

There are two basic types of functioning that are generally considered under the broad heading of psychic or paranormal abilities. These are classically known as *extrasensory perception* (ESP), in which one acquires information through unexplainable means and *psychokinesis*, in which one physically manipulates the environment through unknown means. The SAIC laboratory uses more neutral terminology for these abilities; they refer to ESP as *anomalous cognition* (AC) and to psychoki-nesis as *anomalous perturbation* (AP). The vast majority of work at both SRI and SAIC investigated anomalous cognition rather than anomalous perturbation, although there was some work done on the latter.

Anomalous cognition is further divided into categories based on the apparent source of the information. If it appears to come from another person, the ability is called *telepathy*, if it appears to come in real time but not from another person it is called *clairvoyance* and if the information could have only been obtained by knowledge of the future, it is called *pre-cognition*.

It is possible to identify apparent precognition by asking someone to describe something for which the correct answer isn't known until later in time. It is more difficult to rule out precognition in experiments attempting to test telepathy or clairvoyance, since it is almost impossible to be sure that subjects in such experiments never see the correct answer at some point in the future. These distinctions are important in the quest to identify an explanation for anomalous cognition, but do not bear on the existence issue.

The vast majority of anomalous cognition experiments at both SRI and SAIC used a technique known as *remote viewing*. In these experi-ments, a *viewer* attempts to draw or describe (or both) a *target* location, photograph, object or short video segment. All known channels for receiv-ing the information are blocked. Sometimes the viewer is assisted by a monitor who asks the viewer questions; of course in such cases the *mon-itor* is blind to the answer as well. Sometimes a *sender* is looking at the target during the session, but sometimes there is no sender. In most cases the viewer eventually receives *feedback* in which he or she learns the cor-rect answer, thus making it difficult to rule out precognition as the expla-nation for positive results, whether or not there was a sender.

Most anomalous cognition experiments at SRI and SAIC were of the *free-response* type, in which viewers were simply asked to describe the target. In contrast, a *forced-choice* experiment is one in which there are a small number of known choices form which the viewer must choose. The latter may be easier to evaluate statistically but they have been tradition-ally less successful than free-response experiments. Some of the work done at SAIC addresses potential explanations for why that might be the case.

2.2 Statistical Issues and Definitions

Few human capabilities are perfectly replicable on demand. For example, even the best hitters in the major baseball leagues cannot hit on demand. Nor can we predict when someone will hit or when they will score a home run. In fact, we cannot even predict whether or not a home run will occur in a particular game. That does not mean that home runs don't exist.

Scientific evidence in the statistical realm is based on replication of the same average performance or relationship *over the long run*. We would not expect a fair coin to result in five heads and five tails over each set of ten tosses, but we can expect the proportion of heads and tails to settle down to about one half over a very long series of tosses. Similarly, a good baseball hitter will not hit the ball exactly the same proportion of times in each game but should be relatively consistent over the long run.

The same should be true of psychic functioning. Even if there truly is an effect, it may never be replicable on demand in the short run even if we understand how it works. However, over the long run in well-controlled laboratory experiments we should see a consistent level of functioning, above that expected by chance. The anticipated level of functioning may vary based on the individual players and the conditions, just as it does in baseball, but given players of similar ability tested under similar conditions the results should be replicable over the long run. In this report we will show that replicability in that sense has been achieved.

2.2.1 P–VALUES AND COMPARISON WITH CHANCE

In any area of science, evidence based on statistics comes from comparing what actually happened to what should have happened by chance. For instance, without any special interventions about 51 percent of births in the United States result in boys. Suppose someone claimed to have a method that enabled one to increase the chances of having a baby of the desired sex. We could study their method by comparing how often births resulted in a boy when that was the intended outcome. If that percentage was higher than the chance percentage of 51 percent *over the long run*, then the claim would have been supported by statistical evidence.

Statisticians have developed numerical methods for comparing results to what is expected by chance. Upon observing the results of an experiment, the *p-value* is the answer to the following question: *If chance alone is responsible for the results, how likely would we be to observe results this strong or stronger?* If the answer to that question, i.e. the *p*-value is very small, then most researchers are willing to rule out chance as an explanation. In fact it is commonly accepted practice to say that if the *p*-value is 5 percent (0.05) or less, then we can rule out chance as an explanation. In such cases, the results are said to be *statistically significant*. Obviously the smaller the *p*-value, the more convincingly chance can be ruled out.

Notice that when chance alone is at work, we *erroneously* find a statistically significant result about 5 percent of the time. For this reason and others, most reasonable scientists require replication of non-chance results before they are convinced that chance can be ruled out.

2.2.2 REPLICATION AND EFFECT SIZES

In the past few decades scientists have realized that true replication of experimental results should focus on the *magnitude* of the effect, or the *effect size* rather than on replication of the *p*-value. This is because the latter is heavily dependent on the size of the study. In a very large study, it will take only a small magnitude effect to convincingly rule out chance. In a very small study, it would take a huge effect to convincingly rule out chance.

In our hypothetical sex-determination experiment, suppose 70 out of 100 births designed to be boys actually resulted in boys, for a rate of 70 percent instead of the 51 percent expected by chance. The experiment would have a *p*-value of 0.0001, quite convincingly ruling out chance. Now suppose someone attempted to replicate the experiment with only ten births and found 7 boys, i.e. also 70 percent. The smaller experiment would have a *p*-value of 0.19, and would not be statistically significant. If we were simply to focus on that issue, the result would appear to be a failure to replicate the original result, even though it achieved exactly the same 70 percent boys! In only ten births it would require 90 percent of them to be boys before chance could be ruled out. Yet the 70 percent rate is a more exact replication of the result than the 90 percent.

Therefore, while *p*-values should be used to assess the overall evidence for a phenomenon, they should not be used to define whether or not a replication of an experimental result was "successful." Instead, a successful replication should be one that achieves an effect that is within expected statistical variability of the original result, or that achieves an even stronger effect for explainable reasons.

A number of different *effect size* measures are in use in the social sciences, but in this report we will focus on the one used most often in remote viewing at SRI and SAIC. Because the definition is somewhat technical it is given in Appendix 1. An intuitive explanation will be given in the next subsection. Here, we note that an effect size of 0 is consistent with chance, and social scientists have, by convention, declared an effect size of 0.2 as small, 0.5 as medium and 0.8 as large. A medium effect size is supposed to be visible to the naked eye of a careful observer, while a large effect size is supposed to be evident to any observer.

2.2.3 RANDOMNESS AND RANK-ORDER JUDGING

At the heart of any statistical method is a definition of what should happen "randomly" or "by chance." Without a random mechanism, there can be no statistical evaluation.

There is nothing random about the responses generated in anomalous cognition experiments; in other words, there is no way to define what they would look like " by chance." Therefore, the random mechanism in these experiments must be in the choice of the *target*. In that way, we can compare the response to the target and answer the question: "If chance alone is at work, what is the probability that a *target* would be chosen that matches this *response* as well as or better than does the actual target?"

The SAIC remote viewing experiments and all but the early ones at SRI used a statistical evaluation method known as *rank-order judging*. After the completion of a remote viewing, a judge who is blind to the true target (called a *blind judge*) is shown the response and five potential targets, one of which is the correct answer and the other four of which are "decoys." Before the experiment is conducted each of those five choices must have had an equal chance of being selected as the actual target. The judge is asked to assign a rank to each of the possible targets, where a rank of one means it matches the response most closely, and a rank of five means it matches the least.

The rank of the correct target is the numerical score for that remote viewing. By chance alone the actual target would receive each of the five ranks with equal likelihood, since despite what the response said the target matching it best would have the same chance of selection as the one matching it second best and so on. The average rank by chance would be three. Evidence for anomalous cognition occurs when the average rank over a series of trials is significantly lower than three. (Notice that a rank of one is the best possible score for each viewing.)

This scoring method is conservative in the sense that it gives no extra credit for an excellent match. A response that describes the target almost perfectly will achieve the same rank of one as a response that contains only enough information to pick the target as the best choice out of the five possible choices. One advantage of this method is that it is still valid even if the viewer knows the set of possible targets. The probability of a first place match by chance would still be only one in five. This is important because the later SRI and many of the SAIC experiments used the same large set of *National Geographic* photographs as targets. Therefore, the experienced viewers would eventually become familiar with the range of possibilities since they were usually shown the answer at the end of each remote viewing session.

For technical reasons explained in Appendix 1, the effect size for a series of remote viewings using rank-order judging with five choices is (3.0—average rank)/2½. Therefore, small, medium and large effect sizes (0.2, 0.5 and 0.8) correspond to average ranks of 2.72, 2.29 and 1.87, respectively. Notice that the largest effect size possible using this method is 1.4, which would result if every remote viewing achieved a first place ranking.

2.3 Methodological Issues

One of the challenges in designing a good experiment in any area of science is to close the loopholes that would allow explanations other than the intended one to account for the results.

There are a number of places in remote viewing experiment where information could be conveyed by normal means if proper precautions are not taken. The early SRI experiments suffered from some of those problems, but the later SRI experiments and the SAIC work were done with reasonable methodological rigor, with some exceptions noted in the detailed descriptions of the SAIC experiments in Appendix 2.

The following list of methodological issues shows the variety of concerns that must be addressed. It should be obvious that a well-designed experiment requires careful thought and planning.

- No one who has knowledge of the specific target should have any contact with the viewer until after the response has been safely secured.
- No one who has knowledge of the specific target or even of whether or not the session was successful should have any contact with the judge until after that task has been completed.
- No one who has knowledge of the specific target should have access to the response until after the judging has been completed.
- Targets and decoys used in judging should be selected using a well-tested randomization device.
- Duplicate sets of targets photographs should be used, one during the experiment and one during the judging, so that no cues (like fingerprints) can be inserted onto the target that would help the judge recognize it.
- The criterion for stopping an experiment should be defined in advance so that it is not called to a halt when the results just happen to be favorable. Generally, that means specifying the number of trials in advance, but some statistical procedures

require or allow other stopping rules. The important point is that the rule be defined in advance in such a way that there is no ambiguity about when to stop.

- Reasons, if any, for excluding data must be defined in advance and followed consistently, and should not be dependent on the data. For example, a rule specifying that a trial could be aborted if the viewer felt ill would be legitimate, but only if the trial was aborted before anyone involved in that decision knew the correct target.
- Statistical analyses to be used must be planned in advance of collecting the data so that a method most favorable to the data isn't selected *post hoc*. If multiple methods of analysis are used the corresponding conclusions must recognize that fact.

2.4 Prima Facie Evidence

According to *Webster's Dictionary,* in law *prima facie* evidence is "evidence having such a degree of probability that it must prevail unless the contrary be proved." There are a few examples of applied, non-laboratory remote viewings provided to the review team that would seem to meet that criterion for evidence. There are examples in which the sponsor or another government client asked for a single remote viewing of a site, known to the requester in real time or in the future, and the viewer provided details far beyond what could be taken as a reasonable guess. Two such examples are given by May (1995) in which it appears that the results were so striking that they far exceed the phenomenon as observed in the laboratory. Using a *post hoc* analysis, Dr. May concluded that in one of the cases the remote viewer was able to describe a microwave generator with 80 percent accuracy, and that of what he said almost 70 percent of it was reliable. Laboratory remote viewings rarely show that level of correspondence.

Notice that standard statistical methods cannot be used in these cases because there is no standard for probabilistic comparison. But evidence gained from applied remote viewing cannot be dismissed as inconsequential just because we cannot assign specific probabilities to the results. It is most important to ascertain whether or not the information was achievable in other standard ways. In section 3 an example is given in which a remote viewer allegedly gave code words from a secret facility that he should not have even known existed. Suppose the sponsors could be absolutely certain that the viewer could not have known about those code words through normal means. Then even if we can't assign an exact probability to the fact that he guessed them correctly, we can agree that it would be very small. That would seem to constitute *prima facie* evidence unless an alternative explanation could be found. Similarly, the viewer who described the microwave generator allegedly knew only that the target was a technical site in the United States. Yet, he drew and described the microwave generator, including its function, its approximate size, how it was housed and that it had "a beam divergence angle of 30 degrees" (May, 1995, p. 15).

Anecdotal reports of psychic functioning suffer from a similar problem in terms of their usefulness as proof. They have the additional difficulty that the "response" isn't even well-defined in advance, unlike in applied remote viewing where the viewer provides a fixed set of information on request. For instance, if a few people each night happen to dream of plane crashes, then some will obviously do so on the night before a major plane crash. Those individuals may interpret the coincidental timing as meaningful. This is undoubtedly the reason many people think the reality of psychic functioning is a matter of belief rather than science. Since they are more familiar with the provocative anecdotes than with the laboratory evidence.

The SRI Era

3.1 Early Operational Successes and Evaluation

According to Puthoff and Targ (1975) the scientific research endeavor at SRI may never have been supported had it not been for three apparent operational successes in the early days of the program. These are detailed by Puthoff and Targ (1975), although the level of the matches is not clearly delineated.

One of the apparent successes concerned the "West Virginia Site" in which two remote viewers purportedly identified an underground secret facility. One of them apparently named codewords and personnel in this facility accurately enough that it set off a security investigation to determine how that information could have been leaked. Based only on the coordinates of the site, the viewer first described the above ground terrain, then proceeded to describe details of the hidden underground site.

The same viewer then claimed that he could describe a similar Communist Bloc site and proceeded to do so for a site in the Urals. According to Puthoff and Targ "the two reports for the West Virginia Site, and the report for the Urals Site were verified by personnel in the sponsor organization as being substantially correct (p. 8)."

The third reported operational success concerned an accurate description of a large crane and other information at a site in Semipalatinsk, USSR. Again the viewer was provided with only the geographic coordinates of the site and was asked to describe what was there.

Although some of the information in these examples was verified to be highly accurate, the evaluation of operational work remains difficult, in part because there is no chance baseline for comparison (as there is in controlled experiments) and in part because of differing expectations of different evaluators. For example, a government official who reviewed the Semipalatinsk work concluded that there was no way the remote viewer could have drawn the large gantry crane unless "he actually saw it through remote viewing, or he was informed of what to draw by someone knowledgeable of [the site]. "Yet that same analyst concluded that "the remote viewing of [the site] by subject S1 proved to be unsuccessful" because "the only positive evidence of the railmounted gantry crane was far outweighed by the large amount of negative evidence noted in the body of this analysis." In other words, the analyst had the expectation that in order to be "successful" a remote viewing should contain accurate information only.

Another problem with evaluating this operational work is that there is no way to know with certainty that the subject did not speak with someone who had knowledge of the site, however unlikely that possibility may appear. Finally, we do not know to what degree the results in the reports were selectively chosen because they were correct. These problems can all be avoided with well designed controlled experiments.

3.2 The Early Scientific Effort at SRI

During 1974 and early 1975 a number of controlled experiments were conducted to see if various types of target material could be successfully described with remote viewing. The results reported by Puthoff and Targ (1975) indicated success with a wide range of material, from "technical" targets like a Xerox machine to natural settings, like a swimming pool. But these and some of the subsequent experiments were criticized on statistical and methodological grounds; we briefly describe one of the experiments and criticisms of it to show the kinds of problems that existed in the early scientific effort.

The largest series during the 1973 to 1975 time period involved remote viewing of natural sites. Sites were randomly selected for each trial from a set of 100 possibilities. They were selected "without replacement," meaning that sites were not reused once they had been selected. The series included eight viewers, including two supplied by the sponsor. Many of the descriptions showed a high degree of subjective correspondence, and the overall statistical results were quite striking for most of the viewers.

Critics attacked these experiments on a number of issues, including the selection of sites without replacement and statistical scoring method used. The results were scored by having a blind judge attempt to match the target material with the transcripts of the responses. A large fraction of the matches were successful. But critics noted that some successful matching could be attained just from cues contained in the transcripts of the material, like when a subject mentioned in one session what the target had been in the previous session. Because sites were selected without replacement, knowing what the answer was on one day would exclude the target site from being the answer on any other day. There was no way to determine the extent to which these problems influenced the results. The criticisms of these and subsequent experiments, while perhaps unwelcome at the time, have resulted in substantially improved methodology in these experiments.

3.3 An Overall Analysis of the SRI Experiments: 1973–1988

In 1988 an analysis was made of all of the experiments conducted at SRI from 1973 until that time (May et al. 1988). The analysis was based on all 154 experiments conducted during that era, consisting of over 26,000 individual trials. Of those, almost 20,000 were of the forced choice type and just over a thousand were laboratory remote viewings. There were a total of 227 subjects in all experiments.

The statistical results were so overwhelming that results that extreme or more so would occur only about once in every 10^{20} such instances if chance alone is the explanation (i.e., the p-value was less than 10^{-20}). Obviously some explanation other than chance must be found. Psychic functioning may not be the only possibility, especially since some of the earlier work contained methodological problems. However, the fact that the same level of functioning continued to hold in the later experiments, which did not contain those flaws, lends support to the idea that the methodological problems cannot account for the results. In fact, there was a talented group of subjects (labeled G1 in that report) for whom the effects were stronger than for the group at large. According to Dr. May, the majority of experiments with that group were conducted later in the program, when the methodology had been substantially improved.

In addition to the statistical results, a number of other questions and patterns were examined. A summary of the results revealed the following:

1. "Free response" remote viewing, in which subjects describe a target, was much more successful than "forced choice" experiments, in which subjects were asked to choose from a small set of possibilities.

2. There was a group of six selected individuals whose performance far exceeded that of unselected subjects. The fact that these same selected individuals consistently performed better than others under a variety of protocols provides a type of replicability that helps substantiate the validity of the results. If methodological problems were responsible for the results, they should not have affected this group differently from others.

3. Mass-screening efforts found that about one percent of those who volunteered to be tested were consistently successful at remote viewing. This indicates that remote viewing is an ability that differs across individuals, much like athletic ability or musical talent. (Results of mass screenings were not included in the formal analysis because the conditions were not well-controlled, but the subsequent data from subjects found during mass-screening were included.)

4. Neither practice nor a variety of training techniques consistently worked to improve remote viewing ability. It appears that it is easier to find than to train good remote viewers.

5. It is not clear whether or not feedback (showing the subject the right answer) is necessary, but it does appear to provide a psychological boost that may increase performance.

6. Distance between the target and the subject does not seem to impact the quality of the remote viewing.

7. Electromagnetic shielding does not appear to inhibit performance.

8. There is compelling evidence that precognition, in which the target is selected after the subject has given the description, is also successful.

9. There is no evidence to support anomalous perturbation (psychokinesis), i.e. physical interaction with the environment by psychic means.

3.4 Consistency with Other Laboratories in the Same Era

One of the hallmarks of a real phenomenon is that its magnitude is replicable by various researchers working under similar conditions. The results of the overall SRI analysis are consistent with results of similar experiments in other laboratories. For instance, an overview of forced choice precognition experiments (Honorton and Ferrari, 1989) found an average "effect size" per experimenter of 0.033, whereas all forced choice experiments at SRI resulted in a similar effect size of 0.052. The comparison is not ideal since the SRI forced choice experiments were not necessarily precognitive and they used different types of target material than the standard card-guessing experiments.

Methodologically sound remote viewing has not been undertaken at other laboratories, but a similar regime called the ganzfeld (described in more detail in Section 5) has shown to be similarly successful. The largest collection of ganzfeld experiments was conducted from 1983 to 1989 at the Psychophysical Research Laboratories in Princeton, NJ. Those experiments were also reported by separating novices from experienced subjects. The overall effect size for novice remote viewing at SRI was 0.164, while the effect size for novices in the ganzfeld at PRL was a very similar 0.17. For experienced remote viewers at SRI the overall effect size was 0.385; for experienced viewers in the ganzfeld experiments it was 0.35. These consistent results across laboratories help refute the idea that the successful experiments at any one lab are the result of fraud, sloppy protocols or some methodological problem and also provide an indication of what can be expected in future experiments.

4. The SAIC Era

4.1 An Overview

The review team decided to focus more intensively on the experiments conducted at Science Applications International Corporation (SAIC), because they provide a manageable yet varied set to examine in detail. They were guided by a Scientific Oversight Committee consisting of experts in a variety of disciplines, including a winner of the Nobel Prize in Physics, internationally known professors of statistics, psychology, neuroscience and astronomy and a medical doctor who is a retired U.S. Army Major General. Further, we have access to the details for the full set of SAIC experiments, unlike for the set conducted at SRI. Whatever details may be missing from the written reports are obtainable from the principle investigator, Dr. Edwin May, to whom we have been given unlimited access.

In a memorandum dated July 25, 1995, Dr. Edwin May listed the set of experiments conducted by SAIC. There were ten experiments, all designed to answer questions about psychic functioning, raised by the work at SRI and other laboratories, rather than just to provide additional proof of its existence. Some of the experiments were of a similar format to the remote viewing experiments conducted at SRI and we can examine those to see whether or not they replicated the SRI results. We will also examine what new knowledge can be gained from the results of the SAIC work.

4.2 The Ten Experiments

Of the ten experiments done at SAIC, six of them involved remote viewing and four did not. Rather than list the details in the body of this report, Appendix 2 gives a brief description of the experiments. What follows is a discussion of the methodology and results for the experiments as a whole. Because of the fundamental differences between remote viewing and the other type of experiments, we discuss them separately.

In the memorandum of 25 July 1995, Dr. May provided the review team with details of the ten experiments, including a short title, number of trials, effect size and overall *p*-value for each one. His list was in time sequence. It is reproduced in Table 1, using his numbering system, with the experiments categorized by type, then sequentially within type. The effect size estimates are based on a limited number of trials, so they are augmented with an interval to show the probable range of the true effect (e.g. 0.124 ± 0.071 indicates a range from 0.053 to 0.195). Remember that an effect size of 0 represents chance, while a positive effect size indicates positive results.

Table 1
SAIC Experiments Listed by Dr. Edwin May

Expr	Title	Trials	Effect Size	p-value
	Remote Viewing Experiments			
1	Target dependencies	200	0.124 ± 0.071	0.040
4	AC with binary coding	40	-0.067 ± 0.158	0.664
5	AC lucid dreams, base	24	0.088 ± 0.204	0.333
6	AC lucid dreams, pilot	21	0.368 ± 0.218	0.046
9	ERD AC Behavior	70	0.303 ± 0.120	0.006
10	Entropy II	90	0.550 ± 0.105	9.1×10^{-8}
	Other Experiments			
2	AC of binary targets	300	0.123 ± 0.058	0.017
3	MEG Replication	12,000s	MCE	MCE
7	Remote observation	48	0.361 ± 0.144	0.006
8	ERD EEG investigation	7,000s	MCE	MCE

4.3 Assessing the Remote Viewing Experiments by Homogeneous Sets of Sessions

While Table 1 provides an overall assessment of the results of each experiment, it does so at the expense of information about variability among viewers and types of targets. In terms of understanding the phenomenon, it is important to break the results down into units that are as homogeneous as possible in terms of procedure, individual viewer and type of target. This is also important in order to assess the impact of any potential methodological problems. For example, in one pilot experiment (E6, AC in Lucid Dreams) viewers were permitted to take the targets home with them in sealed envelopes. Table 2 presents the effect size results at the most homogeneous level possible based on the information provided. For descriptions of the experiments, refer to Appendix 2. Overall effect sizes for each viewer and total effect sizes for each experiment are weighted according to the number of trials, so each trial receives equal weight.

Table 2
Individual Effect Sizes

Experiment			Expert Remote Viewers				
	009	131	372	389	518	Unknown/ Other	Total
Static Targets (National Geographics)							
E1: Static	0.424	-0.071	0.424	0.177	0.283	NA	0.247
E9	0.432	NA	0.354	0.177	NA	NA	0.303
E10: Static	0.566	NA	0.801	-0.071	0.778	NA	0.550
E5 (see note)	NA	NA	NA	NA	NA	0.088	0.088
E6 (see note)	NA	NA	NA	NA	NA	0.370	0.370
E4 (see note)	-0.112	NA	0.000	0.112	NA	-0.559	-0.067
Dynamic Targets (Video Film Clips)							
E1: Dynamic	0.000	0.354	-0.283	0.000	-0.071	NA	0.000
E10: Dynamic	0.919	NA	0.754	0.000	0.424	NA	0.550
Overall	0.352	0.141	0.340	0.090	0.271	NA	

Note: Experiment 5 did not include any expert viewers. Experiment 6 included 4 expert viewers but separate results were not provided. Experiment 4 used a specially designed target set and only 4 choices in judging.

4.4 Consistency and Replicability of the Remote Viewing Results

One of the most important hallmarks of science is replicability. A phenomenon with statistical variability, whether it is scoring home runs in baseball, curing a disease with chemotherapy or observing psychic functioning, should exhibit about the same level of success in the long run, over repeated experiments of a similar nature. The remote viewing experiments are no exception. Remember that such events should not replicate with any degree of precision in the short run because of statistical variability, just as we would not expect to always get five heads and five tails if we flip a coin ten times, or see the same batting averages in every game.

The analysis of SRI experiments conducted in 1988 singled out the laboratory remote viewing sessions performed by six "expert" remote viewers, numbers 002, 009, 131, 372, 414 and 504. These six individuals contributed 196 sessions. The resulting effect size was 0.385 (May *et al.*, 1988, p. 13). The SRI analysis does not include information individually by viewer, nor does it include information about how many of the 196 sessions used static versus dynamic targets. One report provided to the review team (May, Lantz and Piantineda, 1994) included an additional experiment conducted after the 1988 review was performed, in which Viewer 009 participated with 40 sessions. The effect size for Viewer 009 for those sessions was 0.363. None of the other five SRI experts were participants.

The same subject identifying numbers were used at SAIC, so we can compare the performance for these individuals at SRI and SAIC. Of the six, three were specifically mentioned as participating in the SAIC remote viewing experiments. As can be seen in Table 2, viewers 009, 131 and 372 all participated in Experiment 1 and viewers 009 and 372 participated in Experiments 4, 9 and 10 as well.

The overall effect sizes for two of the three, viewers 009 and 372, were very close to the SRI effect size of 0.385 for these subjects, at 0.35 and 0.34, respectively, and the 0.35 effect size for Viewer 009 was very similar to his 0.363 effect size in the report by May, Lantz and Piantineda (1994). Therefore, we see a repeated and, more importantly, hopefully a repeatable level of functioning above chance for these individuals. An effect of this size should be reliable enough to be sustained in any properly conducted experiment with enough trials to obtain the long run statistical replicability required to rule out chance.

It is also important to notice that viewers 009 and 372 did well on the same experiments and poorly on the same experiments. In fact the correlation between their effect sizes across experiments is 0.901, which is very close to a perfect correlation of 1.0. This kind of consistency warrants investigation to determine whether it is the nature of the experiments, a statistical fluke or some methodological problems that led these two individuals to perform so closely to one another. If methodological problems are responsible, then they must be subtle indeed because the methodology was similar for many of the experiments, yet the results were not. For instance, procedures for the sessions with static and dynamic targets in Experiment 1 were almost identical to each other, yet the dynamic targets did not produce evidence of psychic functioning (p-value = 0.50) and the static targets did (p-value = 0.0073). Therefore, a methodological problem would have had to differentially affect results for the two types of targets, even though the assignment of target type was random across sessions.

4.5 Methodological Issues in the Remote Viewing Experiments at SAIC

As noted in Section 2.3, there are a number of methodological considerations needed to perform a careful remote viewing experiment. Information necessary to determine how well each of these were addressed is generally available in the reports, but in some instances I consulted Dr. May for additional information. As an example of how the methodological issues in Section 2.3 were addressed, an explanation will be provided for Experiment 1.

In this experiment the viewers all worked from their homes (in New York, Kansas, California, and Virginia). Dr. Nevin Lantz, who resided in Pennsylvania, was the principal investigator. After each session, viewers faxed their response to Dr. Lantz and mailed the original to SAIC. Upon receipt of the fax, Dr. Lantz mailed the correct answer to the viewer. The viewers were supposed to mail their original responses to SAIC immediately, after faxing them to Dr. Lantz. According to Dr. May, the faxed versions were later compared with the originals to make sure the originals were sent without any changes. Here are how the other methodological issues in Section 2.3 were handled:

- *No one who has knowledge of the specific target should have any contact with the viewer until after the response has been safely secured.* No one involved with the experiment had any contact with the viewers, since they were not in the vicinity of either SAIC or Dr. Lantz's home in Pennsylvania.

- *No one who has knowledge of the specific target or even of whether or not the session was successful should have any contact with the judge until after that task has been completed.* Dr. Lantz and the individual viewers were the only ones who knew the correct answers, but according to Dr. May, they did not have any contact with the judge during the period of this experiment.

- *No one who has knowledge of the specific target should have access to the response until after the judging has been completed.* Again, since only the viewers and Dr. Lantz knew the correct target, and since the responses were mailed to SAIC by the viewers before they received the answers, this condition appears to have been met.

- *Targets and decoys used in judging should be selected using a well-tested randomization device.* This has been standard practice at both SRI and SAIC.

- *Duplicate sets of targets photographs should be used, one during the experiment and one during the judging, so that no cues (like fingerprints) can be inserted onto the target that would help the judge recognize it.* This was done; Dr. Lantz maintained the set used during the experiment while the set used for judging was kept at SAIC in California.

- *The criterion for stopping an experiment should be defined in advance so that it is not called to a halt when the results just happen to be favorable. Generally, that means specifying the number of trials in advance, but some statistical procedures require other stopping rules. The important point is that the rule be defined in advance in such a way that there is no ambiguity about when to stop.* In advance it was decided that each viewer would contribute 40 trials, ten under each of four conditions (all combinations of sender/no sender and static/dynamic). All sessions were completed.

- *Reasons, if any, for excluding data must be defined in advance and followed consistently, and should not be dependent on the data. For example, a rule specifying that a trial could be aborted if the viewer felt ill would be legitimate, but only if the trial was aborted before anyone involved in that decision knew the correct target.* No such reasons were given, nor was there any mention of any sessions being aborted or discarded.

- *Statistical analyses to be used must be planned in advance of collecting the data so that a method most favorable to the data isn't selected post hoc. If multiple methods of analysis are used the corresponding conclusions must recognize that fact.* The standard rank-order judging had been planned, with results reported separately for each of the four conditions in the experiment for each viewer. Thus, 20 effect sizes were reported, four for each of the five viewers.

4.6 Was Anything Learned at SAIC?

4.6.1 TARGET SELECTION

In addition to the question of whether or not psychic functioning is possible, the experiments at SAIC were designed to explore a number of hypotheses. Experiments 1 and 10 were both designed to see if there is a relationship between the "change in visual entropy" in the targets and the remote viewing performance.

Each of the five senses with which we are familiar is a change detector. Our visions is most readily drawn to something that is moving, and in fact if our eyes are kept completely still, we cease to see at all. Similarly, we hear because of moving air, and our attention is drawn to sudden changes in sound levels. Other senses behave similarly. Thus, it is reasonable that if there really is a "psychic sense" then it would follow that same pattern.

Experiments 1 and 10 were designed to test whether or not remote viewing performance would be related to a particular type of change in the target material, namely the "change in visual entropy." A target with a high degree of change would be one in which the colors changed considerably throughout the target. A detailed explanation can be found in the SAIC reports of this experiment, or in the article "Shannon Entropy: A Possible Intrinsic Target Property" by May, Spottiswoode and James, in the *Journal of Parapsychology*, December 1994. It was indeed found that there was a correlation between the change in entropy in the target and the remote viewing quality. This result was initially shown in Experiment 1 and replicated in Experiment 10. A simulation study matching randomly chosen targets to responses showed that this was unlikely to be an artifact of target complexity or other features.

It is worth speculating on what this might mean for determining how psychic functioning works. Physicists are currently grappling with the concept of time, and cannot rule out precognition as being consistent with current understanding. Perhaps it is the case that we do have a psychic sense, much like our other senses, and that it works by scanning the future for possibilities of major change much as our eyes scan the environment for visual change and our ears are responsive to auditory change. That idea is consistent with anecdotal reports of precognition, which are generally concerned with events involving major life change. Laboratory remote viewing may in part work by someone directing the viewer to focus on a particular point in the future, that in which he or she receives the feedback from the experiment. It may also be the case that this same sense can scan the environment in actual time and detect change as well.

Another hypothesis put forth at SAIC was that laboratory remote viewing experiments are most likely to be successful if the pool of potential targets is neither to narrow nor too wide in teams of the number of possible elements in the target. They called this feature the "target-pool bandwidth" and described it as the number of "differentiable cognitive elements." They reasoned that if the possible target set was too small, the viewer would see the entire set and be unable to distinguish that information from the psychic information. If the set was too broad, the viewer would not have any means for editing an extensive imagination.

Combining these two results would indicate that a good target set would contain targets with high change in visual entropy, but that the set would contain a moderately-sized set of possibilities. The set of 100 *National Geographic* photographs used in the later days at SRI and at SAIC may have inadvertently displayed just those properties.

4.6.2. REMOTE STARING

Experiment 7, described in Appendix 2, provided results very different from the standard remote viewing work. That experiment was designed to test claims made in the Former Soviet Union and by some researchers in the United States, that individuals could influence the physiology of another individual from a remote location. The study was actually two separate replications of the same experiment, and both replications were successful from a traditional statistical perspective. In other words, it appeared that the physiology of one individual was activated when he or she was being watched by someone in a distant room. If these results are indeed sound, then they may substantiate the folklore indicating that people know when they are being observed from behind.

4.6.3 ENHANCED BINARY COMPUTER GUESSING

Experiment 2 was also very different from the standard remote viewing experiments, although it was still designed to test anomalous cognition. Three subjects attempted to use a statistical enhancement technique to increase the ability to guess forced choice targets with two choices. This clever computer experiment showed that for one subject, guessing was indeed enhanced from a raw rate of just above chance (51.6% instead of 50%) to an enhanced rate of 76 percent. The method was extremely inefficient, and it is difficult to imagine practical uses for this ability, if indeed it exists.

5. External Validation: Replications of Other Experiments

5.1 Conceptual Similarity: Ganzfeld Experiments

While remote viewing has been the primary activity at SRI and SAIC, other researchers have used a similar technique to test for anomalous cognition, called the ganzfeld. As noted in the SAIC Final Report of 29 Sept. 1994, the ganzfeld experiments differ from remote viewing in three fundamental ways, First, a "mild altered state is used," second, senders are [usually] used, so that telepathy is the primary mode, and third, the reviewed (viewers) do their own judging just after the session, rather than having an independent judge.

The ganzfeld experiments conducted at Psychophysical Research Laboratories (PRL) were already mentioned in Section 3.4 Since the time those results were reported, other laboratories have also been conducting ganzfeld experiments. At the 1995 Annual Meeting of the Parapsychological Association, three replications were reported, all published in the peer-received *Proceedings* of the conference.

The ganzfeld experiments differ in the preferred method of analysis as well. Rather than using the sum of the ranks across sessions, a simple count is made of how many first places matches resulted from a series. Four rather than five choices are given, so by chance there should be about 25% of the sessions resulting in first place matches.

5.2 Ganzfeld Results from Four Laboratories

In publishing the ganzfeld results from PRL, Bem and Honorton (1994) excluded one of the studies from the general analysis for methodological reasons, and found that the remaining studies showed 106 hits out of 329 sessions, for a hit rate of 32.2 percent when 25 percent was expected by chance. The corresponding p-value was 0.0002. As mentioned earlier, the hallmark of science is replication. This result has now been replicated by three additional laboratories.

Bierman (1995) reported four series of experiments conducted at the University of Amsterdam. Overall, there were 124 sessions and 46 hits, for a hit rate of 37 percent. The hit rates for the four individual experiments were 34.3 percent, 37.5 percent, 40 percent and 36.1 percent, so the results are consistent across his four experiments.

Morris, Dalton, Delanoy and Watt (1995) reported results of 97 sessions conducted at the University of Edinburgh in which there were 32 successes, for a hit rate of 33 percent. They conducted approximately equal numbers of sessions under each of three conditions. In one condition there was a known sender, and in the other two conditions it was randomly determined at the last minute (and unknown to the receiver) that there would either be a sender or not. Hit rates were 34 percent when there was a known sender and when there was *no* sender, and 28 percent when there was a sender but the receiver did not know whether or not there would be. They did discover *post hoc* that one experimenter was more successful than the other two at achieving successful sessions, but the result was not beyond what would be expected by chance as a *post hoc* observation.

Broughton and Alexander (1995) reported results from 100 sessions at the Institute for Parapsychology in North Carolina. They too found a similar hit rate, with 33 hits out of 100 sessions, or 33 percent hits.

Results from the original ganzfeld work and these three replications are summarized in Table 3, along with the SRI and SAIC remote viewing results. The effect sizes for the ganzfeld replications are based on Cohen's h, which is similar in type to the effect size used for the remote viewing data. Both effect sizes measure the number of standard deviations the results fall above chance, using the standard deviation for a single session.

5.3 Conclusions About External Replication

The results shown in Table 3 show that remote viewing has been conceptually replicated across a number of laboratories, by various experimenters and in different cultures. This is a robust effect that, were it not in such an unusual domain, would no longer be questioned by science as a real phenomenon. It is unlikely that methodological problems could account for the remarkable consistency of results shown in Table 3.

Table 3
Remote Viewing and Ganzfeld Replications

Laboratory	Sessions	Hit Rate	Effect Size
All Remote Viewing at SRI	770	N/A	0.209
All Remote Viewing at SAIC	445	N/A	0.230
PRL, Princeton, NJ	329	32 percent	0.167
University of Amsterdam, Netherlands	124	37 percent	0.261
University of Edinburgh, Scotland	97	33 percent	0.177
Institute for Parapsychology, NC	100	33 percent	0.177

6. Is Remote Viewing Useful?

Even if we were all to agree that anomalous cognition is possible, there remains the question of whether or not it would have any practical use for government purposes. The answer to that question is beyond the scope of this report, but some speculations can be made about how to increase the usefulness.

First, it appears that anomalous cognition is to some extent possible in the general population. None of the ganzfeld experiments used exclusively selected subjects. However, it also appears that certain individuals possess more talent than others, and that it is easier to find those individuals than to train people. It also appears to be the case that certain individuals are better at some tasks than others. For instance, Viewer 372 at SAIC appears to have a facility with describing technical sites.

Second, if remote viewing is to be useful, the end users must be trained in what it can do and what it cannot. Given our current level of understanding, it is rarely 100 percent accurate, and there is no reliable way to learn what is accurate and what is not. The same is probably true of most sources of intelligence data.

Third, what is useful for one purpose may not be useful for another. For instance, suppose a remote viewer could describe the setting in which a hostage is being held. That information may not be any use at all to those unfamiliar with the territory, but could be useful to those familiar with it.

7. Conclusions and Recommendations

It is clear to this author that anomalous cognition is possible and has been demonstrated. This conclusion is not based on belief, but rather on commonly accepted scientific criteria. The phenomenon has been replicated in a number of forms across laboratories and cultures. The various experiments in which it has been observed have been different enough that if some subtle methodological problems can explain the results, then there would have to be a different explanation for each type of experiment, yet the impact would have to be similar across experiments and laboratories. If fraud were responsible, similarly, it would require an equivalent amount of fraud on the part of a large number of experimenters or an even larger number of subjects.

What is not so clear is that we have progressed very far in understanding the mechanism for anomalous cognition. Senders do not appear to be necessary at all; feedback of the correct answer may or may not be necessary. Distance in time and space do not seem to be an impediment. Beyond those conclusions, we know very little.

I believe that it would be wasteful of valuable resources to continue to look for proof. No one who has examined all of the data across laboratories, taken as a collective whole, has been able to suggest methodological or statistical problems to explain the ever-increasing and consistent results to date. Resources should be directed to the pertinent questions about how this ability works. I am confident that the questions are no more elusive than any other questions in science dealing with small to medium sized effects, and that if appropriate resources are targeted to appropriate questions, we can have answers within the next decade.

References

Bem, Daryl J. and Charles Honorton (1994). Does psi exist? Replicable evidence for an anomalous process of information transfer. *Psychological Bulletin*, 115, 4.

Bierman, Dick J. (1995). *The Amsterdam Ganzfeld Series III & IV: Target clip emotionality, effect sizes and openness.* In Proceedings of the 38th Annual Parapsychological Association Convention, 27.

Broughton, Richard and Cheryl Alexander (1995). *Autoganzfeld II: The first 100 sessions.* In Proceedings of the 38th Annual Parapsychological Association Convention, 53.

May, Edwin C. (1995). *AC Technical trials: Inspiration for the target entropy concept.* SAIC Technical Report, May 26.

May, Edwin C., Nevin D. Lantz and Tom Piantineda (1994). *Feedback considerations in anomalous cognition experiments.* Technical Report, November 29.

May, Edwin C., J.M. Utts, V.V. Trask, W.W. Luke, T.J. Frivold and B.S. Humphrey (1988). *Review of the psychoenergetic research conducted at SRI International (1973-1988).* SRI International Technical Report, March 1989.

Morris, Robert L., Kathy Dalton, Deborah Delanoy and Caroline Watt (1995). *Comparison of the sender/no sender condition in the Ganzfeld.* Proceedings of the 38th Annual Parapsychological Association Convention, 244.

Puthoff, Harold E. and Russell Targ (1975). *Perceptual augmentation techniques: Part two – research report.* Stanford Research Institute Final Report, Dec. 1.

Appendix 1: Effect Size Measure Used with Rank Order Judging

In general, effect sizes measure the number of standard deviation the true population value of interest falls from the value that would be true if chance alone were at work. The standard deviation used is for one subject, trial, etc., rather than being the standard error of the sample statistic used in the hypothesis test.

In rank-order judging, let R be the rank for one trial. If the number of possible choices is N, then we find:

$$E(R) = (N + 1)/2$$

and

$$Var(R) = (N^2-1)/12.$$

Therefore, when $N = 5$, we find $E(R) = 3$ and $Var\ (R) = 2$. The effect size is therefore:

$$Effect\ Size = (3.0-Average\ Rank)/2^{\frac{1}{2}}$$

Appendix 2: A Brief Description of the SAIC Experiments

Experiments Involving Remote Viewing

There were six experiments involving remote viewing, done for a variety of purposes.

EXPERIMENT 1: TARGET AND SENDER DEPENDENCIES

Purpose: This experiment was designed to test whether or not a sender is necessary for successful remote viewing and whether or not dynamic targets, consisting of short video clips, would result in more successful remote viewing than the standard *National Geographic* photographs used in most of the SRI experiments.

Method: Five experienced remote viewers participated, three of whom (#s 009, 131 and 372) were included in the experienced group at SRI; their identification numbers were carried over to the SAIC experiments. Each viewer worked from his or her home and faxed the results of the sessions to the principal investigator, Nevin Lantz, located in Pennsylvania. Whether the target was static or dynamic and whether or not there was a sender was randomly determined and unknown to the viewer. Upon receiving the fax of the response, Dr. Lantz mailed the correct answer to the viewer. The original response was sent to SAIC in California, where the results were judged by an analyst blind to the correct target. Standard rank-order judging was used.

Since it is not explicitly stated, I asked Dr. May what measures were taken to make sure the viewer actually mailed the original response to SAIC *before* receiving the correct answer in the mail. He said that the original faxed responses were compared with the responses received by SAIC to make sure they were the same, and they all were.

Results: Each viewer contributed ten trials under each of the four possible conditions (sender/no sender and static/dynamic target), for a total of 40 trials per viewer. There was a moderate difference (effect size = 0.121, p = 0.08) between the static and dynamic targets, with the traditional *National Geographic* photographs faring better than the dynamic video clips. There was no noticeable difference based on whether or not a sender was involved, supporting the same conclusion reached in the overall analysis of the SRI work. Combined over all conditions and all viewers, the effect size was 0.124 (p = 0.04): for the static targets alone it was 0.248 (exact p = 0.0073) while for the dynamic targets it was 0.00 (p = 0.50).

Discussion: The SAIC staff speculated that the dynamic targets were not successful because the possibilities were too broad. They chose a new set of dynamic targets to be more similar to the static targets and performed another experiment the following year to compare the static targets with the more similar set of dynamic ones. That experiment is described below (Experiment 10).

EXPERIMENT 4: ENHANCING DETECTION
OF AC WITH BINARY CODING

Purpose: This experiment was designed to see if remote viewing could be used to develop a message-sending capability by focusing on the presence or absence of five specific features of a target. The target set was constructed in packets of four, with possible combinations of the absence (0) or presence (1) of each of the five features chosen to correspond to the numbers 00000, 01110, 10101, 11011. This is standard practice in information theory when trying to send a two digit number (00, 01, 10 or 11); the remaining three bits are used for "error correction." Different sets of five features were used for each of ten target packs.

Method: Five viewers each contributed eight trials, but the same eight targets were used for all five viewers. There was no sender used, and viewers were told that each target would be in a fixed location for one week. They were to spend 15 minutes trying to draw the target, then fax their responses to SAIC in California. The results were blind-judged and the binary features were coded by both the viewers and an independent analyst.

Results: The results were unsuccessful in showing any evidence of psychic functioning. Neither standard rank-order judging nor analysis based on the binary guesses showed any promise that this method works to send messages.

EXPERIMENT 5: AC IN LUCID DREAMS (BASELINE)

Purpose: Despite its name, this experiment did not involve lucid dreaming. Instead, it was used to test three novice remote viewers who were to participate in an experiment involving remote viewing while dreaming. This baseline experiment was designed to see if these individuals would be successful at standard laboratory remote viewing.

Method: For this baseline experiment, each of the three viewers contributed eight trials using a standard protocol common in the SRI era. For each trial, a target was randomly chosen from the set of 100 *National Geographic* targets used at SRI and SAIC. The target was placed on a table (so no sender was used) while the viewer, in another room, was asked to provide a description. The response was later blind-judged by comparing it to the target and four decoys, and providing a rank-ordering of the five choices.

Results: Of the three novice viewers, one obtained a promising effect size of 0.265, although the result was not statistically significant due to the small number of trials (8). Individual results were not provided for the other two viewers, but the overall effect size was reported as 0.088 for the three viewers.

EXPERIMENT 6: AC IN LUCID DREAMS (PILOT)

Purpose: A lucid dream is a dream in which one becomes aware that he or she is dreaming, and can control subsequent events in the dream. This ability has apparently been successfully trained by Dr. Stephen LaBerge of the Lucidity Institute. He was the Principal Investigator for this experiment. The experiment was designed to see if remote viewing could be successfully employed while the viewer was having a lucid dream.

Method: Seven remote viewers were used; four were experienced SAIC remote viewers and three were experienced lucid dreamers from the Lucidity Institute. The latter three were the novice viewers used in Experiment 5. The experienced SAIC remote viewers were given training in lucid dreaming. The number of trials contributed by each viewer could not be fixed in advance because of the difficulty of attaining the lucid dream state. A total of 21 trials were conducted, with the seven viewers contributing anywhere from one to seven trials each. The report did not mention whether or not the stopping criterion was fixed in advance, but according to Dr. May the experiment was designed to proceed for a fixed time period and to include all sessions attained during that time period.

Unlike with standard well-controlled protocols, the viewers were allowed to take the target material home with them. The targets, selected from the standard *National Geographic* pool, were sealed in opaque envelopes with covert threads to detect possible tampering (there were no indications of such tampering). Viewers were instructed to place the targets at bedside and to attempt a lucid dream in which the envelope was opened and the target viewed. Drawings and descriptions were then to be produced upon awakening.

Results: The results were blind-judged using the standard sum of ranks. Since the majority of viewers contributed only one or two trials, analysis by individual viewer would be meaningless. For the 21 trials combined, the effect size was 0.368 (p = 0.046). Information was not provided to differentiate the novice remote viewers from the experienced ones.

EXPERIMENT 9: ERD AC BEHAVIOR

Purpose: The remote viewing in this experiment was conducted in conjunction with measurement of brain waves using an EEG. The purpose of the experiment was to see whether or not EEG activity would change when the target the person was attempting to describe was briefly displayed on a computer monitor in a distant room. Details of the EEG portion will be explained as experiment 8. Here, we summarize the remote viewing part of the study.

Method: Three experienced remote viewers (#s 009, 372 and 389) participated. Because of the pilot nature of the experiment, the number of trials differed for each viewer based on availability, with viewers 009, 372 and 389 contributing 18, 24 and 28 trials, respectively. Although it is not good protocol to allow an unspecified number of trials, it does not appear that this problem can explain the results of this experiment.

Results: Responses were blind-judged using standard rank-order analysis. The effect sizes for the viewers 009, 372 and 389 were 0.432 (p = 0.033), 0.354 (p = 0.042) and 0.177 (p = 0.175), respectively. The overall effect size was 0.303 (p = 0.006).

EXPERIMENT 10: ENTROPY II

Purpose. The experiment was designed as an improved version of Experiment 1. After the unsuccessful showing for the dynamic targets in Experiment 1, the SAIC team speculated that the "target pool bandwidth" defined as the number of "cognitively differentiable elements" in the target pool might be an important factor. If the possible target material was extremely broad, viewers might have trouble filtering out extraneous noise. If the set of possibilities was too small, as in forced choice experiments, the viewer would see all choices at once and would have trouble filtering out that knowledge. An intermediate range of possibilities, too large to be considered all at once, was predicted to be ideal. The standard *National Geographic* pool seemed to fit that range. For this experiment, a pool of dynamic targets was created with a similar "bandwidth." In both Experiments (1 and 10) the researchers predicted that remote viewing success would correlate with the change in visual entropy of the target, as explained in Section 4.6.1.

Method: Four of the five viewers from Experiment 1 were used (#s 009, 372, 389 and 518). They each contributed equal numbers of sessions with static and dynamic targets, with the viewers blind to which trials had which type. Senders were not used, and all sessions were conducted at SAIC in California, unlike Experiment 1 in which the viewers worked at home. Viewer #372 contributed 15 of each type while the others each contributed 10 of each type. Standard rank-order judging was used.

Results: Table 4 shows the results for this experiment, Unlike in Experiment 1, the static and dynamic targets produced identical effect sizes, with both types producing very successful results. The combined effect size for all trials is 0.55, resulting in a z-score of 5.22.

Table 4
Results for Experiment 10

Viewer	Static Targets			Dynamic Targets		
	Rank	ES	p	Rank	ES	p
009	2.20	0.565	0.037	1.70	0.919	1.8×10^{-3}
372	1.87	0.801	9.7×10^{-4}	1.93	0.754	1.8×10^{-3}
389	3.10	-0.071	0.589	3.00	0.000	0.500
518	1.90	0.778	7.2×10^{-3}	2.40	0.424	0.091
Total	2.22	0.550	1.1×10^{-5}	2.22	0.550	1.1×10^{-5}

The Other Experiments at SAIC

There were four additional experiments at SAIC, not involving remote viewing. Two of them (experiments 3 and 8) involved trying to measure brain activity related to psychic functioning and will be described briefly. Experiment 3 used a magnetoenchephalograph (MEG) to attempt to detect anomalous signals in the brain when a remote stimulus was present. Due to the background noise in the brain measurements and the expected strength of the signal, the experimenters realized too late that they would not be able to detect a signal even if it existed. Experiment 8 utilized an EEG to try to detect the interruption of alpha waves when a remote viewing target was briefly displayed on a computer monitor in another room. The area of the brain tested was that corresponding to visual stimuli. No significant change in alpha was seen.

The remaining two experiments were replications of previous work measuring psychic functioning in areas other than remote viewing. They will be described in detail.

EXPERIMENT 2: AC OF BINARY TARGETS

Purpose: This experiment attempted to replicate and enhance random number generator experiments conducted at SRI. In these types of experiments a computer randomly selects one of two choices to be the target, denoted as 0 and 1 and the subject pushes a mouse button when he or she thinks the internal choice matches the target choice. This process is repeated over many trials. The computer tabulates the results and the experiment is a success if the subject guesses the correct answer more often than would be expected by chance. The purpose is to see if humans can correctly guess computer-selected binary targets, and hopefully by extension, correctly solve binary choice problems in real situations. If that were to be the case, then real problems could be posed as binary ones(e. g. is the lost child still in this city or not) to narrow down possibilities.

Method: This SAIC experiment was designed to enhance the accuracy of binary guessing by using a statistical technique called sequential analysis. Rather than just one guess for each decision, the subject continues to guess until the computer ascertains that a decision has been reached. The computer keeps track of the number of times zero and one have each been guessed and announces a decision when one of the choices has clearly won out over the other, or when it is clear that it is essentially an ongoing tie. In the latter case, no decision is recorded. Three subjects participated (#s 007, 083 and 531) in this experiments at SRI.

Results: Using this method for enhancing the accuracy of the guesses, subject #531, who had been successful in previous similar experiments, was able to achieve 76 correct answers out of 100 tries. This remarkable level of scoring for this type of experiment resulted in an effect size of 0.520 and a z-score of 5.20. The other two subjects did not differ from chance results, with 44 and 49 correct decisions out of 100 or 101. (One subject accidentally contributed an additional trial.)

Although the result for subject 531 is remarkably successful, it does not represent a very efficient method of obtaining the decision. To reach the 100 decisions required a total of 21,337 guesses, i.e. over 200 guesses for each decision. Of the individual guesses, only 51.6 percent were correct, for an effect size of 0.032, similar to other forced choice experiments. Due to the large number of guesses, the corresponding z-score was 4.65. Combined over all three subjects, 56 percent of the 301 decisions were correct and the effect size was 0.123. The combined results were still statistically significant, with $p = 0.017$, as shown in Table 1.

EXPERIMENT 7: REMOTE OBSERVATION

Purpose: It is often reported anecdotally that people know when they are being watched. Two experiments were conducted at SAIC to determine whether or not these anecdotes could be supported by a change in physiology when someone is being observed from a distance. The experimental design was essentially the same for the two experiments. This work was a conceptual replication of results reported by researchers in the Former Soviet Union (FSU), the United States and Scotland. The experiments in the FSU were interpreted to mean that the physiology of the recipient was being manipulated by the sender, an effect that if real could have frightening consequences.

Method: The "observee" was seated in a room with a video camera focused on him or her, and with galvanic skin response measurements being recorded. In a distant room the "observer" attempted to influence the physiology of the observee at randomly spaced time intervals. During those time intervals, an image of the observee appeared on a computer monitor watched by the observer. During "control" periods, the video camera remained focused on the observee but the computer monitor did not display his or her image to the observer. There were 16 "influence" periods randomly interspersed with 16 "control" periods, each of 30 seconds, with blank periods of 0 to 5 seconds inserted to rule out patterns in physiology.

Results: To determine whether or not the galvanic skin response of the observees was activated while they were being watched, the response during the control periods was compared with the response during the "influence" periods for each subject. The results were then averaged across subjects. In both experiments, there was greater activity during the periods of being watched than there was during the control periods. The results were statistically significant in each case ($p = 0.036$ and 0.014) and the effect sizes were similar, at 0.39 and 0.49. As preplanned, the results were combined, yielding an effect size of 0.39 ($p = 0.005$). As an interesting *post hoc* observation, it was noted that the effect was substantially stronger when the observer and observee were of opposite sexes than when they were of the same sex.

Discussion: This experiment differs from the others conducted at SAIC since it involves interaction between two people rather than one person ascertaining information about the environment or the future. It raises substantially more questions than it answers, since the mechanism for the shift in physiology is unknown. Possibilities range from the idea that the observee was able to know when the computer in the distant room was displaying his or her image, not unlike remote viewing, to the possibility that the observer actually did influence the physiology of the observee. Further experimentation as well as a review of similar past experiments may be able to shed light on this important question.

CHAPTER 8

A Laboratory Approach to the Nocturnal Dimension of Paranormal Experience: Report of a Confirmatory Study Using the REM Monitoring Technique

Montague Ullman *and* Stanley Krippner

A study was designed to investigate telepathic effects in REM sleep. A single subject (S), who had produced statistically significant data in a previous study, spent eight nights in the laboratory. On each night, a target (art print) was randomly selected by a staff member (agent) after S was in bed. The agent spent the night in a distant room, attempting to telepathically influence S's dreams when the monitoring experiments signaled that a REM period had begun. At the end of each REM period, S was awakened by the experimenters and a dream report was elicited and tape-recorded. Only the agent was aware of the target content and he remained in his room throughout the night. Transcripts of the eight dream protocols and copies of the eight targets were given to three independent judges who assessed correspondences, on a blind basis, on a 100-point scale. The results were significant at p *<0.001.*

Reprinted with permission from *Biological Psychiatry*, 1969, **1**, 259–270.

Introduction

Parapsychological research, almost without exception, has emphasized techniques applicable to daytime experimentation. The physiological measures now available to monitor dreaming have paved the way for a nocturnal approach to the paranormal in which most of the features of the naturally occurring paranormal event can be included as intrinsic features of the experiment itself. Utilizing the Rapid Eye Movement technique, it becomes possible to program a relationship between an agent looking at a target picture and a sleeping subject who is attempting to incorporate the unknown target into the series of dreams he is having that night. This technique lends itself to the independent judging of the degree of correspondence between dream protocol and target, as well as to the use of statistical techniques to reflect a quantifiable result.

A nocturnal approach of this kind emphasizes the congruence between certain attributes of dreaming and the conditions that characterize the anecdotal accounts of paranormal events. Dreaming is a naturally recurring state characterized by a radical transformation in consciousness, resembling in many ways the dissociated states frequently noted at the time of occurrence of paranormal events. Dreaming also highlights currently significant motivational needs, another important point of congruence with the spontaneous paranormal event.

Critical surveys of the research in telepathy have been made by Soal and Bateman (1954), Murphy (1961), and Rao (1966). A summary of parapsychological research involving personality factors has been presented by Schmeidler and McConnell (1958). The relationships between parapsychology and biology were discussed in a 1955 symposium sponsored by the Ciba Foundation (Wolstenholme and Millar, 1956). Although the reality of paranormal experience is of broad general interest, the focus of psychiatrists has centered about the existence of the so-called telepathic dream, i.e., a dream involving the transfer of information from one person to another, other than through known sensory channels. Associations between parapsychology and psychoanalysis were explored in an anthology which included six papers by Freud (Devereux, 1953).

Although clinical reports of paranormal effects in dreams have appeared in the literature over a period of several decades, there is only one report of an experimental approach to the subject (Bleksley, 1963). In this experiment, a subject attempted to awaken himself at a time indicated by a clock situated 900 miles away. This clock was reset daily at a time randomly selected. A total of 284 trials were attempted, and the results were statistically significant. The subject did better when he awakened from a dream than when he awakened without having been aware of dreaming.

Wallwork (1952) reported the first attempt to relate EEG patterns and paranormal functioning. Wallwork's methodology was repeated by Cadoret (1964) who found that significantly more ESP hits occurred when trials were accompanied by alpha activity than when accompanied by relatively fast activity. Similar findings have been reported by Tart (1963) and Motoyama (1964).

In 1962 a Dream Laboratory was established at the Maimonides Medical Center for the investigation of telepathy and dreaming. The first study to be completed which used a single subject (S) took place in 1964 (Ullman *et al.*, 1966). This was a 7 night study with a male psychologist as S. In earlier screening trials he appeared able to incorporate into his dreams aspects of target pictures that an agent (A) or sender was looking at in another room. Three outside judges rated each of the typed transcripts of the psychologist's dream reports against each of the seven art prints which had been used as target pictures. It was hypothesized that each dream transcript would correspond more closely to the target of that night than to the targets used on other nights of the experiment. Each transcript-target combination was rated by the three judges and the mean of the three ratings was entered on a seven-by-seven matrix. When the matrix was subjected to analysis of variance technique the correct transcript-target combinations received significantly higher mean ratings than the incorrect transcript-target combinations ($p < 0.01$). The results indicated that telepathic effects, as hypothesized, had been incorporated into the dreams of S during a controlled laboratory experiment. On each of the seven nights of the experiment S's dream and associational statements demonstrated a close correspondence to the randomly selected target picture for that particular experimental session.

Procedure

In 1966, the same psychologist was again available as a subject for an experimental study. The staff member who had served as A in the previous study was also available for the attempted replication. The same three outside judges (Js) offered their services to evaluate the material. An eight night series was planned by the Dream Laboratory staff.

It was again hypothesized that S's dream transcript for any given experimental night would reflect the influence of telepathic communication with A. The target selection was made by a team of four staff members who were never present on any of the experimental nights. As a result, the range of possible target pictures to be used was unknown to *S*, to *A*, or to the experimenters (*E*s) who monitored the equipment during each session.

The targets were postcard size prints of famous paintings. One of the staff psychologists examined over 100 art prints from New York museums and from art books, selecting 20 that combined simplicity, highly emotional content, and vivid color, the characteristics which appeared to typify successful telepathy target pictures in previous experimental sessions at the Dream Laboratory. These 20 prints were narrowed to 10 by two other staff members.

In the initial series (1964) the nightly log of *A* indicated that he had spontaneously dramatized or acted out some of the scenes depicted in the target picture. In order to facilitate this, as well as to more deeply involve *A* in the theme and mood of the target picture, a fourth staff member prepared a series of objects relating to each of the target pictures. These objects in conjunction with the picture would, it was hoped, involve *A* in a multisensory involvement with the target both through his physical contact with the objects selected as well as their use as props in acting out aspects of the target picture.

The staff member who selected the multisensory materials sealed each art print in an opaque envelope; this envelope was enclosed in a larger envelope which was sealed. Each envelope had a small latter in its upper right hand corner, matching a letter on an appropriate box of multisensory materials. The staff member who sealed the envelopes affixed his signature on the flap of each envelope. The signature was covered with transparent tape so that any attempt by anyone to open the envelopes prematurely would be detected. The same staff member affixed his signature to the side of each box of multisensory materials. Again, the signature was covered with transparent tape to detect any attempt to tamper with the materials. *S* was not informed as to the presence of the multisensory materials. However, he knew from previous experience that the target material would be prints of famous paintings.

S slept in the Dream Laboratory on nonconsecutive nights. As soon as *S* was in bed, *A* entered an office and selected a single digit from a table of random numbers. At this point he was given a key by one of the *E*s; taking the key he went to an attaché case, unlocked it, and counted down through the stack of target envelopes until he reached the number of the randomly selected digit. If the random number was larger than the number of targets remaining, *S* went through the pool a second time until an envelope was located, the order of which matched the randomly chosen number.

Once the target had been selected the appropriate box of multisensory materials was located. *A* and *E* examined both the target envelope and the box to see if the transparent tape had been broken or if the signatures showed evidence of tampering. Still under the observation of an *E*, *A* placed the remaining targets back into the attaché case and locked it, taking the target materials to his room.

The *A*'s room contained a table, a bed, a loudspeaker, and a buzzer. *S*'s dream report could be heard by *A* on the loudspeaker; this procedure served to maintain *A*'s interest in the experiment and his continued orientation to the sleeping *S*. There was no microphone in *A*'s room, making it impossible for any vocal cues to be transmitted from *A* to *S* or from *A* to *E*s.

Upon arriving in the agent's room, *A* opened the two envelopes and the box of multisensory materials. He spent the remainder of the night in this room which was 98 feet distant from *S*'s sleep room, and which was separated from the sleep room by three doors and two hallways. (*A*'s room was adjoined by a washroom which *A* was permitted to use.)

During the night *E*s monitored *S*'s sleep in order to detect emergent State I REM periods. At the onset of each REM period, *E* signaled *A* by means of a one-way buzzer to awaken and to concentrate on the target. At the end of each REM period, *E* awakened *S* by means of a two-way intercom, and elicited a verbal report. These reports, as well as *S*'s associations to them, were tape recorded and subsequently transcribed. Specifically, *S* was asked:

> Please tell me what has been going through your mind. (Pause) Is there anything else? (Pause) Was there any color? (Pause) Thank you. Please go back to sleep.

Following *S*'s final awakening, toward the end of each experimental session, an *E* conducted a post-sleep interview with *S* in order to obtain additional associational material. At this time *S* was also asked to make a guess as to what he thought the target for that night might have been. Specifically, *S* was asked:

> How do you feel? (Pause) How many dreams do you think you had? (Pause) Do you remember your first dream report? (Pause) Can you elaborate on it? (Pause) What feeling or mood accompanied the dream? (Pause) What thoughts or memories does the dream bring to mind? (Pause) Do you remember your second dream report, etc.? Were there any elements in your night's dream which did not seem to make much sense in terms of your personal life? (Pause) Which ones? (Pause) Please

make a guess as to what you think the target may have been. (Pause) Thank you. I'll be right in to take off the electrodes.

After the post-sleep interview was concluded, a secretarial assistant mailed the tape to a transcriber who typed a transcript of the night's verbal reports and interview. *S* was dismissed until the following experimental session. *A* resealed the envelopes and the box containing the multisensory material, affixing his signature to each seal and covering it with transparent tape. The used materials were filed away until the conclusion of the entire experimental series.

After the transcripts for all eight experimental nights had been collected and transcribed, three outside *J*s (who had not been present for any of the experimental sessions) rated each of the eight target materials against each of the eight transcripts. The *J*s worked blind and independently, using slides of the target and the multisensory material.

The 64 possible target-transcript combinations were submitted to each *J* in a different random order. Eight combinations were judged at a time; following the completion of each set of eight, *J* mailed the ratings to the Dream Laboratory and started another set. The materials were submitted to the *J*s by mail and sent back by mail reducing *J-E* contact, and thus eliminating contamination in the form of *E* bias effects. The following statement was sent to each *J*:

The task that confronts you may be thought of in terms of an individual's dream experience in connection with some stimulating event which has found its way into the dream production. It is taken as axiomatic in psycho-analytic literature that some of what a person experiences during the waking state finds its way into his dreams, more or less transformed. It is also known that stimuli that are experienced by a dreamer while in the sleeping state may be incorporated into his dreams.

You are to consider that the target represents an event that has occurred while the subject was just going to sleep, or has occurred while the subject was in the sleeping state. You must further assume that the event has in fact influenced the dream either in a direct way or through some process of transformation. The task then becomes one of working from the dream back to the event that affected the dream. It is possible that one target was used on any given night, that more than one target was used on any given night, or that no target was used on any given night. Therefore, each of your judgments should be completely independent of any other judgment.

You are to familiarize yourself with each target. Remember that the title of the target picture, the artist, the date, etc. are considered to be part of the target. You are also to familiarize yourself with each transcript as the time comes for you to evaluate target-transcript correspondences.

The actual steps are:

1. Locate the target and the transcript which match the numeral and the letter on the first group of judging forms. Fill in the blanks titled "subject," "judge," and "date." You will notice that three sheets are stapled together in each group.

2. Using the front page of the first group of judging forms, read the dreams on the transcript and color in the space that represents, in your judgment, the correspondence with the target material. This judging is done on the basis of the *dreams alone*.

3. Using the middle page of the first group of judging forms, read the post-sleep interview and color in the space that represents, in your judgment, the correspondence with the target material. This is done on the basis of the *entire transcript*.

4. Using the back page of the first group of judging forms, re-read the summary and color in the space that represents, in your judgment, the correspondence with the target material. This judging is done on the basis of the *summary alone*.

5. Proceed to the secondary group of judging forms and repeat the process. When you have finished a set of eight forms return them, by mail, to the Dream Laboratory.

A number of special precautions were taken in this study to insure that no possible sensory cues bearing on the target could in any way reach *S*. The two rooms used to house *S* and *A* were at opposite sides of the building and were 98 feet apart.

A remained in the room for the entire night, with the exception of visits to the adjoining washroom. *S* remained in the sleep room for the entire night. Communication from *A* to *S* or from *A* to the *E*s was impossible, due to the one-way communication system.

The range of target material was known only to the four staff members who had prepared it. None of these staff members came into contact with *S* until the end of the experimental series.

Judging was undertaken by three *J*s, none of whom came in contact with *S* or *A* until the end of the experimental series. All of the judging forms were sent through the mail. This aspect of the procedure was handled by a secretarial assistant who had not been present during any of the experimental sessions.

The cited precautions taken during the experimental procedure reflect improvements made over the first study done with *S*. For the first study, the target pool was selected by *A* and *E*. Due to a limited staff there was only one *E*. Therefore, *A* emerged from his room at one point during the night to monitor *S*'s dreams while *E* rested. Even so, *A* never spoke to *S* on the intercom; the awakening procedure was always handled by *E*. For the first study *S* became ill on the eighth experimental night and was hospitalized for 3 months. For the second study all eight nights were completed.

Results from the first study were subjected to an analysis of variance technique suggested by Scheffé (1959). For the second study with *S*, a more conservative technique was utilized, consisting of a Latin-square analysis of variance. For the latter procedure the three judges received different randomizations of the 64 possible transcript-target combinations. They worked on sets of eight combinations at a time, mailing each set back to the Dream Laboratory upon its completion.

Results

Statistical analysis consisted of a Latin-square analysis of variance technique. This procedure was employed to compare the ratings of the eight critical parts (e.g., the actual target-transcript combinations for each experimental night) with the 56 noncritical pairs. Means of the three *J*s' ratings were entered in the matrix.

The experimental hypothesis had been made on the basis of correspondences between the targets and the entire transcript for each night. On this basis, an *F* of 6.43 was obtained which is significant at $p < 0.001$ with 7 and 21 degrees of freedom.[*] Therefore, the telepathy hypothesis was confirmed and the results of the previous study were replicated.

A common criticism of the previous study centered around the allegation that dreams are so ambiguous that just about any picture would correspond in some way to a dream transcript. This argument can be countered by pointing out that the *J*s worked blind and that they matched each of the eight targets against each of the eight transcripts.

A further check on this allegation was made. A fourth *J* was given copies of the eight transcripts of the second study as well as the seven

---

[*]*Judgings on the basis of dreams alone were also statistically significant ($F = 2.65$, $p < 0.005$, 7 and 21 df), as were the judgings on the basis of S's guess for the night ($F = 4.96$, $p < 0.005$, 7 and 21 df). It will be noted that the highest level of significance was reached when the entire transcript was utilized in the judging process.*

targets used for the first study, the eight targets used for the second study, and a target used for a pilot session with S. Before the fourth J attempted the 128 ratings, eight transcript-target combinations were randomly assigned using the eight "control" targets. Upon completion of the judging procedure, ratings for the "correct" and the "control" transcript-target combinations were placed in separate analysis of variance matrices and inspected, utilizing the Scheffé technique (1959). The "correct" transcript-target combinations received higher ratings from the fourth judge than did all other combinations on the matrix (F = 8.11, p < 0.01, 8 and 64 df). The "control" combinations did not produce statistically significant data (F = -0.71, 8 and 64 df). Therefore, the allegation that significant results can be obtained from chance target-transcript combinations was not demonstrated.

Examples of Correspondences Between Dream and Target

Several of the targets are described below, as well as the accompanying multisensory materials. Excerpts from the dream reports and postsleep interviews are presented, with especially striking transcript-target correspondences *italicized*. It should be remembered that Js worked from the entire dream transcript, not just the excerpts presented here.

EXPERIMENTAL NIGHT 2

For the second experimental night, Hiroshige's "Downpour at Shono" was randomly selected. It portrays a Japanese man with an umbrella trying to escape a driving rain. The directions in the box of multisensory materials read "Take a shower." A small Oriental umbrella was included in the box.

First Dream Report: No apparent correspondences.

Second Dream Report: "It's as though I was doing some drawing, or some drawing was being done. This was very hazy ... I had the feeling as though it were in a *down position*, like a low table. *Down* on the floor. Seems that's what I meant by *'down'*."

Third Dream Report: "... Something about *an Oriental man* who was ill..."

Fourth Dream Report: "The part I remember—it sort of faded away but *it had to do with fountains—a big fountain*. It would be like one you see in Italy. *A fountain*. Two images and a *water spray* that would shoot up. No color."

Fifth Dream Report: "...*I was in this indoor-outdoor place. I assumed it was outdoors yet at one part of the dream it was indoors*... And there was an air conditioner in it too..."

Sixth Dream Report: No apparent correspondences.

Post-Sleep Interview: "There was a young man. He seemed to be an invalid or something, and he was on a bed. And I just don't remember any more ... I just had the two images this time, one with *the fountain* like the ones in Italy, *the elaborate fountains*, and a giant eye of a needle ... *The fountain makes me think of pictures and scenes I've seen of Rome. In fact, a short time ago I was looking at a book. The book is called 'Fountains in Italy', I think. They have so many fountains ... I remember talking about fountains being renewing of life* ... I was walking on the street. *It seemed it was raining a little bit* and we got to a particular point, and the street was blocked, so we had to walk out into the street and around ... Of course, *it was raining*, and it was night and it had a sort of heavy feeling..."

Guess for the Night: "... In terms of just standing out, I would say *the fountain* and the needle ... Those particularly seem to sort of stand out as being unusual... *For some reason I'm going to say that it had something to do with ... fountains or something ... Fountain. Maybe water ...*"

EXPERIMENTAL NIGHT 4

"Both Members of this Club" by Bellows was the fourth target selected. It portrays two boxers in a savage fight; a crowd watches with glee. A leather boxing glove was the multisensory item which accompanied this painting.

First Dream Report: "... There were *a lot of people ... There was a lot of activity going on.* Conversation between the people ... There were some strange characteristics about them in the way they were dressed ..."

Second Dream Report: No apparent correspondence.

Third Dream Report: "... I was watching some cars parked on the beach being *pounded* in. *One of them was pounded in and hit another car and completely broke it to pieces.* And then I was in the car with my mother and father ... *and the ocean began to pound in and knock the car back ... and the wave pounded and hit the car.* And I thought it was really going to hit the other car hard ..."

Fourth Dream Report: "... The only thing I can remember is cleaning a shoe. Cleaning a shoe with some sort of solution ... and there was the process of going over the entire shoe, cleaning it with this, and then putting an oil on it and polishing it ... And there was a tiger coming out of a drain ... *It was just a black leather shoe.* The process was cleaning a dirty shoe. Just a man's shoe ... Just a lace shoe..."

Fifth Dream Report: "... Well, I was thinking about Viet Nam. Different aspects of it. *The pros and cons* ... Being in Viet Nam and reasons for being there and *arguments* of why we should be there and some of the *arguments* of why we shouldn't."

Post-Sleep Interview: "... *There were a number of people* and the people themselves are not clear ... Something about their attitudes I can't recapture. It would be more ... *competition* ... *That would give me a feeling perhaps of maybe competition in some way* ... It began with the observation of a tremendous storm ... Ships were being *pounded* and driven into the beach ... These huge waves would *pound* these ships ashore... The water would *pound* in a great distance ... *It picked up a car and slammed into another car* and just completely it fell apart. Like if you'd drop a watch, it would go *shattering* in all directions... The waves were *pounding* us in and we were being pushed toward another car ... It was quite an interesting dream and I enjoyed it. *Maybe I enjoyed the violence in the dream* ... The *violence* in the dream—was exciting... The mood was one of awe and grandeur ... The cleaning of the shoe was a process of going over a black shoe, a man's shoe ..., and the whole dream consisted of cleaning the shoe. Now I think this was the dream where I had the other impression about the tiger ... Where in the devil did the tiger come from?"

Guess for the Night: "... I think I was betraying a great deal of *violence, destructiveness, aggressiveness* ... Something to do within nature because the tiger is ... *an independent, powerful creature* to be respected. In terms of the target ... *something that is depicting power*. At the moment, I have the feeling of nature in its broadest sense. *You might say the raw aspects of nature more than the more refined aspects of a human being* ..."

On the sixth experimental night, Beckmann's "Descent From the Cross," a painting which depicts a brown, emaciated Christ being taken down from the Cross, was selected. The box of multisensory materials included a crucifix, a picture of Christ, and a red felt pen so that the agent could color Christ's wounds to simulate red blood.

First Dream Report: No apparent correspondences.

Second Dream Report: No apparent correspondences.

Third Dream Report: No apparent correspondences.

Fourth Dream Report: "It started off with a birthday party ... then went out somewhere ... and we passed by an area where *Winston Churchill* was making a talk ... And the part I remember is my father driving ... and then we drove on home ... and there was a *lot of wine* that I tasted and I think I got a piece of cake. And that was about the end of the dream ... There were *two bottles of wine* ... *Churchill was*, as I said, *old, emaciated*.

I had remembered him as a fat, chubby guy, and *here he was old and getting thinner and drawn...*"

Fifth Dream Report: "It started out in some sort of a native community ... It got to the point ... where we were going to be put in the stewpot. I don't know what was happening. *We were going to be sacrificed,* or something, and there were political overtones. It seemed like there was a speech by *President Johnson* being played to them ... I was trying to figure out how we could change their minds ... and there was one loudspeaker there and *we decided that what we would do is pretend we were the gods* or something, by forbidding this by speaking in the loudspeaker and also ... we could use fireworks ... and use this booming voice to forbid them from doing this. And then when it came time to do it we didn't have any of this stuff ... *Red ... I think red.* Another thing, *I think in looking at the so-called king, chief or whatever the native was ... his skin was a very rich chocolate color* ... Just one other thing that keeps coming back but very hard to describe—the chief ... his head was very strange looking. It would almost be like you were looking at him, looking at *one of these totem-pole gods.* And his eyes were very unusual and it seemed like there was some color there, *reddish-*rimmed ... eyes... *They, too, were going through a whole ceremony to the gods. And the idea was to scare them by speaking through the speaker as though we were the gods forbidding them to kill us...*"

Sixth Dream Report: No apparent correspondences.

Post-Sleep Interview: "... *Churchill seemed to be emaciated.* He was drying up and *he was thinner than what you had remembered him as* ... I remember primarily *the wine* ... And I remember seeing *Churchill* ... The *aggression* was being thrown at different people; although it didn't harm them physically, it would certainly scare *the bejeezus* out of them ... It was sort of a funny dream ... It had a strange quality to it in which I was going about it as though it were possible to do something, and in the dream I didn't provide for it. I mean by that, there were ... these natives and the loudspeaker ... *To make them think the gods had spoken, which was going to save me ... this loudspeaker was there* ... but also there was the planning to use fireworks that didn't exist. As though thinking about it and planning it was in some way going to be just as influential in something happening as though it really did exist ... The last stage of the ceremony, we would be the star participants ... There was just an awareness that *they were going to kill us in some way, that it was part of their ceremony ... It began to have a very ritualistic feeling ...*"

Guess for the Night: "Well, you can say a lot of things in the dreams didn't make sense. After all, I'm not too frequently exposed to seeing *Churchill* ... I'd say the native bit was rather strange ... I'd say that would be outside my daily experience. It seems like I was trying to assert something in the dream that really wasn't there ... *One of the things I dreamed about quite a bit was ... the ceremonial aspect. In the Churchill thing there was a ceremonial thing going on, and in the native dream there was a type of ceremony going on ... leading to whatever the ceremonial would be to sacrificing two victims. I would say the sacrifice feeling in the native dream ... would be more like the primitive trying to destroy the civilized ...* In this instance it seemed to have an element of *cannibalism* in it ... I think I can take it a little further. *I would say the native part, the primitive part, believed in this god authority. Now in terms of what was being said in the dream it believed in the god-authority, or the idea of it, but what was happening in the dream ... was not a real god.* It was the utilization of a lot of ritual. It was the use of the belief. I don't know if I'm making myself clear. In other words, *no god was speaking. It was the use of the fear of this, or the awe of god idea that was to bring about the control. Not that god spoke.*"

Discussion

The methodology here described offers the possibility of the first systematic approach to the study within the laboratory setting of a phenomenon rather elusively revealing itself in occasional anecdotal accounts and even more sporadically in the context of the clinical psychotherapeutic relationship. Within the laboratory setting, one faces many of the same problems that exist *in vivo*, namely, the clustering of paranormal effects in a relatively small percentage of the population, and the general unpredictability of events of this kind. We have the additional problem of so structuring the relationship between A and S that enough of an emotional and motivational balance will be created to cause this type of information flow to occur. In our own work, we have conducted several one night screening studies in an effort at selecting, in a gross and subjective way, the gifted subject whose dreams at a manifest content level have an easily identifiable resemblance to the target picture. We selected, as a result of three such screening studies, three individuals who appeared gifted in this way. Each was then subjected to an individual series of studies carried out and evaluated along the lines described. In only one of the three were the results statistically significant, although in each instance the results were in the right direction and a number of striking correspondences did occur for each subject. The present study was an attempted confirmatory study of the earlier one done with the first successful S.

We interpret the confirmatory study as supporting evidence for an extrasensory effect linked to an altered state of consciousness and not explainable on the basis of sensory leakage. The physical and psychological dimensions of the problem have yet to be explored. With regard to the former there are numerous speculative models but none of any heuristic significance as yet. The situation is somewhat more hopeful with regard to the latter. Murphy (1961) has repeatedly pointed out the applicability to parapsychological research of certain basic axioms that hold in psychology generally, i.e., the influence of set, motivation, belief, the decline effect, etc. Our own work has begun to include the personality and motivational dimensions of the *S-A* interaction.

There are a great many physical and psychological variables which have to be studied in an effort to learn more about the optimal conditions for the manifestation of such paranormal effects. Among the basic ones psychologically are the relevance of genetic relationships, kinship, or friendship as ties between *S* and *A*.

In the experimental series reported, the personal relationship between *S* and *A* was a pleasant and empathic one. Although the two psychologists affirmed the fact that they never saw each other outside the laboratory setting, they spent time together before each experimental session. They resembled each other in a variety of ways. Of approximately the same age, both had been through psychoanalysis, both engaged in psychotherapy, and both had been successful in other professional fields before becoming psychologists. Both had traveled abroad; both wore beards. The literature on successful telepathy experiments demonstrates the importance of close interpersonal relationships (Schmeidler and McConnell, 1958).

A more specific concern was voiced by Freud (1933) when he raised the question of the possible distortion of telepathically perceived messages through unconscious elaboration as part of the dream work. Our judges have thus far been influenced mainly by manifest correspondences, or by transparently obvious symbolic correspondences.

From a physiological point of view, we have no certain knowledge that it is the dream state *per se* which facilitates telepathic transfer. There may well be other critical periods during the sleep cycle that may prove to be more relevant. Starting with the dreaming phase was simply an empirically based choice. Finally, the more refined experimentation possible with animals suggests the possibility of linking REM studies in animals to problems of extrasensory communication.

Acknowledgment

The authors express their appreciation to Rhea White, Patricia

Carrington Ephron, Marian Nester, and Craig Ezell for their services as judges, to Sol Feldstein for serving as the agent, to Dr. William Erwin for serving as the subject, and to Dr. Michael Capobianco who served as statistical consultant for the study.

References

Bleksley, A.H. (1963). An experiment in long-distances ESP during sleep. *J. Parapsychol.* 27:1.
Cadoret, R.J. (1964). An exploratory experiment: EEG recording during clairvoyant card tests. *J. Parapsychol.* 28: 226.
Devereux, G. (ed.) (1953). *Psychoanalysis and the Occult*, International Universities Press, New York.
Freud, S. (1933). *New Introductory Lectures on Psychoanalysis*, W.W. Norton, New York, Chapter 2.
Motoyama, H. (1964). Differences between ESP and mental calculation viewed from electroencephalographic change. *J. Religious Phil.* 3:1.
Murphy, G. (1961). *Challenge of Psychical Research*, Harper, New York.
Rao, R. (1966). *Experimental Parapsychology*, Charles C. Thomas, Springfield, Ill.
Scheffé, H. (1959). *The Analysis of Variance*, John Wiley, New York, Chapter 10.
Schmeidler, G.R., and McConnell, R.A. (1958). *ESP and Personality Patterns*, Yale University Press, New Haven, Conn.
Soal, S.G., and Bateman, F. (1954). *Modern Experiments in Telepathy*, Yale University Press, New Haven, Conn.
Tart, C.T. (1963). Physiological correlates of psi cognition. *Intern. J. Neuropsychiat.* 5: 375.
Ullman, M., Krippner, S., and Feldstein, S. (1966). Experimentally-induced telepathic dreams: two studies using EEG-RMG monitoring technique. *Intern. J. neuropsychiat.* 2: 420.
Wallwork, S.C. (1952). ESP experiments with simultaneous electroenephalographic recordings. *J. Soc. Psychical Res.* 36: 697.
Wolstenholme, G.E.W., and Millar, E.C.P. (1956). *Ciba Foundation Symposium on Extrasensory Perception*, Little, Brown, and Co., Boston.

CHAPTER 9

Psychology and Anomalous Observations: The Question of ESP in Dreams

Irvin L. Child

In recent years, evidence has been accumulating for the occurrence of such anomalies as telepathy and psychokinesis, but the evidence is not totally convincing. The evidence has come largely from experiments by psychologists who have devoted their careers mainly to studying these anomalies, but members of other disciplines, including engineering and physics, have also taken part. Some psychologists not primarily concerned with parapsychology have taken time out from other professional concerns to explore such anomalies for themselves. Of these, some have joined in the experimentation (e.g., Crandall & Hite, 1983; Lowry, 1981; Radin, 1982). Some have critically reviewed portions of the evidence (e.g., Akers, 1984; Hyman, 1985). Some, doubting that the phenomena could be real, have explored nonrational processes that might encourage belief in their reality (e.g., Ayeroff & Abelson, 1976). Still others, considering the evidence substantial enough to justify a constructive theoretical effort, have struggled to relate the apparent anomalies to better established knowledge in a way that will render them less anomalous (e.g., Irwin, 1979) or not anomalous at all (e.g., Blackmore, 1984). These psychologists differ widely in their surmise about whether the apparent anomalies in question will eventually be judged real or illusory; but they appear to agree that the evidence to date warrants serious consideration.

Reprinted with permission from *American Psychologist*, 1985, **40**, 1219–1230.

Serious consideration of apparent anomalies seems an essential part of the procedures of science, regardless of whether it leads to an understanding of new discoveries or to an understanding of how persuasive illusions arise. Apparent anomalies—just like the more numerous observations that are not anomalous—can receive appropriate attention only as they become accurately known to the scientists to whose work they are relevant. Much parapsychological research is barred from being seriously considered because it is either neglected or misrepresented in writings by some psychologists—among them, some who have placed themselves in a prime position to mediate interaction between parapsychological research and the general body of psychological knowledge. In this article, I illustrate this important general point with a particular case, that of experimental research on possible ESP in dreams. It is a case of especially great interest but is not unrepresentative of how psychological publications have treated similar anomalies.

The Maimonides Research

The experimental evidence suggesting that dreams may actually be influenced by ESP comes almost entirely from a research program carried out at the Maimonides Medical Center in Brooklyn, New York. Among scientists active in parapsychology, this program is widely known and greatly respected. It has had a major indirect influence on the recent course of parapsychological research, although the great expense of dream-laboratory work has prevented it from being a direct model.

None of the Maimonides research was published in the journals that are the conventional media for psychology. (The only possible exception is that a summary of one study [Honorton, Krippner, & Ullman, 1972] appeared in convention proceedings of the American Psychological Association.) Much of it was published in the specialized journals of parapsychology. The rest was published in psychiatric or other medical journals, where it would not be noticed by many psychologists. Most of it was summarized in popularized form in a book (Ullman, Krippner, & Vaughan, 1973) in which two of the researchers were joined by a popular writer whose own writings are clearly not in the scientific tradition, and the book departs from the pattern of scientific reporting that characterizes the original research reports.

How, then, would this research come to the attention of psychologists, so that its findings or its errors might in time be evaluated for their significance to the body of systematic observations upon which psychology has been and will be built? The experiments at Maimonides were published between about 1966 and 1972. In the years since—now over a decade—five books have been published by academic psychologists that purport to offer a scholarly review and evaluation of parapsychological research. They vary in the extent to which they seem addressed to psychologists themselves or to their students, but they seem to be the principal route by which either present or future psychologists, unless they have an already established interest strong enough to lead them to search out the original publications, might become acquainted with the experiments on ESP in dreams. I propose to review how these five books have presented knowledge about the experiments. First, however, I must offer a summary of the experiments; without that, my review would make sense only to readers already well acquainted with them.

The experiments at Maimonides grew out of Montague Ullman's observations, in his psychiatric practice, of apparent telepathy underlying the content of some dreams reported by his patients—observations parallel to those reported by many other psychiatrists. He sought to determine whether this apparent phenomenon would appear in a sleep laboratory under controlled conditions that would seem to exclude interpretations other than that of ESP. He was joined in this research by psychologist Stanley Krippner, now at the Saybrook Institute in San Francisco, and a little later by Charles Honorton, now head of the Psychophysical Research Laboratories in Princeton, New Jersey. Encouraged by early findings but seeking to improve experimental controls and identify optimal conditions, these researchers, assisted by numerous helpers and consultants, tried out various modifications of procedure. No one simple description of procedure, therefore, can be accurate for all of the experiments. But the brief description that follows is not, I believe, misleading as an account of what was generally done.

The Experimental Procedure

A subject would come to the laboratory to spend the night there as would-be percipient in a study of possible telepathic influence on dreams. He or she met and talked with the person who was going to serve as agent (that is, the person who would try to send a telepathic message), as well as with the two experimenters taking part that night, and procedures were explained in detail unless the percipient was a repeater for whom that step was not necessary. When ready to go to bed, the percipient was wired up in the usual way for monitoring of brain waves and eye movements, and he or she had no further contact with the agent or agent's experimenter until after the session was completed. The experimenter in the next room monitored the percipient's sleep and at the beginning of each period of rapid eye movements (REM), when it was reasonably certain the sleeper would be dreaming, notified the agent by pressing a buzzer.

The agent was in a remote room in the building, provided with a target picture (and sometimes accessory material echoing the theme of the picture) randomly chosen from a pool of potential targets as the message to be concentrated on. The procedure for random choice of a target from the pool was designed to prevent anyone else from knowing the identity of the target. The agent did not open the packet containing the target until isolated for the night (except for the one-way buzzer communication). Whenever signaled that the percipient had entered a REM period, the agent was to concentrate on the target, with the aim of communicating it telepathically to the percipient and thus influencing the dream the percipient was having. The percipient was oriented toward trying to receive this message. But of course if clairvoyance and telepathy are both possible, the percipient might have used the former—that is, might have been picking up information directly from the target picture, without the mediation of the agent's thoughts or efforts. For this reason, the term *general extrasensory perception* (GESP) would be used today, though the researchers more often used the term *telepathy*.

Toward the approximate end of each REM period, the percipient was awakened (by intercom) by the monitoring experimenter and described any dream just experienced (with prodding and questioning, if necessary, though the percipient of course knew in advance what to do on each awakening). At the end of the night's sleep, the percipient was interviewed and was asked for impressions about what the target might have been. (The interview was of course double-blind; neither percipient nor interviewer knew the identity of the target.) The dream descriptions and morning impressions and associations were recorded and later transcribed.

The original research reports and the popular book both present a number of very striking similarities between passages in the dream transcripts and the picture that happened to be the night's target. These similarities merit attention, yet they should in themselves yield no sense of conviction. Perhaps any transcript of a night's dreaming contains passages of striking similarity to any picture to which they might be compared. The Maimonides research, however, consisted of carefully planned experiments designed to permit evaluation of this hypothesis of random similarity, and I must now turn to that aspect.

Results

To evaluate the chance hypothesis, the researchers obtained judgments of similarity between the dream content and the actual target for the night, and at the same time obtained judgments of similarity between the dream content and each of the other potential targets in the pool from which the target had been selected at random. The person judging, of course, had no information about which picture had been randomly selected as target; the entire pool (in duplicate) was presented together, with no clue as to which picture had been the target and which ones had not. That is, in the experimental condition a picture was randomly selected from a pool and concentrated on by the agent, and in the control condition a picture was left behind in the pool. Any consistent difference between target and nontarget in similarity to dream content, exceeding what could reasonably be ascribed to chance, was considered an apparent anomaly.

The data available for the largest number of sessions came from judgments made by judges who had no contact with the experiment except to receive (by mail, generally) the material necessary for judging (transcripts of dreams and interview and a copy of the target pool). For many sessions, judgments were also available from the dreamer; he or she, of course, made judgments only after completing participation in the experiment as dreamer (except in some series where a separate target pool was used for each night and the dreamer's judgments could be made at the end of the session). For many sessions, judgments were made for the dream transcripts alone and for the total transcript including the morning interview; for consistency I have used the latter, because it involved judges who had more nearly the same information as the subjects.

The only form in which the data are available for all series of sessions is a count of hits and misses. If the actual target was ranked in the upper half of the target pool, for similarity to the dreams and interview, the outcome was considered a hit. If the actual target was ranked in the lower half of the pool, the outcome was considered a miss. The hit-or-miss score is presented separately in Table 1 for judges and for subjects in the first two data column. Where information is not supplied for one or the other, the reason is generally that it was impossible for the researchers to obtain it, and for a similar reason the number of cases sometimes varies.*

*Of course, usable judgments could not be obtained from the subject in precognitive sessions, because at the time of judging he or she would already know what the target had been. For Line F, the single subject was unable to give the extra time required for judging, and for Line O one of the four subjects failed to make judgments. In a few of the pilot sessions (Lines H, K, and N) only the subject's judgment was sought, and in some sessions only that of one or more judges'; in a few, the mean judges' rating was neither a hit nor a miss but exactly at the middle.

Each data row in Table 1 refers to one segment of the research, and segments for the most part are labeled as they were in the table of Ull-man et al. (1973, pp. 275–277). Segments that followed the general pro-cedure I described—all-night sessions, with an agent concentrating on the target during each of the percipient's REM periods—are gathered together in the first eight lines, A through H (in five of these segments, all but A, C, and H, a single percipient continued throughout a series, and in four of these the percipient was a psychologist). Other types of segments are presented in the rest of the table. Lines I, J, and K summa-rize precognitive sessions; here the target was not selected until after the dreaming and interview had been completed. The target consisted of a set of stimuli to be presented directly to the percipient after it had been selected in the morning. Lines L and M represent GESP sessions in which the percipient's dreams were monitored and recorded throughout the night, but the agent was attempting to transmit only before the percipi-ent went to sleep or just after, or sporadically. Line N refers to a few clair-voyance sessions; these were like the standard GESP sessions except that there was no agent (no one knew the identity of the target). Finally, Line O reports on some GESP sessions in which each dream was considered separately; these formed a single experiment with four percipients, com-paring nights involving a different target for each REM period with nights involving repeated use of a single target.

Regardless of the type of session (considering the five types I have described), each session fell into one of two categories: (a) pilot sessions, in which either a new dreamer or a new procedure was being tried out; these appear in lines H, K, and N, or (b) sessions in an experimental series, planned in advance as one or more sessions for each of two or more sub-jects, or as a number of sessions with the same dreamer throughout. Most of the researchers' publications were devoted to the results obtained in the experimental series, but the results of the pilot sessions have also been briefly reported.

A glance at the score columns for judges and for subjects is sufficient to indicate a strong tendency for an excess of hits over misses. If we aver-age the outcome for judges and for subjects, we find that hits exceed misses on every one of the 15 independent lines on which outcome for hits and misses differs. (On Line E hits and misses occur with equal frequency.) By a simple sign-test, this outcome would be significant beyond the 0.0001 level. I would not stress the exact value here, for several reasons. There was no advance plan to merge the outcomes for judges and subjects. More-over, the various series could be split up in other ways. Although I think my organization of the table is very reasonable (and I did not notice this outcome until after the table was constructed), it is not the organization selected by Ullman et al. (1973); their table, if evaluated statistically in this same way, would not yield so striking a result. What is clear is that the tendency toward hits rather than misses cannot reasonably be ascribed to chance. There is some systematic—that is, nonrandom—source of anomalous resemblance of dreams to target.

Despite its breadth, this "hitting" tendency seems to vary greatly in strength. The data on single dreams—Line O—suggest no consistency. At the other extreme, some separate lines of the table look impressive. I will next consider how we may legitimately evaluate the relative statistical significance of separate parts of the data on all-night sessions. (I will not try to take exact account here of the fact that the single-dream data are not significant, though it is wise to have in mind that the exact values I cite must be viewed as slightly exaggerated, in the absence of any explicit advance prediction that the results for all-night sessions and for single dreams would differ greatly.)

Two difficulties, one general and one specific, stand in the way of making as thorough an evaluation as I would wish. The general difficulty is that the researchers turned the task of statistical evaluation over to various consultants—for the most part, different consultants at various times—and some of the consultants must also have influenced the choice of procedures and measures. The consultants, and presumably the researchers themselves, seem not to have been at that time very experienced in working with some of the design problems posed by this research nor in planning how the research could be done to permit effective analysis. Much of the research was not properly analyzed at the time, and for much of it the full original data are no longer available. (The researchers have been very helpful in supplying me with material they have been able to locate despite dispersal and storage of the laboratory's files. Perhaps additional details may be recovered in the future.) The result is that completely satisfactory analysis is at present possible only for some portions of the data.

The specific difficulty results from a feature of the research design employed in most of the experimental series, a feature whose implications the researchers did not fully appreciate at the time. If a judge is presented with a set of transcripts and a set of targets and is asked to judge similarity of each target to each transcript, the various judgments may not be completely independent. If one transcript is so closely similar to a particular target that the judge is confident of having recognized a correct match, the judge (or percipient, of course) may minimize the similarity of that target to the transcripts judged later. Instructions to judges explicitly

Table 1

Summary of Maimonides Results on Tendency for Dreams to Be Judged More Like Target Than Like Nontargets in Target Pool

Series	Judges' score Hit	Miss	Subjects' score Hit	Miss	Z or t resulting from judgments Judges	Subjects	Sources
GESP: Dreams monitored and recorded throughout night; agent "transmitting" during each REM period							
A. 1st screening	7	5	10	2	$z = 0.71^b$	$z = 1.33^b$	Ullman, Krippner, & Feldstein (1966)
B. 1st Erwin	5	2	6	1	$z = 2.53^b$	$z = 1.90^b$	Ullman et al. (1966)
C. 2nd screening	4	8	9	3	$z = -.25^b$	$z = 1.17^b$	Ullman (1969)
D. Posin	6	2	6	2	$z = 1.05^c$	$z = 1.05^c$	Ullman (1969)
E. Grayeb	3	5	5	3	$z = -.63^c$	$z = 0.63^c$	Ullman, Krippner, & Vaughan (1973)
F. 2nd Erwin	8	0	8	0	$t = 4.93^a$		Ullman & Krippner (1969)
G. Van de Castle	6	2	8	0	$t = 2.81^a$	$t = 2.74^a$	Krippner & Ullman (1970)
H. Pilot Sessions	53	14	42	22	$z = 4.20^b$	$z = 2.21^b$	Ullman et al. (1973)
Precognition: Dreams monitored and recorded throughout night; target experience next day							
I. 1st Bessent	7	1			$t = 2.81^a$		Krippner, Ullman, & Honorton (1971)
J. 2nd Bessent	7	1			$t = 2.27^a$		Krippner, Honorton, & Ullman (1972)
K. Pilot sessions	2	0			$z = 0.67^c$		Ullman et al. (1973)

GESP: Dreams monitored and recorded throughout night; agent active only at beginning or sporadically

L. Sensory bombardment	8	0	4	4	$z = 3.11$[b]	$z = 0.00$[c]	Krippner, Honorton, Ullman, Masters, & Houston (1971)
M. Grateful Dead	7	5	8	4	$z = 0.61$[c]	$z = 0.81$[c]	Krippner, Honorton, & Ullman (1973)
Clairvoyance: Dreams monitored and recorded throughout night; concealed target known to no one							
N. Pilot sessions	5	3	4	5	$z = 0.98$[b]	$z = 0.00$[b]	Ullman et al. (1973)
GESP: Single Dreams							
O. Vaughan, Harris, Parise	105	98	74	79	$z = 0.63$[c]	$z = -.32$[c]	Honorton, Krippner, & Ullman (1972)

Note: GESP = general extrasensory perception. Italics identify results obtained with procedures that preserve independence of judgments in a series. For some series, the published source does not use the uniform measures entered in this table, and mimeographed laboratory reports were also consulted. Superscripts indicate which measure was available, in order of priority.

[a]*Ratings.* [b]*Rankings.* [c]*Score (count of hits and misses).*

urged them to avoid this error, but we cannot tell how thoroughly this directive was followed. Nonindependence would create no bias toward either positive or negative evidence of correspondence between targets and transcripts, but it would alter variability and thus render inappropriate some standard tests of significance. I have entered in the two succeeding columns of the table a *t* or a *z* that can be used in evaluating the statistical significance of the departure from chance expectancy (*t* is required when ratings are available, and *z* must be used when only rankings or score counts are available, because sample variability in the former case is estimated from the data but in the latter case must be based conservatively on a theoretical distribution.) If ratings were available, they were used; if not, rankings were used if available; otherwise, score count was used.

Is there likely to have been much of this non-independence in the series where it was possible? A pertinent fact is that the hits were not generally direct hits. That is, there was no overwhelming tendency for the correct target to be given first place rather than just being ranked in the upper half of the target pool. This greatly reduces the strength of the argument that ordinary significance tests are grossly inaccurate because of nonindependence. Because certainty is not possible, however, we need to separate results according to whether the procedures permitted this kind of nonindependence. In the table, I have italicized results that cannot have been influenced by this difficulty (either because each night's ratings were made by a different person or because each night in a series had, and was judged in relation to, a separate target pool) or that closely approximate this ideal condition.

The outcome is clear. Several segments of the data, considered separately, yield significant evidence that dreams (and associations to them) tended to resemble the picture chosen randomly as target more than they resembled other pictures in the pool. In the case of evaluation by outside judges, two of the three segments that are free of the problem of nonindependence yield separately significant results: The pilot sessions (Line H) yield a z of 4.20, and thus a p of .00002. An experiment with distant but multisensory targets (Line L) yields a z of 3.11 and a p of .001. If we consider segments in which judgments may not be completely independent of each other and analyze them in the standard way, we find that the two series with psychologist William Erwin as dreamer are also significant (if nonindependence of judgments does not seriously interfere), Line B with a z of 2.53 (p <.01) and Line F with a t of 4.93 and 7 df (p <.01). The two precognitive series (Lines I and J), each with 7 df, yield ts of 2.81 and 2.27, with p values slightly above and below .05, respectively.

Segment results based on the subjects' own judgments of similarity are less significant than those based on judgments by outside judges. Only two segments reach minimal levels of statistical significance: Line G, where the t of 2.74 with 7 df is significant at the .05 level, and Line H, where the z of 2.21 is significant at the .05 level.

The statistical evaluation of the separate segments of the Maimonides experiments also permits a more adequate evaluation of their overall statistical significance. For judgments by outside judges, three segments are free of the potential nonindependence of successive judgments (Lines H, L, and N). Putting these three together by the procedure Mosteller and Bush (1954, pp. 329–330) ascribed to Stouffer (recommended by Rosenthal [1984, p. 72] as the "simplest and most versatile" of the possible procedures), the joint p value is <.000002. For the subjects' own judgments, six segments are available (Lines A, C, G, H, L, and N), and their joint p value is less than .002. The other segments of the data have the problem of potential nonindependence of successive judgments, and even if the exaggeration of significance may be small for a single line, I would not want to risk compounding it in an overall p. Their prevailing unity of direction, however (direction not being subject to influence by the kind of nonindependence involved here), and the substantial size of some of the differences, justify the inference that the overall evidence of consistency far exceeds that indicated by only those selected segments for which a precise statistical statement is possible. The impression given by the mere count of hits and misses is thus fully confirmed when more sensitive measures are used.

Parapsychological experiments are sometimes criticized on the grounds that what evidence they provide for ESP indicates at most some very small effects detectable only by amassing large bodies of data. Those to whom this criticism has any appeal should be aware that the Maimonides experiments are clearly exempt from it. The significant results on Lines F and G of the table, for example, are each attributable basically to just eight data points.

If replications elsewhere should eventually confirm the statistically significant outcome of the Maimonides experiments, would the fact of statistical significance in itself establish the presence of the kind of anomaly called ESP? Of course not. Statistical significance indicates only the presence of consistency and does not identify its source. ESP, or the more general term *psi*, is a label for consistencies that have no identifiable source and that suggest transfer of information by channels not familiar to present scientific knowledge. A judgment about the appropriateness of the label, and thus about the "ESP hypothesis," is complex. It depends on a variety of other judgments and knowledge—how confidently other possible sources of the consistent effect can be excluded, whether other lines of experimentation are yielding results that suggest the same judgment, and so on.

I believe many psychologists would, like myself, consider the ESP hypothesis to merit serious consideration and continued research if they read the Maimonides reports for themselves and if they familiarized themselves with other recent and older lines of experimentation (e.g., Jahn, 1982, and many of the chapters in Wolman, 1977).

Some parapsychological researchers—among them the Maimonides group—have written at times as though a finding of statistical significance sufficiently justified a conclusion that the apparent anomaly should be classified as ESP. I can understand their choice of words, which is based on their own confidence that their experiments permitted exclusion of other interpretations. But perhaps psychologists who in the future become involved in this area may prefer to use a term such as *anomalies*, so as to avoid variable and possibly confusing connotations about the origin of the anomalies. Zusne and Jones (1982) wisely prepared the way for this usage in speaking of *anomalistic psychology*. But meanwhile, psychologists need not cut themselves off from knowledge of relevant facts because of dissatisfaction with the terminology surrounding their presentation.

Attempted Replications Elsewhere

The Maimonides pattern of controlled experiment in a sleep laboratory, obviously, is extremely time consuming and expensive, and replication seems to have been attempted so far at only two other sleep laboratories. At the University of Wyoming, two experiments yielded results approximately at mean chance expectation—slightly below in one study (Belvedere & Foulkes, 1971), slightly above in the other (Foulkes et al., 1972). In a replication at the Boston University School of Medicine (Globus, Knap, Skinner, & Healey, 1968), overall results were not significantly positive, though in this instance encouragement for further exploration was reported. The researchers had decided in advance to base their conclusions on exact hits— that is, placing the target first, rather than just in the upper half; by this measure, the results were encouraging, though not statistically significant. Moreover, to quote the researchers, "*Post hoc* analysis revealed that the judges were significantly more correct when they were more 'confident' in their judgments.... Further conservatively designed research does seem indicated because of these findings" (Globus et al., 1968, p. 365).

A study by Calvin Hall (1967) is sometimes cited as a replication that confirmed the Maimonides findings; in truth, however, although it provided impressive case material, it was not done in a way that permits evaluation as a replication of the Maimonides experiments. Several small-scale studies, done without the facilities of a sleep laboratory, have been reported that are not replications of even one of the more ambitious Maimonides experiments but each of which reports positive results that might encourage further exploration (Braud, 1977; Child, Kanthamani, & Sweeney, 1977; Rechtschaffen, 1970; Strauch, 1970; Van de Castle, 1971). In the case of these minor studies—unlike the Maimonides studies and the three systematic replications—one must recognize the likelihood of selective publication on the basis of interesting results. Taken all together, these diverse and generally small-scale studies done elsewhere do, in my opinion, add something to the conviction the Maimonides experiments might inspire, that dream research is a promising technique for experimental study of the ESP question.

The lack of significant results in the three systematic replications is hardly conclusive evidence against eventual replicability. In the Maimonides series, likewise, three successive replications (Lines C, D, and E in Table 1) yielded no significant result, yet they are part of a program yielding highly significant overall results.

If results of such potentially great interest and scientific importance as those of the Maimonides program had been reported on a more conventional topic, one might expect them to be widely and accurately described in reviews of the field to which they were relevant, and to be analyzed carefully as a basis for sound evaluation of whether replication and extension of the research were indicated, or of whether errors could be detected and understood. What has happened in this instance of anomalous research findings?

Representation of the Maimonides Research in Books by Psychologists

It is appropriate to begin with C.E.M. Hansel's 1980 revision of his earlier critical book on parapsychology. As part of his attempt to bring the earlier book up to date, he included an entire chapter on experiments on telepathy in dreams. One page was devoted to a description of the basic method used in the Maimonides experiments; one paragraph summarized the impressive outcome of 10 of the experiments. The rest of the chapter was devoted mainly to a specific account of the experiment in which psychologist Robert Van de Castle was the subject (the outcome is summarized in Line G of my Table 1) and to the attempted replication at the University of Wyoming (Belvedere & Foulkes, 1971), in which Van de Castle was again the subject. Another page was devoted to another of the Maimonides experiments that was also repeated at the University of Wyoming (Foulkes et al., 1972). Hansel did not mention the replication by Globus et al. (1968), whose authors felt that the results encouraged further exploration. Hansel gave more weight to the two negative outcomes at Wyoming than to the sum of the Maimonides research, arguing that sensory cues supposedly permitted by the procedures at Maimonides, not possible because of greater care taken by the Wyoming experimenters, were responsible for the difference in results. He did not provide, of course, the full account of procedures presented in the original Maimonides reports that might persuade many readers that Hansel's interpretation is far from compelling. Nor did he consider why some of the other experiments at Maimonides, not obviously distinguished in the care with which they were done from the two that were replicated (e.g., those on Lines E, M, and O of Table 1) yielded a close-to-chance outcome such as Hansel might have expected sensory cuing to prevent.

Hansel exaggerated the opportunities for sensory cuing—that is, for the percipient to obtain by ordinary sensory means some information about the target for the night. He did this notably by misinterpreting an ambiguous statement in the Maimonides reports, not mentioning that his interpretation was incompatible with other passages; his interpretation was in fact erroneous, as shown by Akers (1984, pp. 128-129). Furthermore, Hansel did not alert the reader to the great care exerted by the researchers to eliminate possible sources of sensory cuing. Most important is the fact that Hansel did not provide any plausible account—other than fraud—of how the opportunities for sensory cuing that he claimed existed would be likely to lead to the striking findings of the research. For example, he seemed to consider important the fact that at Maimonides the agent could leave his or her room during the night to go to the bathroom, whereas in Wyoming the agent had a room with its own bathroom, and the outer door to the room was sealed with tape to prevent the agent from emerging. Hansel did not attempt to say how the agent's visit to the bathroom could have altered the details of the percipient's dreams each night in a manner distinctively appropriate to that night's target. The only plausible route of influence of the dream record seems to be deliberate fraud involving the researchers and their subjects. The great number and variety of personnel in these studies—experimenters, agents, percipients, and judges—makes fraud especially unlikely as an explanation of the positive findings; but Hansel did not mention this important fact.

It appears to me that all of Hansel's criticisms of the Maimonides experiments are relevant only on the hypothesis of fraud (except for the mistaken criticism I have mentioned above). He said that unintentional communication was more likely but provided no evidence either that it occurred or that such communication—in any form in which it might have occurred—could have produced such consistent results as emerged from the Maimonides experiments. I infer that Hansel was merely avoiding making explicit his unsupported accusations of fraud. Fraud is an interpretation always important to keep in mind, and it is one that could not be entirely excluded even by precautions going beyond those used in the Wyoming studies. But the fact that fraud was as always, theoretically possible hardly justifies dismissal of a series of carefully conducted studies that offer important suggestions for opening up a new line of inquiry into a topic potentially of great significance. Especially regrettable is Hansel's description of various supposed defects in the experiments as though they mark the experiments as being carelessly conducted by general scientific criteria, whereas in fact the supposed defects are relevant only if one assumes fraud. A reader who is introduced to the Maimonides research by Hansel's chapter is likely to get a totally erroneous impression of the care taken by the experimenters to avoid various possible sources of error. The one thing they could not avoid was obtaining results that Hansel considered a priori impossible, hence evidence of fraud; but Hansel was not entirely frank about his reasoning.

An incidental point worth noting is that Hansel did not himself apply, in his critical attack, the standards of evidence he demanded of the researchers. His conclusions were based implicitly on the assumption that the difference of outcome between the Maimonides and the Wyoming experiments was a genuine difference, not attributable to random variation. He did not even raise the question, as he surely would have if, in some parallel instance, the Maimonides researchers had claimed or implied statistical significance where it was questionable. In fact, the difference of outcome might well have arisen from random error; for the percipient's own judgments the difference is significant at the 5% level (2-tailed), but for the outsiders' judgments it does not approach significance.

Another 1980 book is *The Psychology of Transcendence*, by Andrew Neher, in which almost 100 pages are devoted to "psychic experience." Neher differed from the other authors I refer to in describing the Maimonides work as a "series of studies of great interest" (p. 145), but this evaluation seems to be negated by his devoting only three lines to it and four lines to unsuccessful replications.

A third 1980 publication, *The Psychology of the Psychic*, by David Marks and Richard Kammann, provides less of a general review of recent parapsychology than Hansel's book or even Neher's one long chapter. It is largely devoted to the techniques of mentalists (that is, conjurers specializing in psychological rather than physical effects) and can be useful to anyone encountering a mentalist who pretends to be "psychic." Most readers are not likely to be aware that parapsychological research receives only limited attention. The jacket blurbs give a very different view of the book, as do the authors in their introductory sentences:

> ESP is just around the next corner. When you get there, it is just around the next corner. Having now turned over one hundred of these corners, we decided to call it quits and report our findings for public review [Marks & Kammann, 1980, p. 4].

Given this introduction to the nature of the book, readers might suppose it would at least mention any corner that many parapsychologists have judged to be an impressive turning. But the Maimonides dream experiments received no mention at all.

Another volume, by psychologist James Alcock (1981), quite clearly purports to include a general review and evaluation of parapsychological research. Alcock mentioned (p. 6) that Hansel had examined the Maimonides experiments, but the only account of them that Alcock offered (on p. 163) was incidental to a discussion of control groups. By implication he seemed to reject the Maimonides experiments because they included no control groups. He wrote that "a control group, for which no sender or no target was used, would appear essential" (p. 163). Later he added, "One could, alternatively, 'send' when the subject was not in the dream state, and compare 'success' in this case with success in dream state trials" (p. 163). The first of these statements suggests a relevant use of control groups but errs in calling it essential; in other psychological research, Alcock would have doubtless readily recognized that within-subject control can, where feasible, be much more efficient and pertinent than a separate control group. His second statement suggests a type of experiment that is probably impossible (because in satisfactory form it seems to require the subject to dream whether awake or asleep and not to know whether he or she was awake or asleep). This second kind of experiment, moreover, has special pertinence only to a comparison between dreaming and waking, not to the question of whether ESP is manifested in dreaming.

Alcock, in short, did not seem to recognize that the design of the Maimonides experiments was based on controls exactly parallel to those used by innumerable psychologists in other research with similar logical structure (and even implied, curiously enough, in his own second suggestion). He encouraged readers to think that the Maimonides studies are beyond the pale of acceptable experimental design, whereas in fact they are fine examples of appropriate use of within-subject control rather than between-subjects control.

The quality of thinking with which Alcock confronted the Maimonides research appeared also in a passage that did not refer to it by name. Referring to an article published in *The Humanist* by Ethel Grodzins Romm, he wrote,

> Romm (1977) argued that a fundamental problem with both the dream telepathy research and the remote viewing tests is that the reports suffer from what she called "shoe-fitting" language; she cited a study in which the sender was installed in a room draped in white fabric and had ice cubes poured down his back. A receiver who reported "white" was immediately judged to have made a "hit" by an independent panel. Yet, as she observed, words such as "miserable," "wet," or "icy" would have been better hits…. Again, the obvious need is for a control group. Why are they not used? [p. 163].

What Romm described as "shoe fitting" (misinterpreting events to fit one's expectations) is an important kind of error that is repeatedly made in interpretation of everyday occurrences by people who believe they are psychic. But the dream telepathy research at Maimonides was well protected against this kind of error by the painstaking controls that Alcock seemed not to have noticed. Surely Romm must be referring to some other and very sloppy dream research?

Not at all. The details in this paragraph, and even more in Romm's article, point unmistakably, though inaccurately, to the fifth night of the first precognitive series at Maimonides. The actual details of target and response would alone deprive it of much of its value as an example of shoe fitting. As reported by Krippner, Ullman, & Honorton (1971), the target was a morning experience that included being in a room that was draped with white sheets. The subject's first dream report had included the statement, "I was just standing in a room, surrounded by white. Every imaginable thing in that room was white" (p. 201). There is more similarity here than Romm and Alcock acknowledged in mentioning from this passage only the single word "white."

More important, however, is the fact that the experiment they were referring to provided no opportunity for shoe fitting. The procedures followed in the experiment were completely misrepresented in a way that created the illusion that the possibility existed. There was no panel, in the sense of a group of people gathered together and capable of influencing each other. The judges, operating independently, separately judged every one of the 64 possible combinations of target and transcript yielded by the eight nights of the experiment, not just the eight correct pairings, and they had no clues to which those eight were. Their responses are hardly likely to have been immediate, as they required reading the entire night's transcript. Because each judge was working alone and was not recording times, there would have been no record if a particular response had been immediate, and no record of what particular element in the transcript led to an immediate response.

I looked up in a 1977 issue of *The Humanist* the article by Romm that Alcock cited. The half page on shoe-fitting language gave as examples this item from the Maimonides research and also the SRI remote-viewing experiments (Puthoff & Targ, 1976) done at SRI International. In both cases what was said was pure fiction, based on failure to note what was done in the experiments and in particular that the experimenters were well aware of the danger of shoe-fitting language and that the design of their experiments incorporated procedures to ensure that it could not occur. Romm's ignorance about the Maimonides research and her apparent willingness to fabricate falsehoods about it should be recognized by anyone who had read any of the Maimonides research publications. Yet Alcock accepted and repeated the fictions as though they were true. His presentation in the context of a book apparently in the scientific tradition seems to me more dangerous than Romm's original article, for anyone with a scientific orientation should be able to recognize Romm's article as propaganda. Its title, for example, is "When You Give a Closet Occultist a Ph.D., What Kind of Research Can You Expect?" and it repeatedly speaks of "cult phuds," meaning people with PhDs who are interested in parapsychological problems. Alcock's repetition of Romm's misstatements in a context lacking these clues may well be taken by many a reader as scholarly writing based on correct information and rational thought. Paradoxically, both Alcock's paragraph and Romm's article are excellent examples of the shoe-fitting error that both decry in others who are in fact carefully avoiding it.

The last of the five books that bring, or fail to bring, the Maimonides research to the attention of psychologists and their students is *Anomalistic Psychology: A Study of Extraordinary Phenomena of Behavior and Experience*, a 1982 volume by Leonard Zusne and Warren H. Jones. This is in many ways an excellent book, and it is also the one of the five that comes closest to including a general review of important recent research in parapsychology. Its brief account of the Maimonides dream experiments, however, misrepresented them in ways that should seriously reduce a reader's interest in considering them further.

Zusne and Jones's description of the basic procedure made three serious errors. First, it implied that one of the experimenters had a chance to know the identity of the target. ("After the subject falls asleep, an art reproduction is selected from a large collection randomly, placed in an envelope, and given to the agent" p. 260). In fact, precautions were taken to ensure that no one but the agent could know the identity of the target. Second, the authors stated that "three judges ... rate their confidence that the dream content matches the target picture" (p. 260), leading the reader to suppose that the judges were informed of the identity of the target at the time of rating. In fact, a judge was presented with a dream transcript and a pool of potential targets and was asked to rate the degree of similarity between the transcript and each member of the pool, while being unaware of which member had been the target. Third, there was a similarly, though more obscurely, misleading description of how ratings were obtained from the dreamer.

This misinformation was followed by even more serious misrepresentation of the research and, by implication, of the competence of the researchers. Zusne and Jones (1982) wrote that Ullman and Krippner (1978) had found that dreamers were not influenced telepathically unless they knew in advance that an attempt would be made to influence them. This led, they wrote, to the subject's being "primed prior to going to sleep" through the experimenter's

> Preparing the receiver through experiences that were related to the content of the picture to be telepathically transmitted during the night. Thus, when the picture was Van Gogh's Corridor of the St. Paul Hospital, which depicts a lonely figure in the hallways of a mental hospital, the receiver: (1) heard Rosza's *Spellbound* played on a phonograph; (2) heard the monitor laugh hysterically in the room; (3) was addressed as "Mr. Van Gogh" by the monitor; (4) was shown paintings done by mental patients; (5) was given a pill and a glass of water; and (6) was daubed with a piece of cotton dipped in acetone. The receiver was an English "sensitive," but it is obvious that no psychic sensitivity was required to figure out the general content of the picture and to produce an appropriate report, whether any dreams were actually seen or not [pp. 260–261].

If researchers were to report positive results of the experiment described here by Zusne and Jones and were to claim that it provided some positive evidence of ESP, what would a reader conclude? Surely, that the researchers were completely incompetent, but probably not that they were dishonest. For dishonesty to take such a frank and transparent form is hardly credible.

Incompetence of the researchers is not, however, a proper inference. The simple fact, which anyone can easily verify, is that the account Zusne and Jones gave of the experiment is grossly inaccurate. What Zusne and Jones have done is to describe (for one specific night of the experiment) some of the stimuli provided to the dreamer the next morning, *after* his dreams had been recorded and his night's sleep was over. Zusne and Jones erroneously stated that these stimuli were provided *before* the night's sleep, to prime the subject to have or falsely report having the desired kind of dream. The correct sequence of events was quite clearly stated in the brief reference Zusne and Jones cited (Ullman & Krippner, 1978), as well as in the original research report (Krippner, Honorton, & Ullman, 1972).

I can understand and sympathize with Zusne and Jones's error. The experiment they cited is one in which the nocturnal dreamer was seeking to dream in response to a set of stimuli to be created and presented to him the next morning. As may be seen in Table 1, results from such precognitive sessions (all done with a single subject) were especially strong. This apparent transcendence of time as well as space makes the precognitive findings seem at least doubly impossible to most of us. An easy misreading, therefore, on initially scanning the research report, would be to suppose the stimuli to have been presented partly in advance (because some parts obviously involved a waking subject) and partly during sleep.

This erroneous reading on which Zusne and Jones based their account could easily have been corrected by a more careful rereading. In dealing with other topics, they might have realized the improbability that researchers could have been so grossly incompetent and could have checked the accuracy of their statements before publishing them. Zusne and Jones are not alone in this tendency to quick misperception of parapsychological research through preconception and prejudice; we have already seen it in Alcock's book. Alcock (1983) wrote the review of Zusne and Jones's book for *Contemporary Psychology*, the book-review journal of the American Psychological Association, and he did not mention this egregious error, even though very slight acquaintance with the Maimonides research should suffice to detect it.

Discussion

The experiments at the Maimonides Medical Center on the

possibility of ESP in dreams clearly merit careful attention from psychologists who, for whatever reason, are interested in the question of ESP. To firm believers in the impossibility of ESP, they pose a challenge to skill in detecting experimental flaws or to the understanding of other sources of error. To those who can conceive that ESP might be possible, they convey suggestions about some of the conditions influencing its appearance or absence and about techniques for investigating it.

This attention is not likely to be given by psychologists whose knowledge about the experiments comes from the books by their fellow psychologists that purport to review parapsychological research. Some of those books engage in nearly incredible falsification of the facts about the experiments; others simply neglect them. I believe it is fair to say that none of these books has correctly identified any defect in the Maimonides experiments other than ones relevant only to the hypothesis of fraud or an inappropriate statistical reasoning (easily remedied by new calculations from the published data). I do not mean that the Maimonides experiments are models of design and execution. I have already called attention to a design flaw that prevents sensitive analysis of some of the experiments; and the control procedures were violated at one session, as Akers (1984) pointed out on the basis of the full information supplied in the original report. (Neither of these genuine defects was mentioned in any of the five books I have reviewed here, an indication of their authors' general lack of correct information about the Maimonides experiments.)

Readers who doubt that the falsification is as extreme as I have pictured it need only consult the sources I have referred to. Their doubt might also be reduced by familiarity with some of James Bradley's research (1981, 1984). In his 1984 article, he reported similar misrepresentations of fact on a topic, robustness of procedures of statistical inference, on which psychologists would not be thought to have nearly the strength of preconception that many are known to have about ESP. How much more likely, then, falsification on so emotionally laden a topic as ESP is for many psychologists! In the earlier article, Bradley (1981) presented experimental evidence (for college students, in this case, not psychologists) that confidence in the correctness of one's own erroneous opinions is positively correlated with the degree of expertise one believes oneself to have in the field of knowledge within which the erroneous opinion falls. This finding may help in understanding why the authors of some of these books did not find it necessary to consider critically their own erroneous statements.

A very considerable proportion of psychologists have a potential interest in the question of ESP. In a recent survey (Wagner & Monnet, 1979) of university professors in various fields, 34% of psychologists were found to consider ESP either an established fact or a likely possibility, exactly the same proportion as considered it an impossibility. In this survey, psychologists less frequently expressed a positive opinion than did members of other disciplines, a finding that may be attributable to psychologists' better understanding of sources of error in human judgment. There seems to be no equally sound reason for the curious fact that psychologists differed overwhelmingly from others in their tendency to consider ESP an impossibility. Of natural scientists, only 3% checked that opinion; of the 166 professors in other social sciences, not a single one did.

Both of these groups of psychologists have been ill served by the apparently scholarly books that seem to convey information about the dream experiments. The same may be said about some other lines of parapsychological research. Interested readers might well consult the original sources and form their own judgments.

References

Akers, C. (1984). Methodological criticisms of parapsychology. In S. Krippner (Ed.), *Advances in parapsychological research* (Vol. 4, pp. 112-164). Jefferson, NC: McFarland.

Alcock, J.E. (1981). *Parapsychology, science or magic? A psychological perspective.* New York: Pergamon Press.

Alcock, J.E. (1983). Bringing anomalies back into psychology. *Contemporary Psychology,* 28, 351-352.

Ayeroff, F., & Abelson, R.P. (1976). ESP and ESB: Belief in personal success at mental telepathy. *Journal of Personality and Social Psychology,* 34, 240-247.

Belvedere, E., & Foulkes, D. (1971). Telepathy and dreams: A failure to replicate. *Perceptual and Motor Skills,* 33, 783-789.

Blackmore, S.J. (1984). A psychological theory of the out-of-body experience. *Journal of Parapsychology,* 48, 201-218.

Bradley, J.V. (1981). Overconfidence in ignorant experts. *Bulletin of the Psychonomic Society,* 17, 82-84.

Bradley, J.V. (1984). Antinonrobustness: A case study in the sociology of science. *Bulletin of the Psychonomic Society,* 22, 463-466.

Braud, W. (1977). Long-distance dream and presleep telepathy. In J.D. Morris, W.G. Roll, & R.L. Morris (Eds.), *Research in parapsychology 1976* (pp. 154-155). Metuchen, NJ: Scarecrow.

Child, I.L., Kanthamani, H., & Sweeney, V.M. (1977). A simplified experiment in dream telepathy. In J.D. Morris, W.G. Roll, & R.L. Morris (Eds.), *Research in parapsychology 1976* (pp. 91-93). Metuchen, NJ: Scarecrow.

Crandall, J.E., & Hite, D.D. (1983). Psi-missing and displacement: Evidence for improperly focused psi? *Journal of the American Society for Psychical Research,* 77, 209-228.

Foulkes, D., Belvedere, E., Masters, R.E.L., Houston, J., Krippner, S., Honorton, C., & Ullman, M. (1972). Long-distance "sensory-bombardment" ESP in dreams: A failure to replicate. *Perceptual and Motor Skills*, 35, 731-734.

Globus, G., Knapp, P., Skinner, J., & Healey, J. (1968). An appraisal of telepathic communication in dreams. *Psychophysiology*, 4, 365.

Hall, C. (1967). Experimente zur telepathischen Beeinflussung von Traumen. [Experiments on telepathic influence on dreams]. *Zeitschrift fur Parapsychologie und Grenzgebiete der Psychologie*, 10, 18–47.

Hansel, C.E.M. (1980). *ESP and parapsychology: A critical reevaluation*. Buffalo, NY: Prometheus.

Honorton, C. Krippner, S., & Ullman, M. (1972). Telepathic perception of art prints under two conditions. *Proceedings of the 80th Annual Convention of the American Psychological Association*, 7, 319–320.

Hyman, R. (1985). The ganzfeld psi experiment: A critical appraisal. *Journal of Parapsychology*, 49, 3-49.

Irwin, H.J. (1979). *Psi and the mind: An information processing approach*. Metuchen, NJ: Scarecrow.

Jahn, R.G. (1982). The persistent paradox of psychic phenomena: An engineering perspective. *Proceedings of the Institute of Electrical and Electronics Engineers*, 70, 136-170.

Krippner, S., Honorton, E., & Ullman, M. (1972). A second precognitive dream study with Malcolm Bessent. *Journal of the American Society for Psychical Research*, 66, 269-279.

Krippner, S., Honorton, C., & Ullman, M. (1973). An experiment in dream telepathy with "The Grateful Dead." *Journal of the American Society of Psychosomatic Dentistry and Medicine*, 20, 9-17.

Krippner, S., Honorton, C., Ullman, M., Masters, R., & Houston, J. (1971). A long-distance "sensory-bombardment" study of ESP in dreams. *Journal of the American Society for Psychical Research*, 65, 468-475.

Krippner, S., & Ullman, M. (1970). Telepathy and dreams: A controlled experiment with electroencephalogram-electro-oculogram monitoring. *Journal of Nervous and Mental Disease*, 151, 394-403.

Krippner, S., Ullman, M., & Honorton, C. (1971). A precognitive dream study with a single subject. *Journal of the American Society for Psychical Research*, 65, 192-203.

Lowry, R. (1981). Apparent PK effect on computer-generated random digit series. *Journal of the American Society for Psychical Research*, 75, 209-220.

Marks, D., & Kammann, R. (1980). *The psychology of the psychic*. Buffalo, NY: Prometheus.

Mosteller, F., & Bush, R.R. (1954). Selected quantitative techniques. In G. Lindzey (Ed.), *Handbook of social psychology* (Vol. 1, pp. 289-334). Cambridge, MA: Addison-Wesley.

Neher, A. (1980). *The psychology of transcendence*. Englewood Cliffs, NJ: Prentice-Hall.

Puthoff, H.E., & Targ, R. (1976). A perceptual channel for information transfer over kilometer distances: Historical perspective and recent research. *Proceedings of the Institute of Electrical and Electronic Engineers*, 64, 329-354.

Radin, D.I. (1982). Experimental attempts to influence pseudorandom number sequences. *Journal of the American Society for Psychical Research*, 76, 359-374.

Rechtschaffen, A. (1970). Sleep and dream states: An experimental design. In R. Cavanna (Ed.), *Psi favorable states of consciousness* (pp. 87-120). New York: Parapsychology Foundation.

Romm, E.G. (1977). When you give a closet occultist a Ph.D., what kind of research can you expect? *The Humanist*, 37 (3), 12-15.

Rosenthal, R. (1984). *Meta-analytic procedures for social research*. Beverly Hills, CA: Sage.

Strauch, I. (1970). Dreams and psi in the laboratory. In R. Cavanna (Ed.), *Psi favorable states of consciousness* (pp. 46-54). New York: Parapsychology Foundation.

Ullman, M. (1969). Telepathy and dreams. *Experimental Medicine & Surgery*, 27, 19-38.

Ullman, M., & Krippner, S. (1969). A laboratory approach to the nocturnal dimension of paranormal experience: Report of a confirmatory study using the REM monitoring technique. *Biological Psychiatry*, 1, 259-270.

Ullman, M., & Krippner, S. (1978). Experimental dream studies. In M. Ebon (Ed.), *The Signet handbook of parapsychology* (pp. 409-422). New York: New American Library.

Ullman, M., Krippner, S., & Feldstein, S. (1966). Experimentally induced telepathic dreams: Two studies using EEG-REM monitoring technique. *International Journal of Neuropsychiatry*, 2, 420-437.

Ullman, M., Krippner, S., & Vaughan, A. (1973). *Dream telepathy*. New York: Macmillan.

Van de Castle, R.L. (1971). The study of GESP in a group setting by means of dreams. *Journal of Parapsychology*, 35, 312.

Wagner, M.W., & Monnet, M. (1979). Attitudes of college professors toward extra-sensory perception. *Zetetic Scholar*, no. 5, 7-16.

Wolman, B.B. (Ed.). (1977). *Handbook of parapsychology*. New York: Van Nostrand Reinhold.

Zusne, L., & Jones, W.H. (1982). *Anomalistic psychology: A study of extraordinary phenomena of behavior and experience*. Hillsdale, NJ: Erlbaum.

CHAPTER 10

Experimenter Effects and the Remote Detecting of Staring

Richard Wiseman *and* Marilyn Schlitz

> *...the experimenter effect is the most important challenge facing modern experimental parapsychology. It may be that we will not be able to make too much progress in other areas of the field until the puzzle of the experimenter effect is solved* [Palmer, 1986, pp. 220–221].

The apparent detection of an unseen gaze (i.e., the feeling of being stared at, only to turn around and discover somebody looking directly at you) is a common type of ostensible paranormal experience, with between 68% and 94% of the population reporting having experienced the phenomenon at least once (Braud, Shafer, & Andrews, 1993a; Coover, 1913).

Some parapsychologists have attempted to assess whether this experience is based, at least in part, on genuine psi ability. Such studies use two participants: a "sender" and a "receiver." These individuals are isolated from one another, but in such a way that the sender can see the receiver. Early experiments had the sender sitting behind the receiver (Coover, 1913; Poortman, 1959; Tichener, 1898); some later studies have used one-way mirrors (Peterson, 1978) or a closed-circuit television system (Braud, Shafer, & Andrews, 1993a, 1993b; Williams, 1983). The experimental session in this type of study is divided into two sets of randomly ordered "stare" and "non-stare" trials. During stare trials the sender directs his/her attention toward the receiver; during non-stare trials the

Reprinted with permission from *Journal of Parapsychology*, 1997, **61**, 197–207.

sender directs his/her attention away from the receiver. Either during or after each trial a response is made by the receiver. In early studies, the receivers made verbal guesses as to whether they believed they had been stared at; later studies have measured receivers' electrodermal activity (EDA) throughout each trial. A number of studies have obtained statistically significant differences between responses to stare and non-stare trials and in a recent review of this work, Braud, Shafer, and Andrews (1993b) concluded:

> We hope other investigators will attempt to replicate these studies. We recommend the design as one that is straightforward, has already yielded consistent positive results, and addresses a very familiar psi manifestation in a manner that is readily communicable and understandable to the experimental participants and to the public at large [p. 408].

Both authors of the present paper previously attempted to replicate this staring effect. The first author (R.W.) is a skeptic regarding the claims of parapsychology who wished to discover whether he could replicate the effect in his own laboratory. The second author (M.S.) is a psi proponent who has previously carried out many parapsychological studies, frequently obtaining positive findings. The staring experiments carried out by R.W. showed no evidence of psychic functioning (Wiseman & Smith, 1994; Wiseman, Smith, Freedman, Wasserman, & Hurst, 1995). M.S.'s study, on the other hand, yielded significant results (Schlitz & LaBerge, 1997).

Such "experimenter effects" are common within parapsychology and are open to several competing interpretations (see Palmer, 1989a, 1989b). For example, M.S.'s study may have contained an experimental artifact absent from R.W.'s procedure. Alternatively, M.S. may have worked with more psychically gifted participants than R.W. had, or may have been more skilled at eliciting participants' psi ability. It is also possible that M.A. and R.W. created desired results via their own psi abilities, or fraud. Little previous research has attempted to evaluate these competing hypotheses. This is unfortunate, because it is clearly important to establish why experimenter effects occur, both in terms of assessing past psi research and attempting to replicate studies in the future. For these reasons, the authors agreed to carry out a joint study in the hope of learning why our original studies obtained such dramatically different results.

Method

Design

Our joint study required M.S. and R.W. to act as separate experimenters for two different sets of trials. The two sets of trials were carried out at the same time (early October, 1995) and in the same location (R.W.'s laboratory at the University of Hertfordshire in the U.K.). In addition, the experimenters used the same equipment, drew subjects from the same subject pool, and employed exactly the same methodological procedures. The only real difference between the trials was that one set was carried out by M.S. and the other set was run by R.W. We were curious to discover if, under these conditions, we would continue to obtain significantly different results. Each study had one independent variable with two levels—stare and non-stare. The dependent variables were the receivers' EDA during the experimental season and their responses to a "belief-in-psi" questionnaire.

Participants

Thirty-two subjects (10 males and 22 females; mean age of 25.72, age range 18–49) acted as receivers. Thirty of these were undergraduate psychology students studying at the University of Hertfordshire. The remaining two were the authors' colleagues. M.S. and R.W. acted in a dual capacity as both experimenter and sender.

Apparatus and Materials

LAYOUT OF ROOM

It was clearly important to minimize the possibility of any sensory leakage between sender and receiver during the experimental sessions. For this reason the receiver was located in the University's Social Observation Laboratory while the sender was located in a small room approximately 20 meters away from the laboratory (see Figure 1).

VIDEO EQUIPMENT

A Panasonic AG-450 video camera was positioned in front of the receiver and relayed an image (via a long cable connecting the two rooms) to a 14-inch JVC color TV monitor in the sender's room. This one-way closed circuit television system allowed the experimenter to see the subject, but not vice versa.

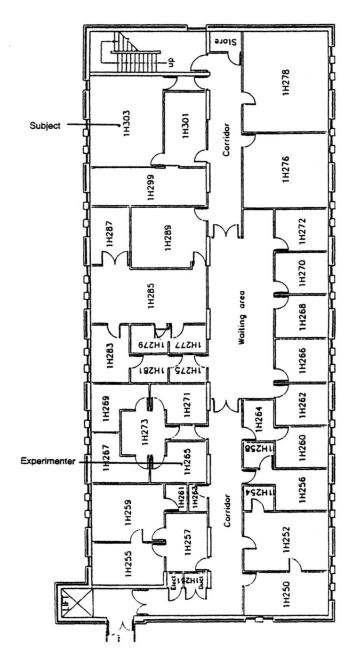

Figure 1. Locations of experimenter and subject during session.

EDA measurement. The receivers' EDA (electrodermal activity) was recorded by the RelaxPlus system (a commercially available hardware and software package produced by UltraMind, Ltd.). This system measures skin resistance level by placing a constant current across two stainless steel electrodes and then recording the resistance encountered by that current at a rate of 10 samples per second. The system filters for possible artifacts (caused, for example, by movement) and records data to the computer's hard disk. The equipment (i.e., electrodes, input device, computer, computer monitor) was located next to the receiver throughout the experiment. The part of the program involved in storing the details of subjects and their physiological data could be accessed only via a password known only to M.S. and R.W. Data from the Relax-Plus system were then fed into a spreadsheet (Microsoft's Excel) in order to calculate the mean EDA for each 30-second trial. All statistical analyses were carried out using the Statview software package.

Belief-in-psi questionnaire. The receivers were asked three questions concerning their attitudes toward psi (see Appendix). They indicated their responses on a seven-point scale ranging from −3 to +3. A general "belief-in-psi" score was obtained by summing the receiver's responses over all three questions. Low scores on this questionnaire were taken to indicate strong belief in psi.

Trial randomization. The receivers' EDA may decline during a session for several reasons (e.g., the apparatus measuring EDA may warm up or the participants may habituate to their surroundings). This decline could lead to artifactual evidence for psi if stare trials tend to precede non-stare trials. The following randomization procedure was devised to minimize this possible artifact.

Prior to the experiment, an individual not involved in running the experiment (Matthew D. Smith) prepared a set of 32 sheets, each of which contained the order of the 32 stare or non-stare trials for one session. For 16 of these sheets the trial orders were generated in the following way: M.D.S. first opened the random number table (Robson, 1983, Appendix Three), chose a number as an entry point into the table, and then threw a die twice. The numbers that came up determined how he moved from this entry point to an actual starting point. The eight consecutive numbers located in the row to the right of this starting point determined the order of the stare and non-stare trials. An even number translated into an ABBA (stare, non-stare, non-stare, stare) order while an odd number translated into a BAAB (non-stare, stare, stare, non-stare) order. The trial order for the remaining 16 sheets was determined by counterbalancing the orders of the randomized sheets just described. Thus, a stare, non-stare, non-stare, stare on a randomized sheet became a non-stare, stare, stare, non-stare on a counterbalanced sheet. All 32 sheets were then mixed together, placed in an opaque folder, and kept in a locked drawer in R.W.'s office. M.D.S. was aware of the experimental hypotheses prior to carrying out the above randomization procedure.

Procedure

The receivers were run individually. On arriving at the laboratory, each one was met by either R.W. or M.S. Most were run by whichever of the experimenters was free to carry out the session; however, on a few occasions (e.g., when a receiver was a friend or colleague of one of the experimenters) the experimenter would be designated in advance of the trial. Thus most subjects were assigned to experimenters in an opportunistic way, rather than by one that was properly randomized (e.g., via random number tables or the output of a random number generator). The experimenter showed the subject to the receiver's room and explained the purpose of the experiment. Next, the experimenter attached electrodes to the first and third fingers of the participant's nondominant hand and made sure that the RelaxPlus system was correctly monitoring their EDA. The receivers were asked not to move their hand unnecessarily, nor to try to guess when they might be being stared at, but instead to simply remain as open as possible to any remote influence. The experimenter entered the receiver's personal data in a computerized database, initiated the recording of EDA, started a stopwatch, and left the receiver's room.

It was important that receivers were not aware of the order of the stare and non-stare trials *before* the start of the experimental session. For this reason, the list of trial orders was only selected by the experimenter only *after* he or she had left the receiver's room. The experimenter then went to R.W.'s office, retrieved the folder containing the lists of trial orders, selected any sheet he or she wanted, and proceeded to the sender's room.

Two minutes after initiating the recording of the receiver's EDA, the experimenter started to carry out the designed order of stare and non-stare trials; this order was presented to the experimenters in the form of a list. During stare trials, the experimenter quietly directed his/her attention toward the receiver; during non-stare trials the experimenter quietly directed this attention away from the receiver. Each trial lasted 30 seconds. Throughout this time the receiver completed the belief-in-psi questionnaire and then read some magazines. All of the magazines were selected to be relatively bland in content in order to minimize possible effects on the receivers' EDA.

On completion of all 32 trials, the experimenter returned to the receiver's room, thanked the participant, and told him or her that feedback of the overall results would be given within the next few weeks.

At the end of each experimental day, both experimenters copied that day's data (from their own participants as well as from the other experimenter's participants) onto their own floppy disk.

Results[1]

Primary Analyses

All analyses were preplanned. A Wilcoxon signed rank test was used to compare receivers' total EDA for the 16 stare trials with their total EDA during the 16 non-stare trials.[2] Receivers run by R.W. did not differ from chance expectations (Wilcoxon z = .44, df = 15, p = .64, two-tailed). In contrast, receivers run by M.S. showed a significant effect (Wilcoxon z = -2.02, df = 15, p = .04, two=tailed).

A "detect score" was then calculated for each subject by subtracting the total EDA during the stare trials from the total EDA for the non-stare trials. An unpaired t test revealed that the detect scores of M.S.'s subjects were not significantly different from those of R.W.'s (df = 30, t = 1.39, p = .17, two-tailed).

Secondary Analyses

Table 1 contains the correlation coefficients between participants' belief-in-psi questionnaire scores and their detect scores. Spearman rank correlation coefficients revealed that none of these correlations were significant. Table 1 also contains the means (and standard deviations) of the questionnaire scores for R.W.'s group. M.S.'s group, and all participants.

This experiment was first reported at the 1996 Convention of the Parapsychological Association (Wiseman & Schlitz, 1996). While preparing the paper for journal publication, the authors reviewed the data and discovered an error in the way one subject's data had been transferred into the statistical package used for the analyses. For this reason the results reported here are slightly different from those reported in Wiseman and Schlitz (1996).

†*Previous studies (e.g., Braud et al., 1993a, 1993b) have assessed their results by creating a "psi score" (the sum of EDA during stare trials divided by the sum of the total EDA) for each participant and then using a one-sample t test to determine the degree to which these scores deviate from chance expectation. This procedure obscures the question of whether an overall result is caused by a very small number of participants performing extremely well. The Wilcoxon sign rank test is more conservative than the one-sample t test because it is less influenced by the size of the deviation between participants' scores.*

Table 1
Means and Standard Deviations for the Belief in PSI Questionnaire and Correlation Coeffcients and p Values Between Subjects' Questionnaire Scores and Detect Scores

	R.W.'s participants	M.S.'s participants	All participants
Mean	1.94	-.81	.56
Standard deviation (*SD*)	4.22	4.12	4.33
Correlation (*r*) (Corrected for ties)	-.15	.32	.15
z score	-.58	1.23	.84
p value, two-tailed	.56	.22	.39

Discussion

Subjects run by R.W. did not respond differently to stare and non-stare trials. In contrast, participants run by M.S. were significantly more activated in stare than non-stare trials. These findings can be interpreted in several ways.

First, one might argue that M.S.'s significant results were caused by some type of experimental artifact. Several steps were taken to guard against this possibility. For example, neither the receivers nor the experimenters knew the order of the stare and non-stare trials before the start of the experiment; the location of the rooms minimized the possibility of any sender-to-receiver sensory leakage; and the randomization procedure ensured that the results were unlikely to be caused by progressive errors. Thus, coupled with the fact that one would expect any artifact to influence the results of both studies, suggests that M.S.'s significant results are unlikely to have been caused by a methodological error.

Second, one could argue that either R.W.'s or M.S.'s results were caused by receivers' cheating. For example, subjects could have discovered the order of stare and non-stare trials before the experimental session and altered their EDA accordingly. Alternatively, participants could have altered their data files so that they coincided with the order of stare and non-stare trials. Several factors mitigate against these possibilities. First, such cheating would have been far from straightforward. For example, the selection of trial order was carried out a few moments before the start of the experimental session and it could only have been accessed by a participant who had installed some kind of covert monitoring equipment in the sender's room. Likewise, the computer could only be accessed if a participant had discovered a password which was known only to the experimenters. Also, neither R.W.'s or M.S.'s significant results are due to one exceptional participant, and one would therefore have to hypothesize that several participants successfully cheated.

Third, the results could have been caused by experimenter fraud. Although the experiment was not designed to make such fraud impossible, its design does mean that certain types of cheating would have been extremely unlikely. For example, neither experimenter could have decided to include data only from certain subjects because the full list of all subjects was known to both experimenters. However, more sophisticated forms of cheating were *theoretically* possible. For example, one experimenter could have substituted false sets of EDA values for subjects' actual values before the data were analyzed. Although possible, this would have been far from straightforward because subjects were frequently scheduled back-to-back (thus cutting to a minimum the time available for recording a false replacement session), and each experimenter made a back-up disk of all the day's sessions at the end of each day (thus minimizing the possibility of an experimenter's substituting data after the day they had been recorded). In addition, no evidence of any cheating was uncovered during the running of the experiment or analysis of the data.

Fourth, one could argue that M.S. was working with a more "psychically gifted" population than R.W. was. This also seems unlikely because the receivers were assigned to the two experimenters in an opportunistic fashion.

Fifth, it is possible that M.S. was more skilled at eliciting subjects' psi ability than R.W. was. Interestingly, M.S.'s subjects scored higher on the "belief-in-psi" questionnaire than R.W.'s subjects did (although this difference just failed to reach significance: unpaired t value = 1.86, df = 30, p = .072, 2-tailed). Given that participants were opportunistically assigned to experimenters, this difference might be a reflection of the different ways in which R.W. and M.S. oriented receivers at the start of the experiment. It seems quite possible that the experimenters' own level of belief/disbelief in the existence of psi caused receivers to express different levels of belief/disbelief in psi and to have different expectations about the success of the forthcoming experimental session. Videotapes of R.W.'s and M.S.'s induction procedures are currently being analyzed to identify differences in interaction and content.

Finally, it is also possible that both R.W. and M.S. used their own psi abilities to create the results they desired. This interpretation, if genuine, supports past research which suggests that successful experimenters (i.e., those who consistently obtain significant effects in psi studies) outperform unsuccessful ones on a variety of psi tasks (see Palmer, 1986, for a review of the literature supporting this notion).

In conclusion, this study reveals the value of developing collaborative relationships between skeptics and psi proponents. Both authors view this study as an initial step in the investigation of experimenter effects in psi research. Additional experiments would further aid our understanding of such effects. For example, it would be useful to carry out an experiment in which one experimenter interacted with the receiver and the other carried out the stare and non-stare trials during the experimental session. Such a study would help discover whether our initial interactions with the receiver or our behavior during the experimental session caused the results reported in this paper. We, the authors, hope to carry out such a study in the near future, and we urge other psi proponents and skeptics to run similar studies.

References

Braud, W., Shafer, D., & Andrews, S. (1993a). Reactions to an unseen gaze (remote attention): A review, with new data on autonomic staring detection. *Journal of Parapsychology*, 57, 373–390.

Braud, W., Shafer, D., & Andrews, S. (1993b). Further studies of autonomic detection of remote staring: replications, new control procedures, and personality correlates. *Journal of Parapsychology*, 57, 391–409.

Coover, J.E. (1913). The feeling of being stared at. *American Journal of Psychology*. 24, 570–575.

Palmer, J. (1986). ESP research findings the process approach. In H.L. Edge, R.L. Morris, J. Palmer, & J.H. Rush (Eds.), *Foundations of parapsychology* (pp. 184–222). London: Routledge & Kegan Paul.

Palmer, J. (1989a). Confronting the experimenter effect. *Parapsychology Review*, 20, 1–4.

Palmer, J. (1989b). Confronting the experimenter effect. Part 2. *Parapsychology Review*, 20(5), 1–5.

Peterson, D.M. (1978). Through the looking glass: an investigation of extrasensory detection of being stared at M.A. Thesis, University of Edinburgh.

Poortman, J.J. (1959). The feeling of being stared at *Journal of the Society for Psychical Research*, 40, 4–12.

Robson, C. (1983). Experiment, design and statistics in psychology. London: Penguin Books.

Schlitz, M.J., & LaBerge, S. (1997). Covert observation increases skin conductance in subjects unaware of when they are being observed: A replication. *Journal of Parapsychology*, 61, 185–196.

Titchener, E.B. (1898). The feeling of being stared at. *Science*, 8, 895–897.

Williams, L. (1983). Minimal cue perception of the regard of others: The feeling of being stared at. Paper presented as the 10th Annual Conference of the Southeastern Regional Parapsychological Association, West Georgia College, Carrolton, GA. See *Journal of Parapsychology*, 47, 59–60.

Wiseman, R. & Smith, M.D. (1994). A further look at the detection of unseen gaze. *Proceedings of the Parapsychological Association 37th Annual Convention*, 465–478.

Wiseman, R., Smith, M.D., Freedman, D., Wasserman, T., & Hurst, C. (1995). Two further experiments concerning the remote detection of an unseen gaze. *Proceedings of the Parapsychological Association 38th Annual Convention*, 480–492.

CHAPTER 11

Personality Characteristics of ESP Subjects: III. Extraversion and ESP

B.K. Kanthamani *and* K. Ramakrishna Rao

Extraversion-introversion is undoubtedly one of the most widely explored dimensions of personality so far in ESP research. Eysenck (1967) surveys a surprisingly large number of studies that seem to have direct or indirect bearing on this. Accepting the view that psi is an "ancient and primitive form of perception" and that conditions of high cortical arousal are therefore unfavorable to it, Eysenck goes on to deduce the hypothesis that extraverts are likely to do better on psi tests than introverts, because the introverts habitually are in a state of greater cortical arousal than the extraverts.

Some of the several studies that have involved physiological measures in relation to ESP may be interpreted as measures of cortical arousal. For example, when Otani (1965) used skin resistance as a measure of relaxation, he found that positive ESP scoring is likely to occur when the subject is in a relaxed condition and that negative results may be obtained when he is in an excited condition. Another physiological indicator that is influenced by cortical arousal is the alpha rhythm in the EEG pattern, which is especially evident in relaxed wakefulness. Stanford (1965) reported in his preliminary study that ESP correlated significantly with alpha activity in the EEG, although this was not confirmed in his later

Reprinted with permission from *Journal of Parapsychology*, 1972, 36, 198–212.

study. Honorton (1969) reported a strong positive correlation between ESP scores and alpha levels of his subjects. These reports are used as examples; it is not necessary for present purposes to discuss all of the many studies using alpha as an indicator of ESP success. However, the findings suggest that cortical arousal, which has been accepted as being higher in introverts than in extraverts, correlates negatively with ESP.

A number of experiments have been conducted in the past to relate ESP with extraversion as measured by different personality tests. In 1945, Humphrey reported an attempt to correlate the ESP scores of her subjects in three series of experiments with ratings on the Bernreuter Personality Inventory (BPI). She found no significant relationship between extraversion-introversion scores and ESP scores. In a later attempt (Humphrey, 1951), she divided her subjects into two groups. Those scoring above the 50th percentile on the extraversion-introversion scale were called extraverts and those scoring below the 50th percentile were called introverts. In the first series the extraverts gave a highly significant positive deviation ($p < .00003$) and the introverts scored at chance. The difference between the rate of scoring of the extraverts and introverts was significant at the .03 level.

A similar analysis of two other series of experiments showed that the extraverts scored positively and the introverts scored negatively. The difference between the two groups was significant ($p < .005$). Pointing out that more than 70% of the extraverts gave positive ESP scores and more than 70% of the introverts gave negative ESP scores, Humphrey (1951, pp. 259–60) claimed: "Thus far in ESP personality research, no other measure of personality has distinguished high and low ESP scores with this degree of accuracy."

Casper (1952) used a more or less similar procedure to confirm Humphrey's findings. The extraverts, those who obtained scores above the 50th percentile on Bernreuter's E-I scale, gave a positive deviation, and the introverts, those scoring below the 50th percentile, gave a negative deviation. The difference in the rate of scoring was significant at the .03 level.

More recently, better constructed and validated scales for the measurement of extraversion-introversion than the BPI have been used. Astrom (1965) gave 48 of his subjects a group GESP test with ESP cards and administered the Maudsley Personality Inventory (MPI) to them. It was found that the extraverts, defined as those who were one standard deviation above average on the E-scale, scored significantly more hits than the introverts, defined as those who were one standard deviation below average on the E-scale. The extraverts obtained an average of 6.65 hits per run and the introverts, 2.80 hits per run. The difference between the two groups was statistically significant.

Green (1966a; 1966b), however, did not find in two of her experiments a significant relationship between E-scores on the MPI and ESP scores. But Eysenck (1967) referred to some of her unpublished work and reported that it was more successful.

Nicol and Humphrey (1953) in one study used the Guliford STDCR Inventory, which gives information on five personality factors, those of social introversion-extraversion, thinking introversion-extraversion, depression, cycloid depression, and rhathymia (happy-go-lucky behavior). These factors are generally considered to be different aspects of introversion-extraversion. Correlations were worked out between the total ESP scores and several personality factors. It was observed that all of the obtained correlations were in the direction to be expected by the previous studies, even though the result was significant only for Factor D, freedom from depression ($r = +.37$, $P = .05$).

Nash (1966) used the Minnesota Multiphasic Personality Inventory (MMPI) in his work with college students and obtained several correlations with ESP scores. However, only the measure of social introversion correlated with ESP to a significant degree, and that was a negative relationship. This indicated that those who were more introverted obtained lower scores on ESP tests than those who were less introverted. A similar tendency was observed in a study by Black (quoted by Eysenck, 1967) in which a negative relationship was found between MMPI scores on social introversion and ESP.

Even if we assume that the variety of tests that purport to measure extraversion-introversion measure a comparable, if not identical, dimension, there is still no uniformity among the studies with regard to the criterion that distinguishes the extraverts from the introverts for the purpose of understanding their ESP ability. In Humphrey's study (1945) the 50th percentile mark distinguished the extraverts from the introverts. Astrom (1965) used one standard deviation above or below average on the E-scale as the criterion. Green's (1966 a; 1966 b) was yet another criterion. If the extraversion scores had been directly correlated with the ESP scores, the problem would have been much simpler, but in many studies no such correlation was obtained or expected. However, not all of the relationships are linear. Therefore, while extraverts generally may be superior to introverts as performers on ESP tests, the highly extraverted subjects are not necessarily the best, and vice versa. These different studies using different criteria make apparently different assumptions about the nature of the relationship between extraversion and ESP. Therefore, any meaningful comparison of them becomes difficult.

Although the evidence in these studies that involve the direct measurement of extraversion and introversion is suggestive of some relationship with ESP, there is also a considerable amount of indirect evidence from the study of traits known to relate to extraversion.

Sociability is one of the most common characteristics of extraversion, and its relationship to ESP among children has been tested. Shields (1962), in her work with children, used a battery of personality tests to diagnose whether her subjects were "withdrawn" or "not withdrawn." Her ESP test was a game with Popeye picture cards. The withdrawn group scored below chance to a degree that was marginally significant ($p < .05$), the nonwithdrawn (or sociable) group scored above chance to a significant degree ($p < .001$), and the difference in the rate of scoring between the two groups was highly significant ($p < .001$).

In Shield's second experiment an ESP test known as the "Matching Abacus Test" was used. On this test the withdrawn children obtained on the average 4.59 hits per run and the non-withdrawn children obtained 6.17 hits per run. The difference between the two groups in their rate of scoring was significant far beyond the .01 level. The above two studies suggest that sociability seems to be related to ESP, at least in children.

Van de Castle (1958) studied the relationship between psi in a psychokinesis experiment and spontaneity, using the Rorschach. He reported a suggestive correlation between high spontaneity and positive PK scores. In another PK experiment Scherer (1948) found that conditions that favored spontaneity seemed to facilitate psi. Therefore, if spontaneity is a characteristic of extraverts rather than of introverts, there is sufficient evidence that it is related to ESP.

Eilbert and Schmeidler (1950), in still a different kind of differentiation, related subjects' work habits and their ESP scores by dividing them into two groups, those of the ego-involved and the task-oriented. They found that the subjects rated as ego-involved generally scored below mean chance expectation (MCE) and those rated as task-oriented generally scored above MCE. The difference between the rate of scoring of the ego-involved and the task-oriented was statistically significant. Because introverts tend to be more easily ego-involved in their work than extraverts, this study also may be considered as evidence in favor of the hypothesis that extraverts tend to obtain more hits than introverts.

Schmeidler (1964), in a computer experiment with still another variation, used the Time Metaphor Test (TMT), which elicits attitudes toward time and the future. The items of this test were found to cluster under three groups by factor analysis: dynamic-hasty metaphors, naturalistic-passive metaphors, and humanistic metaphors. Among the obtained correlations there was only a suggestive relationship between ESP scores and dynamic-hasty scores ($r = +.27$) and between ESP scores and naturalistic-passive scores ($r = -.28$). According to Knapp and Garbutt (1958), strong preference for dynamic-hasty metaphors indicates a high competitive tendency, which we can consider as a characteristic of extraverts; thus, this study also has a bearing on the relationship between ESP and introversion-extraversion.

In a later experiment Heyman and Schmeidler (1967) administered a shortened version of the TMT to a group of subjects and divided them into two groups, the dynamic-hasty and the naturalistic-passive. They found that the dynamic-hasty subjects made more 1+ hits. We can reasonably assume that extraverts generally tend to be more dynamic-hasty than introverts.

Because self-confidence is considered to be a characteristic of extraverts rather than of introverts, there is evidence that it is related to ESP. In a study by Nicol and Humphrey (1953) the self-confidence scores obtained through the Guilford-Martin Inventory correlated significantly with ESP scores ($r = +.55$, $p = .01$). The positive relationship suggested that the subjects noted as highly self-confident tended to score positively and those rated low obtained fewer hits.

There also have been studies of the relationship between ESP and general activity, which is a characteristic of extraverts. The Nashes (1967) used the Guilford-Zimmerman Temperament Survey and obtained correlations between ESP scores and the 10 personality traits it measures. In the first experiment, with 24 subjects, the Factor G (general activity) gave a correlation of +.36, which is not significant. However, the following study, with 412 subjects, gave a significant positive correlation of .13 ($P = .01$) between ESP scores and scores on Factor G, which indicated that subjects with higher general activity scores obtained more ESP hits than those who scored less on this scale.

Present Study

The review of these studies indicates that although there is sufficient evidence to suggest that extraversion is positively related to the ESP scoring trend, it does not show whether the whole dimension is related to ESP or only the several primary factors of which it is composed. The present study is focused to make that comparison. The data for it are derived from the larger investigation described in detail elsewhere (Kanthamani and Rao, 1971).

As can be recalled, the whole investigation considered of four experiments, which included a pilot study and three confirmatory series, namely, experiments A, B, and C. The subjects were young boys and girls studying in English medium schools at Waltair, India. They were tested individually for ESP in two sessions with the regular ESP cards. Each subject completed eight standard runs following the blind-matching technique. In the third session the High School Personality Questionnaire (HSPQ) was administered to them to obtain scores on different personality factors.

In the previous paper (Kanthamani and Rao, 1972) it was observed that although several single personality traits were significantly related to ESP scoring, a combination of such traits together predicted psi-hitters and missers much better. The present paper considers another question raised in the first report (Kanthamani and Rao, 1971), namely, whether the personality factors known to be related to ESP affect psi individually or insofar as they are a part of a cluster representing the broad spectrum of personality, that is, extraversion. To study this question, the several individual factors that together determine the score on the extraversion scale must be compared with the extraversion scale with regard to their efficiency in predicting the ESP performance. The following paragraphs describe in detail such analyses made on the present data.

Derivation of Extraversion Scores

The method used to derive the E-score is essentially the same as the standard method described in the HSPQ manual (Cattell and Beloff, 1962). According to this method four primary factors, namely, Cyclothymia (A), Parmia (H), Surgency (F), and Lack of Self-sufficiency (Q_2) are regarded as the component parts of the E-scale. In other words, persons with the cyclothymic temperament, who are also of the happy-go-lucky type and are adventurous and who go with the group rather than alone tend to score high on the extraversion scale. The scores on these facts are given different weightages as shown in Table 1. It can be recalled that the raw scores on the primary factors are first converted into the standard scores ("sten" scores) before they are used to give a score on extraversion (E-scale). Factors A, H, and F are given more weightage in their contribution to the E-score than Factor Q_2. The sten scores on the first three factors are multiplied by 2, but the sten score on Q_2 is just subtracted from 11. The E-score is the sum of the resultants. The minimum score possible by this method would be 7 and the maximum 70, with a mean of 38.5. Higher scores on this scale indicate greater extraversion and lower scores indicate relative degrees of introversion.

Table 1
Computation of Extraversion Scores

| Extravert Traits | Treatment of Sten Score | Range of Score | |
		Low	High
A (Cyclothymia)	Multiply by 2	2	20
H (Parmia)	Multiply by 2	2	20
F (Surgency)	Multiply by 2	2	20
Q₂ (Lack of self-sufficiency)	Subtract from 11 and add without multiplication	1	10
Total		7	70

Theoretical Mean = 38.5

Table 2
ESP Scores in Relation to the E-Scale

| | Pilot | | Exp. A | | Exp. B | | Exp. C | |
	Ext.	Intr.	Ext.	Intr.	Ext.	Intr.	Ext.	Intr.
N	14	8	19	31	17	19	14	24
Runs	112	64	152	248	136	152	112	192
Deviation	+50	-40	+20	-45	+64	-23	-6	-104
Mean hits Per run	5.45	4.37	5.13	4.82	5.47	4.85	4.95	4.46

$t = 3.31$ (20df); $p < .01$[a] $t = 1.42$ (n.s.) $t = 3.24$ (34df); $p < .005$[b] $t = 2.17$ (36df); $p < .025$[b]

[a]Two-tailed.
[b]One-tailed.

The extraversion scores were obtained in this manner for each subject. The analysis of the results consisted of comparing the four primary factors with the extraversion factor to study their relative efficiency in separating the hitting and missing tendencies of the subjects on the ESP tests. More specifically, the predictions on Factors A, H, F, and Q_2 are compared with the predictions made by the E-scale.

Statistical Analysis

As in the previous papers (Kanthamani and Rao, 1971 and 1972) the subjects were allotted to two groups on every primary factor with their theoretical mean as the cutting-point, and then their ESP scores were compared by the t test.

On the E-scale the theoretical mean of 38.5 was used to classify the subjects as extraverts or introverts. Subjects who scored more than 38.5

belonged to the extravert group and those with scores less than 38.5 were included in the introvert group. The difference in their scoring rate was tested by the *t* test.

Results

Tables 2 and 3 summarize the analyses of all the four experiments (pilot and three confirmatory series) in terms of primary factors and the E-scale.

Considering the E-scale first (Table 2), in the pilot experiment there were, in all, 14 extraverts and 8 introverts. The extraverts scored a total of 610 hits in 112 runs. This gives a deviation of +50 from the MCE. The introverts obtained 280 hits in 64 runs, which gives a deviation of −40. The average run scores for the extravert and introvert groups are 5.45 hits and 4.37 hits, respectively. The difference in the rate of scoring between the two groups of subjects gives a *t* ratio of 3.31 (20 *df*), which is significant beyond the .01 level. Thus, the extraverts scored significantly higher than the introverts.

Of 50 subjects in Experiment A, 19 were classified as extraverts and 31 as introverts. The extraverts obtained 780 hits in 152 runs, which gives a deviation of +20 from the MCE. The introverts obtained 1,195 hits in 248 runs, which is 45 less than the chance score. In terms of averages, the extraverts obtained 5.13 hits per run and the introverts, 4.82 hits per run. Even though the results are in the same direction as before, the difference between the two groups is not significant (t = 1.42, 48 *df*; n.s.).

In Experiment B there were 17 subjects in the extravert group and 19 in the introvert group. The extraverts scored a total of 744 hits in 136 runs, which gives a deviation of +64 from the MCE. The introverts obtained 737 hits in 152 runs, which gives a deviation of −23. In terms of averages, the extraverts obtained 5.47 hits per run and the introverts, 4.85 hits. The difference between the two groups in their scoring direction gives a *t* of 3.24, with 34 *df*, significant beyond the .005 level. So here again the extraverts in general scored more than introverts.

Experiment C consisted of 14 extraverts and 24 introverts. The extraverts scored, in all, 554 hits in 112 runs (-6), which gives an average of 4.95 hits per run. The introverts obtained 856 hits (-104) in 192 runs, with an average of 4.46 hits per run. The extraverts scored higher than the introverts even though neither exceeded the chance level. However, the difference between their scoring rates is statistically significant, with a *t* of 2.17, 36 *df*; *p* < .025, which suggests that the extraverts scored more than introverts, although both of them were below chance.

Table 3
ESP Scores in Relation to the Primary Factors

Personality Factor	Pilot			Exp. A			Exp. B			Exp. C		
	Mean Hits Per Run	t^c	p^a	Mean Hits Per Run	t^d	p^b	Mean Hits Per Run	t^e	p^b	Mean Hits Per Run	t^f	p^b
A-	4.37	3.31	<.01	4.88	0.66	n.s.	4.88	2.20	<.025	4.56	0.69	n.s.
A+	5.45			5.03			5.33			4.72		
F-	4.31	4.66	<.001	4.74	1.54	n.s.	4.93	2.31	<.025	4.58	0.67	n.s.
F+	5.58			5.08			5.41			4.73		
H-	4.66	2.04	n.s.	5.04	0.97	n.s.	5.06	0.89	n.s.	4.63	0.66	n.s.
H+	5.38			4.83			5.25			4.65		
Q_2^-	5.27	0.68	n.s.	4.97	0.17	n.s.	5.54	2.87	<.005	4.99	1.90	<.05
Q_2^+	4.98			4.92			4.95			4.51		

[a]Two-tailed. [b]One-tailed. [c]Each t is associated with 20 df. [d]Each t is associated with 48 df. [e]Each t is associated with 34 df. [f]Each t is associated with 36 df.

These results clearly indicate that extraverts generally obtained higher ESP scores than introverts. This tendency is seen consistently in all the experiments, including the last one, in which the overall psi evidence was one of significant psi-missing (Kanthamani and Rao, 1971, p. 201). The average scoring rate of introverts was less than chance in all experiments, but that of the extraverts was above chance in the first three. The difference in the scoring rate of extraverts and introverts reaches statistical significance in all of the experiments except A.

Table 3 gives the results of ESP scores in terms of primary factors which together make up the E-scale. In the pilot experiment Factors A and F showed a significant relation to ESP scores, in that "plus" groups scored positively and "minus" groups negatively; the t ratio was highly significant. However, Factors H and Q_2 failed to make significant contributions.

In Experiment A none of the primary factors showed any significant predictions. In Experiment B, however, Factors A, F, and Q_2 reached significance and H failed. On the other hand, only Q_2 turned out to be significant in Experiment C. These varying results indicate that none of the primary factors is related to ESP in any consistent way throughout these four experiments. Factor A was significant in two experiments, Factor F in two others, Factor H was not significant in any, and Factor Q_2 was significant in two. Thus, whatever relationship one finds in any experiment as far as primary factors are concerned, seems to be true only in a limited sense. However, it should be noted that the respective "plus" and "minus" groups in each factor held up in the same direction in their relation with ESP in all the experiments. This suggests that although there seems to be some relationship between primary factors and ESP, it is not strong enough to be seen in all the experiments.

The comparison between the primary factors and the E-scale with regard to their efficiency in separating psi-hitting and psi-missing subjects can also be made by taking the combined evidence (z statistic) of all the experiments. The different t's of the confirmatory series were used as described elsewhere (Kanthamani and Rao, 1971) to yield a z statistic for each factor. (The pilot experiment was not included in this analysis.) The obtained results are given in Table 4. The z for Factor A is 2.05, which has a p smaller than .025. For Factors F and Q_2, the respective z values are 2.61 and 2.85, both significant beyond the .005 level, but the combined evidence for Factor H is not significant (Z = 1.11). Thus, among the four primary factors, three show a significant relationship to the ESP score. However, the z value for the E-scale is found to be the highest (z = 3.95), which is highly significant (p <.00005).

Table 4
Combined Evidence of the Confirmatory Series

Personality Factor	t Ratio Between Plus and Minus Groups			z	P[a]
	Exp. A	*Exp. B*	*Exp. C*		
A	0.66	2.20	0.69	2.05	<.025
F	1.54	2.31	0.67	2.61	<.005
H	0.97	0.89	0.06	1.11	n.s.
Q_2	0.17	2.87	1.90	2.85	<.005
Extraversion	1.42	3.24	2.17	3.95	<.00005

[a]*One-tailed.*

Discussion

The above results confirm the fact that extraversion is one of the useful dimensions in separating psi-hitting and psi-missing, because subjects rated as extraverts tended to score higher than subjects rated as introverts on the E-scale. The results also suggest that even though the primary factors are not significant in every series, their overall predictions seem to be consistent, and therefore they reach a significant level in their combined effect. Factor Q_2, which was not significant in the pilot study and in Experiment A, turned out to be marginally significant in Experiment C and highly significant in Experiment B. However, Factor H was not significant in any of the experiments, including the pilot. This suggests that although there are certain primary factors that are successful in predicting the direction of hitting and missing, not all of them are necessarily related to ESP. Nevertheless, their combined predictions make the separation much better than any of them taken singly. Because some of the primary factors are significantly related to ESP and others are not, caution should be taken to avoid an improper selection of the personality tests for use in ESP research. It seems that these unitary traits affect psi more because of their relationship to the broader dimension (extraversion) and less in their own right. The greater the relationship between these traits and extraversion, probably the more reliable is their prediction of ESP scoring direction. This point throws light on some of the controversies existing in the past between extraversion and ESP. Since most of the earlier studies involved different unitary traits of extraversion rather than the whole dimension as such, the obtained results may have been dependent on the degree to which they were related to extraversion as a broad dimension.

The results bearing on the relationship between the E-scale and ESP scores are unambiguous and provide positive confirmation of the earlier findings. The tendency for the extraverts to score consistently higher than the introverts was observed in all four experiments, including the pilot. However, although the results of E-scale predictions were independently significant in three experiments, they did not reach the usual conventional level of significance in Experiment A. This finding raises the important question of whether extraversion as measured by the HSPQ is a dimension at all independent of the other known dimensions. A detailed discussion of these points will be presented in following papers.

References

Astrom, Jan. GESP and the MPI measures. Paper read at 8th Annual Parapsychological Convention, New York, 1965 (Abstract). *Journal of Parapsychology*, 1965, 29, 292–93.

Casper, G.W. Effect of the receiver's attitude toward the sender in ESP tests. *Journal of Parapsychology*, 1952, 16, 212–18.

Cattell, R.B., and Beloff, Halla. *Handbook for the Junior-Senior High School Personality Questionnaire.* (2nd ed.) Illinois: Institute for Personality and Ability Testing, 1962.

Eilbert, L., and Schmeidler, Gertrude R. A study of certain psychological factors in relation to ESP performance. *Journal of Parapsychology*, 1950, 14, 53–74.

Eysenck, H.J. Personality and extra-sensory perception. *Journal of the Society for Psychical Research*, 1967, 44, 55–71.

Green, Celia E. Extra-sensory perception and the Maudsley Personality Inventory. *Journal of the Society for Psychical Research*, 1966, 43, 285–86. (a)

Green, Celia E. Extra-sensory perception and the extraversion scale of the Maudsley Personality Inventory (Abstract). *Journal of the Society for Psychical Research*, 1966, 43, 337. (b)

Heyman, S., and Schmeidler, Gertrude R. Attitudes toward time and the impatience effect. Paper read at 10th Annual Convention of the Parapsychological Association, New York, 1967 (Abstract). *Journal of Parapsychology*, 1967, 31, 316.

Honorton, C. Relationship between EEG alpha activity and ESP card-guessing performance. *Journal of the American Society for Psychical Research*, 1969, 63, 365–74.

Humphrey, Betty M. An exploratory correlation study of personality measures and ESP scores. *Journal of Parapsychology*, 1945, 9, 116–23.

Humphrey, Betty M. Introversion-extraversion ratings in relation to scores in ESP tests. *Journal of Parapsychology*, 1951, 15, 252–62.

Kanthamani, B.K., and Rao, K.R. Personality characteristics of ESP subjects. I. Primary personality characteristics and ESP. *Journal of Parapsychology*, 1971, 35, 189–207.

Kanthamani, B.K., and Rao, K.R. Personality characteristics of ESP subjects. II.

The combined personality measure (CPM) and ESP. *Journal of Parapsychology*, 1972, 36, 56–70.

Knapp, R.H., and Garbutt, J.T. Time imagery and the achievement motive. *Journal of Personality*, 1958, 26, 426–34.

Nash, C.B. Relation between ESP scoring level and the Minnesota Multiphasic Personality Inventory. *Journal of the American Society for Psychical Research*, 1966, 60, 56–62.

Nash, C.B., and Nash, Catherine S. Relations between ESP scoring level and the personality traits of the Guilford-Zimmerman Temperament Survey. *Journal of the American Society for Psychical Research*, 1967, 61, 64–71.

Nicol, J.F., and Humphrey, Betty M. The exploration of ESP and human personality. *Journal of the American Society for Psychical Research*, 1953, 47, 133–78.

Otani, S. Some relations of ESP scores to change in skin resistance. In *Parapsychology: From Duke to FRNM*. Durham: Parapsychology Press, 1965.

Scherer, W.B. Spontaneity as a factor in ESP. *Journal of Parapsychology*, 1948, 12, 126–47.

Schmeidler, Gertrude R. An experiment on precognitive clairvoyance: Part III. Precognitive scores related to the subjects' ways of viewing time. *Journal of Parapsychology*, 1964, 28, 93–101.

Shields, Eloise. Comparison of children's guessing ability (ESP) with personality characteristics. *Journal of Parapsychology*, 1962, 26, 200–210.

Stanford, R.G. A study of the relationship between ESP scoring and "brain waves." In *Parapsychology: From Duke to FRNM*. Durham: Parapsychology Press, 1965.

Van de Castle, R.L. An exploratory study of some personality correlates associated with PK performance. *Journal of the American Society for Psychical Research*, 1958, 52, 134–50.

CHAPTER 12

Extraversion and ESP Performance: A Meta-Analysis and a New Confirmation

Charles Honorton, Diane C. Ferrari, *and* Daryl J. Bem

The relationship between ESP performance and individual differences in psychological traits has been explored in many studies since the 1940s. Extraversion is one of the most frequently studied trait variables and three narrative reviews of the ESP/extraversion literature have concluded that ESP performance is positively related to extraversion (Eysenck, 1967; Palmer, 1977; Sargent, 1981). We present a meta-analysis of the extraversion/ESP literature. The purpose of the meta-analysis is to (1) update earlier narrative reviews of the ESP/extraversion relationship, (2) estimate the magnitude of the relationship, (3) assess potential threats to validity, and (4) identify procedural and other variables that moderate the relationship. We will then present a new confirmation of the ESP/extraversion relationship and compare its magnitude to that estimated from the meta-analysis.

The Meta-Analysis

Previous parapsychological meta-analyses have focused on evidence

Reprinted with permission from *Journal of Parapsychology*, 1998, 62, 255–276.

for psi functioning in such research domains as ganzfeld communication (Honorton, 1985), precognition (Honorton & Ferrari, 1989), and studies of the impact of conscious intention on random number generators (Radin & Nelson, 1989). In such cases the effect size index is based on the proportion of hits and the unit of analysis is the trial. In the present case, we are interested in the relationship between psi performance and a predictor variable, extraversion, rather than overall psi performance. The effect size index is the correlation coefficient between the two variables and the subject is the unit of analysis.

Method

Retrieval of Studies

We attempted to retrieve all English-language studies of the relationship between extraversion and performance in experimental ESP tasks. The source of studies includes the bibliographies of three narrative reviews (Eysenck, 1967; Palmer, 1977; Sargent, 1981) and inspection of the principal English-language outlets for publication of parapsychological research, including the *Journal of Parapsychology, Journal of the American Society for Psychical Research, Journal of the Society for Psychical Research*, and *Research in Parapsychology*. In addition, we conducted a computer search of *Psychological Abstracts* using the keywords "extraversion," "extroversion," "introversion," "intraversion," "sociability," and "outgoing."

Investigator Definition

For the purpose of the meta-analysis, we defined independent investigators as investigators who have not worked with other investigators in the data base. In cases of multiple authorship, studies are identified by the senior author of the earliest publication in the data base. For example, studies by Kanthamani (1966), Kanthamani and Rao (1972) and Krishna and Rao (1981) are all identified as Kanthamani studies. While Kanthamani and Krishna did not work together, they share Rao as a co-author and are therefore considered to represent a single investigator set. Similarly, studies by Humphrey (1945, 1951) and by Nicol and Humphrey (1953, 1955) are all identified as Humphrey studies. Laboratory affiliation was not used to identify independent investigators since several investigators worked in different laboratories and several generations of investigators worked in one laboratory.

Procedural Features

Besides bibliographical data identifying the investigator, publication source and date, we coded various procedural, sampling, and statistical features for each study. The procedural features include the type of ESP task (forced-choice or free-response), test setting (individual or group testing), ESP mode (telepathy, clairvoyance, precognition, mixed), and amount of feedback in the ESP task. Procedural features relevant to assessing research quality are described in the following section. Sampling and statistical features coded include the number of subjects, the subject population used, the instrument used for measuring extraversion, and the inferential statistics reported for testing the relationship between ESP performance and extraversion.

Criteria for Assessing Research Quality

Methodological variables were coded in terms of procedural description (or their absence) in the research reports. This approach was used in an earlier meta-analysis of the ESP ganzfeld domain (Honorton, 1985), resulting in study quality ratings that were generally in agreement (r_{26} = .77, p = 10^{-6}) with independent "flaw" ratings by an outside critic (Hyman, 1985). Two sets of criteria were used. One set assessed threats to the validity of the ESP measure. The other set assessed threats to the validity of the relationship between the ESP and extraversion measures.

The ESP quality analysis includes four criteria. One point was given (or withheld) for each of the following:

Control Against Sensory Leakage

Credit was given to GESP (telepathy) studies if the report specified that each of the following criteria were met: sender and receiver were located in separate rooms, the test situation prohibited auditory or other cues from sender to receiver, the sender and receiver were monitored by experimenters, and in free-response studies involving subject judging, duplicate target sets were employed. Credit was given to clairvoyance studies if the report specified that cues from the targets were prohibited by means of physical distance, screens, or opaque packaging. Precognition studies were considered to be immune to sensory leakage problems.

Randomization

Studies received credit if random number tables, random number generators, or mechanical shufflers were used to randomize the targets.

Studies using informal methods of randomization such as hand shuffling and dice throwing, or in which there was no randomization, received no credit. Reports failing to identify the method of randomization received no credit.

DUPLICATE RECORDING

Studies reporting duplicate recording of targets and responses received credit. Reports that failed to describe their data recording procedures and those in which data recording was performed by a single experimenter, received no credit.

DUPLICATE SCORING

Studies reporting duplicate checking of hits received credit. Reports that failed to describe their scoring procedures and those in which scoring was performed by a single experimenter, received no credit.

We assessed two aspects of methodology that could result in a spurious correlation between ESP scores and measures of extraversion: advance specification of the criteria used to define extraversion and the order in which the ESP task and extraversion measure were administered.

A PRIORI DEFINITION OF EXTRAVERSION

An inflated relationship between ESP and extraversion scores could occur if the investigator selected an "optimal" extraversion/introversion breakdown after observing the data, without correcting for multiple analysis. We coded studies as to whether the classification of extraversion/introversion appeared to be predetermined or post hoc. No credit was given for studies using nonstandard classifications (e.g., ± 1 sd, median split, etc.) unless the report explicitly stated that the method of classification was preplanned.

ORDER OF ADMINISTRATION OF EXTRAVERSION AND ESP MEASURES

A spurious correlation between ESP scores and extraversion could arise if subjects' responses on the extraversion scale were influenced by knowledge of their performance in the ESP task. There is some evidence that subjects' responses to psychological tests may be influenced by feedback concerning their ESP performance (Palmer & Lieberman, 1975). We coded studies as to whether the extraversion scale was given before or after the ESP test. This information was available for 45 of the 60 studies.

Meta-Analysis of Correlation Coefficients

We combined correlations across independent studies using the procedures described by Hedges and Olkin (1985) and Rosenthal (1984). All statistics were converted to indices of association; t tests were converted to point-biserials and phi coefficients were computed from 2×2 contingency tables.* We estimated unreported correlations from the reported p values (with results reported only as "nonsignificant" obtained in 13 cases set equal to .00). The signs of the correlations were adjusted if necessary to insure that positive correlations reflect positive relationships between extraversion and ESP performance. The correlations were pooled across studies but within categories based on methodological features associated with the studies. The correlations were transformed to their Fisher's z equivalents, weighted by their df, and averaged. We determined the two-tailed significance levels and 95% confidence intervals (Cos; Hedges and Olkin, 1985). Finally, we conducted chi-square tests of homogeneity (Hedges and Olkin, 1985; Rosenthal, 1984) and transformed mean z's back to the r metric.

The chi-square homogeneity test assesses the consistency of study outcomes, providing a quantitative index of replicability. A set of studies are exact replicates if their effect sizes are identical. They are homogeneous if the variability of effect sizes can be explained by sampling error. A significant but nonhomogeneous effect indicates the presence of moderating variables and homogeneity tests are used to identify moderating variables by subdividing studies into smaller, methodologically similar subgroups (Hedges, 1987).

Results

We retrieved 60 independent studies contained in 35 publications by 17 independent investigators. The studies were reported over a span of 38 years, between 1945 and 1983. The data base comprises 2,963 subjects. Forty-five studies involve ESP card-guessing tasks or similar forced-choice tasks. Fourteen studies employed free-response ESP tasks, and one involved a remote physiological influence task.

The unweighted correlations range from -0.44 to .91. Figure 1 shows

---

Two studies provided only trial-based tests (Cr_d). Correlations were estimated for these studies using a method for estimating effect sizes from critical ratios reported by McCarthy & Schechter (1986). Their method provides an estimate of Cohen's d which we then converted to the r metric.

-.4	4
-.3	6
-.2	5 2
-.1	7 4 1
-.0	9 2 0 0
.0	0 5 8 9
.1	0 0 1 2 2 7 8 8
.2	0 3 3 8
.3	0 0 4 4 4 5 7 8 8
.4	0 6 6 9 9
.5	3 4 8
.6	6 7
.7	
.8	
.9	1

Figure 1. Stem-and-leaf frequency distribution of correlation coefficients between extraversion and ESP performance (N = 47).

a stem-and-leaf display (Tukey, 1977) of the correlation coefficients. (The 13 studies that were assigned *r*'s of zero because of insufficient information are omitted). Unlike other methods of displaying frequency distributions, the stem-and-leaf plot retains the numerical data precisely. (Turned on its side, the stem-and-leaf plot is a histogram.) Each number includes a stem and one or more leaves. For example, the stem .2 is followed by leaves of 0, 3, 3, 8 representing *r*s of .20, .23, .23, and .28.

The meta-analysis is summarized in Table 1. The study grouping is identified in the first column. Columns two through four show, respectively, the number of studies, investigators, and subjects. The mean weighted effect size *r* is shown in column five and columns six and seven show, respectively, the lower and upper 95% (CI) for the effect size. The cumulative *z* score and its associated two-tailed *p* value are shown in columns eight and nine. The chi-square homogeneity statistic is presented in the last column.

Overall Results

The results for all 60 studies are shown in the first row. The mean weighted *r* is 0.09 ($z = 4.63$, $p = .000004$, two-tailed). The 95% CI is an *r* from .05 to .12. While significant, the study effect sizes are nonhomogeneous ($\chi^2_{59}=126.21$, $p <.05$). The second row shows the same analysis, omitting the 13 studies that were assigned *r*s of zero.

Forced-Choice Studies

The ESP/extraversion correlations for the 45 forced-choice (FC) studies are presented in row three of Table 1. These studies were contributed by 13 independent investigators and include 2169 subjects. The mean weighted r is .06 ($z = 2.86$, $p = .0042$, 95% CI from .02 to .11). The FC correlations are significantly nonhomogeneous ($\chi^2_{44} = 92.82$, $p < .05$).

FC STUDIES INVOLVING INDIVIDUAL TESTING

Twenty-one of the FC studies involved individual testing (Table 1, row 4). These studies were performed by 11 independent investigators and included 920 subjects. The mean weighted r is .15 ($z = 4.54$, $p = .000006$, 95% CI from .09 to .22). The correlations are nonhomogeneous ($\chi^2_{20} = 42.99$, $p < .05$).

FC STUDIES INVOLVING GROUP TESTING

The remaining 24 FC studies involved group testing. These studies were conducted by eight independent investigators and included 1249 subjects. They yield a mean weighted r of -0.00 ($z = -0.12$, $p = .904$, 95% CI from -.06 to .05). The group FC studies are homogeneous ($\chi^2_{23} = 37.35$, $p > .05$). Thus, the FC studies involving group testing yielded uniformly null correlations between ESP performance and extraversion.

INDIVIDUAL VERSUS GROUP TESTING

Evidence for a relationship between extraversion and forced-choice ESP performance is limited to FC studies involving individual testing. The difference between the ESP/extraversion correlations for individual and group testing is significant (Cohen's $q = .14$, $z = 3.47$, $p = .00052$, two-tailed).

Free-Response Studies

The results for the 14 free-response (FR) studies are shown in row six of Table 1. The FR studies were contributed by four independent investigators and included 612 subjects. The mean weighted r is .20 ($z = 4.82$, $p = .0000015$, two-tailed). The 95% CI is an r from .12 to .28. The overall FR outcomes, while highly significant, are significantly nonhomogeneous ($\chi^2_{13} = 23.40$, $p < .05$). This nonhomogeneity is due to a moderating variable, test setting.

FREE-RESPONSE STUDIES INVOLVING INDIVIDUAL TESTING

Twelve FR studies employed individual testing Table 1, row 7). These

Table 1
Summary of Extraversion-ESP Meta-Analysis

	Number of Independent Effect Sizes	Number of Independent Investigators	Total Number of Subjects	Mean Effect Size (r)	95% Confidence Interval From	95% Confidence Interval To	z	p	$\chi^{2(k-1)}$
Overall, all studies	60	17	2963	.09	.05	.12	4.63	.000004	126.21*
Studies with r available	47	14	1853	.14	.10	.19	5.90	<.000001	115.91*
Forced-choice guessing tasks	45	13	2169	.06	.02	.11	2.86	.0042	92.82*
Individual testing	21	11	920	.15	.09	.22	4.54	.000006	42.99*
Group testing	24	8	1249	-.00	-.06	.05	-0.12	.904	37.35
Free-response imaging tasks[a]	14	4	612	.20	.12	.28	4.82	.0000015	23.40*
Individual testing	12	3	512	.20	.11	.29	4.46	.0000083	15.85
Group testing	2	1	100	.19	-.01	.37	1.83	.067	7.53*

*Significant nonhomogeneity at $p < .05$, according to χ^2 test.
[a]One study (Haraldsson, 1970) involving remote physiological influence does not fit into either forced-choice or free-response category.

Notes: r is the weighted average correlation coefficient (Hedges & Olkin, 1985). k represents the number of independent effect sizes. χ^2 is the within group homogeneity statistic (Rosenthal, 1984).

studies were contributed by three independent investigators and include 512 subjects. The results are both significant and homogeneous. The mean weighted r is .20 (z = 4.46, p = .0000083, 95% CI from .11 to .29, χ^2_{11} = 15.85, p >.05).

FREE-RESPONSE STUDIES INVOLVING GROUP TESTING
Only two FR studies involved group testing (Table 1, row 8). Both studies were contributed by the same investigator. The mean weighted r is .19 (z = 1.83, p = .067, 95% CI from -.01 to .37). The results are significantly nonhomogeneous (χ^2_1 = 7.53, p<.05).

Free-Response versus Forced-Choice Studies

The mean correlation between ESP performance and extraversion is significantly larger in studies with free-response ESP tests than in those using forced-choice tests (Cohen's q = .14, z = 3.11, p = .0019, two-tailed).

Quality Analysis of Forced-Choice Studies

SENSORY LEAKAGE
Thirty-one of the FC studies describe the use of methods that satisfy our criteria for adequate control against sensory leakage in the ESP task. The ESP/extraversion relationship is not significant for these studies; the mean weighted r is .04 (z = 1.47, p =.142, two-tailed). The ESP/extraversion relationship is significant in the 14 FC studies that are amenable to sensory leakage (r = .14, z = 3.20, p = .0014, two-tailed). The difference between the two correlations is significant (Cohen's q = -.10, z = -2.03, p = .042, two-tailed).

RANDOMIZATION
Thirteen FC studies satisfy our criteria for randomization. The mean weighted r for these studies is .13 (z = 2.27, p = .023). Thirty-two FC studies failed our randomization criteria; they yielded a mean weighted r of .05 (z = 2.13, p = .033, two-tailed). The ESP/extraversion correlation is nonsignificantly *lower* in these studies than in studies using formal randomization methods (Cohen's q = .08, z = 1.40, p = .162, two-tailed).

DUPLICATE RECORDING
Six FC studies employed duplicate recording of targets and responses. The mean weighted r for these studies is .31 (z = 3.52, p = .00043, two-tailed). The 39 studies without duplicate recording yielded a mean

weighted r of .05 (z = 2.01, p = .0444, two-tailed). The ESP/extraversion relationship is significantly stronger in studies with duplicate recording (Cohen's q = .27, z = 3.02, p = .0025).

DUPLICATE CHECKING

Eighteen FC studies reported using methods for duplicate checking of hits. These studies are associated with a mean weighted r of .27 (z = 5.72, p <10^{-6}, two-tailed). The 27 FC studies that did not use methods for duplicate checking yielded a nonsignificant r of .01 (z = 0.23, p = .59). The difference between the two correlations is significant (Cohen's q = .27, z = 5.20, p <10^{-6}, two-tailed).

A PRIORI DEFINITION OF EXTRAVERSION

Thirty-seven FC studies satisfied our criteria for a priori definition of extraversion. These studies had a mean weighted r of .05 (z = 2.20, p = .028). The remaining eight FC studies failed our criteria for a priori definition of extraversion (r = .10, z = 2.00, p = .046, two-tailed). The two correlations do not differ significantly (Cohen's q = -.05, z = 0.92, p = .358, two-tailed).

ORDER OF ADMINISTRATION OF EXTRAVERSION AND ESP MEASURES

Evidence for a relationship between forced-choice ESP performance and extraversion is entirely dependent upon the outcomes of studies in which extraversion was measured after the ESP test (N = 18 studies, r = .17, z = 3.51, p = .00045). The correlation between FC ESP performance and extraversion in studies in which extraversion was measured *before* the ESP task is not significant (N = 16 studies, r = -.02, z = -0.78, p = .782) and the difference between the two correlations is significant (Cohen's q = .19, z = 3.58, p = .00034, two-tailed). This difference is not attributable to methodological features of the two groups such as test setting, the extraversion measure, or ESP mode.

Degree of ESP feedback is documented in nine of the 18 studies that measured extraversion after the ESP task and subjects received feedback of their ESP performance in each of these studies (r = .29, z = 4.59, p = .0000045, two-tailed). Seven of the nine studies where feedback is undocumented were group studies which usually involve delayed feedback or no feedback at all. These studies yield a nonsignificant correlation between performance and extraversion (r = .05, z = 0.64, p = .522, two-tailed) which is significantly lower than that for the studies known to involve feedback (Cohen's q =.25, z = 2.54, p = .011, two-tailed). The relationship between forced-choice ESP performance and extraversion thus appears to be artifactual.

PATTERNS OVER TIME

The forced-choice studies were reported between 1945 and 1982. There is a significant decline in the magnitude of the ESP/extraversion relationship over this period (r = -.40, t = -2.89, 43 df, p = .006, two-tailed). Moreover, methodological quality, as assessed in terms of threats to the validity of the ESP measure, has not improved over the survey period (r = .01, t = 0.03, p = .976, two-tailed). These results are contrary to the patterns found in meta-analyses of three other parapsychological domains, which exhibit constant effect sizes and significant methodological improvement over time (Honorton, 1985; Honorton & Ferrari, 1989; Radin & Nelson, 1989). There has been substantial improvement with regard to threats to the validity of the ESP/extraversion relationship; more recently reported studies have generally involved administration of the extraversion measure before the ESP task (r = .78, t = 7.02, 32 df, p <10^{-6}). These findings are consistent with the conclusion that the FC ESP/extraversion relationship is artifactual.

FC Outcomes by Investigator

The FC study outcomes by investigator are shown in Table 2. The order of ESP and extraversion testing is indicated following the investigator's name for investigators with single studies or multiple studies involving uniform testing order. Separate breakdowns are given for investigators with studies involving different testing orders. Significant outcomes were obtained by four of the 13 FC investigators (31%); using the investigator as the unit of analysis, the overall results are significant (z = 3.49, p = .00048, two-tailed) but nonhomogeneous (χ^2_{12}=41.20, p<.05). The effect of testing order accounts for the overall significance and non-homogeneity. The five investigators who measured extraversion before the ESP task have outcomes that are nonsignificant and homogeneous (z =-0.71, p = .761, two-tailed, χ^2_4=3.97, p>.05), while the outcomes of the eight investigators who measured extraversion after the ESP task are significant and nonhomogeneous (z=3.51, p=.00045, two-tailed, χ^2_7=17.29, p <.05). Thus, the impact of ESP/extraversion testing order is consistent across investigators and is not attributable to idiosyncratic research styles or other characteristics of a single prolific investigator.

Quality Analysis of Free-Response Studies

SENSORY LEAKAGE

All 14 FR studies satisfied our criteria for adequacy of control against sensory leakage.

Table 2
Forced-Choice Outcomes by Investigator

Investigator	N Studies	N Subjects	r	z	p
Astrom-?	1	48	.24	1.63	.103
Casper-A	1	20	.53	2.46	.014
Green	2	148	.00	0.00	.500
?	1	108	.00	0.00	.500
A	1	40	.00	0.00	.500
Humphrey	6	138	.26	2.86	.0042
?	3	55	.27	1.84	.0658
A	3	83	.22	1.95	.051
Kanthamani	7	301	.21	3.59	.00033
?	1	60	.00	0.00	.500
A	3	108	.38	4.03	.000056
B	3	133	.02	0.25	.400
McElroy-A	1	31	.00	0.00	.500
Nash	8	207	.14	1.92	0.54
?	2	60	.29	2.22	.026
A	6	147	.08	0.86	.390
Nielsen	3	60	-.04	-0.29	.771
A	2	48	.00	0.00	.500
B	1	12	-.23	-0.69	.755
Sargent	3	85	.17	1.46	.144
B	2	40	-.02	-0.12	.548
M	1	45	.31	2.07	.038
Shields-?	2	99	.30	2.98	.0029
Shrager-B	2	76	.18	1.48	.139
Szczygielski-A	1	17	-.36	-1.42	.922
Thalbourne-B	8	939	-.04	-1.28	.90

Overall forced-choice z by investigators = 3.49, p = .00048, two-tailed, $\chi^2_{12}=41.20$, p <.05. Extraversion measured before ESP test (5 investigators): z by investigators-0.71, p = .761, two-tailed, $\chi^2_4=3.97$, p>.05. Extraversion measured after ESP test (8 investigators): z by investgators = 3.51, p = .00045, two-tailed, $\chi^2_7=17.29$, p<.05.

Notes: r is the weighted average correlation coefficient (Hedges & Olkin, 1985). The letters B and A following the investigator's name indicate whether the extraversion/introversion measure was administered before (B) or after (A) the ESP task. Studies where this information is not available are indicated by a question mark (?). Testing order was mixed (M) in one study. X^2 is the within group homogeneity statistic (Rosenthal, 1984).

RANDOMIZATION

Nine FR studies satisfied our criteria for randomization (r =.38, z=4.74, p=.0000022, two-tailed). Five FR studies employed informal randomization procedures or failed to document their method of randomization (r=.14, z=2.86, p=.0042, two-tailed). The difference between the two correlations is significant (Cohen's q=.26, z=2.86, p=.0042, two-tailed).

DUPLICATE RECORDING

Thirteen of the 14 FR studies employed duplicate recording methods ($r=.29$, $z=4.62$, $p=.0000039$, two-tailed).

DUPLICATE CHECKING

All 14 FR studies employed duplicate checking methods.

A PRIORI DEFINITION OF EXTRAVERSION

Eleven FR studies satisfied our criteria for a priori definition of extraversion ($r=.16$, $z=3.72$, $p=.0002$, two-tailed). Three studies failed to document their basis of classification ($r=.48$, $z=4.01$, $p=.000061$, two-tailed). The two correlations differ significantly (Cohen's $q=.36$, $z=2.77$, $p=.0056$, two-tailed).

ORDER OF ADMINISTRATION OF EXTRAVERSION AND ESP MEASURES

The extraversion scale was administered before the ESP task in 11 of the FR studies ($r=.21$, $z=4.57$, $p=.000005$, two-tailed). The remaining three FR studies failed to report the order in which the ESP and extraversion measures were given ($r=.15$, $z=1.64$, $p=.101$, two-tailed). The difference between the two correlations is not significant (Cohen's $q=.06$, $z=0.62$, $p=.532$). Thus, for the free-response studies, the evidence for a relationship between ESP performance and extraversion is not susceptible to explanation in terms of an order artifact.

PATTERNS OVER TIME

The free-response studies were reported between 1960 and 1982. Unlike the forced-choice studies, the magnitude of the ESP/extraversion relationship has increased over time, though not significantly so ($r=.19$, $t=0.66$, 12 df, $p=.524$, two-tailed). The methodological quality of the free-response studies has also improved over time ($r=.36$, $t=1.35$, 12 df, $p=.202$, two-tailed).

Confirmation of Differences in Research Quality in Relation to Test Setting

Honorton & Ferrari (1980), in a meta-analysis of forced-choice precognition experiments, found that studies involving individual testing were of significantly higher methodological quality than studies involving group testing ($t=3.08$, 137 df, $p = .003$, two-tailed). We have confirmed this finding in the ESP/extraversion meta-analysis ($t=2.27$, 39 df, $p =.015$, one-tailed). This analysis excludes the 12 precognition studies which overlap with the earlier meta-analysis.

Since we have determined that there is no ESP/extraversion relationship in the forced-choice studies when the effects of task order are
considered, the remaining analyses are restricted to the free-response studies.

Consistency Across Investigators

Table 3 shows the overall FR results by investigator. Three of the
four investigators have significant ESP/extraversion correlations and the
results of the fourth investigator (Braud) approach significance. The z by
investigator is 5.11, a result that should arise by chance less than one time
in 3.3 million. The results are homogeneous across investigators (χ^2_3=2.51,
p>.05). Although 10 of the 14 FR studies were contributed by one investigator (Sargent), evidence for the relationship between free-response ESP
performance and extraversion is not dependent upon that investigator.
When Sargent's work is eliminated, the results of the three remaining
investigators still strongly support a relationship between ESP performance and extraversion (z = 3.35, p =.0008, two-tailed). Therefore, we
conclude that the ESP/extraversion relationship is consistent across investigators.

Extraversion Measures

Each FR investigator used a different scale for measuring extraversion. Marsh used the Bernreuter Personality Inventory (Super, 1942); Sargent and his group used the Cattell 16PF (Cattell, Eber, & Tatsuoka,
1970); Braud and Bellis & Morris used scales constructed by the investigators (with no psychometric validation provided). It is impossible to isolate the effects of the instruments for measuring extraversion from the
ensemble of procedures and research styles associated with the investigators. All that can be said is that a relationship between extraversion and
ESP performance is evident in studies using four different measures of
extraversion.

Selective Reporting

In order to assess the vulnerability of these studies to selective reporting, we used Rosenthal's (1984) "Fail-safe N" statistic to estimate the
number of unreported studies averaging null outcomes necessary to reduce
the known data base to nonsignificance. The Fail-safe N is 140 studies.
In other words, if we were to assume that the observed outcomes arise

Table 3
Free-response Outcomes by Investigator

Investigator	N studies	N subjects	r	z	p
Bellis & Morris	1	23	.47	2.26	.024
Braud	2	100	.19	1.86	.063
Marsh	1	311	.13	2.30	.021
Sargent	10	178	.31	3.85	.00012

z by investigators = 5.11, p = 3 × 10⁻⁷, two-tailed. χ^2_3=2.51, p>.05

Notes. r is the weighted average correlation coefficient (Hedges & Olkin, 1985). χ^2 is the within group homogeneity statistic (Rosenthal, 1984).

from selective reporting, it would be necessary to postulate 10 unreported studies averaging null outcomes for each reported study. Therefore, we conclude that the free-response ESP/extraversion relationship cannot be explained on the basis of selective reporting.

Power Analysis

The FR mean *r* of .20 is equivalent to an average ESP scoring advantage for extraverts over introverts of 0.14 standard deviations. The FR studies average sample size is 44 subjects and the likelihood of detecting a correlation of .2 at the five percent significance level with this sample size—the statistical power—is 37 percent (Cohen, 1977, p. 87). Thus, in a sample of 14 studies, the expected number of statistically significant studies is 5.2; the actual number of significant studies is seven (exact binomial probability, with *p* = .37 & *q* =.63, *r* = .23, one-tailed). Thus, the observed rate of significant outcomes is consistent with a correlation of .2.

Achievement of statistical significance, assuming a correlation of .2, is essentially a coin toss with sample size less than 68 subjects; a sample size of 180 is necessary to achieve 85 percent power.

In the following section, we explore the predictive validity of the ESP/extraversion meta-analysis by comparing the meta-analytic estimate to the outcome of a new data set.

A New Confirmation

Extraversion data is available for 221 of the 241 subjects in a series of ESP ganzfeld studies reported by Honorton, Berger, Varvoglis, Quant,

Derr, Hansen, Schechter, & Ferrari (1990) and conducted at the Psychophysical Research Laboratories (PRL) in Princeton, NJ. The experimental procedures are described in detail in the Honorton, et al. (1990) report.

Subjects

The subjects were 131 women and 90 men. Their average age is 37 years (sd = 11.7). This is a well-educated group; the mean formal education is 15.5 years (sd = 2.0) and belief in psi is strong in this population. On a seven-point scale where "1" indicates strong disbelief and "7" indicates strong belief in psi, the mean is 6.20 (sd = 1.03). Personal experiences suggestive of psi were reported by 88 percent of the subjects; eighty percent reported ostensible telepathic experiences. Eighty percent have had some training in meditation or other techniques involving internal focus on attention. One hundred and sixty-three subjects contributed a single ESP ganzfeld session and 58 contributed multiple sessions.

Extraversion Measure

Extraversion was measured using the continuous scores of the Extraversion/Introversion (EI) Scale in Form F of the Myers-Briggs Type Indicator (MBTI; Briggs & Myers, 1957). The MBTI was not used in any of the meta-analysis studies. The MBTI EI Scale is constructed so that scores below 100 indicate extraversion and scores above 100 indicate introversion. (For consistency with the meta-analysis, we have reversed the signs so that positive correlations reflect a positive relationship between ESP performance and extraversion.) The mean EI score for the PRL subjects is 100.36 (sd = 25.18).

ESP Measure

ESP performance was measured using the standardization ratings of the target and decoys (Stanford's z scores; Stanford and Sargent, 1983). Stanford z's were averaged for subjects with multiple sessions.

Results

OVERALL RESULTS

The correlation between ESP performance and extraversion in the PRL series is significant (r =.18, 219 df, t = 2.67, p =.008, two-tailed, 95%

CI from .05 to .30). This outcome is very close to the meta-analytic estimate for free-response studies ($r = .20$) and the difference between the two correlations is nonsignificant (Cohen's $q = .02$, $z = -0.26$, $p = .793$, two-tailed).

GANZFELD NOVICES

The results are similar if we restrict our analysis to the five PRL Novice series with inexperienced subjects who each completed a single ganzfeld session. MBTI data is available for 190 of the 205 Novices and the mean weighted r for the five series is .17 ($z = 2.25$, $p = .024$, two-tailed, 95% CI from .02 to .31). The ESP/extraversion correlations are homogeneous across the five series ($\chi^2_4 = 2.88$, $p > .05$). Eleven subjects in the first Novice series (Series 101) completed the MBTI between six and eighteen months after their ESP ganzfeld session and we did not maintain records of their identity. However, the results are essentially the same when this series is eliminated. The mean weighted r for the remaining four Novice series is .19 ($z = 2.30$, $p = .021$, two-tailed, 95% CI from .03 to .34).

OUTCOME BY EXPERIMENTER

Eight experimenters contributed to the PRL data base (Honorton et al., 1990). Table 4 shows the ESP/extraversion correlation by experimenter for the five Novice series. The mean weighted r for the eight experimenters is .16 ($z = 2.09$, $p = .037$, two-tailed, 95% CI from .01 to .30). The results are homogeneous across the eight experimenters ($\chi^2_7 = 6.43$, $p > .05$).

OUTCOME IN RELATION TO EI STATUS OF EXPERIMENTER

It is possible that the relationship between ESP performance and extraversion is moderated by personality characteristics of the experimenter. The last column of Table 4 shows the MBTI EI scores for each experimenter. Only two experimenters (Derr and Schlitz) are extraverts. Two others (Honorton and Quant) are borderline introverts. While the above analyses indicate that the ESP/extraversion correlation is consistent across experimenters, there is a nonsignificant tendency for the relationship to be stronger in the data of less introverted experimenters ($r = .47$, 6 *df*, $p = .235$, two-tailed).

Combined Estimate of the Relationship between Free-Response ESP Performance and Extraversion

Combining the new confirmation with the meta-analysis, the overall mean weighted r is .19 ($z = 5.50$, $p = 3.8 \times 10^{-8}$, 95% CI from .13 to

.26). The "Fail-safe N" for the combined estimate is 181 studies, or a ratio of 12 unreported studies averaging null effects for each known study. Four of the five investigators have overall significant outcomes and the outcomes are homogeneous across investigators ($\chi^2_4 = 6.03$, $p > .05$).

Discussion

The Meta-Analysis

FORCED-CHOICE STUDIES

The meta-analysis challenges the conclusions from earlier narrative reviews of the relationship between extraversion and forced-choice ESP performance (Eysenck, 1967; Palmer, 1977; Sargent, 1981). The apparent relationship between extraversion and ESP performance in these studies appears to be due to the influence of subjects' knowledge of their ESP performance on their subsequent responses to the extraversion measures. Evidence for a relationship between ESP and extraversion occurs only when extraversion was measured after the ESP test; no evidence of an ESP/extraversion relationship is found in studies where extraversion was measured before the ESP task.

Evidence for a nonzero effect in the forced-choice studies is also limited to the subset of studies involving ESP testing procedures that were vulnerable to potential sensory leakage. There is reason to believe, however, that this may result from a procedural confound: six of the eight studies in this subgroup for which information on the order of testing is available also involved extraversion testing following ESP feedback.

Table 4
ESP/Extraversion Correlations by
Experimenter in the PRL Novice Series

Experimenter	N Subjects	r	z	Experimenter EI scores
Honorton	41	.27	1.71	101
Quant	69	.29	2.38	103
Derr	22	.03	0.68	81
Berger	13	-.37	-1.18	115
Varvoglis	21	.08	0.32	133
Schechter	7	-.05	-0.10	125
Ferrari	10	-.20	-0.54	133
Schlitz	7	.15	0.92	69

Note. r is the weighted average correlation coefficient (Hedges & Olkin, 1985).

The apparent biasing effect of ESP feedback probably arises from one of two possibilities. Awareness of "success" or "failure" may lead subjects to later perceive themselves as more extraverted or introverted. Or, the problem may arise from an experimenter expectancy effect (Rosenthal & Rubin, 1978), in which subjects respond to the investigator's expectations that extraverts are more successful in ESP tests than introverts. Obviously, further research will be necessary to clarify the problem.

The existence of this problem, however, necessarily arouses concern over the viability of reported relationships between ESP performance and other personality factors such as neuroticism (Palmer, 1977). Much of the research in these areas was conducted by the same investigators, and it is likely that similar methods were used. We believe that conclusions regarding the relationship between ESP performance and other personality variables should be suspended until the relevant study domains can be examined with respect to this problem.

FREE-RESPONSE STUDIES

The meta-analysis does support the existence of a relationship between extraversion and free-response ESP performance. The free-response studies are not amenable to explanation in terms of an order artifact or other identifiable threats to validity. The overall correlation of .20 would be expected to occur only about one time in 674,000 by chance. Three of the four investigators contributing to this data base obtained significant ESP/extraversion relationships and the fourth investigator's results approach significance. The correlations are homogeneous across investigators, and across the largest grouping of studies in which subjects were tested individually. The effect remains highly significant even when 71 percent of the studies, contributed by one investigator, are eliminated from consideration. Thus, the relationship seems to be robust. Estimation of the filedrawer problem (Rosenthal, 1984), indicates that it would be necessary to postulate 10 unreported studies averaging null results for every retrieved study in order to account for the observed effect on the basis of selective reporting.

The New Confirmation

The results of the confirmation, involving a new set of investigators and a new scale of extraversion, support the meta-analytic findings and increase their generalizability. The relationship between free-response ESP performance and extraversion now spans 833 subjects and five independent investigator teams. The homogeneity of the effect across the eight experimenters in the confirmatory study further increases our confidence that the effect is replicable and not dependent upon unknown characteristics of individual investigators. A nonsignificant trend in the data does suggest that the ESP/extraversion relationship may, to some extent, be moderated by the experimenter's extravertedness and it may be advisable for future investigators to record and report extraversion/introversion scores of the experimenters.

The Predictive Validity of Meta-Analysis

Meta-analysis is a powerful tool for summarizing existing evidence. It enables more precise estimation of the significance and magnitude of behavioral effects than has been possible with traditional narrative reviews, and is useful in identifying moderating variables. In the present case, meta-analytic techniques revealed a serious source of bias that had been overlooked in earlier narrative reviews of the ESP/extraversion domain. Moreover, the meta-analysis identified a subset of the domain that is not amenable to the discovered bias and provided an estimate of the magnitude of the relationship between ESP and extraversion in that subset.

Ultimately, the usefulness of meta-analysis will be judged by its ability to predict new outcomes and in this regard we consider the results of the confirmation study to be especially noteworthy. The correlation between ESP performance and extraversion in the confirmation study is very close to that predicted by the meta-analysis. This is the second test of the predictive validity of meta-analysis in parapsychological problem areas; we have previously reported that ESP ganzfeld performance in a new series of studies (Honorton et al., 1990), closely matched the outcomes of earlier studies in a meta-analysis (Honorton, 1985). Predictability is the hallmark of successful science and these findings lead us to be optimistic concerning the prospect that parapsychology may be approaching this more advanced stage of development.

References

Studies used in meta-analyses are indicated by an asterisk. Some reports contain more than one study; for reports with multiple studies, the number of studies is indicated in brackets following the reference.

*Ashton, H.T., Dear, P.R., & Harley, T.A. (1981). A four-subject study of psi in the ganzfeld. *Journal of the Society for Psychical Research*, 51, 12–21.

*Astrom, J. (1965). GESP and the MPI measures. *Journal of Parapsychology*, 29, 292–293.

*Bellis, J., & Morris, R.L. (1980). Openness, closedness and psi [Abstract]. In W.G. Roll (Ed.), *Research in Parapsychology 1979*, 98-99. Metuchen, NJ: Scarecrow Press.
*Braud, L.W. (1976). Openness vs. closedness and its relationship to psi [Abstract]. In J.D. Morris, W.G. Roll, & R.L. Morris (Eds.), *Research in Parapsychology 1975*, 155-159. Metuchen, NJ: Scarecrow Press.
*Braud, L.W. (1977). Openness vs. closedness and its relationship to psi [Abstract]. In J.D. Morris, W.G. Roll, & R.L. Morris (Eds.), *Research in Parapsychology 1976*, 162-165. Metuchen, NJ: Scarecrow Press.
Briggs, K.C., & Myers, I.B. (1957). *Myers-Briggs Type Indicator Form F:* Palo Alto, CA: Consulting Psychologists Press, Inc.
*Casper, G.W. (1952). Effects of the receiver's attitude toward the sender in ESP tests. *Journal of Parapsychology*, 16, 212-218.
Cattell, R.B., Eber, H.W., & Tatsuoka, M.M. (1970). *Handbook for the Sixteen Personality Factor Questionnaire*. Champaign, IL: Institute for Personality and Ability Testing.
Cohen, J. (1977). *Statistical power analysis for the behavioral sciences* (Rev. Ed.). New York: Academic Press.
Eysenck, H.J. (1967). Personality and extra-sensory perception. *Journal of the Society for Psychical Research*, 44, 55-70.
*Fisk, G.W. (1960). The Rhodes experiment. Linkage in extra-sensory perception by M.C. Marsh. *Journal of the Society for Psychical Research*, 40, 219-239.
*Fisk, G.W., & Marsh, M.C. *Linkage in Extra-Sensory Perception*. Unpublished doctoral dissertation, Rhodes University, Grahamstown, South Africa.
*Green, C.E. (1966a). Extra-sensory perception and the Maudsley Personality Inventory. *Journal of the Society for Psychical Research*, 43, 285-286.
*Green, C.E. (1966b). Extra-sensory perception and the extraversion scale of the Maudsley Personality Inventory. *Journal of the Society for Psychical Research*, 43, 337.
*Haraldsson, E. (1970). Psychological variables in a GESP test using plethysmograph recordings. *Proceedings of the Parapsychological Association*, 7, 6-7.
*Harley, T.A., & Sargent, C.L. (1980). Trait and state factors influencing ESP performance in the ganzfeld [Abstract]. In W.G. Roll (Ed.), *Research in Parapsychology 1979*, 126-127. Metuchen, NJ: Scarecrow Press.
Hedges, L.V. (1987). How hard is hard science, how soft is soft science? The empirical cumulativeness of research. *American Psychologist*, 42, 443-455.
Hedges, L.V., & Olkin, I. (1985). *Statistical methods for meta-analysis*. New York: Academic Press.
Honorton, C. (1985). Meta-analysis of psi ganzfeld research: A response to Hyman. *Journal of Parapsychology*, 49, 51-92.
Honorton, C., & Ferrari, D.C. (1989). "Future telling": A meta-analysis of forced-choice precognition experiments, 1935-1987. *Journal of Parapsychology*, 53, 281-308.
Honorton, C., Berger, R.E., Varvoglis, M.P., Quant, M., Derr, P., Hansen, G., Schechter, E.I., & Ferrari, D.C. (1990). Psi communication in the ganzfeld: Experiments with an automated testing system and a comparison with a meta-analysis of earlier studies [Abstract]. In L.A. Henkel & J. Palmer (Eds.) *Research in Parapsychology 1989*, 25-32. Metuchen, NJ: Scarecrow Press.

Hyman, R. (1985). The psi ganzfeld experiment: A critical appraisal. *Journal of Parapsychology*, 49, 3–49.

*Humphrey, B.M. (1945). An exploratory correlation study of personality measures and ESP scores. *Journal of Parapsychology*, 9, 116–123. [3 studies].

*Humphrey, B.M. (1951). Introversion-extraversion ratings in relation to scores in ESP tests. *Journal of Parapsychology*, 15, 252–262.

*Kanthamani, B.K., & Rao, K.R. (1972). Personality characteristics of ESP subjects: III. Extraversion and ESP. *Journal of Parapsychology*, 36, 198–212.

*Kanthamani, B.K. (1966). ESP and social stimulus. *Journal of Parapsychology*, 30, 31–38.

*Krishna, S.R., & Rao, K.R. (1981). Personality and "belief" in relation to language ESP scores [Abstract]. In W.G. Roll & J. Beloff (Eds.), *Research in Parapsychology 1980*, 61–63. [2 studies]. Metuchen, NJ: Scarecrow Press.

McCarthy, D., & Schechter, E.I. (1986). Estimating effect size from critical ratios [Abstract]. In D.H. Weiner & D.I. Radin (Eds.), *Research in Parapsychology 1985*, 95–96. Metuchen, NJ: Scarecrow Press.

*McElroy, W.A., & Brown, W.K.R. (1950). Electric shocks for errors in ESP card tests. *Journal of Parapsychology*, 14, 257–266.

*Nash, C.B. (1966). Relation between ESP scoring level and the Minnesota Multiphasic Personality Inventory. *Journal of the American Society for Psychical Research*, 60, 56–62. [8 studies].

*Nicol, J.F., & Humphrey, B.M. (1953). The exploration of ESP and human personality. *Journal of the American Society for Psychical Research*, 47, 133–178.

*Nicol, J.F., & Humphrey, B.M. (1955). The repeatability problem in ESP-personality research. *Journal of the American Society for Psychical Research*, 49, 125–156.

*Nielsen, W. (1970a). Relationships between precognition scoring level and mood. *Journal of Parapsychology*, 34, 93–116.

*Nielsen, W. (1970b). Studies in group targets: A social psychology class. *Proceedings of the Parapsychological Association*, 7, 55–57.

*Nielsen, W. (1970c). Studies in group targets: An unusual high school group. *Proceedings of the Parapsychological Association*, 7, 57–58.

Palmer, J. (1977). Attitudes and personality traits in experimental ESP research. In B.B. Wolman (Ed.), *Handbook of Parapsychology*. New York: Van Nostrand Reinhold.

Palmer, J., & Lieberman, R. (1975). The influence of psychological set on ESP and out-of-the-body experiences. *Journal of the American Society for Psychical Research*, 68, 193–213.

Radin, D.I., & Nelson, R.D. (1989). Evidence for Consciousness-related anomalies in random physical systems. *Foundations of Physics*, 19, 1499–1514.

Rosenthal, R. (1984). *Meta-analytic procedures for social research*. Beverly Hills, CA: Sage.

Rosenthal, R., & Rubin, D.B. (1978). Interpersonal expectancy effects: The first 345 studies. *Behavioral and Brain Sciences*, 3, 377–386.

*Sargent, C.L. (1978). Hypnosis as a psi-conducive state: A controlled replication study. *Journal of Parapsychology*, 42, 257–275. [2 studies].

*Sargent, C.L. (1980). *Exploring psi in the ganzfeld*. New York: Parapsychology Foundation, Inc. [2 studies].

Sargent, C.L. (1981). Extraversion and performance in "extra-sensory perception" tasks. *Personality and Individual Differences*, 2, 137–143.

*Sargent, C.L., & Harley, T.A. (1981). Three studies using a psi-predictive trait variable questionnaire. *Journal of Parapsychology*, 45, 199–214.

*Sargent, C.L., & Matthews, G. (1982). Ganzfeld GESP performance with variable-duration testing [Abstract]. In W.G. Roll, J. Beloff, & R.A. White (Eds.), *Research in Parapsychology 1981*, 159-160. Metuchen, NJ: Scarecrow Press.

*Sargent, C.L., Bartlett, H.J., & Moss, S.P. (1982). Response structure and temporal incline in ganzfeld free-response GESP testing. *Journal of Parapsychology*, 46, 85–110. [2 studies].

*Sargent, C.L., Harley, T.A., Lane, J., & Radcliffe, K. (1981). Ganzfeld psi-optimization in relation to session duration [Abstract]. In W.G. Roll & J. Beloff (Eds.), *Research in Parapsychology 1980*, 82-84. Metuchen, NJ: Scarecrow Press.

*Shields, E. (1962). Comparison of children's guessing ability (ESP) with personality characteristics. *Journal of Parapsychology*, 26, 200-210. [2 studies].

*Shrager, E.F. (1978). The effects of sender-receiver relationship and associated personality variables on ESP scores. *Journal of the American Society for Psychical Research*, 72, 35–47. [2 studies].

Stanford, R.G., & Sargent, C.L. (1983). Z scores in free-response methodology: Comments on their utility and correction of an error. *Journal of the American Society for Psychical Research*, 77, 319–326.

Super, D.E. (1942). The Bernreuter Personality Inventory: A review of research. *Psychological Bulletin*, 39, 94–125.

*Szczygielski, D., & Schmeidler, G.R. (1975). ESP and two measures of introversion [Abstract]. In J.D. Morris, W.G. Roll, & R.L. Morris (Eds.), *Research in Parapsychology 1974*, 15-17. Metuchen, NJ: Scarecrow Press.

*Thalbourne, M.A., & Jungkuntz, J.H. (1983). Extraverted sheep versus introverted goats: Experiments VII and VIII. *Journal of Parapsychology*, 47, 49–51. [2 studies].

*Thalbourne, M.A., Beloff, J., & Delanoy, D. (1982). A test for the "extraverted sheep versus introverted goats" hypothesis [Abstract]. In W.G. Roll, J. Beloff, & R.A. White (Eds.), *Research in Parapsychology 1981*, 155–156. [2 studies]. Metuchen, NJ: Scarecrow Press.

*Thalbourne, M.A., Beloff, J., Delanoy, D., & Jungkuntz, J.H. (1983). Some further tests of the extraverted sheep versus introverted goats hypothesis [Abstract]. In W.G. Roll, J. Beloff, & R.A. White (Eds.), *Research in Parapsychology 1982*, 199–200. [4 studies]. Metuchen, NJ: Scarecrow Press.

Tukey, J.W. (1977). *Exploratory data analysis*. Reading, MA: Addison-Wesley.

CHAPTER 13

Comments on the Extraversion- ESP Meta-Analysis by Honorton, Ferrari, and Bem

John Palmer *and* James C. Carpenter

Among the most important contributions made by the late Charles Honorton were meta-analyses involving psi effects that had been studied in a sufficiently large numbers of experiments to merit such treatment (Honorton, 1985; Honorton & Ferrari, 1989; Honorton, Ferrari, & Bem, 1998). All of them had been published in the *Journal of Parapsychology* except the one involving ESP and the psychological trait of extraversion, a deficiency we are pleased to remedy in this issue. The principal conclusion from this latter meta-analysis was that there exists a positive relationship between extraversion and ESP scores, for both forced-choice and free-response measures of ESP, that is statistically significant ($p = 4 \times 10^{-6}$) although small in magnitude ($r = +.09$). More refined analyses led Honorton and his co-authors to conclude that for forced-choice ESP tests, the result was due to an artifact, namely, the effect of "subjects' knowledge of their ESP performance upon their responses to the extraversion measure" (Honorton et al., 1998, p. 255). The purpose of this short paper is to challenge this latter conclusion, or, to put it conversely, defend the legitimacy of the extraversion-ESP relationship for forced-choice experiments.

The general problem that underlies our disagreement with Honorton et al. has to do with confounded predictors. When we compare the

Reprinted with permission from *Journal of Parapsychology*, 1998, **62**, 277–282.

performance of two groups of subjects in a single experiment that is properly conducted, the two groups differ (whether in terms of their individual traits or the treatments administered to them) on only one factor or independent variable. Therefore, significantly different scores on the dependent variable can be attributed only to this one independent variable or predictor. However, such is not the case when the results of two groups of experiments are compared in a meta-analysis. Because such databases usually include studies designed by many different investigators who generally do not seek to address in a controlled fashion the relationship of interest to the meta-analyst, such comparability on extraneous variables is not to be expected. In other words, the two groups of studies may differ in many other ways besides the one the meta-analyst seeks to assess, and one of these may be the real cause of differences in scores on the dependent variable.

In the extraversion meta-analysis by Honorton et al., one independent variable of interest to the authors was whether subjects completed the extraversion questionnaire before or after they learned their ESP scores. They found that the positive extraversion-ESP correlation was only significant for those subjects who completed the extraversion scale after they took the ESP test, and thus after they knew their ESP scores. The authors offered two explanations for the results of these compromised studies. First, subjects' perception of their success or failure in the ESP task might have influenced how extraverted or introverted they perceived themselves to be. Second, the *experimenters'* knowledge of the ESP scores might have led to experimenter expectancy effects.

With regard to these explanations, it should be noted that the authors provided no rationale for their plausibility, nor did they provide any evidence that extraversion scales are susceptible to such biases. We were first moved to look into the authors' claim of an artifactual relationship because their explanations did not appear plausible to us. This is not for parapsychological reasons, but because of the nature of the measures of extraversion that the studies employed. Personality inventories have been constructed in such a way as to meet the criterion that the scores they produce are very nonreactive to a person's ongoing experiences—changes of mood or state of mind, etc. This psychometric aim has generally been achieved (e.g., Cattell, 1957; Gough, 1957; Kelly, 1955). Another way of putting this is to say that these instruments have high test-retest reliability. The proposed interpretations would require us to believe that feedback about an ESP test resulted in sizable mean shifts in scores that are known to be nonreactive to such minor perturbations.

A more direct test of Honorton et al.'s subject bias hypothesis was provided by Krishna and Rao (Experiment 2, 1991), who gave a forced-choice ESP test followed by Cattell's High School Personality Questionnaire (HSPQ) to 80 female Indian students, ranging in age from 15 to 19, in a group setting. Prior to taking the HSPQ half of the students were falsely told that they had all scored well above chance on the ESP test, whereas the other half were falsely told they had scored well below chance. The means of the two groups on the HSPQ extraversion scale did not differ significantly from each other (p = .53), which means that ESP feedback did not influence how subjects described themselves with respect to extraversion. Similar results were found with the HSPQ neuroticism scale.

Coding Changes

Honorton kindly gave copies of the raw data files used in the meta-analysis to Carpenter. He went through the reports of all 60 studies used in the meta-analysis to check on the accuracy of the coding with respect to order of testing. Of the 45 forced-choice studies, Honortor et al. had coded 16 as having given the extraversion test before the ESP test (EIPRE), and 18 as having given the extraversion test after the ESP test (EIPOST). Insufficient information was provided in the reports of the other 11 studies, which were classified as UNKNOWN.

Carpenter found no coding errors in the free-response studies, but he concluded that three of the forced-choice studies coded as UNKNOWN should have been coded as EIPRE (Sargent & Harley, 1981; Shields, 1962*), thereby raising the size of this group from 16 to 19 studies. This adjustment also raises the extraversion-ESP correlation in the EIPRE group from r = -.02 to r = +.01. The associated z is raised from −0.78 to +0.43, and the corresponding p-value is reduced from .782 to .334, one-tailed. Cohen's q, which the authors used to evaluate the difference between the correlation in the EIPRE group (+.01) and the corresponding one in the EIPOST group (+.17), is reduced from .25 to .16, z = 2.98, p = .003. The effect of these coding changes is trivial and they do not alter the authors' conclusions.

Confounded Predictors

Honorton et al. reported that the significant correlation between

The Shields (1962) report described two experimental series.

extraversion and ESP in the EIPOST group was entirely attributable to the 9 (of 18) studies where the degree of feedback was specified in the report. The authors noted that the 9 studies in which degree of feedback was not reported were mostly group experiments in which feedback, if given at all, is ordinarily delayed. It therefore seemed best to reclassify these studies as UNKNOWN, leaving the remaining 9 to constitute the EIPOST group (a decision made before the following analyses were undertaken).

Elsewhere in their paper, the authors noted that among forced-choice experiments in their meta-analysis there is a highly significant difference between studies in which subjects were tested individually and those in which they were tested in groups ($p = 5.2 \times 10^{-4}$). The significant extraversion-ESP correlation is contributed entirely by the studies using individual testing. Could this be a possible confound with order? To find out, we compared the group-testing status ("test setting") of the EIPRE and EIPOST subgroups. We found that all 9 of the EIPOST studies used individual testing whereas only 8 of the 19 EIPRE studies did. The resulting 2×2 contingency table yielded $p = .004$ by Fisher's Exact Test. Thus, there clearly is a confound between order of testing and test setting status as predictors of the extraversion-ESP relationship. Using the z-transformed correlation coefficients between extraversion and ESP as the dependent variable, we found that among the 19 EIPRE studies the correlation for the individual-testing studies was $r=+.21$, compared to $r=-.05$ for the group-testing studies. The difference is significant, $t(17) = 2.17$, $p = .045$. Finally, we combined order and test setting as predictors of the transformed extraversion-ESP correlations in a multiple regression analysis. The contribution of test setting is significant, $t = 2.22$, $p = .036$, whereas the contribution of order is not, $t = 0.93$, $p = .364$.

Disconfounding the Confound

The preceding analyses suggest that group-testing status, rather than order of testing, is the true mediator of the extraversion-ESP correlation. In this section, we report additional evidence in support of this conclusion. Three of the 9 studies in the EIPOST group were actually series in a larger experiment reported by Kanthamani and Rao (1972). All used very similar methodology, as did a fourth series in which the extraversion test was given before the ESP test. This series was appropriately placed in the EIPRE group by the authors. With the exception of different experimenters giving the ESP test, the only methodological difference that seemed to exist between Series 4 and the other three was order of testing (Kanthamani & Rao, 1971). Therefore, these studies, treated collectively, closely approach the kind of unconfounded manipulation of the order of testing that we ordinarily would find only in a single experiment. The results of the four series are presented in Table 1, which is a reproduction of Table 2 in Kanthamani and Rao (1972). Note that the outcome in "Ext. C" (the EIPRE series) is quite comparable to the net result of the other three series. The difference of 0.49 between the ESP means of extraverts and introverts in Exp. C is very similar to the mean difference of 0.56 in the combined results of the other three series. The published data only allowed a comparison of the two groups of series using the run as the unit of analysis. We compared the difference between the proportion of hits obtained by extraverts and introverts in the combined EIPOST (.023) series to the corresponding difference in the one EIPRE series (.020). The difference between the differences proved to be statistically negligible, $z = 0.12$, $p = .904$.*

These results from an unconfounded comparison reinforce the conclusion that in the Honorton et al. meta-analysis, the order effect upon the extraversion-ESP relationship is itself an artifact of test setting. That is to say, the reason why the EIPOST studies were more successful than the EIPRE studies is that they uniformly used individual testing, whereas most of the EIPRE studies used group testing. This view is also reinforced by the fact that individual testing was found to be superior to group testing in Honorton's meta-analysis of precognition experiments (Honorton & Ferrari, 1989). It is also possible that other, unrecognized confounding variables contributed to the problem.

The above outcomes mean that the order of testing artifact cannot be used as a basis for discounting the legitimacy of the positive extraversion-ESP correlation for forced-choice studies. The one other basis on which its legitimacy might be challenged is Honorton et al.'s finding that studies using suboptimal methods of preventing sensory cues yielded a significantly higher extraversion-ESP correlation than did studies using optimal methods ($p = .042$). However, we selected this marginal p-value post hoc from among a total of four methodological flaws evaluated, and it cannot withstand a correction for multiple analyses. Moreover, a correlation between the z-transformed correlation coefficients of the 45 forced-choice studies in the database and their overall quality codings was slightly positive, $r +.04$. Nonetheless, we do not think the finding

For the sake of completeness, it should be noted that Exp. B differed from all the other series in that the subjects were males rather than females. Removing Exp. B from the analysis would only serve to make the EIPRE-EIPOST difference even smaller.

Table 1
ESP Scores in Relation to Extraversion (From Kanthamani & Rao, 1972, p. 205)

	Pilot		Exp. A		Exp. B		Exp. C	
	Ext.	*Intr.*	*Ext.*	*Intr.*	*Ext.*	*Intr.*	*Ext.*	*Intr.*
N	14	8	19	31	17	19	14	24
Runs	112	64	152	248	136	152	112	192
Deviation	+50	-40	+20	-45	+64	-23	-6	-104
Mean hits per run	5.45	4.37	5.13	4.82	5.47	4.85	4.95	4.46
	t = 3.31 (20 *df*); P<.01[a]		t = 1.42 (*ns*)		t = 3.24 (34 *df*); P<.005[b]		t = 2.17 (36 *df*); P.025[b]	

[a]*Two-tailed.* [b]*One-tailed.*

about sensory cues can be completely discounted in assessing the validity of the extraversion-ESP relationship for forced-choice studies.

References

Cattell, R.B. (1957). *Personality and motivation: Structure and measurement.* Yonkers-on-Hudson, NY: World Books.

Gough, H.G. (1957). *Manual for the California Psychological Inventory.* Palo Alto, CA: Consulting Psychologists Press.

Honorton, C. (1985) Meta-analysis of psi ganzfeld research: A reply to Hyman. *Journal of Parapsychology*, 49, 51–92.

Honorton, C., & Ferrari, D.C. (1989). "Future Telling": A meta-analysis of forced-choice precognition experiments, 1935-1987. *Journal of Parapsychology*, 53, 281–308.

Honorton, C., Ferrari, D.C., & Bem, D.J. (1998). Extraversion and ESP performance: A meta-analysis and a new confirmation. *Journal of Parapsychology*, 62, 257–278.

Kanthamani, B.K., & Rao, K.R. (1971). Personality characteristics of ESP subjects: I. Primary personality characteristics and ESP. *Journal of Parapsychology*, 35, 189–207.

Kanthamani, B.K., & Rao, K.R. (1972). Personality characteristics of ESP subjects: III. Extraversion and ESP. *Journal of Parapsychology*, 36, 198–212.

Kelly, E.L. (1955). Consistency of the adult personality. *American Psychologist*, 10, 659–681.

Krishna, S.R., & Rao, K.R. (1991). Effect of ESP feedback on subjects' responses to a personality questionnaire. *Journal of Parapsychology*, 55, 147–158.

Sargent, C., & Harley, T.A. (1981). Three studies using a psi-predictive trait variable questionnaire. *Journal of Parapsychology*, 45, 199–214.

Shields, E. (1962). Comparison of children's guessing ability (ESP) with personality characteristics. *Journal of Parapsychology*, 26, 200–210.

CHAPTER 14

Further Studies of Relaxation as a Psi-Conducive State

Lendell W. Braud *and* William G. Braud

Introduction

In a recent paper in this *Journal* (Braud and Braud, 1973), we pre-sented preliminary data which suggested that progressive muscular relax-ation facilitates the receptive psi process. Subjects in states of deep muscular and mental relaxation (induced by a modified form of Jacob-son's progressive relaxation technique [1938]) scored dramatically high in seven GESP (free response; art print target) experiments. In those pre-liminary experiments, induction of actual physical and mental relaxation was confounded with *suggestions* of mental and physical relaxation and with suggestions that the induced state of relaxation was optimal for psi functioning. Additionally, we made no attempt to actually measure the degree of physical and mental relaxation produced in our subjects via the taped state-inducing instructions. In the two experiments reported here, we explored the role of relaxation in a more analytical manner. In Exper-iment 1, we found successful psi function to be related to degree of relax-ation when the latter was self-rated on a ten-point scale. In Experiment 2, an objective measure of degree of relaxation (electromyographic [EMG] recording from the frontalis muscle group) was found to be positively and significantly related to successful psi performance. Thus, these studies

Reprinted with permission from *Journal of the American Society for Psychical Research*, 1974, 68, 229–245.

begin to indicate that the relaxed state itself is conducive to good receptive psi functioning, when confounding factors such as different moods, attitudes, or expectancies are either eliminated or directly assessed.

Experiment 1: Psi and Self-Rated Degree of Relaxation

Subjects

The subjects were sixteen black students (six female, ten male) enrolled in an experimental psychology class at Texas Southern University. They were all junior or senior psychology majors and they were required to participate in the study as a course requirement. About their willingness to take part in the experiment, it might be said that they were interested but not wildly enthusiastic. None of the subjects had participated before in psi experimentation nor had they had any striking personal psi experiences; however, they would all be classified as "sheep."

Procedure

The subjects were tested individually, with L.W.B. serving as agent. Subject and agent occupied separate rooms, which were separated by a third intervening classroom (approximately forty feet wide). A session began with the subject sitting in a regular classroom desk-chair. It was explained that the purpose of the experiment was to investigate the effect of relaxation on the psi process. A tape recording containing instructions for physical and mental relaxation, identical to that appearing in Appendix 1 of our previous report (Braud and Braud, 1973), was played once so that the subject might become familiar with its contents. The procedure by which the subject would later rank target correspondences was then explained. Next, L.W.B. asked the subject to follow the taped instructions, started the tape recorder, then left the room, closing and locking the door behind her.

While L.W.B. walked to the agent's room, closed and locked the door behind her, and randomly selected the target for that session (see below), the tape recorder played instructions the subject was to follow in order to relax his entire musculature using an abbreviated version of Jacobson's progressive relaxation procedure. This procedure involved alternately tensing then relaxing each part of the body in turn until a profound state of muscular relaxation was produced. The subject then attempted to mentally relax, at first employing imagery of pleasant and relaxing scenes, then blanking his mind and becoming as passive as possible. Before achieving this relaxed state, the subject had been told that a particular target picture would be "transmitted" by L.W.B. and that he was to try to receive impressions about that picture. He was told that the state he was to enter was optimal for psychic functioning, that he would experience impressions of the target picture, and that he would be able to remember these impressions perfectly. The procedures and instructions played for fifteen minutes. There followed a five-minute impression period, indicated on the tape by a very low intensity "white noise." The subject was then instructed to return to his normal state of consciousness and was told (via the tape recorder) to remember his impressions and to record them (via written narrative and drawings) on specially prepared sheets which were to be used in later judging. The subject had been urged to distinguish true impressions from associations elicited by those impressions; i.e., he was urged not to interpret, intellectualize, analyze, or synthesize impressions. He also had been asked to attempt to distinguish target-relevant impressions from the sort of images evoked by the state itself—i.e., conventional meditation imagery. After recording his impressions, the subject indicated his degree of relaxation during the impression period on a ten-point scale (1 = extremely relaxed; 10 = extremely tense).

While the subject was relaxing, agent L.W.B., in her office, randomly selected a visual target from a pool of postcard-sized art reproductions and pictures clipped from magazines, without seeing any of the targets not selected. The targets were prepared and selected in a manner different form that described by Braud and Braud (1973). Here, the target pool consisted of twenty target sets or packs, each pack containing six pictures. The target packs had been prepared beforehand by W.G.B., who had attempted to use simple yet striking pictures and tried to make the six pictures within any given pack as dissimilar as possible (especially in *form*). Each picture (identified by a pressure sensitive label with a letter from *A* through *F*) was sealed in an opaque envelope (identified by a number from 1 through 6). Six such envelopes were enclosed in each of twenty larger opaque envelopes, each bearing a number between 1 and 20. After leaving the subject, agent L.W.B. randomly selected first a pack, then an envelope within that pack, through the use of a 40 row × 40 column table of random numbers in which the entry point was determined by two cuts of a well-shuffled deck of cards (bearing the numbers 1 through 40) and a coin toss (to determine row vs. column). The chosen envelope contained the target for that session; the pictures in the unchosen and unseen five envelopes within the same pack became the control alternative pictures.

The agent, while in a normal state of consciousness, opened the chosen envelope and concentrated for five minutes upon the selected target picture in terms of its raw sensory information (shapes, colors) and avoided "intellectualizing" the picture (i.e., she did not attempt to put the parts of the picture into words, did not try to associate to the picture, etc.). In addition to looking at the picture, the agent traced the outlines of the major shapes in the picture with her finger and also attempted to hallucinate textures, tastes, odors, and sounds that were portrayed in the picture but could not be directly sensed. This was done in an effort to involve all sensory modalities, not merely vision. During the impression period, the target was covered with a one-eighth inch thick sheet of glass to prevent sensory contamination of the target via heat, sweat, oil, or markings that might otherwise identify it. When she had concluded her five-minute attempt to "send" correct impressions, the agent recorded the letter of the target, returned it to its envelope, and replaced all six envelopes in the larger pack envelope (in proper numerical order). She then quietly placed the sealed pack of six pictures on a stool outside the subject's still-closed room, and returned to her office without sensorily encountering the subject.

After recording his impressions and rating his degree of relaxation, the subject opened the door, took the envelope into his room, opened it, and began judging the degree of correspondence between his own impression protocol and each of the six pictures. He had been asked to assign the rating of 1 to the picture which corresponded most to his impressions, and the rating of 6 to the one that corresponded least. The remaining four rankings were given to the intermediate correspondences. No ties or omissions were allowed. His ratings completed, the subject went to the agent's office, was given feedback about his success, and then was dismissed.

It had been decided to test each subject twice, with one day between sessions. The mean psi score and the mean relaxation score would serve as the data to be analyzed. When the subject returned for his second session, the procedure just described was repeated exactly.

Results

For statistical analysis, mean rankings of the correct target of 1 through 3 were classified as hits; rankings of the target of 4 through 6 were classed as misses. By this definition, there were 12 hits and 4 misses overall, yielding a binomial probability of .038. Thus, significant psi-hitting occurred in the experiment as a whole. The mean ranking for the correct target (across all subjects) was 2.78. There were three direct hits (rankings of 1 for the correct target).

When the subjects were dichotomized at the median into "good psi performers" (the eight subjects with the best mean psi scores) and "poor psi performers" (the eight subjects with the poorest mean psi scores), it was found that the good psi performers were significantly more relaxed than were the poor psi performers (Mann-Whitney $U = 14.5$, $n_1 = n_2 = 8$, $p < .04$). The good psi performers had a mean psi score of 1.69 and a mean self-rated relaxation score of 1.81, while the poor psi performers had a mean psi score of 3.88 and a mean self-rated relaxation score of 3.12.

Discussion

The results of this first experiment replicate and extend the earlier findings of Braud and Braud (1973) that a state of relaxation is conducive to good psi performance. While the subjects in the original study were all close friends and associates of the experimenters, those of the present study were unselected college students. The importance of this experiment lies in the finding that although all subjects listened to the same instructions, followed the same procedures and suggestions, and had similar expectancies about a successful outcome, they apparently responded to the tape differently (i.e., relaxed in different degrees) and these degrees of relaxation were in turn significantly related to degree of psi performance.

Experiment 2: Psi and EMG-Defined Relaxation

Since it might be argued that, in Experiment 1, relaxation was not adequately measured by the subjects' self-ratings, a more objective measure of relaxation was employed in Experiment 2. Degree of physical relaxation was measured by means of EMG recordings from the frontalis muscle group of the subjects. One group listened to tape recorded relaxation-inducing instructions, while another group listened to tension-inducing instructions. Thus, degree of relaxation was manipulated, objectively measured, and related to psi performance. A 16-item questionnaire (see Table 1 below) was administered which assessed self-rated physical and mental relaxation during various phases of the experiment and also taped several subjective variables believed to have an important effect upon psi performance: e.g., subjects' beliefs about ESP, mood and attitude (general and about certain specific aspects of the experiment), and certain "state" variables.

Subjects

The subjects were twenty white students (six female, fourteen male) enrolled at the University of Houston. Ten subjects were tested under relaxation conditions and ten under tension conditions. Random assignment to groups was done on the basis of a coin toss performed after the experimenter had instructed the subject and had left the room. Thus, the experimenter did not interact with the subject at any time (except after the session was completed) while knowing the group membership of that subject. Some of the subjects volunteered to serve; others served in order to fulfill various course requirements.

Procedure

The procedure was identical to that described in Experiment 1, with the following exceptions: (*a*) subjects were tested while sitting in a comfortable reclining chair in a soundproof, electrically shielded room; (*b*) the relaxation subjects listened to a relaxation tape identical to that used in Experiment 1, but with the muscular tension components removed; (*c*) there was added a tension group that listened to a tension-inducing tape (described below); (*d*) EMG recordings were taken throughout the session; (*e*) the ten-point scale used to indicate degree of relaxation was replaced by the 16-item questionnaire referred to above; and (*f*) the number of sessions per subject was reduced to one.

Two tape recordings were used in this experiment: one induced relaxation, the other induced tension. A new relaxation tape was recorded in which, as indicated above, instructions to tense muscle groups were omitted. Subjects were simply instructed to relax all muscle groups systematically from foot to head. Mental relaxation instructions and suggestions that relaxation was an optimal state for psi functioning remained on the tape. A new tension-inducing tape was recorded in which, essentially, all mentions of the word "relaxation" were replaced by the word "tension," along with appropriate changes in other wording where necessary. Subjects were instructed to tense all muscle groups in turn, from foot to head. There followed instructions for mental tension, alertness, activity, and arousal. Subjects listening to this tape were told that a tense, alert, ready state was optimal for psi functioning. The relaxation instructions were recorded in a slowly speaking voice and lasted twenty-five minutes; the tension instructions were recorded in a quickly speaking voice and lasted fifteen minutes. This reduction in the playing time of the tension tape was necessary so that the content would be the same as that covered in the relaxation tape, and so that subjects would not have to maintain tension for too long (and hence uncomfortable) a period.*

Before listening to the relaxation- or tension-inducing tapes, the subject completed the 16-item questionnaire designed to determine certain subjective factors believed to affect the psi process in an important manner. The questionnaire included three items which concerned belief in ESP; four items concerning the subject's mood and attitude toward the experiment, the experimenter (L.W.B., who was also the agent in this experiment), and the target picture; and nine items concerning the subject's "state" during various periods of the experiment. The state cluster included questions about the subject's feelings of physical and mental relaxation or tension at the beginning of the session and during the impression period, about his belief that the induced state was conducive to psi functioning, and about his state of consciousness and body awareness during the impression period. Subjects self-rated each item on a ten-point scale. They did not rate items 9, 12, 14, 15, and 16 (which concerned the impression period) until after they had returned to a normal state of consciousness at the end of the session, but before they recorded their impressions. Item 7 (which concerned the target picture) was not rated until after the impression-target correspondences were judged, but before the subject was informed which picture was actually the target. The entire questionnaire appears in Table 1.

Electromyographic activity was recorded through the use of a system similar to that described by Budzynski and Stoyva (1969) and by Green, Walters, Green, and Murphy (1969), with the important exception that feedback was not provided the subject. Electrical activity of the frontalis muscle group was amplified, filtered, and recorded on an oscillograph. We defined EMG activity as bioelectrical activity within the range 20-200 H_z and greater than a minimal amplitude which was adjusted for each subject. The minimal amplitude was determined during a pre-baseline adjustment period, lasting one to three minutes, and consisted of that amplitude (in microvolts) which the subject exceeded twenty per cent of the time. In practice, a sensitivity (threshold) control in a detector circuit was adjusted to a level which showed the presence of EMG activity (indicated by the running of a cumulative clock) for twelve seconds out of each minute. The apparatus remained at this setting throughout the session. The frontalis group was chosen because its tension level is believed to be a good index of general physical and mental

*Transcripts of these two tapes are on file at the A.S.P.R. Photocopies are available at cost upon request. — Ed.

Table 1
Questionnaire Items Regarding Belief, Mood, Attitude, and State

1. Do you believe in ESP?
2. Do you believe that scoring greater than chance (good scoring due to good ESP) can occur in an experiment such as the one you are now participating in?
3. Do you believe that you will score above chance in *this* experiment?
4. How is your mood today?
5. To what extent are you in the mood to participate in this ESP experiment?
6. Rate your attitude or feeling concerning the experimenter in this experiment.
7. How well do you like the target picture?
8. Describe your physical state right now, at this very moment.
9. Describe your physical state during the five-minute impression period.
11. Describe your mental state right now, at this very moment.
12. Describe your mental state during the five-minute impression period.
14. How much do you believe that the state you were in during the impression period could facilitate ESP?
15. During the impression period, was your state of consciousness about the same as it normally is or was it different? How similar or how different?
16. During the impression period, was your awareness of your body (feelings, sensations, etc.) the same as usual or was it altered?

Note: All items were rated by the subjects on a ten-point scale beneath each item.

activity (Budzynski and Stoyva, 1973). The twenty per cent "EMG threshold" was used so that the relative sensitivity of our apparatus would be the same for all subjects and so that their EMG activity could be more directly compared. Absolute EMG amplitude was also available as an ink-written readout on chart paper which could later be measured in terms of its microvoltage. Our major EMG measurement was "number of tension seconds during a five-minute epoch." This measure was read directly from a cumulative electric clock (accurate to 1/100 sec.) and indicated the amount of time a subject's EMG level exceeded his own twenty per cent threshold amplitude during the immediately preceding five minutes. Such "tension seconds" measures were recorded during a five-minute baseline period in which the subject sat quietly, with eyes open, in the dimly illuminated shielded room; then during successive five-minute periods during which the subject followed the taped state-inducing instructions (five such periods for relaxation subjects and three periods for tension subjects). Finally, EMG was recorded during the five-minute impression period.

At the end of the session, the tape directed the subject to remove the forehead electrodes and gave instructions concerning the judging of the target correspondences. The procedures for selecting the targets, conveying the packets to the subjects, and judging and scoring correspondences were all identical to those already described in Experiment 1.

Results

In order to facilitate communication, we will present the results of this experiment in several numbered sections:

1. The overall experiment yielded evidence for significant psi hitting: fifteen subjects obtained hits (rankings of 1 through 3) while five subjects obtained misses (rankings of 4 through 6), yielding a binomial probability of .021.

2. The tape-recorded instructions were effective in altering the subjects' physical and subjective states. The relaxation tape produced a significant within-subjects decrement from beginning to end of session in EMG-defined muscle tension (Wilcoxon matched-pairs signed-ranks test, $T = 0$, $p < .005$, one-tailed), while the tension tape produced a significant within-subjects increment in EMG-defined muscle tension (Wilcoxon $T = 7$, $p < .025$, one-tailed). During the impression period, the EMG-defined muscle tension of relaxation subjects was significantly lower than that of tension subjects (Mann-Whitney $U = 8$, $p < .001$, one-tailed).

The relaxation tape produced a significant within-subjects decrement in self-rated physical tension (Wilcoxon $T = 3.5$, $p < .01$), while the tension tape produced a significant within-subjects increment in self-rated physical tension ($T = 0$, $p < .005$). During the impression period, the self-rated physical tension of relaxation subjects was significantly lower than that of tension subjects ($U = 3$, $p < .001$).

The relaxation tape produced a slight, nonsignificant within-subjects decrement in self-rated mental tension, while the tension tape produced a significant within-subjects increment in self-rated mental tension ($T = 0$, $p < .005$). During the impression period, the self-rated mental tension of relaxation subjects was significantly lower than that of tension subjects ($U = 2.5$, $p < .001$).

These tape-induced changes in EMG, physical state rating, and mental state rating are presented graphically in Figure 1.

3. Subjects listening to relaxation instructions performed significantly better on the psi task than did subjects listening to tension instructions. Relaxation subjects scored nine hits and one miss (binomial $p = .011$), while tension subjects scored six hits and four misses (binomial $p = .377$). The psi performance of the relaxation subjects (mean score =

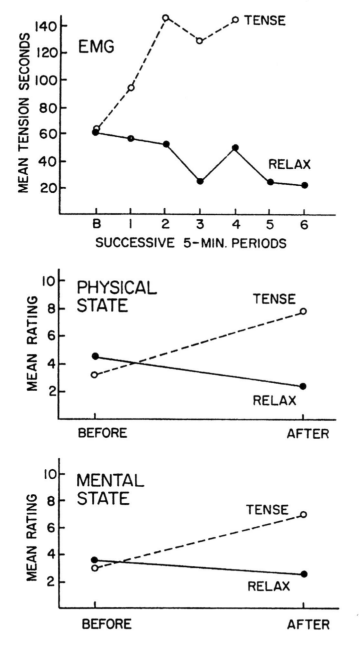

Figure 1. Changes in EMG-defined tension, self-rated physical state, and self-rated mental state measures for relaxation versus tension subjects.

2.0) was significantly superior ($U = 21$, $p < .025$) to that of the tension subjects (mean score = 3.4).

4. The relaxation and tension groups did *not* differ significantly in terms of other variables which might have important influences on the psi process (i.e., belief, mood, attitude, certain other states). Thus, the relaxation/tension effect was *not* confounded by differences between the two groups in expectancy or other subjective variables. The means, Mann-Whitney U values, and probabilities for all variables measured are given in Table 2. It was predicted that the two randomly constituted groups would not differ on any of the variables measured except those that would be altered through following the taped instructions. The groups did indeed differ only in terms of the predicted variables (those marked by asterisks).

5. There was a significant positive correlation between psi performance (over all twenty subjects) and (*a*) degree of EMG-defined, subjectively-rated physical relaxation and subjectively-rated mental relaxation during the impression period; and (*b*) degree of *shift* toward more relaxed

Table 2
Summary of Questionnaire Responses, EMG Measures, and Psi Scores for the Tension and Relaxation Groups of Experiment 2

Variable	Mean Scores Relaxation	Tension	U	p
1. Belief in ESP	2.3	3.3	30	n.s.
2. ESP possible in this experiment	3.1	2.5	46	n.s.
3. Personal success in this experiment	4.9	5.7	36.5	n.s.
4. General mood today	3.2	3.6	46	n.s.
5. Mood to participate in this experiment	2.8	1.9	28.5	n.s.
6. Attitude toward experimenter	2.1	2.1	49	n.s.
7. Liking for the target picture	3.7	4.2	43.5	n.s.
8. Initial physical state	4.6	3.1	29.5	n.s.
9. Impression physical state*	2.3	7.9	3	<.001
10. Physical state shift*	-2.3	+4.8	2	<.001
11. Initial mental state	3.6	3.0	31.5	n.s.
12. Impression mental state*	2.7	7.0	2.5	<.001
13. Mental state shift*	-0.9	+4.0	4	<.001
14. Belief that state is conducive to psi	2.4	3.5	33.5	n.s.
15. State of consciousness (impression period)	4.7	5.7	35	n.s.
16. Body awareness (impression period)	5.9	5.0	42	n.s.
17. Initial EMG (tension-seconds)	57.5	94.0	27	=.05
18. Impression EMG*	23.9	146.2	8	<.001
19. EMG shift*	-33.6	+52.2	11	<.01
20. Psi score*	2.0	3.4	21	<.025

	Relaxation	Tension
	9 hits	6 hits
Note: Predicted variables are	1 miss	4 misses
marked by asterisks.	$p = .011$	$p = .377$

EMG-defined, self-rated physical relaxation and self-rated mental relaxation values from beginning to end of the session. There was no significant correlation between initial EMG level, initial physical relaxation rating, or initial mental relaxation rating and psi performance. These Spearman rank-order correlations and their associated probability values are given in Table 3.

      6. EMG level, physical state rating, and mental state rating all intercorrelated positively and significantly, whether measured in terms of their initial values, their impression period values, or their degree of shift from beginning to end of the session. This indicates that the subjects were accurately aware of their tension or relaxation levels and that their subjective ratings correlate well with objective bioelectrical measurements of degree of relaxation. The most interesting of these correlations are reported in the correlation matrix of Table 3.

Discussion

      The results of this second experiment further confirm and extend the earlier findings of Braud and Braud (1973) and the findings of the first experiment reported above. Subjects without any prior history of striking psychic experiences are shown to demonstrate reliable psi abilities while in a state of physical and mental relaxation. This psi-conducive state was induced through the simple expedient of having the subjects listen to and follow tape-recorded instructions involving progressive relaxation of all muscle groups and imaging of pleasant relaxing scenes. While Braud and Braud earlier merely demonstrated that the "relaxation state" *may* be psi-conducive, it was not until the first experiment reported here that psi performance was directly related to the degree to which the relaxed state was present in the subjects. In the second experiment, the problem of confounded variables was attacked more systematically. The relaxed subjects did not differ from the tense subjects in their belief about the possibility of ESP (generally, or in themselves in this particular experimental setting), or in their belief that the state they were in was conducive to psi success. The two groups did not differ in terms of their moods or their attitudes toward the experiment, the experimenter, or the target picture. Thus, various important subjective (psychological) factors which previously have been shown to influence psi performance were equated in our two groups. As far as we are presently able to determine, our groups differed only in terms of the degree to which they entered a relaxed state. In our work, we have indexed this relaxed state by EMG measurements

Table 3
Spearman Rank-Order Correlation Matrix

	Psi	Initial EMG	Impression EMG	EMG shift	Initial physical state	Impression physical state	Physical state shift	Initial mental state	Impression mental state	Mental state shift
Psi										
Initial EMG	+.12									
Impression EMG	+.49*									
EMG shift	+.52*									
Initial physical state	−.25									
Impression physical state	+.53*	+.67†								
Physical state shift	+.49*		+.67†							
Initial mental state	−.14				+.72†					
Impression mental state	+.49*	+.57†				+.81†				
Mental state shift	+.49*		+.52*				+.82†			

*p <.05. †p<.01

and by subjects' self-ratings of degree of physical and mental relaxation (or tension).

We suggest that a relaxed state is favorable to the occurrence of receptive psi (telepathy, clairvoyance, precognition). We believe that the measures we employed are only a few of a large number of valid indices or "symptoms" of what we are calling the "relaxation state." Other indices which either have already been used or might be used in future research include: lowered frequency and increased amplitude of EEG activity (i.e., a shift toward alpha, alphoid, and theta frequencies); lowered sympathetic arousal, as measured by a decrement in heart- or pulse-rate, blood pressure, or vasomotor activity; lowered spontaneous or elicited skin response activity; heightened basal skin resistance; reduced oxygen consumption; reduced breathing rate; reduced blood lactate level; and so on. These various physiological indications would constitute a *syndrome*, the presence of which is hypothesized to be psi-conducive.

At the psychological level, the presence of the relaxation syndrome would be revealed through the manifestations of Deikman's "receptive mode" (1971): diffuse attending, paralogical thought processes, decreased boundary perception, dominance of the sensory over the formal, and decreased negative emotionality (e.g., anger, anxiety). There should also occur a shift in dominance away from left-hemispheric and toward right-hemispheric functioning (Ornstein, 1972). Such a shift would be indicated (or could be measured) by a reduction in verbal, mathematical, temporal, abstract, analytical, lineal, digital, rational, and conscious functioning; with a concomitant increase in imagery, spatial, concrete, holistic, non-lineal, analogical, intuitive, and unconscious functioning. Behaviorally, the left- to right-hemisphere shift should be accompanied by an increased incidence of "left-looking," i.e., movement of the eyes to the left while engaging in reflective thought (see Bakan, 1971). Phenomenologically, the relaxation state should be accompanied by the types of mental content typically elicited by various meditative and biofeedback procedures: changes in body awareness, a more inward focusing of attention, feelings of unity, changes in the sense of time, experience of the void, ineffable experiences, and so on. Additionally, the relaxation state might be accompanied by increased hypnotic susceptibility, increased dreaming or reverie, and increased creativity.

Since the relaxation state itself is hypothesized to be psi-conducive, any of its manifestations should facilitate the psi process. Several of these manifestations have been measured and have been positively related to good psi performance by various parapsychologists; others await documentation. Similarly, any technique which induces a shift toward a greater relaxation state should also facilitate psi. The technique employed successfully in the present experiments is progressive muscular relaxation, along with suggestions of mental quietude. Other investigators have facilitated ESP through the use of hypnosis, meditative exercises, biofeedback, and other consciousness-altering devices. We suggest that all such attempts are successful to the extent that they produce a shift toward the relaxation state. The greater the number of effective techniques used and the greater the number of indices which actually change, the more dramatic the shift and the more dramatic should be the degree of psi-facilitation obtained.

Finally, some speculations are in order regarding the mechanism of action and the adaptive significance of relaxation as a psi-conducive state. One model which might clarify the role of relaxation in psi functioning is the "optimal level of arousal" model so frequently noted in motivational psychology (Hebb, 1966). According to this model, there is an optimal level of arousal or activation for the efficient performance of a task, and this optimal level decreases as a function of task difficulty. Difficult or relatively unpracticed tasks are disrupted by even moderate increments in arousal, while easy or well-practiced tasks suffer only when arousal is very greatly increased. We would expect a task such as ESP, since it does appear to be so difficult and is practiced so little, to function best at very low activation levels. Even the activation level of normal consciousness, which is low enough to be optimal for many difficult non-psi tasks, may be too high for effective psi performance. We speculate that procedures which induce the relaxation state reduce activation or arousal to a level low enough so that psi is no longer disrupted. Stated in other words, an inverted U-shaped function should be found to relate good psi performance to level of arousal, and the peak of such a nonmonotonic curve should correspond to an extremely low activation level, much lower than levels previously found to be optimal for very difficult non-psi tasks. At present, we are attempting to determine the exact nature of this function by relating psi performance to degree of activation or arousal as measured by EMG, EEG, and autonomic nervous system activity.

Another finding of motivational psychology which is of interest to us is the observation that ordinary sensory functioning improves with increased arousal or activation (up to a point, of course). Thus, our regular senses function best and we can process external information best when our organisms are in states of relatively high arousal (Budzynski and Stoyva, 1973; Fuster, 1959). But if all information input channels functioned in this way, organisms in deeply relaxed states (characterized by extremely low arousal or activation) such as sleep, etc., would be deprived of information about the external world during these episodes and would be virtually helpless. It is reasonable to assume that the selective pressure of evolution would have favored the development of other types of information processors (the so-called "extrasensory" processes) which not only did not decline in efficiency with decrements in arousal, but even *increased* in efficiency. These information processors (which have come to be recognized as the various receptive psi processes) would serve the very adaptive function of detecting (especially) information about threatening environmental events and (at the very least) alerting the relaxed organism to a higher level of arousal at which the regular senses could now provide the organism with life-saving information. Such speculation assumes that effective psi functioning is present not only in man, but in any living organism in which a (low arousal, low activation) metabolic trough might reduce regular sensory ability and render that organism helpless to deal with external threats to its well-being (especially predation). A testable prediction of this model is that psi should occur most in those species which enter low arousal states frequently and which are especially vulnerable to predation. Psi should occur least in species which enter low arousal states very infrequently and/or are not likely to be preyed upon. Another prediction is that any variable or set of variables which reduce normal sensory functioning should also increase psi functioning. Studies of sensory isolation, pattern deprivation, or sensory overload suggest themselves as interesting tests of the model.

References

Bakan, P. The eyes have it. *Psychology Today*, 1971, 4, 64.

Braud, W.G., and Braud, L.W. Preliminary explorations of psi-conducive states: Progressive muscular relaxation. *Journal of the American Society for Psychical Research*, 1973, 67, 26–46.

Budzynski, T.H., and Stoyva, J.M. An instrument for producing deep muscle relaxation by means of analog information feedback. *Journal of Applied Behavior Analysis*, 1969, 2, 231–237.

Budzynski, T.H., and Stoyva, J.M. Biofeedback techniques in behavior therapy. In D. Shapiro and others (Eds.), *Biofeedback and Self-Control*, 1972. Chicago: Aldine, 1973. Pp. 437–459.

Deikman, A. Bimodal consciousness. *Archives of General Psychiatry*, 1971, 25, 481–489.

Fuster, J.M. Effects of stimulation of brain stem on tachistoscopic perception. *Science*, 1958, 127, 150.

Green, E.E., Walters, E.D., Green, A.M., and Murphy, G. Feedback technique for deep relaxation. *Psychophysiology*, 1969, 6, 371–377.

Hebb, D.O. *A Textbook of Psychology.* Philadelphia: Saunders, 1966.
Jacobson, E. *Progressive Relaxation.* (2nd ed.) Chicago: University of Chicago Press, 1938.
Ornstein, R. *The Psychology of Consciousness.* San Francisco: Freeman, 1972.

CHAPTER 15

ESP Card Tests of College Students with and without Hypnosis

Jarl Fahler *and* Remi J. Cadoret

Introduction

The research reported here is a continuation of earlier experiments by J.F. with ESP cards in Finland (Faher, 1957). In that work, tests were conducted with four selected adults in an attempt to get better ESP results when the subjects were under hypnosis than when they were in the waking state. On the strength of the findings of that investigation, it seemed safe to suggest that hypnosis might provide the experimenter with a way of helping the subject to concentrate his efforts upon the ESP task and to strengthen his interest in his performance. However, it was clear that there was still room for different opinions about the exact role of hypnosis in psi experiments with ESP cards.

After the experiments in Finland, J.F. was invited to spend some time in the Parapsychology Laboratory of Duke University for the purpose of doing further work along the same lines. The first objective of the American work was to see if the highly significant scoring obtained by hypnotized subjects in the Finnish experiment could be maintained in the new situation. An affirmative answer to this question would have great importance at the present stage of ESP research because of its possible relevance to the problem of reliably controlling psi performance.

Reprinted with permission from *Journal of Parapsychology*, 1958, **22**, 125–136.

General Procedure

The experiments presented in this paper were conducted in the Parapsychology Laboratory between the end of August, 1957, and the beginning of February, 1958. The subjects were college students who volunteered their services. Their volunteering for the tests and continuing to participate probably depended on numerous factors, such as their interest in psi and social atmosphere set by the experimenters. The experiments can be divided into three sections which are roughly chronological, but with some overlapping within the total period covered by the work.

The aim of the first tests (Section A) was to see if successful ESP performance could be obtained in the experimental situation when informal test conditions were used. Most of this first work was done as GESP tests in which either the experimenter or a co-experimenter acted as "sender," or agent, and was in the same room with the subject. But there were also some tests for clairvoyance using either a BT or DT technique. No effort was made at this stage to test each subject with an equal number of runs in the waking state and in hypnosis. However, the results were impressive enough to justify going on to the more formal tests for clairvoyance subsequently introduced in Sections B and C. The results of Section A are presented as a background for this research and not as the basis for any conclusion.

Sections B and C represented two general advances beyond the exploratory conditions of Section A. In the first place all of the tests were for clairvoyance (either the BT or DT technique). In the second place, each subject was tested to the same extent in the waking state and under hypnosis within the same session. In section B, the number of runs varied from session to session, but they were always equally divided between the two conditions. In half of the sessions hypnosis was used first and in the others it was used last. In Section C all sessions were of the same length: three runs in the waking state followed by three in hypnosis, or vice versa. Thus during both B and C, half of each subject's trials in each session were made in the waking state and half under hypnosis. The co-experimenter in Section B was sometimes an undergraduate and sometimes R.J.C. or another laboratory staff member. In Section C, the co-experimenter was always R.J.C. During the sessions of Section C the subjects were in a Faraday cage, and an electroencephalogram was taken in the attempt to find out if there is any relationship between ESP and changes in the alpha brain wave pattern. The results of the EEG investigation are not included here, but will be given in a later paper.

Test Methods and Conditions

Closed packs of the standard ESP cards were used for all the tests. Before each run, the pack was given five dovetailed shuffles followed by a cut. A detailed description of the conditions in the three sections follows:

Section A

This section consisted primarily of exploratory GESP tests designed to introduce the subjects to card-calling. The subject was screened from the cards although the agent remained in the same room with the subject. The experimenter recorded the subject's calls and, as soon as the run was finished, recorded the target order with the agent looking on. The agent in most cases was a university student. In some few sessions, when no agent was available, J.F. acted both as agent and as recorder of the calls and cards.

Tests for clairvoyance were done with the BT or the DT technique in which the cards were screened from the sight of the subject. In the majority of sessions, both an experimenter and a co-experimenter were present. Either the experimenter handled the cards while the co-experimenter recorded the subject's calls, or vice versa. When there was no co-experimenter, the experimenter handled the cards and recorded at the same time. At the end of the session, the card order was recorded and the hits were checked by the experimenter, with the subject (and the co-experimenter if there was one) observing.

In the BT tests, here and throughout the whole experiment, a special box was used to hold the cards during the run and to facilitate the one-by-one removal of the top cards from the pack as the calls progressed. The box was shallow and long enough to accommodate the shuffled pack in one end and the cards that had already been called in the other end. These two sections of the box were separated by a low, curved middle partition; and as each card on the top of the pack was called by the subject, it was removed and placed in position in the other section of the box by the experimenter. Each card was transferred by merely touching the back lightly with one finger and sliding it across the partition into the other section of the box. The use of this apparatus served two purposes: it facilitated the handling of the cards; and it provided assurance against sensory cues from the face of the card since there was no need to lift the cards at all in handling them.

Section B

The tests in Section B, which were all clairvoyance, were also carried out with the subject screened from the sight of the cards. Sometimes the experimenter recorded the subject's calls and the co-experimenter handled the cards; sometimes they exchanged roles. The co-experimenter on almost all occasions was an undergraduate student assistant, and since the same student was not available for all of the tests, several different co-experimenters were used. In most sessions, however, the co-experimenter was Mr. Charles Egerton. After each session, the experimenter, the co-experimenter, and the subject checked the hits.

Section C

In this section of the investigation, two members of the research staff were present at all times during the tests. The subject was inside the Faraday cage lying prone in a deck chair. J.F. was inside the cage with him. The other experimenter, R.J.C., who operated the EEG apparatus outside the cage, shuffled and cut a pack of ESP cards and placed them on a table or chair in the special open box previously described. The sides of this box were high enough so that, when it was at the same level as the subject's head, the subject could not see the backs of the cards even if his eyes were open. (Since EEG records were taken concurrently with the subject's ESP calls, the subjects were kept in a prone position with their eyes closed.)

When the face-down pack was in the box ready to be used, R.J.C. handed the box to J.F. in the cage and the subject proceeded to go through the ESP run. As J.F. moved each card from the top of the pack to the second compartment of the box, he indicated to the subject, by saying "Now" or "Next," that the card was in position and he was ready to record the subject's call. When the run was completed, the box containing the target cards was passed out of the cage to R.J.C., who recorded the target order. He then reshuffled, cut, and returned the pack to the box for the next run. At the conclusion of the six runs of the session (three in the waking state and three in hypnosis, or vice versa), the target card order was given to J.F., who covered the call record for each run and recorded the target order on his record sheet with both R.J.C. and the subject witnessing. The hits were circled and the score was then counted for each run. This procedure was followed in all BT runs.

One subject made his calls with the DT method. In these tests, R.J.C. alone handled the cards, shuffling and cutting them for each run, placing them in the box used for the BT tests, and keeping the box somewhere out of sight of the subject. J.F., in the Faraday cage, recorded the subject's calls as usual, and the run of 25 trials was made without removing any of the cards from the top of the pack. At the conclusion of each run, R.J.C. recorded the target card order, both experimenters checked the hits, and R.J.C. reshuffled the cards for the next run. These DT tests, then, where even the experimenter did not see the backs of the cards, represent the most thoroughly controlled part of the experiment. As may be seen in Table 5, the hypnosis results of the subject who used the DT method were independently significant and were comparable in scoring level to the results of the other subjects with the BT method.

During all of these tests in which the EEG record was taken, the subject was in a prone position, as previously noted, and was required to make his calls softly and without overt movement in order that a good EEG record could be obtained. In both the waking and hypnotic states, the subject's eyes were closed, and during the hypnotic part of the session the room was partly darkened.

Results

Section A: Introductory and Exploratory

The total of 46 runs in hypnosis in the clairvoyance part of the experiment gave a deviation of +48, which, with a standard deviation of 13.56, corresponds to a significant critical ratio* of 3.54, as shown in Table 1. The tests in the waking state (46 runs) produced a deviation of +36 and a CR of 2.65, which is also significant. The hypnosis and waking parts together gave a deviation of +84. The standard deviation here is 19.18 and there is a highly significant CR of 4.38. The GESP part of the experiment is also shown in Table 1.

Table 1
GESP and Clairvoyance Results of Section A with Subjects in Waking and Hypnotic States

Method	Waking State				Hypnotic State			
	Runs	*Hits*	*Dev.*	*CR*	*Runs*	*Hits*	*Dev.*	*CR*
Clairvoyance	46	266	+36	2.65	46	278	+48	3.54
GESP	67	378	+43	2.63	102	638	+128	6.34

*In this report, critical ratios have been given for those results that are significant with a probability of .01 or smaller. The probability value in every instance has not been given.

As already mentioned, no conclusions should be drawn from the results presented in Table 1, except that this exploratory work certainly justified the investigations in sections B and C, the results of which are presented in Tables 2-5.

Section B: Waking-Hypnosis Tests
with Different Co-experimenters

The 105 runs in the hypnotic state gave a deviation of +118, which, with a standard deviation of 20.50, yields a highly significant CR of 5.76, as shown in Table 2. The tests in the waking state gave only chance results (a deviation of +6) although some of the subjects' individual results in the waking state may be of interest from the psi-missing point of view. (See Table 3.) Table 2 also shows the evaluation of the difference between the results in the waking and the hypnotic states (CR = 3.85).

An examination of the data of Table 3 shows that the tendency for higher scores to occur in the hypnotic state is significant even when the session is taken as the statistical unit of observation. Out of 20 sessions for all subjects, there were 16 in which hypnosis gave higher scores than the waking state; one session in which they were equal; and only three in which the waking state gave the higher scores. A chi-square test of the 16-3 distribution where equality is expected gives $x^2 = 8.89$ (1 d.f.), $p = .003$.

Of interest and perhaps importance is the contrast between the hypnotic state and the waking state among the individual subjects. Table 3 shows that 8 of the 10 had higher scores in hypnosis than in the waking state. There were four sessions in the hypnosis section that were significantly positive and none in the waking section. The results of subject K.G. are especially noteworthy. In the waking state she made a significant negative total deviation of -24 in 17 runs (and a positive but insignificant total deviation of 9 in 17 runs in hypnosis). Also, the subject F.T. had a negative total deviation in her waking state runs, while her total results in hypnosis gave a significant positive deviation. All of the

Table 2
Clairvoyance Results of Section B, with
Subjects in Waking and Hypnotic States

States	Runs	Hits	Dev.	CR	
Waking	105	531	+ 6		$\left.\begin{array}{l} \\ \end{array}\right\}$ Cr$_d$=3.85
Hypnosis	105	643	+118	5.76	

Table 3
Section B Scores of Individual Subjects for Each Session

Subject	Waking State				Hypnotic State			
	Runs	*Hits*	*Dev.*	*CR*	*Runs*	*Hits*	*Dev.*	*CR*
B.B.	5	31	6		5	37	12	2.69
	5	31	6		5	26	1	
	4	24	4		4	22	2	
Total	14	86	16		14	85	15	
H.B.	5	21	-4		5	28	3	
K.G.	10	33	-17	2.69	10	55	5	
	4	17	-3		4	19	-1	
	3	11	-4		3	20	5	
Total	17	61	-24	2.91	17	94	9	
S.H.	3	11	-4		3	18	3	
A.L.	3	18	3		3	22	7	
H.L.	5	29	4		5	30	5	
M.M.	5	29	4		5	39	14	3.13
	3	17	2		3	20	5	
Total	8	46	6		8	59	19	3.36
L.O.	5	26	1		5	39	14	3.13
J.T.	5	34	9		5	38	13	2.91
F.T.	10	40	-10		10	61	11	
	10	54	4		10	60	10	
	5	26	1		5	26	1	
	5	24	-1		5	27	2	
	5	29	4		5	33	8	
Total	35	173	-2		35	207	32	2.70
S.W.	5	26	1		5	23	-2	

	Hypnosis Higher	Waking State Higher
Sessions with Unequal Scores	16	3

$\chi^2=8.89$ (1 d.f.)
$p = .003$

striking psi effects of the subjects are in the hypnotic state except for the impressive negative deviation by the subject K.G. in the waking state.

Section C: Confirmatory Tests with Two Laboratory Staff Experimenters

This part of the investigation was carried out with both J.F. and R.J.C. present. It was designed at the start to include 10 subjects. The plan was that the subjects should be tested in DT or BT clairvoyance (as each preferred) in four sessions, with six runs in each session. These six runs were divided into three waking runs and three runs in hypnosis. The section was designed for a total of 240 runs, but because of unforeseen circumstances it was not possible to complete four sessions with all subjects. Accordingly, the number of total runs was brought up to 240 by collecting more sessions from subjects who were willing to continue the tests. The results presented in Tables 4 and 5 consist of all the data obtained under the prescribed conditions.

The 120 runs in the hypnotic state gave a deviation of +187, which, with a standard deviation of 21.90, has a highly significant CR of 8.54. (See Table 4.) The tests in the waking state produced only chance results (a deviation of -1), although some of the individual subjects' results as shown in Table 5 deserve further discussion.

In Section C, as in the foregoing part of the experiment, there is a strong tendency favoring the results in the hypnotic state. The difference between the results in the waking state and those in hypnosis has a CR of the difference of 6.07. But the more proper statistical basis of comparison is in terms of the session scores. There were 35 sessions in which the scores were not equal in hypnosis and in the waking state. In 30 of these, the hypnosis score was the higher. This distribution gives a chi square of 17.86 (1 d.f.) with $p = .00002$.

Perhaps one of the most interesting facts shown in Table 5 is the performance of subject L.L. Out of five sessions in the waking state, she had four with negative deviations and one with a zero deviation. In the

Table 4
Clairvoyance Results of Section C, with Subjects in Waking and Hypnotic States

States	Runs	Hits	Dev.		CR
Waking	120	599	-1		$CR_d=6.07$
Hypnosis	120	783	+187	8.54	8.54

Table 5
Section C Scores of Individual Subjects for Each Session

Subject	Waking State				Hypnotic State			
	Runs	Hits	Dev.	CR	Runs	Hits	Dev.	CR
S.W.	3	17	2		3	23	8	
	3	16	1		3	20	5	
	3	13	−2		3	24	9	2.60
	3	15	0		3	20	5	
Total	12	61	1		12	87	27	3.90
M.K.	3	17	2		3	17	2	
L.L.	3	7	−8		3	24	9	2.60
	3	11	−4		3	19	4	
	3	8	−7		3	17	2	
	3	13	−2		3	21	6	
	3	15	0		3	19	4	
Total	15	54	−21	2.71	15	100	25	3.23
A.L.	3	13	−2		3	17	2	
	3	17	2		3	25	10	2.89
	3	14	−1		3	14	−1	
	3	17	2		3	21	6	
Total	12	61	1		12	77	17	
H.C.	3	14	−1		3	15	0	
	3	15	0		3	13	−2	
Total	6	29	−1		6	28	−2	
J.C.*	3	21	6		3	27	12	3.47
	3	19	4		3	19	4	
	3	15	0		3	18	3	
	3	10	−5		3	18	3	
Total	12	65	5		12	82	22	3.18
H.L.	3	18	3		3	14	−1	
	3	12	−3		3	13	−2	
Total	6	30	0		6	27	−3	
S.H.	3	9	−6		3	17	2	
	3	20	5		3	19	4	
Total	6	29	−1		6	36	6	
F.T.	3	16	1		3	13	−2	
	3	17	2		3	20	5	
	3	16	1		3	19	4	
	3	12	−3		3	26	11	3.18
Total	12	61	1		12	78	18	2.60

Table 5 (continued)

Subject	Waking State				Hypnotic State			
	Runs	Hits	Dev.	CR	Runs	Hits	Dev.	CR
C.B.	3	13	−2		3	18	3	
	3	12	−3		3	22	7	
	3	21	6		3	22	7	
	3	14	−1		3	25	10	2.89
Total	12	60	0		12	87	27	3.90
J.T.	3	12	−3		3	25	10	2.89
	3	19	4		3	24	9	2.60
	3	14	−1		3	20	5	
	3	19	4		3	18	3	
	3	14	−1		3	16	1	
	3	17	2		3	17	2	
	3	20	5		3	27	12	3.47
Total	21	115	10		21	147	42	4.58
M.M.	3	17	2		3	17	2	

*Always DT.

	Hypnosis Higher	Waking State Higher
Sessions with Unequal Scores	30	5

χ^2=17.86 (1 d.f.)
p = .00002

hypnosis sessions, on the other hand, all five deviations were positive. L.L.'s performance in the waking state ended with the deviation of -21 in her 15 runs, which is significant (CR = 2.71). In hypnosis, she has a deviation of +25 in 15 runs, which gives a CR of 3.23. This is sufficient to raise the question whether, for this one subject at least, the conditions of the experiment were conducive to psi-missing in the waking state.

Discussion

Something, at least, may be said in favor of the usefulness of hypnosis in improving the scoring rate of the subjects. Out of the four significant positive deviations of the individual sessions in Section B, all four were produced during hypnosis, while the only significant session deviation in the waking state was the negative one produced by K.G. Of the nine significant positive session deviations in Section C, all were made during the hypnotic state. In a word, significant ESP effects did accompany the hypnotic treatment, whatever the responsible conditions may have been.

Perhaps the subjects were usually not equally motivated to perform at their best rate in the waking state. Hypnosis seems to provide the experimenter with a way of concentrating the subject's effort upon his task and improving his interest in his performance. Moreover, with the aid of hypnosis, the subject can be relaxed by the experimenter before the testing begins. Disturbing noises, very common during our experiments, did not usually bother the subjects when they were hypnotized. We cannot, of course, rule out the possibility that equally high results might have been produced in the waking state if special methods of improving the effort of the subject had been used. But so far, we do not know of such a method.

In the experiments reported here, there are strong indications that the subjects were stabilized by hypnosis as such, although we must be careful in our interpretation of the results. The role of the experimenters is very important in such a situation. The subject, if he has enough interest in the work, usually tries to satisfy the experimenter. The whole atmosphere in the experimental room is of the greatest importance; and a person without a strong interest in his task had better not try an experiment in parapsychology, especially not with hypnosis where the subject is very sensitive to the attitude of the experimenter (Björkhem, 1943).

References

Björkhem, J. *De Hypnotiska Hallucinationerna.* Stockholm: Litteraturförlaget, 1943.

Fahler, J. ESP card tests with and without hypnosis. *J. Parapsychol.*, 1957, 21, 179–85.

CHAPTER 16

Hypnotic Induction vs. Control Conditions: Illustrating an Approach to the Evaluation of Replicability in Parapsychological Data

Ephraim I. Schechter

Introduction

Some phenomena are robust, based on effects that occur in a wide variety of conditions. Introductory textbook demonstrations are often chosen precisely because of their robustness; few people fail to detect their retinal blind spot. Other phenomena are very sensitive to surrounding conditions and cannot be evoked casually; in order to study these we must know what conditions enhance or inhibit them so that we can produce them when we need to.

The effects we call psi phenomena are clearly not robust; if they were, their replicability would not be in question. This does not mean that they are not replicable, but it does suggest that we should evaluate their replicability by asking about the conditions under which they occur rather than simply "do they occur?" This paper illustrates some of the processes

Reprinted with permission from *Journal of the American Society for Psychical Research*, 1984, 78, 1–27.

involved in analyzing research on the conditions that affect psi performance, using studies comparing ESP performance after hypnotic induction with performance in control conditions as an example.

The first step in such an analysis is to ask whether the performance
appears to be reliably stronger when the variable is present than when it
is absent. We will see that, at this level of analysis, hypnotic induction
does appear to facilitate performance.

The next step is to ask whether the effect occurs primarily in studies in which the ESP testing techniques are flawed or potentially flawed,
since it could be that these flaws, rather than the experimental variable,
are producing results. If the data survive this test, we can go on to ask
whether the effect occurs primarily when some confounding varaible is
present—if, for example, the hypnotic induction condition were always
tested last, the effect might be due to practice and familiarity with the
ESP test and not to the induction at all. Here we will see that the effect
holds up fairly well but that it is not clear whether the scoring differences
are due to the induction itself or to the percipients' and experimenters'
expectations about induction.

(Notice the difference between asking about replicability and asking about the process involved. Should it turn out that increased scoring
after an induction experience occurs because percipients expect to do better then, we would stop talking about "an apparently reliable effect of
induction" and start talking about "an apparently reliable effect of percipient expectancies"—but we would still be talking about an apparently
reliable effect.)

Analyses: Stage 1

The research literature contains 25 comparisons of psi performance
following induction with performance in control conditions, in 20
papers by 12 researchers and research teams at 10 different laboratories.*
All 25 involve ESP testing. Table 1 lists the comparisons, indicating
for each whether ESP performance was stronger after induction or
under control conditions and whether the difference was statistically
significant.[†,‡]

*See Honorton (1977), Honorton and Krippner (1969), and Van de Castle (1969) for earlier
reviews.
†Since Table 1 distinguishes between Induction>Control and Control>Induction, significance decisions were based on two-tailed probabilities even if the original report used one-tailed tests.
Wherever possible, statistical tests involving subject means (or sums) and variances were used in
preference to tests based on overall condition sums (see, e.g., Stanford and Palmer, 1972)* [continued]

Two of the five studies listed as "Comparison Unclear" are described in such a way that the overall Induction/Control difference cannot be evaluated (Casler, 1971; Krippner, 1968). The other three studies in this category are there because interactions between the Induction/Control variable and other experimental variables make a simple Induction/Control comparison hard to interpret. Honorton (1964, 1966) used scores on an interest inventory to predict whether each of his percipients would score above or below chance levels in the ESP test. Scores following induction were higher than control-condition scores for the predicted high-scorers and lower than control-condition scores for the predicted low scorers; the difference was significant for the predicted low-scorers in both studies. In other words, in both studies induction appeared to enhance scoring in the predicted direction. Both can be considered as conceptually supporting the overall Induction/Control effect suggested by Table 1, but combining the scores of the predicted low-scorers and the predicted high-scorers for an overall Induction/Control comparison seems inappropriate.

Braud and Mellen (1979) used a within-subjects design to compare scoring in a control condition with scoring in five different induction conditions. In four of these, the induction included age-regression suggestions. There was nonsignificantly higher scoring after induction without suggestions than there was in the control condition, but the scoring after

and only data included in the published reports were involved in making new calculations. The significance criterion was adjusted appropriately whenever more than one statistical test was used to compare Induction and Control performances. As a result of these recalculations and adjustments, two studies reported as statistically significant by their author are classified as nonsignificant for the present analysis (Casler, 1962 Expt. 1, 1967). Nash and Durkin's (1959) data are classified as nonsignificant, following the recalculation of the CRd given by Honorton (1977, p. 446). Moss et al. (1970) indicate that their Induction-condition percipients performed significantly above chance levels (p<.001) while the Control percipients performed "only at chance" (p. 51). There were different numbers of trials in the two conditions but the actual number of trials per condition is not given, so there is no way to determine from the report whether the Induction/Control difference was significant. However, even the worst case, with the fewest Control trials and most Induction trials consistent with Moss et al.'s description, has a higher percentage of hits in the Induction condition than in the Control condition. Hence this study is classified as "Induction>Control" and, conservatively, "difference not significant." For Casler (1962), see also Casler (1982). For a more detailed description of Van de Castle and Davis (1962), see Honorton and Krippner (1969, pp. 224–225).
‡Novinski and Wineman's (1978) study is not included in Table 1 nor in the later analyses. This study did involve both "self-hypnosis" and control tests, but it is not clear whether the self-hypnosis procedure was comparable to the inductions used in the other studies. (If this study had been included, it would have been listed as "Comparison Unclear." Probabilities for self-hypnosis and control runs for a single percipient are reported, but we cannot tell how the proportion of hits in the self-hypnosis condition compares to that in the control condition since the numbers of trials involved in the p-values are not given.)

induction plus age-regression suggestions was nonsignificantly lower than in the control condition. None of the other studies used age-regression suggestions, and while the difference between the performances in Braud and Mellen's control and simple induction comparisons does fit the Induction/Control pattern shown by Table 1, the study's design is not factorial and it does not seem appropriate to extract this comparison from the overall results.

The study by Grela (1945) is listed twice. This study involved a within-subjects comparison of a noninduction condition, an induction involving suggestions for positive scoring, and an induction plus suggestions for negative scoring. There was also a separate group of percipients who were given suggestions for positive scoring but no formal induction. This is not a factorial design; rather, it is two studies, a within-subjects one with scoring suggestions as a variable and a between-subjects one with positive scoring suggestions in both induction and control conditions. It seems appropriate to treat the two comparisons separately.

That leaves 20 of the 25 comparisons readily interpretable, and Table 2 summarizes their results. At a quick glance, one might say "Seven studies show significantly stronger ESP performance after induction but the other 13 do not. If anything, that's tilted against the hypothesis."

However, we'd expect only one of the 20 studies to show significantly greater performance after induction by chance. The probability that seven of the studies would have this outcome by chance is only 0.000034 (one-tailed Binomial Test with $p = .05$ and $q = .95$).

Also, "significant support vs. everything else" may not be the most appropriate comparison. Nine of the 13 *non*significant differences also show higher performance after induction, and there are no cases in which performance after induction was significantly below control-condition performance. In other words, all of the significant comparisons and 69% of the nonsignificant ones have stronger performance following induction.

It is true, of course, that any one of the nonsignificant results is likely to be a chance effect. But in assessing replicability, we are evaluating *across* studies, not one study at a time. As an extreme example, if there were 100 nonsignificant studies dealing with some variable, but every one of them had higher scores when the variable was present than when it was absent, we'd interpret the data as showing a weak but reliable effect, not as indicating "no significant effect."

If there were nothing but chance effects in these data, we would expect as many results in one direction as in the other. The likelihood that 16 out of the 20 comparisons would have stronger performance after induction by chance is 0.006 (one-tailed Binomial Test with $p=q=.5$).

Table 1
Comparison of ESP Performance Following Hypnotic Induction with ESP Performance Under Control Conditions

Results[a]	Comparison	Interaction with Another Variable?
Induction > Control, difference significant	(1) Casler, 1962, Expt. 2[b] (2) Casler, 1964[b] (3) Fahler & Cadoret, 1958, Expt. 1[b] (4) Fahler & Cadoret, 1958, Expt. 2[b] (5) Fahler & Cadoret, 1958, Expt. 3[b] (6) Rao, 1964 (7) Sargent, 1978	
Induction > Control, difference not significant	(8) Casler, 1962, Expt. 1[b] (9) Casler, 1967[b] (10) Casler, 1976[b] (11) Fahler, 1957[b] (12) Grela, 1945[b, c] (13) Moss et al., 1970 (14) Rao, 1979, 1st series[b] (15) Rao, 1979, 2nd series (16) Van de Castle & Davis, 1962	 type of motivating instructions used presence/absence of suggestions for high scoring
Control ≥ Induction, difference not significant	(17) Edmunds & Joliffe, 1965[b] (18) Grela, 1945[b, d] (19) Honorton, 1972 (20) Nash & Durkin, 1959[b]	 percipient's suggestibility
Control > Induction, difference significant		
Induction/Control comparison unclear	(21) Braud & Mellen, 1979 (22) Casler, 1971[e] (23) Honorton, 1964 (24) Honorton, 1966 (25) Krippner, 1968[e]	whether induction involved age-regression whether high or low ESP scoring predicted whether high or low ESP scoring predicted

[a]*Two-tailed, corrected for multiple analyses.* [b]*Classification based on re-analysis of data in published report.* [c]*Between-subjects portion of experiment.* [d]*Within-subjects portion of experiment.* [e]*Report does not contain information needed to assess overall Induction/Control difference.*

Table 2
Summary of Results of Comparisons of ESP Performance Following Hypnotic Induction with ESP Performance Under Control Conditions

	Induction > Control	Control ≥ Induction
$p < .05$	7	0
n.s.	9	4

(The control vs. simple-induction comparison in the Braud and Mellen [1979] study strengthens the pattern, and Honorton's 1964 and 1966 studies add still more support if we think in terms of the percipient's expected scoring direction rather than in terms of ESP "hits" per se.)

Overall, then, the first stage of our analysis indicates that the apparent difference between ESP hitting after hypnotic induction and under control conditions is not likely to be a chance effect. How this difference is to be interpreted, however, depends on the relationship between the performances and mean chance expectation (MCE); Induction performances predominantly above MCE and Control performances near or below MCE lead to a different conclusion than would Induction performances near MCE and Control performances well below MCE.

The reports of 19 of 20 interpretable Induction/Control comparisons contain the information needed to compare individual-condition performances with MCE.* Table 3 shows that performance after induction is above MCE in 79% of the comparisons and significantly above MCE in 48%, while performance under control conditions varies widely in direction and strength.† This suggests that scoring is facilitated in the induction condition.

Analyses: Stage 2

The next step in the analysis is to see whether the studies responsible for these patterns are those containing potential flaws in the psi testing or in the Induction/Control comparison. Twenty-two of the 25 comparisons used forced-choice testing, and two of the three which did not fall into the "Comparison Unclear" category (Braud and Mellen, 1979;

The significance levels are reported by Grela (1945, between-subjects comparison), Moss et al. (1970), and Sargent (1978, Induction condition); the others have been calculated using data in the published reports. The direction of Moss et al.'s Control-condition data is not clear from their report; that condition has been assigned to the "=MCE" category.
†*Table 3A in the Appendix indicates which studies fall in each cell of Table 3. The Appendix gives this information for Tables 3, 4, 5, 6, 7, 9, 10, 12, 13, and 14.*

Table 3
Induction and Control Performances
Compared to Mean Chance Expectation

		Induction				
C		>MCE p<.05	>MCE n.s.	=MCE	<MCE n.s.	<MCE p<.05
O	>MCE p<.05	2 (11%)				
N	>MCE n.s.	4 (21%)			2 (11%)	
T	=MCE	1 (5%)		1 (5%)		
R	<MCE n.s.	2 (11%)	5 (26%)			
O	<MCE p<.05		1 (5%)		1 (5%)	
L		9 (48%)	6 (31%)	1 (5%)	3 (16%)	

Krippner, 1968: see also Honorton, 1972). It makes sense, then, to focus on possible problems in forced-choice procedures.

The experimenters in all of the comparisons knew whether the percipients were being tested under induction or control conditions. This makes it crucial to look for ways in which the experimenters could have inadvertently affected the ESP-test results.

For example, there is the possibility of "sensory leakage"—information about the target might have passed from the experimenter to the percipient by way of conventional sensory cues. Nineteen of the 22 forced-choice comparisons were described fully enough to be evaluated for sensory-leakage problems, and 18 of the 19 had appropriate controls. When the testing involved both an agent and a percipient, the percipient was in one room and the targets and the agent were in another. When there was no agent—when no one was looking at the targets while the percipient was trying to guess them—either the targets were hidden from both the percipient and the experimenter or both the experimenter and the targets were hidden from the percipient. The poorly-controlled study (Fahler and Cadoret, 1958, Expt. 1) was an exploratory series which involved several testing techniques. Slightly over half of the trials involved GESP procedure in which the percipient, the agent, and the experimenter were within sight of each other so that inadvertent sensory cueing may have occurred.

Table 4 compares the outcomes of the forced-choice comparisons that were protected against sensory leakage with the outcomes of those whose descriptions are either unclear or indicate possible sensory leakage. The proportion of comparisons with greater ESP hitting after induction is no higher when the controls are weak or unclear than when they are strong—in other words, the possibility of sensory leakage does not appear to be related to the overall pattern of results.

Since the experimenters knew whether an induction or control test was being given, it is possible that unintentional scoring errors might have biased the results to favor the induction condition. Fourteen of the 22 forced-choice comparisons contain description of how the scores were checked. In four, the experimenter was both the only person who recorded the percipients' calls and the only person who checked them against the target order. In seven others, the experimenter was the only one who recorded the calls, but two or more people independently checked them against the targets. Tables 5 and 6 compare the outcomes of these studies with the outcomes of studies whose descriptions made it clear that the calls were independently recorded (Table 6) and checked (Table 5) by two or more people.

Table 5 indicates that having two or more people independently check the scores does not appear to interfere with the general pattern. And, as Table 6 shows, performance after induction was stronger than performance under control conditions in all three of the studies whose descriptions make it clear that two or more people independently recorded the percipients' calls, indicating that introducing this control does not destroy the pattern. However, six of the eight *single*-recorder studies with stronger performance after induction produced significant Induction/Control differences, suggesting that this variable should be studied more intensively

Table 4
Effect of Potential Sensory Cues on Results of Induction/Control Comparison

	Protection Against Sensory Cueing	
Induction/Control Comparison	*Weak or Unclear*	*Satisfactory*
Induction>Control, $p<.05$	1 (25%)	6 (33%)
Induction>Control, n.s.	2 (50%)	7 (39%)
Control ≥ Induction, n.s.	0	3 (17%)
Control>Induction, $p<.05$	0	0
Not Clear	1 (25%)	2 (11%)
Total	4 (100%)	18 (100%)

Table 5
Effect of ESP Scoring Technique on Results of Induction/Control Comparison

	Number of People Checking Scores	
Induction/Control Comparison	*Experimenter Only*	*2 or More*
Induction>Control, *p*<.05	0	7 (59%)
Induction>Control, n.s.	2 (50%)	3 (25%)
Control ≥ Induction, n.s.	2 (50%)	1 (8%)
Control>Induction, *p*<.05	0	0
Not Clear	0	1 (8%)
Total	4 (100%)	12 (100%)

Table 6
Effect of ESP Scoring Technique on Results of Induction/Control Comparison

	Number of People Recording Calls	
Induction/Control Comparison	*Experimenter Only*	*2 or More*
Induction>Control, *p*<.05	6 (54%)	1 (33%)
Induction>Control, n.s.	2 (18%)	2 (67%)
Control ≥ Induction, n.s.	2 (18%)	0
Control>Induction, *p*<.05	0	0
Not Clear	1 (10%)	0
Total	11 (100%)	3 (100%)

before conclusions are drawn. More studies with two or more recorders (or, given today's technology, using automated recording techniques) are clearly needed.

Another potential trouble spot in forced-choice testing is the method used to randomize the target sets. The randomization method was specified for 18 or the 22 forced-choice comparisons; 15 used hand shuffling of cards containing the target material and the other three used random number tables to determine the target order. Both systems have their problems (for discussions see, e.g., Davis and Akers, 1974; Morris, 1978), but it is clear that it is harder to obtain adequate randomization with hand shuffling.

Table 7 indicates that one of the three studies using random number tables produced significantly higher performance after induction than under control conditions, while another produced postinduction performance

Table 7
Effects of Method for Randomizing ESP Targets on Results of Induction/Control Comparison

Induction/Control Comparison	Hand Shuffle	Random Number Table
Induction>Control, $p<.05$	6 (40%)	1 (33.3%)
Induction>Control, n.s.	6 (40%)	0
Control ≥ Induction, n.s.	2 (13%)	1 (33.3%)
Control>Induction, $p<.05$	0	0
Not Clear	1 (33.3%)	1 (33.3%)
Total	15 (100%)	3 (100%)

that was nonsignificantly below control-condition performance. The third is Honorton's 1966 study in which scores following induction were above control-condition scores for predicted high-scorers and significantly below control-condition scores for predicted low scorers. While it is clear that more studies using random number tables to determine the target order are needed, this technique does not seem to have destroyed the apparent effect of induction on ESP performance in the few studies that have been done.

In additions, if we ask *how* inadequate randomization might be responsible for the difference between performance following induction and performance in control conditions, it becomes apparent that the use of hand shuffling could not have been responsible for the overall pattern. In fact, the evaluation of the possible effects of randomization technique serves as an excellent example of the delicacy with which such analyses must be done.

The randomization technique might be responsible for overall above-chance ESP scoring, but why would it have different effects on performance in the induction and control conditions? There would have to be some way for inadequate randomization to make it easier for the percipient to guess correctly in the induction test than in the control test. Only Rao's 1964 study seems to contain such a possibility. At the end of each run in this within-subjects comparison, the percipient was shown which calls had been hits, and the postinduction test was given immediately after the control test was finished. The detailed feedback may have biased the percipient's guessing tendencies, and if the hand shuffling did not change the card sequence thoroughly between the tests, this bias could have led to excess hitting in the induction test. The other comparisons involved one or more protections against this kind of problem—between-subjects designs, counterbalanced testing orders in within-subjects designs, running the induction and control tests in separate sessions, and/or withholding feedback until both tests were completed. My point here is that, often, counting the outcomes of studies that do and do not contain a particular potential problem may not be sufficient. As in this example, it may be the combination of design flaws and safeguards that determines the final conclusion.

To check this possibility, I gave each comparison a "flaw rating" by counting the number of potential procedural problems it had. Where the presence or absence of a problem was unclear I considered that it might have been there and counted it for that study. Then I rated how strongly each comparison supported the idea that ESP hitting is stronger after induction, giving three points to comparisons in which performance after induction was significantly stronger than control performance, two points to comparisons in which performance after induction was nonsignificantly stronger, and one point to those in which control performance was the same as or significantly stronger than induction performance. (There are no comparisons in which control performance was significantly stronger than induction performance, so there were none that got zero points. I did not rate the forced-choice studies whose Induction/Control comparisons were unclear [Casler, 1971; Honorton, 1964, 1966].)

The results can be seen in Table 8. A rank-order correlation of this "success rating" and the cumulative flaws" score gave a nonsignificant correlation coefficient of −0.141 with 17 df (t = −0.59, nowhere near statistical significance). In other words, there was no systematic relationship between the number of potential ESP-testing flaws and the studies' outcomes.*

Similar analyses can be done with other aspects of the ESP testing. It might be, for example, that the other positive results come primarily from studies in which only a few percipients were tested or in which relatively few trials were used.

Low numbers of percipients and trials are not like the variables discussed earlier. Sensory leakage, possible recording errors, and the possibility that percipients may become aware of patterns in the target order are flaws in the ESP testing procedure; if the apparent Induction/Control difference had tended to occur when these factors were present but not when the appropriate controls were used, we would probably have concluded that something other than psi was responsible for the pattern. The

---

*The numbers should not be taken too seriously here. Both scales are coarse and yield many tied ranks, which tends to wash out subtle relationships. The safest interpretation of the correlation coefficients in Tables 8 and 11 is that there is no strong relationship between the "success rating" and "cumulative flaws" scores of Table 8 or the "potential design problems" of Table 11.

fact that controlling these flaws does not appear to have destroyed the tendency for Induction performance to be stronger than Control performance in the studies that have been done so far does not, of course, force a psi interpretation, but it does leave it as a possible and perhaps even a plausible one.

The use of relatively few percipients and/or trials introduces a different kind of problem. Small distributions tend to be more sensitive to the effects of uncontrolled, unsystematic variables. If the apparent Induction/Control difference occurred when there were few data points but not in studies with many data points, we might suspect that what appeared to be a trend was simply a chance effect. If this continued to occur as the number of studies grew, however, we'd be more inclined to suspect that something about using many participants and/or large number

Table 8
Relationship Between Number of Potential Flaws in ESP-Testing Procedures and Outcome of Induction/Control Comparison

Comparison*	No. of Flaws	Outcome Rating**
1	2	3
2	2	3
3	3	3
4	2	3
5	2	3
6	1	3
7	1	3
8	4	2
9	3	2
10	3	2
11	1	2
12	2	2
13	3	2
14	3	2
15	1	2
16	4	2
17	3	1
18	2	1
20	2	1
	Range: 1–4	Range: 1–3
	Mean = 2.32	Median = 2.22
	Std. Dev. = 0.95	IQR = 1.13

Rank-Order Correlation: $r = -0.141$ ($df=17$)
($t = -0.59, p > .05$)

*Numbers refer to Table 1. # Flaws: Possibility of Sensory Leakage. Experimenter as Only Recorder. Experimenter as Only Checker. Randomizing by Hand Shuffling. **3 = Induction > Control, p < .05 2 = Induction > Control, n.s.; 1 = Control ≥ Induction, n.s.; 0 = Control > Induction, p < .05.*

of trials, such as prolonged testing or less select participant pools, was interfering with a real effect. In other words, finding a difference primarily in the studies with few data points would not necessarily lead to a non-psi interpretation, and the use of large numbers of participants and/or trials is not a "control procedure" in the sense that eliminating sensory leakage is. Still, even with the relatively small number of studies available at this point, a look at the relationships between the studies' outcomes and the numbers of data points involved may be informative.

Tables 9 and 10 indicate that the tendency for Induction performance to be stronger than Control performance is not concentrated in the studies with low numbers of percipients or trials. There are fewer significant Induction/Control differences in the studies with the most participants and the highest numbers of trials per condition, but the direction of the Induction/Control difference does not appear to be related to these factors.*

Table 11 shows the results of including low numbers of percipients and low numbers of trials per condition in a "success rating x number of potential design problems" analysis like the "success x cumulative flaws" analysis of Table 8. The six potential problems evaluated are the four procedural flaws of Table 8 plus low numbers of percipients and trials per condition. The correlation between the "potential design problems" score and the "success rating" is small and far from statistical significance (rank-order $r[17]+ -.09$, $t[17]= -0.37$, p >.05); there is no apparent systematic relationship between the two variables. (See Footnote on page 272.)

Table 9
Effect of number of Percipients on Results of Induction/Control Comparison

Induction/Control Comparison	Number of Percipients		
	<10	*10–20*	*>20*
Induction>Control, p<.05	2 (29%)	3 (38%)	1 (17%)
Induction>Control, n.s.	2 (29%)	2 (25%)	5 (83%)
Control ≥ Induction, n.s.	2 (29%)	1 (12%)	0
Control>Induction, p<.05	0	0	0
Not Clear	1 (13%)	2 (25%)	0
Total	7 (100%)	8 (100%)	6 (100%)

*Interestingly, there does not seem to be any relationship between the number of participants in a study and the total number of trials per condition in the 19 forced-choice studies for which both figures were reported (Pearson r = +0.039, df = 17, p > .05).

Analyses: Stage 3

Although more studies are needed before we can be sure about some of the variables, it does not appear from the data so far that the tendency for Induction performance to be stronger than Control performance should be attributed to problems in the design of the ESP tests. We can go on, then, to the third stage of the analysis, i.e., asking whether the Induction/Control differences are really related to the presence or absence of induction by checking to see whether they occur primarily when some confounding variable is present.

Since it is the characteristics of the Induction/Control manipulation we are concerned with here, and not the characteristics of the ESP test, we can use both the forced-choice and the free-response studies for these analyses.

Twenty of the comparisons used within-subjects designs, and the first step is to ask whether the Induction/Control difference occurred primarily in these studies, since even with the order of testing counterbalanced, the fact that percipients had already taken some tests or were anticipating taking more tests later may have affected their performance (see Sargent, 1978), for further discussion of the use of within-subjects designs in psi research). The first step in evaluating the effects of within-subjects testing is to ask whether the apparent Induction/Control difference occurs primarily in within-subject studies.

Table 12 indicates that the pattern is not exclusive to the within-subjects designs. With 80% of the comparisons within-subjects, though, it is wise to look more closely. Order effects are a common problem in within-subjects designs. If an examination of the within-subjects comparisons shows that the apparent Induction/Control differences occur mainly when there is a fixed order of testing, we would then have to redo Table 12, comparing the between-subjects designs only to the within-subjects designs in which the testing order was balanced.

The testing order was described for 16 of the 20 within-subjects comparisons, and Table 13 divides them into those with fixed testing orders and those with balanced testing orders. The apparent Induction/Control difference does not appear to be due to order effects.

It seems that the difference between the ESP performances in the induction and control conditions is a reliable effect—it occurs more often than would be expected by chance and it does not appear to be due to faulty ESP testing or experimental design. But it is not at all clear what it is about the induction experience that is responsible for the difference.

For example, it does not appear that the Induction/Control difference

Table 10

Effect of number of Trials in Each Condition on Results of Induction/Control Comparison

No. of Trials/Conditions

Induction/Control Comparison	Quartile: Range: 500–1100	$Q_1=1112$ 1125–2033	Median=2067 2100–2625	$Q_3=2813$ 3000–4800
Induction>Control, $p<.05$	2 (40%)	2 (40%)	2 (40%)	1 (20%)
Induction>Control, n.s.	1 (20%)	1 (20%)	2 (40%)	3 (60%)
Control ≥ Induction, n.s.	1 (20%)	1 (20%)	0	1 (20%)
Control>Induction, $p<.05$	0	0	0	0
Not Clear	1 (20%)	1 (20%)	1 (20%)	0
Total	5 (100%)	5 (100%)	5 (100%)	5 (100%)

Table 11
Relationship Between Number of Potential Design Problems and Outcome of Induction/Control Comparison

Comparison*	No. of Problems	Outcome Rating**
1	4	3
2	4	3
3	4	3
4	3	3
5	3	3
6	3	3
7	2	3
8	4	2
9	3	2
10	3	2
11	2	2
12	3	2
13	4	2
14	5	2
15	2	2
16	6	2
17	4	1
18	4	1
20	4	1

Range: 1–6 Range: 1–3
Mean = 3.53 Median = 2.22
Std. Dev. = 1.02 IQR = 1.13
Rank-Order Correlation: $r = -0.09$ ($df = 17$)
($t = 0.37, p > .05$)

*Numbers refer to Table 1. # Design Problems: Possibility of Sensory Leakage. Experimenter as Only Recorder. Experimenter as Only Checker. Randomization by Hand Shuffling. Number of Percipients ≤ 20. Number of Trials/Condition<Median. **3 = Induction>Control, p<.05. 2 = Induction>Control, n.s. 1 = Control ≥ Induction, n.s. 0 = Control>Induction, p<.05.*

depends on the type of induction that is used. Information about the induction procedure is available for 17 of the 25 comparisons. The techniques used can be divided into two broad classes, those that involved only relaxation instructions and those that also included instructions for sensory hallucinations, arm levitation, and/or eye catalepsy. (It is difficult to divide the latter group further, since some investigators used different methods for different participants.) Table 14 indicates that, except for the "Comparison Unclear" category, the outcomes of these two sets of studies are not particularly different.

Hypnotic depth is another factor that might be related to the Induction/Control difference. However, while a number of authors reported monitoring depth during induction, only two (Casler, 1976; Honorton,

Table 12
Effect of Experimental Design on Results of Induction/Control Comparison

Induction/Control Comparison	Within-Subjects Design	Between Subjects Design
Induction>Control, $p<.05$	6 (30%)	1 (20%)
Induction>Control, n.s.	6 (30%)	3 (60%)
Control ≥ Induction, n.s.	3 (15%)	1 (20%)
Control>Induction, $p<.05$	0	0
Not Clear	5 (25%)	0
Total	20 (100%)	5 (100%)

Table 13
Effect of Fixed vs. Balanced Testing Order in Within-Subjects Designs on Results of Induction/Control Comparison

Induction/Control Comparison	Control Condition First	Order Balanced
Induction>Control, $p<.05$	1 (14%)	4 (40%)
Induction>Control, n.s.	4 (58%)	2 (20%)
Control ≥ Induction, n.s.	1 (14%)	1 (10%)
Control>Induction, $p<.05$	0	0
Not Clear	1 (14%)	3 (30%)
Total	7 (100%)	10 (100%)

1972) report their participants' standing on normed scales of hypnotic depth, so there are not enough data to evaluate this possibility.

There are also aspects of the Induction/Control comparison that have little to do with hypnosis per se. For instance, it might be that the ESP

Table 14
Effect of Type of Induction on Results of Induction/Control Comparison

Induction/Control Comparison	Relaxation plus Sensory &/or Motor Suggestion	Relaxation Only
Induction>Control, $p<.05$	2 (18%)	1 (17%)
Induction>Control, n.s.	3 (28%)	4 (66%)
Control ≥ Induction, n.s.	2 (18%)	1 (17%)
Control>Induction, $p<.05$	0	0
Not Clear	4 (36%)	0
Total	11 (100%)	6 (100%)

differences are related to the percipients' expectations about induction. Studies of the relationship between belief in ESP and performance on ESP tests indicate that whether a person believes in ESP in a general sense is less important than whether he or she expects to do well in the particular ESP test being given (Palmer, 1971). The percipients knew that both induction and control conditions were being tested in all of the within-subjects comparisons and in two of the four between-subjects comparisons (Honorton, 1972; Moss, Paulson, Chang, and Levitt, 1970). Both popular and technical literature often link hypnosis and ESP, and the percipients may simply have expected to perform better after induction.* But since only two comparisons had the percipients blind to the Induction/Control manipulation (Krippner, 1968; Sargent, 1978), and one of those falls into the "Comparison Unclear" category, there aren't enough data at the moment to permit us to analyze the effects of the percipient's expectations.

While the experimenters' expectations may not have led to sensory leakage or inadvertent scoring errors, it is possible that the interpersonal interaction between the experimenter and the percipients and not the fact of induction is what influenced the performances. Unfortunately, the experimenters knew whether induction or control tests were being given in all of the 25 comparisons, so no analysis is possible.

Honorton's 1964 and 1966 data do offer some hope. In these studies, an independent test was used to predict whether each percipient would score above or below the chance level. The experimenter knew whether an induction test or a control test was being given, but he did not know whether the percipient being tested was expected to score above or below chance. Nonetheless, percipients who were expected to score above chance did so after induction but not in the control tests, while those expected to score below chance got below-chance scores after induction but not in the control tests. This is promising, though not a final answer; more studies of the effects of experimenter expectation in Induction/Control comparisons are needed.

Concluding Remarks

In any field of research "more studies are needed" is a familiar end to the evaluation of a body of data, just as the methods used to do the

*Casler (1964, 1967, 1976) and Honorton (1966) asked their percipients to predict their ESP scores at the end of each run; in all four studies, the percipients predicted higher scoring in the induction condition than in the control condition. However, the induction procedures in these studies included suggestions for high ESP scoring, so these predictions do not necessarily reflect a pre-existing expectation.

evaluation have been familiar ones. None of this is unique to parapsychology. The most critical problems in this kind of analysis are those that can result from the analyzer's uncertainty about the analysis process itself, and I have tried to stress key points and assumptions. What are our criteria for lack of replicability—what would we expect to see if there really is no effect at all? Are we looking for the replicability of a robust phenomenon, or are we asking whether our phenomenon is affected by certain conditions? Which question we ask will determine what comparisons we are willing to make. What stage of the analysis are we involved in? Asking whether there appears to be an overall effect calls for different comparisons than asking whether an apparent effect is an artifact of sloppy measurements or poor design. Are we asking about replicability or process? The same comparisons may yield different conclusions depending on which question is asked. In evaluating relationships between procedural variables and the studies' outcomes, are we paying attention to the way various procedures interact with each other? Experimenters often have favorite procedures—have we checked to see whether an apparent procedural effect might actually be an experimenter or laboratory effect?

The frustrations are also familiar. Published descriptions are too often incomplete, and most comparisons cannot use all of the studies. Some studies produce interactions that appear to change the direction of the effect, and cannot be included in any simple way. And even satisfying answers to replicability questions do not mean that we understand the processes involved.

A further frustration is the need for more sensitive measures of the studies' outcomes. The analyses in this paper are, at best, a first step; they are too coarse to be statistically satisfying. (See, e.g., Hedges and Olkin [1980] for a discussion of the statistical power of the "vote counting" approach.) The use of effect size, a standardized measure of the difference between condition means, would yield far more detailed information about outcomes, information which could then be used in inferential meta-analyses (statistical analyses across studies) of the relationships between the studies' procedures and their outcomes. (See, e.g., Glass, McGaw, and Smith [1981], Hunter, Schmidt, and Jackson [1982], and Rosenthal and Rubin [1982] for detailed discussions of this approach.) This would permit much stronger conclusions than do the descriptive and coarse inferential analyses presented here.

However, the reports of six of the 20 interpretable Induction/Control comparisons do not contain either the raw data or the summary statistics (such as condition means and standard deviations, t's, F's) from which effect sizes can be computed. Three of the six do give Z-scores based on condition sums (*CRd*'s), a common way of reporting results in parapsychological research. Effect sizes based on these Z-scores would be estimates rather than true effect sizes. Appropriate correction factors can be derived from simulated runs of various lengths; this work is under way, and, when it is completed, the more delicate meta-analyses can be begun.

Meanwhile, the analyses that have been possible so far are heartening—while it may not be clear how the induction experience affects performance in ESP tests, the effect does seem reliable, which is a step towards improving overall replicability.

References

Braud, W.G., and Mellen, R.R. (1979). A preliminary investigation of clairvoyance during hypnotic age regression. *European Journal of Parapsychology*, 2, 371–380.

Casler, L, (1962). The improvement of clairvoyance scores by means of hypnotic suggestion. *Journal of Parapsychology*, 2, 371–380.

Casler, L. (1964). The effects of hypnosis on GESP. *Journal of Parapsychology*, 28, 126–134.

Casler, L. (1967). Self-generated hypnotic suggestions and clairvoyance. *International Journal of Parapsychology*, 9, 125–128.

Casler, L. (1971). Hypnotically induced interpersonal relationships and their influence on GESP. *Proceedings of the Parapsychological Association 1969*, 6, 14–15. (Abstract)

Casler, L. (1976). Hypnotic maximization of ESP motivation. *Journal of Parapsychology*, 40, 187–193.

Casler, L. (1982). Letter to the editor. *Journal of Parapsychology*, 46, 289–290.

Davis, J.W., and Akers, C. (1974). Randomization and tests for randomness. *Journal of Parapsychology*, 38, 393–407.

Edmunds, S., and Joliffe, D. (1965). A GESP experiment with four hypnotized subjects. *Journal of the Society for Psychical Research*, 43, 192–194.

Fahler, J. (1957). ESP card tests with and without hypnosis. *Journal of Parapsychology*, 21, 179–185.

Fahler, J., and Cadoret, R.J. (1958). ESP card tests of college students with and without hypnosis. *Journal of Parapsychology*, 22, 125–136.

Glass, G.V., McGaw, B., and Smith, M.L. (1981). *Meta-Analysis in Social Research*. Beverly Hills, CA: Sage.

Grela, J.J. (1945). Effect on ESP scoring of hypnotically induced attitudes. *Journal of Parapsychology*, 9, 194–202.

Hedges, L.V., and Olkin, I. (1980). Vote-counting methods in research synthesis. *Psychological Bulletin*, 88, 359–369.

Honorton, C. (1964). Separation of high- and low-scoring ESP subjects through hypnotic preparation. *Journal of Parapsychology*, 28, 250–257.

Honorton, C. (1966). A further separation of high- and low-scoring ESP subjects through hypnotic preparation. *Journal of Parapsychology*, 30, 172–183.

Honorton, C. (1972). Significant factors in hypnotically-induced clairvoyant dreams. *Journal of the American Society for Psychical Research*, 66, 86–102.

Honorton, C. (1977). Psi and internal attention states. In B.B. Wolman (Ed.). *Handbook of Parapsychology* (pp. 435–472). New York: Van Nostrand Reinhold.

Honorton, C., and Krippner, S. (1969). Hypnosis and ESP performance: A review of the experimental literature. *Journal of the American Society for Psychical Research*, 63, 214–252.

Hunter, J.E., Schmidt, F.L., and Jackson, G.B. (1982). *Meta-Analysis: Cumulating Research Findings Across Studies.* Beverly Hills, CA: Sage.

Krippner, S. (1968). Experimentally-induced telepathic effects in hypnosis and non-hypnosis groups. *Journal of the American Society for Psychical Research*, 62, 387–398.

Morris, R.L. (1978). A survey of methods and issues in ESP research. In S. Krippner (Ed.), *Advances in Parapsychological Research. Vol. 2: Extrasensory Perception* (pp. 7–58). New York: Plenum Press.

Moss, T., Paulson, M.J., Chang, A.F., and Levitt, M. (1970). Hypnosis and ESP: A controlled experiment. *American Journal of Clinical Hypnosis.* 13, 46–56.

Nash, C.B., and Durkin, M.G. (1959). Terminal salience with multiple digit targets. *Journal of Parapsychology*, 23, 49–53.

Novinski, M.V., and Wineman, J.A. (1978). Relaxation through hypnosis and ESP scoring. *Journal of Parapsychology*, 42, 60–61. (Abstract)

Palmer, J. (1971). Scoring in ESP tests as a function of belief in ESP. Part I: The sheep-goat effect. *Journal of the American Society for Psychical Research*, 65, 373–408.

Rao, K.R. (1964). The differential response in three new situations. *Journal of Parapsychology*, 28, 81–92.

Rao, K.R. (1979). Language ESP tests under normal and relaxed conditions. *Journal of Parapsychology*, 43, 1–16.

Rosenthal, R., and Rubin, D.B. (1982). Comparing effect sizes of independent studies. *Psychological Bulletin*, 92, 500–504.

Sargent, C.L. (1978). Hypnosis as a psi-conducive state: A controlled replication study. *Journal of Parapsychology*, 42, 257–275.

Stanford, R.G., and Palmer, J. (1972). Some statistical considerations concerning process-oriented research in parapsychology, *Journal of the American Society for Psychical Research*, 66, 166–179.

Van de Castle, R.L. (1969). The facilitation of ESP scores through hypnosis. *American Journal of Clinical Hypnosis*, 12, 37–56.

Van de Castle, R.L., and Davis, K.R. (1962). The relation of suggestibility to ESP scoring levels. *Journal of Parapsychology*, 26, 270–271. (Abstract)

Appendix

The tables in the Appendix indicate which studies fall in each cell of Tables 3, 4, 5, 6, 7, 9, 10, 12, 13, and 14. The numbers used to identify the individual studies are taken from Table 1.

Table 3A
Induction and Control Performances Compared to Mean Chance Expectation

		INDUCTION				
		>MCE p<.05	>MCE n.s.	=MCE	<MCE n.s.	<MCE p<.05
C	>MCE p<.05	3,18				
O **N**	>MCE n.s.	4, 5 7, 12			17, 20	
T **R**	=MCE	13		19		
O	<MCE n.s.	1,9	2, 8, 11 14, 15			
L	<MCE p<.05		6		10	

Table 4A
Effect of Potential Sensory Cues on Results of Induction/Control Comparison

	Protection Against Sensory Cueing	
Induction/Control Comparison	Weak or Unclear	Satisfactory
Induction > Control, p<.05	3	1, 2, 4 5, 6, 7
Induction > Control, n.s.	8, 16	9, 10, 11, 12 13, 14, 15
Control ≥ Induction, n.s. Control > Induction, p<.05		17, 18, 20
Not Clear	22	23, 24

Table 5A
Effect of ESP Scoring Technique on Results of Induction/Control Comparison

	Number of People Checking Scores	
Induction/Control Comparison	Experimenter Only	2 or More
Induction > Control, p<.05		1, 2, 3 4, 5, 6, 7
Induction > Control, n.s.	8, 10	11, 12, 15
Control ≥ Induction, n.s. Control > Induction, p< .05	17, 20	18
Not Clear		24

Table 6A
Effect of ESP Scoring Technique on Results of Induction/Control Comparison

	Number of People Recording Calls	
Induction/Control Comparison	*Experimenter Only*	*2 or More*
Induction>Control, $p<.05$	1, 2, 3	6
	4, 5, 7	
Induction>Control, n.s.	8, 10	11, 15
Control ≥ Induction, n.s.	17, 20	
Control > Induction, $p<.05$		
Not Clear	24	

Table 7A
Effect of Method for Randomizing ESP Targets on Results of Induction/Control Comparison

Induction/Control Comparison	*Hand Shuffle*	*Random Number Table*
Induction > Control, $p<.05$	1, 2, 3	7
	4, 5, 6	
Induction > Control, n.s.	9, 10, 11	
	12, 14, 15	
Control ≥ Induction, n.s.	17, 18	20
Control > Induction, $p<.05$		
Not Clear	23	22, 24

Table 9A
Effect of Number of Percipients on Results of Induction/Control Comparison

	Number of Percipients		
Induction/Control Comparison	*<10*	*10–20*	*>20*
Induction>Control, $p<.05$	5, 6	1, 2, 4	7
Induction>Control, n.s.	11, 14	15, 16	8, 9
			10, 12, 13
Control ≥ Induction, n.s.	17, 20	18	
Control>Induction, $p<.05$			
Not Clear	23	22, 24	

Table 10A
Effect of Number of Trials in Each Condition on Results of Induction/Control Comparison

Induction/Control Comparison	Range:	No. of Trials/Condition			
		500–1100	*1125–2033*	*2100–2625*	*3000–4800*
Induction > Control, $p<.05$		6, 7	1, 2	3[a], 4	5
Induction > Control, n.s.		14	12	8[a], 9	10, 11[a], 15
Control ≥ Induction, n.s.		20	18[a]		17[a]
Control > Induction, $p<.05$					
Not Clear		23	22	24	

$Q_1 = 1112$
$Median = 2067$
$Q_3 = 2813$

*No. of trials in Induction & Control conditions not equal; mean no. of trials/condition used.

Table 12A
Effect of Experimental Design on Results of Induction/Control Comparison

Induction/Control Comparison	Within-Subjects Design	Between-Subjects Design
Induction > Control, $p<.05$	1, 2, 3 4, 5, 6	7
Induction > Control, n.s.	9, 10, 11 14, 15, 16	8, 12, 13
Control ≥ Induction, n.s. Control > Induction, $p<.05$	17, 18, 20	19
Not Clear	21, 22, 23 24, 25	

Table 13A
Effect of Fixed vs. Balanced Testing Order in Within-Subjects Designs on Results of Induction/Control Comparison

Induction/Control Comparison	Control Condition First	Order Balanced
Induction > Control, $p<.05$	6	1, 2, 4, 5
Induction > Control, n.s.	10, 11, 14, 16	9, 15
Control ≥ Induction, n.s. Control > Induction, $p<.05$	18	17
Not Clear	21*	22, 23, 24

*One additional comparison (no. 25) with the Induction condition always tested first falls into the "not clear" category.

Table 14A
Effect of Type of Induction on Results of Induction/Control Comparison

Induction/Control Comparison	Relaxation plus Sensory &/or Motor Suggestion	Relaxation Only
Induction > Control, *p*<.05	1, 2	7
Induction > Control, n.s.	6, 9, 10	12, 13, 14, 15
Control ≥ Induction, n.s.	17, 19	18
Control > Induction, *p*<.05		
Not Clear	21, 22, 23, 24	

CHAPTER 17

Yogic Meditation and Psi Scoring in Forced-Choice and Free-Response Tests

K. Ramakrishna Rao, Hamlyn Dukhan, *and* P.V. Krishna Rao

Theoretical Background

The belief that by practicing yoga one could attain psychic abilities is a very old one in India. By the time of Panini, the great grammarian who lived probably before the Buddha, yoga came to be identified with a method of achieving concentration and controlling sensory inputs. While the word yoga, in this sense of a method, appears in some of the later upanishads such as *Maitrayani Svetasvatara* and *Katha* it was in Patanjali's *Yoga Sutras* (Woods, 1927) that we find its first systematic treatment. Patanjali is not, however, the founder of yoga. As Dasgupta (1922) points out, Patanjali collected the different yoga practices, systematized diverse ideas on the subject, and "grafted them on Samkhya metaphysics" (p. 229).

There is some controversy on Patanjali's dates and whether he is the same person as the author of *Mahabhashya*, a commentary on Panini's grammar. If the authority of Dasgupta is relied on, the grammarian, Patanjali and the Patanjali of *Yoga Sutras* is one and the same and he lived in the second century B.C. Vyasa of fourth century A.D. wrote a commentary on

Reprinted with permission from *Journal of Indian Psychology*, 1978, **1**, 160–175.

Yoga Sutras and Vacaspati and Vijnana Bhiksu commented extensively on the *Vyasabhasya*. Together these works constitute the original and primary sources of much of the yoga literature in Patanjali tradition. In the *Yogatattva Upanisad* four kinds of yoga, *raja yoga, hatha yoga, laya yoga,* and *mantra yoga* are mentioned. *Raja yoga*, which is the subject of *Yoga Sutras*, is regarded as the highest of all. In *hatha yoga* the emphasis is on physical exercises. *Mantra yoga* involves meditation on certain mystical syllables. Thus, it was recognized that different techniques could be employed to achieve a state of psychic concentration which, it was believed, would enable the practitioner to attain all kinds of *siddhis* or supernatural powers.

Yoga Sutras is in four parts. The first three parts describe the doctrines of the Yoga. The part is devoted, among other things, to criticizing the views of Buddhists. Several scholars, including Dasgupta (1922), argued convincingly that the fourth part is a subsequent addition to the three original parts of Patanjali.

It should be emphasized that yoga is not merely a method having psychical and psycho-physiological implications. Together with Samkhya it is also a full-fledged system of philosophy. Therefore, to understand and grasp the full significance of Patanjali's yoga, it is necessary to be aware of its metaphysical context. Some minor differences of detail notwithstanding, Yoga as a system of philosophy shares, with Samkhya the basic assumptions concerning the nature of man. Therefore, Samkhya and Yoga are traditionally treated as one system in Indian Philosophy.

Samkhya-Yoga system admits two principles, *purusha* and *prakriti*, which may be roughly translated as *self* and *matter*. Selves are many in nature. They cannot be characterized as this or that. Their nature is pure consciousness—consciousness devoid of any representations. *Purusha*, the principle of our consciousness, illumines the various types of sensory data and ideational images, but it is different from them. The contents of our cognitions are the manifestations of *prakriti*, while their awareness is a result of their coming into contact with *purusha*. Awareness is *cit* and is distinguished from the cognitive data of the *buddhi*. Our knowledge of a thing consists, then, in the awareness made possible by the association of the *purusha* with the *buddhi* which is a subtle manifestation of the *prakriti*.

Prakriti has three characteristics or aspects to it. They are *sattava, rajas* and *tamas. Tamas* is mass or inertia. *Rajas* is energy. These are predominant in gross matter. *Sattva* is the subtlest of all matter. It is variously translated as intelligence-stuff, thought-stuff, and so on. It is that which is predominant in all activities and processes that are referred to as psychical or mental. While these *gunas*, as they are called, are the abstract forms of matter, they do not exist independently of each other. They combine in various proportions to give us the variety of objects and thoughts we find in the universe. Their disequilibrium is at the root of the process of evolution and change. While *rajas* and *tamas* dominate in things that we describe as material, *sattva* and *rajas* predominate in what we call thought. But it should be noted that even in the subtlest of our thoughts there is an element of *tamas* and in the grossest of matter there is *sattva*.

It is in virtue of the *sattva* element that the *purusha* is able to partake in the knowledge process and illumine, as it were, the *buddhi* which represents the contents of our consciousness. In emphasizing that the *buddhi* contents—sensory data, images and ideas—are subtle manifestations of matter, Samkhya-Yoga thinkers account for much of our mental life in physicalistic terms. The *purusha*, the transcendental and nonphysical principle is postulated primarily to account for awareness.

The *buddhi* with its greatest preponderance of *sattva* is among the first to evolve out of *prakriti*. In virtue of the dominant *sattva* aspect, the *buddhi* not only resembles the *purusha*, but more importantly it reflects the illumination of *purusha* and, therefore, its contents manifest awareness. We will not be too wrong in interpreting that our brain processes are manifestations of subtle matter, and though insufficient to completely account for our conscious mental life, they are essential for it. The Samkhya view that *purusha* is known, not by observation, but by inference implies that Samkhya-Yoga thinkers postulated a distinct principle of consciousness because they felt that that aspect of our mental life which involves awareness cannot be accounted for without such a principle.

The *sattva* element is what makes it possible for the *purusha* to interface with *prakriti*. Such an interfacing generates the notion of ego and self-consciousness and the *purusha* confuses the ongoing changes of the *buddhi* as its own. The *buddhi* interacts with external objects through the senses and assumes the form of the object of its perception. In fact, Yoga holds that the mind "goes out" through the senses to the objects and assumes their form. The mind, or *citta*, includes the *buddhi*, *ahamkara* (ego) as well as the senses. Like the flame of a lamp, it undergoes incessant changes through its interactions. These changes are interpreted as the experiences of a person.

The concept of *buddhitattva* is very important for an understanding of the extrasensory functioning of the mind. *Buddhitattva* is an aggregate of all *buddhis*. It is, in a sense, the collective mind. "It is a state which holds or comprehends within it the *buddhis* of all individuals" (Dasgupta, 1922, p. 249). Again, as Dasgupta puts it, "Each *buddhi* with its own group of ahamkara (ego) and sense-evolutes thus forms a microcosm separate from similar other buddhis with their associated groups" (p. 250). It seems reasonable to assume, then, that while customarily the individual *buddhi* interacts with the external objects through the involvement of the senses, the archaic connection of all the *buddhis* in the *buddhitattva* makes extrasensory interaction between *buddhis* possible.

Thus, according to Samkhya, the psychic apparatus comprises of *buddhi, ahamkara* and *manas.* These together are often called *citta* in yoga. *Citta* is described as incessantly undergoing changes like the flame of a lamp. It pervades the whole body and can pervade everything (*vibhu*). *Citta* in itself is unconscious. The whole psychic apparatus, a product of *prakriti*, would remain unconscious but for the presence of *purusha.* The psyche is like a painted canvas exhibited in darkness. The sense data get imprinted on the canvas. But the printed canvas requires the light of the *purusha* to illumine it.

The *citta* or the psyche is in a state on continuous change or fluctuations. These fluctuations are called *citta vrittis.* These *vrittis* are limitless in number, but are classified into three categories. The first category comprises false perceptions, errors, illusions and hallucinatory experiences in dreams and waking states. The second category includes all normal experiences of a nonyogin. In the third category are the paranormal experiences achieved through the practice of yoga. The *citta* functions at five levels, resulting in five modalities of consciousness. They are, according to Vyasa, (1) *ksipta* (unstable), (2) *mudha* (obscure), (3) *viksipta* (stable-unstable), (4) *ekagra* (single-pointed) and (5) *niruddha* (fully controlled).

The purpose of Patanjali's yoga is to attain the *niruddha* state where the psychic fluctuations are completely restrained and controlled. This can be achieved by practicing certain psycho-physical exercises that include meditation and concentration.

The *citta* is set in fluctuations not only by the sensory stimulations, but also by the subliminal forces called *samskaras* that include *vasanas.* The *vasanas* are dispositional latencies. *Samskaras* are preconscious and unconscious states that influence one's thoughts and actions. Having their own dynamism, they constantly strive for expressions in consciousness and precipitative *vrittis.* A good deal of man's experience is determined by these latent tendencies. Unless these *samskaras* and *vasanas* are revealed, controlled and eradicated, the *citta* cannot be restrained. Yoga practice therefore aims not only at the shutting of the external inputs provided by sensory stimulation, but also the "burning" of the subliminal latencies so that the *niruddha* state is attained.

The *citta* is not merely a canvas which takes on impressions, not merely a passive plastic state that takes on various forms. As Dasgupta (1930) puts it, "there is also the reserve power in it called the sakti, by virtue of which it can reflect and react back upon itself and change the passivity of its transformations into active states associated with will and effort. Thus, man's thoughts and actions are pure psychological determinations. But there in the *citta* is the reserve force by which it can act upon itself and determine itself. This force gets its full play in the strong effort required in meditation by which a particular state is sought to be kept in a study condition as a check against the natural flowing tendency" (pp. 286–87).

In order that the psyche can act on its own, it is necessary that the fluctuations of the psyche are controlled. Yoga formulates a psycho-physiological method which would help us restrict the fluctuations that obstruct the psyche from acting independently of the senses. Patanjli defines yoga as that which controls the fluctuations of the psyche.

Yoga prescribes an eightfold way to control the fluctuations in the psyche. The first two are *yama* and *niyama* which include certain moral commandments such as truthfulness, non-stealing, continence, cleanliness and contentment. The next two, *asana* and *pranayama*, are physical exercises that involve sitting in comfortable postures and practicing breath control. The fifth stage, *pratyahara*, is simple introspection designed to understand the workings of the psyche. The last three *dharana* (concentration), *dhyana* (meditation) and *samadhi*, a standstill state of the psyche, are the most important ones in attaining the yogic state.

The first five are preparatory and the last three are the essential stages of yoga. The need for the ethical and physiological practices in the yogic training is not difficult to understand. Desires and sensory indulgence encourage further involvement in the sensory processes that result in the constant fluctuations of the psyche which are precisely those yoga seeks to control. The physical exercises are also designed, on one hand, to control internal processes in the body from causing fluctuations in the psyche and, on the other, to reduce the sensory input from outside. Whether or not one takes the yoga physiology of *kundalini* and *chakras* seriously, it is not difficult to see that the practice of breath control, for example, could result in a greater control of the physiological processes in the body. Certain studies (Anand, et al. 1961) have already shown that some yogins are able to exercise a measure of control on their autonomic nervous system, could reduce heart beat, cause sweat on certain parts of the body, etc.

The *pratyahara* or introspective stage is quite important. It seems to focus on certain internal monitoring processes, some sort of biofeedback. It is what appears to be the connecting link between the physiological and the psychological exercises. It is by introspection that the practitioner of yoga is able to regulate the body to suit the requirements of his mental states. Such introspection, it would seem, enables the yogin to isolate those experiences which he is seeking and to produce them later at will.

Now, the object of all these exercises is to enable one to concentrate. There are some who could achieve desired levels of concentration without these exercises. They, of course, could skip them. Concentration or *dharana* produces in us a state in which the natural wandering of our thoughts, the fluctuations of the psyche are brought under control. In a state of concentration, the psyche attends to one thing so that there is intensification of activity of the mind in one direction. In a state of concentration the focus of attention is narrowed. This focus is expanded when one goes from concentration to meditation or *dhyana*. Meditation helps to concentrate longer and to fix our attention on any object for a length of time. When this is achieved, the psyche progresses to a standstill state, where the mind is steady and becomes one with the object of concentration. The triple effort of *dharana-dhyana-samadhi* is called *samyama*. According to *Yoga Sutras* one could achieve supernormal powers by doing *samyama* on a variety of things.

If the physical exercises help the inhibition of cerebral activities, concentration, it would seem, enables us to reverse the cognitive process. When the designed levels of concentration are achieved, the psyche is no longer affected by stimuli acting on it. Concentration not only helps to inhibit stimuli exciting the psyche and causing fluctuations in it, but enables the individual to focus attention on desired objects. When this is achieved, the psyche can make a contact directly with the object and apparently obtain extrasensory knowledge of it. There are thus three important aspects to yoga. Firstly, there is the inhibition of cerebral activity, withdrawing of the senses. Secondly, the psyche is activated by concentration. And, finally, the expansion of concentration reverses the role of psyche from one of receiving impressions through senses to one of acting directly so as to take the form of objects independent of the senses.

It has been said that yoga involves some sort of autohypnosis (Zorab, 1963). It may well be. The one-pointed concentration and meditation can cause fatigue and the desired monotony to produce a hypnotic state. There are also unquestionable similarities between the two states. In both the general cerebral activity can be suppressed at will. In both the attention can be focused on the desired object to a degree that is definitely superior to the waking state. It is possible that the yogic concentration in its early phases generates hallucinatory imagery similar to that obtained under hypnosis.

Even if we conclude from these similarities that yogic concentration produces a state similar to hypnotic state, it must be admitted that yoga does more. Yoga involves also further training to which claims of para-normality could be attributed. It is in this context, we could see the similarities between yoga and Ryzl's technique. Ryzl (1966) describes the state of mind specially favorable for the manifestation of psi in the following words. "It is a particular state of consciousness, defying adequate description, between sleep and walking, which we most likely could characterize as a state of appeasement of mental activity and of depriving the mind of arrival of normal sensory impressions with a simultaneous intensive directing of attention in one direction." This is precisely what yoga claims to do by means of physical exercises and concentration.

Moreover, the process of hallucinating by the subject may be quite relevant to the training. The *modus operandi* involved in creating hallucinations and in having extrasensory perceptions may be the same, even though the source is different. The suggestion of Ryzl that the subject should be able to hallucinate in order that he may be successfully trained to get ESP impressions is, therefore, something that deserves further explorations.

Empirical Studies

There has been a recent upsurge of interest among psychologists in the study of meditation (e.g., Benson & Klipper, 1976; Deikman, 1966, 1969; Goleman, 1971; Green & Green, 1971; Maupin, 1969; Naranjo & Ornstein, 1971, Ornstein, 1973; Tart, 1969; 1975). In the last few years a number of parapsychologists have also shown interest in meditation as a psi facilitative technique.

Schmeidler (1970), who was the first to attempt a systematic study of meditation and psi, found her subjects scoring high on an ESP task following a brief instruction in meditation and breathing. The subjects in this study did an ESP run first by calling the symbols. Then they listened to a swami's lecture on meditation, performed the prescribed breathing exercises, and made a second ESP run. The results of this study showed that while the performance in the first run was close to chance the scores in the second run were significantly more than chance expectation, suggesting that meditation may have been responsible for psi hitting in the second run.

Osis and Bokert (1971) carried out three correlational studies and found meditation and ESP to be related in a complex manner. The meditative practices of the subjects in this study varied as they were encouraged to use their own preferred techniques. Some subjects employed Zen and Raja yoga methods, while others adopted self-hypnosis, depth imagery or concentration. The ESP tests employed were both forced choice and free response tasks. The forced choice test is a version of Burgmans' checkerboard test with a close-circuit TV adaptation. The free response test involved guessing pictorial slides. Questionnaires designed to measure changes in the state of consciousness were administered before and after each session. The ESP tests themselves were given after a period of meditation.

A factor analysis of the questionnaire material revealed three stable factors. Of these the factor of "self-transcendence and openness to experience" was found to be associated significantly with ESP scores. The investigators expressed that, among other possibilities, the meager correlations between meditative experiences and ESP might be due to subjects' experiencing the ESP tests as interruptions to their meditation, causing, "task rivalry" and possibly a preferential effect.

Roll and associates carried out a series of experiments to explore the possible effects of Eno meditation on ESP scores. Eno, we are told, is a "philosophy-free" meditation technique which resembles Zen. In their first study, by integrating the ESP task into the experience of meditation itself, Roll and Solfvin (1976a) were able to control for "task rivalry" which was a problem in the study by Osis and Bokert (1971). The design of the study is unfortunately too complicated with so many variables that it is difficult to reasonably estimate the effect of meditation on ESP. The authors conclude, however, that "meditation items were related to free-response GESP results and not to clairvoyance..." (p. 97). An attempted replication (Roll & Solfvin, 1976b) failed to support the hypothesis that GESP scoring is related to meditation. But a post-hoc analysis revealed significant difference between scores on preferred and non-preferred targets.

In another study, Roll, Solfvin and Kreiger (1978) reported a significant correlation between group target ranking in a remote viewing experiment and the group's liking or disliking for the agent as arrived at by majority decision. The same investigators (1978b) attempted a replication of this finding with a somewhat altered procedure. The subjects in this experiment meditated with halved Ping-Pong balls placed over their open eyes. The results did not confirm their previous results.

Stanford and Palmer (1973) administered an ESP test, which involved describing twenty remote target persons, to Malcolm Bessent after he meditated for a period of 15-20 minutes. The results gave no overall evidence of psi, but post-hoc analysis revealed some effects linking psi and mean alpha frequency monitored from the right occipital.

In one investigation Rao and Puri (1978) explored the effect of transcendental meditation on ESP performance with student subjects using Rao's Subsensory Psi Test. Though meditation did not substantially alter ESP performance from pre- to post-meditation sessions, a post-hoc analysis utilizing variance scores provided some suggestive evidence that transcendental meditation may enhance one's psi ability.

In a PK study by Matas and Pantas (1971) subjects who had experience with some form of meditation, meditated for 15 minutes before they attempted to influence by PK a random event generator. The results of the meditators were found to be significantly better than those of control subjects who performed identical tasks without meditating. In three series of experiments, Schmidt and Pantas (1971) found that a single subject performed significantly on a PK task after practicing Zen meditation for 20 minutes prior to the test.

While the results of the experiments reviewed so far do suggest ESP on the part of meditating subjects, it is difficult to conclude that meditation has a facilitating influence on psi. There is an inherent difficulty in designing experiments in this area so as to control for other possibly relevant variables. In Schmeidler's experiment, the subjects' success in post-meditation sessions may have been due to subject's expectancy. The results of the study of Osis and Bokert are, by no means, unequivocal in supporting a meditation—ESP interaction, especially because the subjects' questionnaire response may have been influenced by the knowledge of their success. The studies of Roll and associates also do not provide the necessary evidence. By far the most impressive results are those reported by Schmidt and Pantas. But then, Schmidt had obtained equally impressive if not better results with other non-meditating subjects. Thus, while none of the studies reviewed so far provide convincing evidence that meditation would facilitate psi manifestation, the experiments by Schmeidler and by Matas and Pantas do suggest such a possibility. In the latter, the subject expectancy is controlled for by an independent-subjects design, but the effects of experimenter expectancy are not ruled out.

The traditional belief that supernormal abilities could be acquired through the practice of yoga, together with the suggestive evidence we reviewed above, and the findings that yogins could exercise voluntary control over some of their autonomic processes, suggest the possibility that we may encounter psi more readily among the practitioners of yoga. Therefore, we find many writers (Atreya, 1957; Good, 1963; Kalghati, 1973; Pandey, 1963; Rao 1965; Sharma, 1964; Thouless, 1963) urge very strongly that we undertake investigations in India to test the validity of these claims. The research reported here was in response to these demands to verify the claims of the paranormal among the yoga practitioners through controlled data collection. The project began in 1971 and a first report of the findings incorporating one part of the results was presented in 1972 at the fifteenth annual convention of the Parapsychological Association held in Edinburgh.

Any research attempts with yogins have to take note of several problems. First, there is the difficulty of finding genuine yogins. There are not too many around just waiting for us to test. In the very nature of it we should not expect a true yogin wandering around gathering disciples and giving public demonstrations. Second, the practitioner of yoga is warned that his paranormal abilities stand in the way of his spiritual development and that he should, therefore, scrupulously avoid using them (Atreya, 1954; Bhat, 1964; Bharathi, 1974; Kanthamani, 1971; Woods, 1927). The efforts by the senior author to find yogins who could provide demonstrable evidence for any form of psi did not succeed. Therefore, a compromise was worked out, which consisted of testing relatively normal people at different stages of yogic expertise before and after they entered into a meditation state believed to enhance one's psi ability.

The term "meditation," in this study, refers to a combination of several aspects of yoga practice which enable the subjects to attain a meditative state. These include *mandala* gazing, *pranayama* (breath control), *laya yoga* (*Kundalini* arousal) and *japa yoga* (mantra chanting). Swami Gitananda, the founder and mentor of the Ananda Ashram where this research was carried out says: "The Yoga concept of meditation is not one of mysticism, but rather is an open approach through the human mind to the higher states of consciousness" (personal communication). Meditation was also defined by other yogins as the expulsion of thoughts (Ramana Maharshi, 1968) or the act of detaching the mind from the senses (Bhoomananda Thirtha, 1968). It should be mentioned also that all the subjects daily practiced hatha yogic exercises in addition to their chosen form of meditation.

Method

Subjects

The subjects are students of the Ananda Ashram run by Swami Gitananda at Pondicherry and Bangalore in South India. For the purposes of this experiment, the subjects were classified into juniors and seniors depending on how long they had practiced meditation before the experiment. A junior subject was one who was only recently inducted into yoga practice. A senior subject was one who had already attained some experience in yoga and practiced it for at least a couple of months under supervision. In cases of doubt, Swami Gitananda was consulted. In all cases, the decision whether a subject was a junior or senior was decided before administering the ESP tests.

A total of 59 subjects participated. Of these, 31 were juniors and 28 were seniors. They were tested in three series of experiments. There were 36 men and 23 women who either resided in the Ashram or came daily for the yoga practice to the Ashram. Their ages ranged from 18 to 69 years. Juniors in the pilot series participated in the first confirmatory series as senior subjects. In the pilot and the first confirmatory series all the subjects were Westerners, whereas in the second confirmatory study all the subjects were Indians and Hindus.

Procedure

The subjects in each of the three series were tested by H.D. in eight sessions during a period when they were undergoing intensive training in the practice of yoga and meditation. In each of these sessions, they were administered ESP tests just before they started meditation and immediately after they had meditated. The subjects in the pilot series were tested individually and on the average once in every three days. The experimenter resided in the Ashram throughout the period of investigation and operated within the framework of the Ashram programme. By mutual agreement between the experimenter and the subjects, the time for testing was pre-arranged. Each subject decided for himself what meditative approach he would use on a particular day.

ESP Tests

A forced choice ESP card test and a free response picture target test were used to assess the subject's psi ability. The card test was a double blind matching clairvoyance technique which consisted of two runs of 50 cards, i.e., 4 standard ESP runs, or 100 trials. In this test the experimenter randomly inserted five ESP cards (key cards), one of each kind, into opaque black envelopes out of subject's sight, thoroughly shuffled the deck containing the 50 ESP cards (target cards) and asked the subject to match the cards in the deck with those in the envelopes. This the subjects attempted to do without knowing the identity of the symbols on the cards in the envelope and without seeing the faces of the cards they were matching. Thus, the subject was blind to the key cards as well as the target cards while he sorted the cards. The free response test was a picture target clairvoyance test which involved the subject guessing a single picture enclosed in an opaque envelope. Each subject guessed a different picture in each session, one picture before meditating and another after meditating. The target-picture packets were prepared in the following way.

The staff of the Department of Psychology and Parapsychology of Andhra University, was responsible for the preparation of the targets for the picture test. The experimenter had no knowledge of the picture inside the envelope when he gave the tests. P.D., a lecturer in the Department of Psychology and Parapsychology, selected several hundred black and white pictures with some affective content, from Indian newspapers. She placed one picture each in 6" × 9" manila envelopes, initialed the lid of the envelope, and over her initials, placed a strip of scotch tape to seal the envelopes. She then numbered each target envelope consecutively beginning with one. The number on the envelope was the identifying number of that particular picture target.

The concealed targets were then passed on to B.P., another staff member, who randomized them, placed each in a larger manila envelope, and sealed the envelopes. He then randomized these picture target packets, as they are now called, and labeled each with consecutive numbers again beginning with one. The complete set of targets was then handed over to the experimenter for use with the subjects. A similar procedure was followed to replenish the target packets for use in subsequent series.

The testing was done in a closed room or in the "mandir" of the Ashram. Both experimenter and subject sat facing each other on a straw mat on the floor. No one else was allowed in the room during testing sessions and all necessary precautions were taken against sensory cues. The experimenter used a high table situated at the back of the subject to insert the key cards in black opaque envelopes before the commencement of each double run. This manipulation was completely out of the visual range of the subject. In the first session the subjects were told precisely what they had to do. By the third session there was hardly any need to repeat the instructions. Good rapport existed between experimenter and subjects. Motivation was minimal. No rewards were offered or suggested. After each run, checking and recording of hits on the card test was done by the experimenter in the presence of the subject. At the conclusion of the test, the subject noted his total score and signed the sheet. When the experimenter returned from the Ashram to the department of Psychology and Parapsychology, all the score sheets were independently rechecked.

During the free response tests each subject attempted to describe the target by writing on a sheet of paper attached to the target-packet. The experimenter brought these back to the department with their seals intact. Later, the response sheets were separated from the targets by an assistant who made typed copies of them, substituting code numbers for the purpose of identifying them later. These typed copies, the protocols, were given to two judges for independent evaluation.

Results

Card Tests

The results of the card test data are given in Table 1 separately for the three series. The first was a pilot and the other two were the confirmatory series. It was planned to test the subjects individually in eight sessions, each session consisting of 100 trials before meditation and 100 trials after they meditated. A few subjects, however, could not complete all the eight sessions.

The 15 junior subjects did 464 standard ESP runs of 25 trials each during the pre-meditation session and an equal number of runs in the post-meditation session. They obtained 2,198 hits (-122) in the pre-meditation and 2,411 hits (+91) in the post-meditation session. The difference was significant (t = 2.97; 14 df; p<.01). The 12 senior subjects did 376 runs before and 376 runs after meditation and scored 1,891 (+11) and 1,860 (-20) hits respectively. The difference between pre-and post-meditation scores is insignificant. From these results it appeared that the junior group alone tended to obtain better ESP scores during the post-meditation sessions. We wondered whether the failure of the senior group to show this effect might have been due to their greater awareness of the stigma attached against the acquisition of paranormal powers by yogins.

Two confirmatory experiments were subsequently carried out. The first was again conducted at the Pondicherry branch of the Ashram, and used the same procedure as before. The nine seniors were originally the juniors of the pilot experiment. The nine juniors were new students at the Ashram. Again, all the subjects were Westerners. Testing of each group was done on alternate days until the eight sessions were completed. The junior subjects obtained 1,292 hits (-148) in 288 pre-meditation runs and 1,580 hits (+140) in 288 post-meditation runs (t = 7.57; 8 df; P<.001). The seniors obtained 1,345 hits (-75) and 1,501 hits (+81) in 284 pre- and 284 post-meditation runs respectively (t = 3.92; 8 df; p<.01.

Since the seniors in this experiment were from the junior group of the pilot experiment, we needed to see whether a fresh batch of seniors

Table 1
Results of Card Tests

Experiment	Group	n	No. of Runs	Pre-meditation Scores				Post-meditation Scores						
				No. of Hits	Deviation	CR	p	No. of Hits	Deviation	CR	p	t	df	p
Pilot	Juniors	15	464	2198	-122	2.83	.044	2411	+91	2.11	.03	2.97	14	<.01
	Seniors	12	376	1891	+11	.28	ns	1860	-20	.52	ns	0.85	11	ns
Conf. I	Juniors	9	288	1292	-148	4.36	.00002	1580	+140	4.12	.00004	7.57	8	<.001
	Seniors	9	284	1345	-75	2.2	.02	1501	+81	2.4	.01	3.92	8	<.01
Conf. II	Juniors	7	216	998	-82	2.79	.005	1127	+47	1.6	ns	2.62	6	<.05
	Seniors	7	224	1043	-77	2.57	.01	1235	+115	3.84	.001	4.13	6	<.01

would show the same effect. The second confirmatory study was carried out at the Bangalore branch of the Ananda Ashram, also taught by Swami Gitananda. This time, the subjects were all Indians and practicing Hindus. They did not live at the Ashram; most of them were working people, and lived in their homes. All 14 subjects (seven seniors and seven juniors) were tested daily, usually after work. Testing was done in the Mandir where there was adequate provision for meditation. The junior subjects obtained 998 hits (−82) in 216 pre-meditation and 1,127 hits (+47) in 216 post-meditation runs ($t = 2.62$; 6 df; $p<.05$). The senior subjects did 224 runs before and 224 runs after meditation and obtained 1,043 hits (−77) and 1,235 hits (+115) respectively ($t = 4.13$; 6 df; $p<.01$). Thus this group, like all the previous ones except the seniors in the pilot experiment, supported the hypothesis that the meditators' ESP scores would be better when they tested after they had meditated than before.

Free Response Picture Tests

The picture tests were evaluated by two judges independently. Both of them evaluated the protocols against the target pictures in the following way. They were given the 16 protocols of each subject and the sixteen target pictures. The judges attempted to rank and rate each protocol against the sixteen potential target pictures. The judges operated without any knowledge of whether the protocols belonged to pre-meditation sessions or post-meditation sessions. The target which appeared to be identical or closest to a given protocol was given a rank of 1, while the other targets were awarded ranks in a descending order so that the protocol which had least resemblance to any of the picture targets received a rank of 16. Rating of the protocols was also done with a 100-point scale in such a way that the picture which seemed to match the protocol perfectly would get 100 points and the picture which had no resemblance to the protocol would have a score of 0.

After the ratings and rankings were given to all the items, the rank

Table 2
Results of Picture Tests

Mode of Evaluation	Pre-meditation Scores Mean	Post-meditation Scores Mean	t	df	p
Rank	8.79	8.19	2.00	58	<.05
Rating	20.02	22.60	2.08	58	<.05

and rating scores given to the target picture by the two judges are taken as the ESP score for the trial. The scores of the two judges were averaged. Then the pre-meditation scores were separated from the post-meditation scores and were averaged for each subject. Thus, we have the post-meditation and pre-meditation rank and rating scores for each of the 59 subjects.

The scoring of the picture tests took place several months after the results of the card tests were known. Therefore, it was planned to analyze the results with picture tests of all the subjects in all the three sessions together without separating them into juniors and seniors. The results are given in Table 2.

Both the rank order and rating scores indicated that the subjects guessed the pictures relatively better after they meditated.

The mean rank score during the pre-meditation session is 8.79. It is 8.19 for the post-meditation. The mean chance expectation is 8.50. A t test of the difference gives a t of 2.00 which, with 58 degrees of freedom, is significant at the five per cent level. The pre- and post-meditation rating scores also differed significantly. The judges gave a mean rating of 20.02 for the pre-meditation trials and 22.60 for the post-meditation trials. The t of the difference is 2.08 (58 df), $p<.05$. Thus, the results of picture tests seem to confirm those obtained in the card tests.

Discussion

From the aphorisms of Patanjali to the matching of cards and guessing of concealed pictures in our experiments, the descent is rather steep and by no means smooth. Testing of esoteric ideas within a laboratory set up is what we have attempted to do. In the process we made a number of assumptions. Some of them may be dubious and questionable. For instance, we assumed that our subjects had acquired a measure of skill in the art of meditation which we hoped to manipulate in the two conditions of testing. We had, however, no objective criteria to measure the depth or even genuineness of their "meditative" states. Therefore, other interpretations of the results such as the life style in the Ashram setting, the expectancy set of the subjects and their obviously favorable belief that meditation would enhance psi ability are not ruled out.

Again, our design utilized the same subjects in both the conditions. Some have questioned whether the same-subjects design is appropriate for research of this sort (Honorton, 1977). While we do concede that subject's expectations and motivation are relevant variables which were not controlled in this study, it appears to us that independent-subjects design will not be wholly free either from some of these contaminating variables. It will not be easy to match subjects for their motivation. Also, studies have shown that experimenter expectancies could be just as contaminating as subject expectancies.

While interpreting our results, a point that should be kept in mind is that the subjects in the pre-meditation session did not score at chance. They tended, in a highly significant manner, to psi-miss or to avoid the targets in the card tests. Even in picture tests the same trend is apparent from the rank scores. Since avoidance presumes the knowledge of the target in some sense, we must assume that the subjects are giving evidence of psi even during pre-meditation testing. Therefore, it would be difficult to maintain that the meditating exercises are, by themselves, psi conducive. It would be more appropriate to think that the meditators (whether or not they meditated before participating in a psi test) have a better control of psi which they could use to miss or hit, than to assume that the meditation exercises preceding the ESP tests enabled the subjects to enhance their psi. This hypothesis could easily be tested in future experiments.

Another possibility is that the subject who was about to meditate found the ESP task a distraction and her psychological set at this time was conducive to psi-missing. Sailaja and Rao (1973) reported that their subjects who were called for an interview but given ESP tests before the interview tended to psi-miss. Their post-interview ESP scores, like the post-meditation ESP scores in this study, tended to be positive and were significantly different from the pre-interview scores. Thus, we wonder whether the results of these experiments may not be better explained by the familiar differential effect, an often observed tendency for the subject to score differentially when confronted with contrasting conditions by hitting in one condition and missing in the other.

Even assuming that what we have here is the differential effect, we could still consider meditation as psi facilitating in that the rather strong and consistent effect we have observed may have been due to meditation. This argument would be strong if the results would show that one's progress in meditation is accompanied by a concomitant improvement in post-meditation ESP scores. Therefore, we made the following post-hoc analysis.

The junior subjects who by definition have not yet reached a satisfactory state of yogic development may be expected to improve during the period of testing. For instance, testing in the pilot series took nearly four weeks and each subject was tested in 8 sessions spread over this period. It was the period when the subjects were going through intensive training in yoga. If we assume that the subjects had learned to meditate better in the latter half of the period of testing when compared to the first, we should expect them to perform better in the ESP tests during the last four sessions in comparison to the first four sessions. The junior subjects obtained an average of 20.92 hits per session during the first four post-meditation sessions and an average of 21.43 hits per session during the last four post-meditation sessions. Though the t value for the difference between these two means does not reach an acceptable level of significance ($t = 1.13$, $df = 30$), the tendency is in the expected direction. It is also interesting to note that the senior subjects have not shown a similar tendency. They have obtained an average of 20.41 hits in the first four sessions and an average of 20.67 hits in the last four sessions ($t = .042$, $df = 27$).

Thus, our results do not provide a conclusive case for any intrinsic relationship between psi and meditation. Rather they together with the traditional belief that yoga enables one to control the natural wanderings of the mind, a control that is claimed necessary for acquiring paranormal abilities, warrant further investigations with better controls and design that permit unambiguous interpretation of the results.

In fact, a review by Charles Honorton (1977) of some 80 experimental studies involving what he called the internal attention states which include states of mind induced by hypnosis, relaxation, Ganzfeld stimulation and meditation, suggests that psi research in these areas is about the most promising in terms of results. He concluded:

> Psi functioning is enhanced (i.e., is more easily detected and recognized) when the receiver is in a state of sensory relaxation and is minimally influenced by ordinary perception and proprioception (1977, p. 466).

If yoga is a method of reducing external as well as internal noise of the human system and if such a noise reduction is psi facilitative, then the possibilities of controlling psi through yoga techniques is definitely suggested.

References

Anand, B.K., Chinna, G.S. and Singh, B. Some aspects of electroencephalographic studies in yogis. *Electroencephalography & Clinical Neurophysiology,* 1961, 13. 452–456.

Atreya, B.L. *The philosophy of yogavasistha* (Rev. Ed.) Banaras: Indian Book Shop, 1954.

Atreya, B.L. *An introduction to parapsychology* (2nd Ed.). Banaras: International Standard Publications, 1957.

Benson, H. & Klipper, M.Z. *The relaxation response*. London: Collins, 1976.

Bharathi, A. The ontological status of psychic phenomena in Hinduism and Buddhism. In A. Angoff and D. Barth (Eds.) *Parapsychology and Anthropology*. New York: Parapsychology Foundation, 1974.

Bhat, V.M. *Yogic powers and God realization*. Bombay: Bharatiya Vidya Bhavan, 1964.

Bhoomananda Thirtha. *Brahma Vidyabhyasa*. Kerala: Narayanasram Thapovanam, 1968.

Dasgupta, S. *History of Indian philosophy*, Vol. 1, London: George Allen and Unwin, 1922.

Dasgupta, S. *Yoga philosophy in relation to other systems of Indian thought*. Calcutta: University of Calcutta, 1930.

Deikman, A.J. Deautomatization and the mystic experience. *Psychiatry*, 1966, 29, 324–338.

Deikman, A.J. Experimental meditation. In C.T. Tart (Ed.), *Altered states of consciousness*. New York: Wiley, 1969.

Goleman, D. Meditation as meta–therapy: Hypotheses towards a proposed fifth state of consciousness. *Journal of Transpersonal Psychology*, 1971, 3, 1–25.

Good, I.J. Quantum mechanics and yoga. *Research Journal of Philosophy and Social Sciences*. 1963, 1, 92–98.

Green, E.E. & Green, A.M. On the meaning of transpersonal: Some metaphysical perspectives. *Journal of Transpersonal Psychology*, 1971, 3, 27–46.

Honorton, C. Psi and internal attention states. In Benjamin B. Wolman (Ed.), *Handbook of Parapsychology*. New York: Van Nostrand Rheinhold Company, 1977.

Kalghati, T.G. A new look at paranormal phenomena. *Research Journal of Philosophy and Social Sciences*, 1963, 1, 99–106.

Kanthamani, B.K. Psychical study in India: Past and present. In A. Angoff and B. Shapin (Eds.) *A century of psychical research: The continuing doubts and affirmations*. New York: Parapsychology Foundation, 1971.

Matas F. & Pantas, L. A PK experiment comparing meditating versus non–meditating subjects. *Proceedings of the Parapsychological Association*, 1971, 8, 12–13.

Maupin, E.W. On meditation. In C.T. Tart (Ed.) *Altered states of consciousness*. New York: Wiley, 1969.

Naranjo, C. & Ornstein, R.E. *On the psychology of meditation*. New York: Viking, 1971.

Ornstein, R.E. (Ed.) *The nature of human consciousness. A book of readings*. San Francisco: Freeman, 1973.

Osis, K. & Bokert, E. ESP and changed states of consciousness induced by meditation. *Journal of the American Society for Psychical Research*, 1971, 65, 17–65.

Pandey, R.C. ESP and yoga. *Research Journal of Philosophy and Social Sciences*, 1963, 1, 92–98.

Ramana Maharshi. *The collected works*. Tiruvanamalai: Sri Ramanasram, 1968.

Rao, K.R. Bidirectionality of psi. *Proceedings of the Parapsychological Association*, 1965, 2, 37–59.

Rao, K.R. & Puri, I. Subsensory perception (SSP), extrasensory perception (ESP) and transcendental meditation. *Journal of Indian Psychology*, 1978, 1, 69–74.

Roll, W.G. & Solfvin, G.F. Meditation and ESP. In J.D. Morris, W.G. Roll and R.L. Morris (Eds.), *Research in Parapsychology* 1975, 92–97. Metuchen: Scarecrow, 1976.

Roll, W.G., Solfvin, G.F. & Krieger, J.B. Meditation and ESP: A comparison of conditions. Abstracted in *Journal of Parapsychology*, 1978, 43, 53–54.

Ryzl, M. *Application of hypnosis in ESP* Research paper read at the Parapsychology Seminar, Andhra University, Waltair, 1966.

Sailaja, P. & Rao, K.R. *Experimental studies of the differential effect in life setting.* *Parapsychological Monographs*, No. 13. New York: Parapsychology Foundation, 1973.

Schmeidler, G.R. High ESP scores after a swami's brief instruction in meditation and breathing. *Journal of the American Society for Psychical Research*, 1970, 64, 100–103.

Sharma, R. (Ed). Parapsychology and yoga. Review by B.K. Kanthamani. *Journal of Parapsychology*, 1964, 28, 141–142.

Solfvin, G.F., Roll, W.G. & Krieger, J.B. Meditation and ESP: Remote viewing. In W.G. Roll J.D. Morris and R.L. Morris (Eds.), *Research in Parapsychology*, 1977, 151–157, Metuchen, NJ: Scarecrow Press, 1978.

Stanford, R.G. & Palmer, J. Meditation prior to the ESP task: An EEG study with an outstanding ESP subject. In W.G. Roll, R.L. Morris & J.D. Morris (Eds.), *Research in Parapsychology*, 34–36. 1972. Metuchen: Scarecrow Press, 1973.

Tart, C.T. (Ed.) *Altered states of consciousness: A book of readings.* New York: Wiley, 1969.

Tart, C.T. *States of consciousness*, New York: Dutton, 1975.

Thouless, R.H. The control of psi phenomena. *Research Journal of Philosophy and Social Sciences*, 1963, 1, 71–74.

Woods, J.H. *The yoga system of Patanjali,* Cambridge: Harvard University Press, 1927.

Zorab, G. Yoga and parapsychology. *Research Journal of Philosophy and Social Sciences.* 1963, 1, 78–83.

CHAPTER 18

Meta-Analysis of Psi Ganzeld Research: A Response to Hyman

Charles Honorton

In the early 1970s, a number of investigators were independently led to explore the effects of perceptual isolation techniques on performance in an ESP task (Braud, Wood, & Braud, 1975; Honorton & Harper, 1974; Parker, 1975). The psi ganzfeld research developed out of earlier research suggesting that successful performance in psi tasks is frequently associated with internal attention states brought about through dreaming, hypnosis, induced physical relaxation, and related procedures involving perceptual restriction. (For reviews, see Braud, 1978; Honorton, 1977; Honorton & Krippner, 1969.) The initial success of several different investigators with the ganzfeld technique stimulated wider interest, which led to a shift in emphasis from the process-oriented origins of the research to one focusing on replication rates. Earlier reviews of ganzfeld replication rates suggested a success rate over 50 percent in studies using the technique (e.g., Blackmore, 1980; Honorton, 1978).

Hyman's critique of the psi ganzfeld research (Hyman, 1985) is concerned with two issues: (a) whether the psi ganzfeld experiment supplies evidence for the existence of psi and (b) whether the effects obtained in psi ganzfeld experiments are replicable. I believe the existence of psi will remain in dispute until putative psi effects can be produced and studied with some specifiable degree of replicability. I am therefore primarily concerned with the extent to which the psi ganzfeld paradigm represents a

Reprinted with permission from *Journal of Psychology*, 1985, 49, 51–91.

step in that direction. The central claim under discussion is a replicability claim and, as such, will eventually be resolved through future replications.

The data base I am using comprises the 42 psi ganzfeld studies reported between 1974 and 1981 that reflect the scope of Hyman's review. Subsequent to the time I received Hyman's request for assistance with his review, I learned of additional studies that either had been unknown to me or were reported later; but because Hyman elected to freeze his analysis to the initial set of 42 studies, I shall do so too.

To facilitate comparison of the two papers, I am also adopting Hyman's format of referring to specific studies by the use of study numbers and an appendix for referencing the studies. Since there are numerous and often major points of disagreement between us over the interpretation of individual studies, I have documented my coding and major analyses in a way that will allow readers to reconstruct the process by consulting the original reports.

The following discussion is divided into four major sections. In the first section, I focus on whether there is, in fact, a statistically significant effect in the psi ganzfeld data base. The second section assesses the likely impact of reporting bias in psi ganzfeld studies. The relationship between study outcomes and various potential threats to their internal validity is explored in the third section. Finally, in the fourth section, I shall discuss Hyman's classification and analysis of flaws.

Is There an Effect?

Hyman devotes over half of his paper to the question of whether, after taking into account the effects of multiple analysis, choice of sampling units, and possibilities of selective reporting bias, there is an aggregate psi ganzfeld effect. He suggests on the basis of his assessment of these factors that the actual rate of success (i.e., proportion of "significant" experiments) is at most 30% and that owing to multiple testing options, the true chance rate may be 25% or higher, not 5% as assumed in earlier replication rate estimates. In this section, I present an evaluation that is not influenced by multiple analysis.

Sampling Units

Hyman (pp. 9–11) raises a valid concern regarding ambiguities in the definition of study units where multiple conditions are involved. This problem, unfortunately, is endemic to meta-analysis, and there is no easy solution. As Cooper (1984) comments, "Obviously there will be some subjectivity in the reviewer's judgment of what constitutes a study. For instance, one reviewer might consider all results in a single report as one study. But another reviewer might consider a report that divides results into separate studies as containing more than one study" (p. 75).

Raburn's study (Studies 16 and 17) illustrates the problem. Ten subjects were assigned to each of four cells, in a 2 × 2 factorial design. One factor varied the presence of a sender (sender/no sender), and the other varied subjects' awareness of the ESP task (informed/uninformed). As in all of the other psi ganzfeld studies in this data base, subjects in the informed condition knew they were participating in an ESP task. Subjects in the uninformed condition, however, were led to believe that the experiment was "merely an attempt to elucidate physiological functions associated with sensory deprivation" (Raburn, 1975, pp. 11–12). This represented a radical departure from the standard ganzfeld procedure, one that is unique within the ganzfeld data base. I therefore excluded the uninformed condition, considering only the two cells in which subjects knew they were participating in an ESP task as valid ganzfeld studies.

Inevitably, there will be differences of opinion on decisions of this sort, and Hyman (p. 9) disagrees with my exclusion of Raburn's uninformed condition. Adrian Parker (personal communication, January 10, 1983), on the other hand, agrees that the uninformed condition should be excluded, and he would also exclude the informed–no-sender condition on the grounds that, unlike other ganzfeld studies with clairvoyance procedures, subjects in Raburn's no-sender group were misinformed that there would be a sender.

Though acknowledging that my classification of Raburn's study has, in itself, little effect on the overall evaluation of the data base as a whole, Hyman (pp. 9–11) suggests that similar ambiguities exist in the classification of all studies with multiple conditions. Readers are invited to examine the original study descriptions and draw their own conclusions about the appropriateness of study classifications over which Hyman and I disagree.

Indices of Success

Five indices of success have been used in psi ganzfeld research. Four are based on blind-judging procedures in which the subject or judge is presented with a set of pictures ("judging pool") consisting of the target and a number of control pictures ("decoys"). The judge ranks (or rates) the degree of similarity between each picture and the verbal impressions ("mentation report") elicited during the ganzfeld session.

DIRECT HITS

The most widely used variation is the direct-hits index. Here credit is given only when the target is correctly identified from a judging pool of N elements; so the probability of a hit on each trial is $1/N$. The overall success rate for a series is estimated through the binomial critical ratio (CR) or the exact binomial probability is calculated directly. The direct-hits measure is the simplest index of success, but also the most conservative since it discards most of the rank data.

BINARY (PARTIAL) HITS

The binary-hits index represents a crude weighting scheme that gives credit if the target is in the lower half of the ranks. If, for example, there are six elements in the judging pool, a partial hit is counted when a rank of 1, 2, or 3 is assigned to the target, and the probability of a hit is $1/2$. Though giving some weight to partial hits, this measure still discards half of the rank data, and direct hits receive no more credit than partial ones.

SUM OF RANKS

The sum-of-ranks statistic is the most powerful rank index because it uses all the rank data and differentially rewards lower rank values. It became widely used following publication of the paper by Solfvin, Kelly, and Burdick (1978), which provided formulas and convenient tables.

STANDARDIZED RATINGS

A related index, which has been used in a few studies, uses standardized ratings (Stanford & Sargent, 1983). Here the target and decoys are rated, for example, on a scale from 0 to 100; and the rating assigned to the actual target is standardized. This measure has primarily been used to provide more continuous psi scores in studies correlating psi performance with psychological variables. Standardized ratings can also be reduced to ranks for analysis by one of the rank methods described above.

BINARY CODING

A very different index, used in eight studies in this data base, involved the Maimonides binary coding system (Honorton, 1975). This required a specially constructed target set defined in terms of the presence or absence of features in each of 10 categories such that the content of each target could be encoded as a 10-digit binary number. In contrast to the other indices described above, determination of success with this method does not involve comparison with decoys. The subject's mentation is coded with respect to the 10 target descriptors, thus producing a 10-bit response, which is simply matched against the target code. Because the target is selected from a pool containing all possible combinations of the presence or absence of the 10 features, each experimental trial constitutes 10 independent binary trials with a chance expectation of 5.

A number of factors could influence the relative sensitivity of the various indices. Although a detailed consideration of these issues is beyond the purview of our present discussion, one example, the composition of judging pools in studies with blind-judging procedures, illustrates some of the problems. Except for studies using the binary coding system, each investigator contributing to this data base has used a different target set and uniquely composed judging pools. To maximize the subject's ability to distinguish targets from decoys, the investigator must make the content of pictures in the judging pool as dissimilar as possible. If the subject's mentation report includes impressions of people and there are people in several pictures in the judging pool, there is a judging problem. Indices based on binary hits, sum of ranks, or standardized ratings are likely to be more sensitive than a direct-hits measure in such cases since lower ranks (or ratings) can be spread over the pictures containing mentation-related content. Avoiding overlap of content among the elements in a judging pool becomes more of a problem as the number of pictures in the judging pool increases, and it is probably for this reason that most investigators have limited their judging pools to four elements.

Multiple Analysis

There is no doubt that many investigators have applied multiple statistical tests or indices without adjusting their significance criteria for the number of tests used. This practice *could*, as Hyman argues, dramatically alter our estimates of overall significance. Although Hyman and I agree that there is a multiple-analysis problem in this data base, we have taken different approaches to evaluating its impact.

MULTIPLE-ANALYSIS FLAW RATINGS

Hyman's approach has been to assign flaw ratings to studies that used unadjusted multiple analysis. He has coded studies for the presence or absence of six categories of multiple-analysis errors. Many of these "flaws" are irrelevant since they do not affect assessment of an overall effect. For example, multiple groupings, which Hyman finds to be one of the most frequent causes of multiple-testing errors in this data base, was charged against a study "whenever the study [had] more than one condition" (p. 22). This would be an appropriate charge if we were concerned with assessment of statistical significance of any kind in these studies, but is irrelevant to the assessment of an overall psi ganzfeld effect.

Though comparisons between ganzfeld and other conditions often supplied the motivation for the original investigators in conducting their studies, the previous reviews of psi ganzfeld research, which serve as the source of claims for a psi ganzfeld effect, have counted only overall effects in their estimates of psi ganzfeld success rate (Blackmore, 1980; Honorton, 1977, 1978). I do not believe it is appropriate to charge studies with multiple-analysis flaws simply because the interest of the reviewer differs from that of the original investigator, and this seems to be what Hyman has done in his multiple-grouping and multiple-baseline flaw assignments.

It is not necessary to pursue Hyman's sixfold approach to multiple analysis much further because he found that "no significant differences on any of these six categories of multiple testing exist between the studies classified as 'significant' and those classified as "nonsignificant'" (p. 23). (Curiously, he then describes three "scenarios" to explain why his six categories should not be expected to predict psi ganzfeld success in the first place, leaving this writer somewhat baffled about the purpose of the exercise.)

There remains, however, a genuine multiple-testing problem in this data base. A number of authors did use multiple tests or indices without applying suitable corrections. I have taken two approaches in evaluating the impact of multiple analysis on the assessment of overall outcome: (a) adjusting alpha levels to correct for the number of analyses of overall success rate in studies originally classified as significant, and (b) focusing on studies that use a uniform index. The first approach was included in my response to Hyman's (1983) earlier critique (Honorton, 1983) and constitutes what he refers to as my revised classification; the second approach is presented in this paper.

ALPHA ADJUSTMENT FOR MULTIPLE TESTING

This approach used the Bonferroni inequality (Rosenthal & Rubin,

1984) to guarantee an alpha level no larger than 5%. The adjusted alpha level is calculated by dividing the criterion of significance (i.e., .05) by the number of tests from which an overall effect might be claimed. The Bonferroni correction requires that at least one of the tests remain significant at the adjusted level. If, for example, three separate (albeit not necessarily independent) tests were conducted to assess an overall effect, at least one must be associated with a *p* level not larger than .05/3 (i.e., .0167) for the study to survive the adjustment for multiple testing.

This analysis led to a revision of the number of significant studies in this data base from 23/42 to 19/42; that is, approximately 45% of the studies remained significant at the 5% level. Hyman's response (personal communication, November 29, 1982) was that it is possible to extract a much larger number of analyses (implying a substantially larger correction factor) by counting *all possible* analyses in a given study, including those that are irrelevant to assessment of an overall effect. In one case (Study 22), he counted 513 "implicit" analyses in the study!

Uniform Test and Index

Fortunately, there is another solution, one that removes all reasonable doubt about the nonchance status of the psi ganzfeld effect. This is to apply a uniform test on a single index across all studies that used that index. The direct-hits index was chosen because it was by far the most popular index and could be applied to the largest number of studies. Direct hits was also the index used in the first published psi ganzfeld study (Study 8), which Hyman and others have taken as the model or prototypical psi ganzfeld experiment.

The Direct-Hits Studies

Of the 42 studies included in Hyman's review, 14 did not provide direct hits. These include 10 blind-judging studies in which the primary analysis was based on sum of ranks, binary hits, or standardized ratings (Studies, 3, 5, 6, 9, 13–15, 22, 35, 36). In four other studies, the Maimonides binary coding system provided the only index possible (Studies 20, 32, 37, 40). The number of direct hits is available for the remaining 28, or two thirds of the 42 studies examined by Hyman (Studies, 1, 2, 4, 7, 8, 10–12, 16–19, 21, 23–31, 33, 34, 38, 39, 41, 42).

These 28 studies were reported by investigators in 10 different laboratories and comprise a total of 835 psi ganzfeld sessions. The reports

Table 1
Comparison of Three Z Score Estimates

	Z score estimates		
	Hyman	*CR*	*Exact p*
Mean	1.31	1.37	1.25
Median	1.05	1.03	.95
SD	1.61	1.54	1.57
Stouffer Z	6.95	7.22	6.60
File-drawer	472	512	423

Note. Z (Hyman) was estimated from Freeman-Tukey test. Z (CR) is the binomial CR with correction for continuity when np < 10. Z (exact p) was obtained by converting the exact binomial p into a Z score.

appeared in the following forms: 12 (43%) were published in journals, 11 (39%) were reported at Parapsychological Association conventions with abstracts appearing in *Research in Parapsychology*, and 5 (18%) appeared in a monograph.

Test of Direct-Hits Index

Several options are available for obtaining Z scores based on the number of direct hits in each study. The authors of the studies generally used the binomial *CR* approximation, though some calculated the exact binomial probabilities. Hyman uses an approximation based on the Freeman-Tukey effect-size estimate (Freeman & Tukey, 1950). The Z scores produced by these three methods are almost perfectly correlated, although the magnitude of individual Z scores does vary somewhat. In one case (Study 4), Hyman's estimate yields a Z of −2.71, and the exact binomial gives a much smaller Z of −1.71. In another case (Study 38), the differences alter the study's classification as significant or nonsignificant. For this study, Hyman obtains a Z of 1.7, which is significant on a one-tailed test. The *CR* approximation is also significant (Z = 1.67). The Z score based on the exact binomial probability, however, falls short of significance (Z = 1.62). Both the *CR* and Hyman's method are approximations, and considering the relatively small sample sizes of the studies in this data base, the use of the exact binomial would seem to be the most appropriate method. Therefore, I calculated the exact binomial probability for each study and obtained its associated Z score. As shown in Table 1, this produces slightly more conservative estimates of overall significance and tolerance for the file-drawer problem (to be discussed later) than either the *CR* method or Hyman's method.

The expected Z score, on the null hypothesis, is zero. Of the 28

Table 2
Publication Source and Success Rate

Source of publication	No. of studies	Mean Z score	Stouffer Z	% Sig. .05	1-Way ANOVA, source × Z
Journals	12	1.02	3.53	42%	
Monograph	5	1.61	3.60	60%	$F(2,25) = 0.28$
Research in Parapsychology	11	1.33	4.41	36%	
All sources	28	1.25	6.60	43%	

studies, 23 (or 82%) have positive Z scores (p = .00046, exact binomial test with p = q = .5). The mean Z score is 1.25 (SD = 1.57). The one-tailed 95% confidence interval (Kirk, 1982) yields .76 as the estimate of the lower limit of the true population mean. (When Hyman's Z estimate is used, the 95% confidence interval gives a lower limit of .81.)

A composite Z score was computed by the Stouffer method recommended by Rosenthal (1978). This involves dividing the sum of the Z scores for the individual studies by the square root of the number of studies. The resulting Z score is 6.60 ($p < 10^{-9}$). (If we assume average Z scores of *zero* for the 10 additional blind-judging studies, which did not provide direct-hits information, the combined result across all 38 studies to which direct hits *could possibly have been applied* gives Stouffer Z of 5.67 [p = 7.3 $\times 10^{-9}$]. Thus, whether we stick to the studies for which the relevant information is available or include a null estimate for the additional studies where the information is not available, the aggregate result cannot reasonably be attributed to chance fluctuation.)

Of the 28 studies, 12 (or 43%) have Z scores independently significant at the 5% level (Studies 1, 7, 8, 16, 24–26, 30, 31, 33, 39, 42; p = 3.5 $\times 10^{-9}$, exact binomial test with p = .05 and q = .95). Twenty-five percent of the studies (7/28) are significant at the 1% level (Studies 7, 16, 26, 31, 33, 39, 42; p=9.8 $\times 10^{-9}$, exact binomial test with p = .01 and q = .99).

It is clear that the cumulative outcome of this set of studies cannot be attributed to the inflation of alpha levels through multiple analysis. When a single test is used on a uniform index of success, the result indicates a strong and highly significant overall psi ganzfeld effect.

SUCCESS RATE AND SOURCE OF PUBLICATION

As indicated above, there were three different sources of publication for these 28 studies: journals, monograph reports, and *Research in Parapsychology* abstracts. Table 2 shows the number of studies for each source along with the mean and combined Z scores and the percentage of significant studies. A one-way analysis of variance (source of publication × study Z score) shows no significant effect of publication source ($F[2,25] = 0.28$).

INTERLABORATORY REPLICABILITY

A valid objection made to estimates such as this is that they are based on the success rate of studies rather than on the number of successful investigators or laboratories (Parker, 1978). Since experimenter effects appear to play a prominent role in psi research, high success rates by a small proportion of the contributing investigators are less germane to an assessment of replicability than are the estimates based on success rates across investigators.

Following Rosenthal (1984, p. 128), a combined (Stouffer) Z score was obtained individually for each investigator. These results are shown in Table 3. Significant outcomes are reported by 6 of the 10 investigators and the combined result across investigators yields a Z of 6.16 ($p < 10^{-9}$). Even though half of the studies ($n = 14$) were contributed by two investigators, Carl Sargent and me, and account for 8/12 (67%) of the significant studies, the interlaboratory replicability of the psi ganzfeld effect does not depend on Sargent's work or my own: if we remove the Sargent and Honorton studies, the Stouffer Z across the eight other investigator teams remains safely significant ($Z = 3.67$; $p = .0001$). Four (29%) of these studies (Studies 16, 31, 33, 42) are significant at the 1% level ($p = 9.2 \times 10^{-6}$; binomial test with $n = 14$, $p = .01$, and $q = .99$), and *each* was contributed by a different investigator.

Table 3
Outcome (Direct-Hits Studies) by Investigator

Investigator	No. of studies	Study[a]	Stouffer Z by investigator
Child & Levi	1	4	−1.71
Schmitt & Stanford	1	31	3.11
Sondow	1	33	3.41
York & Morris	1	42	2.89
Braud & Wood	2	2,41	− .04
Raburn	2	16,17	3.38
Palmer et al.	3	10–12	−1.69
Rogo	3	18,19,21	1.04
Honorton et al.	5	7,8,34,38,39	4.82
Sargent et al.	9	1,23–30	4.28

Stouffer Z (investigators) = 6.16

[a]*Study refers to the study number used in Appendix A.*

Thus, though the total number of investigators in this data base is small (n = 10), a majority of them have reported significant studies, and the significance of the overall effect is not dependent on one or two investigators.

Summary on Existence of an Effect

I have limited my analysis to a subset of psi ganzfeld studies to resolve issues raised by Hyman concerning multiple analysis and the effective error rate (alpha level). The analysis was restricted to the blind-judging psi ganzfeld studies that supplied the number of direct hits. A uniform test (Z score associated with the exact binomial probability) was applied to a uniform index (proportion of direct hits). The analysis shows that (a) the cumulative Z score across all studies that met or could in principle have met these criteria is associated with a probability not larger than one part in 100 million, (b) the cumulative Z score by investigators is likewise highly significant and does not depend on any one or two laboratories or investigators, and (c) 43% of the studies (by 60% of the investigators) are significant with the expected chance level safely set at 5%.

Reporting Bias

The File-Drawer Problem

Can a good case be made for attributing these findings to selective reporting of "successful studies? The question is a reasonable one. Selective reporting is a well-known and pervasive problem in the behavioral sciences (Bozarth & Roberts, 1972; Sterling, 1959) and there have been numerous calls for remedial action from investigators in fields ranging from the neurochemistry of learning (Dunn, 1980) to abnormal and developmental psychology (Sommer & Sommer, 1983).

In this regard, parapsychology has set a precedent that other areas of behavioral research would do well to emulate. Recognizing the importance of negative results in assessing research findings, the Parapsychological Association Council in 1975 adopted a policy opposing the selective reporting of positive outcomes. As a consequence, negative findings are routinely reported at Parapsychological Association meetings and in its affiliated journals and other publications.

It is therefore not surprising that approximately half of the known psi ganzfeld studies have, in fact, reported nonsignificant outcomes. Nor is it surprising that Blackmore's (1980) survey of unreported psi ganzfeld studies failed to support the hypothesis that we are dealing here with a biased sample of studies. Blackmore found that, of the 19 completed but then unreported studies elicited through her survey, 7 (or 37%) claimed significant overall outcomes, and she reported a chi-square analysis indicating that the outcome status (significant or nonsignificant) was not significantly related to publication status. She concluded that "the bias introduced by selective reporting of ESP ganzfeld studies is not a major contributor to the overall proportion of significant results, and the apparent success of the technique" (pp. 217–218).[*,†]

Taken to an extreme, the appeal to unknown or unreported studies is a fundamentally nonfalsifiable claim. We can never know, with anything approaching finality, the extent of reporting bias in any research domain. The viability of such claims can be evaluated by attention to the research and reporting practices in the research domain being examined and through estimation of the extent of selective reporting that would be necessary to jeopardize the existing data base. Rosenthal's "file-drawer" statistic (Rosenthal, 1979) estimates the number of unreported studies with Z scores averaging zero that would be required to cancel out the significance of an existing data base. For the direct-hits ganzfeld studies, the file-drawer statistic leads to an estimate of 423 such studies needed to raise the cumulative probability of the 28 known studies to a p of .05 that is, a ratio of unreported-to-reported studies of approximately 15 to 1. Given the mean ganzfeld duration for the existing studies of approximately 28 min, an additional time expenditure of 30 min per session for set-up, instructions, randomization, judging, feedback, and so forth, and an average of 30 trials per study, this translates into more than 12,000 fugitive sessions—one psi ganzfeld session per hour for over 6 years, assuming 40-hour weeks and no vacations! (As for Hyman's comment that "strangely, no contributions have come from Honorton and his laboratory during the latter 4 years of the span covered by the present data base" [p. 35], I draw your attention to Study 34.)

---

*It is inappropriate to add these 19 studies to the current data base as Hyman has done in obtaining his "adjusted count" (p. 11) because some of these studies were subsequently published and they duplicate those already in the data base of 42 studies (personal communication, S.J. Blackmore, November 3, 1982). As for the 11 other studies Hyman includes (p. 11) in his "adjusted count," I simply point out that it was he, and not I, who decided to freeze the analysis to the 42 studies I initially sent to him.

†Readers who know of other unreported psi ganzfeld studies that were not registered in Blackmore's survey should contact the Editor of the Journal, who will send them a questionnaire for documenting details of their study.

Hyman's "Retrospective Study" Hypothesis

Hyman reports a significant negative relationship between sample size and study outcome.* Dividing the studies into four classes of sample size and performing a power analysis, he finds a significant tendency for studies in the class with the smallest sample sizes (< 20 trials, $n = 7$) to have significant outcomes.[†,‡] Since, as he says (p. 13), "We would normally expect to find the probability of obtaining a significant result, all other things being equal, to increase with the square root of the sample size," his reaction to the negative relationship is that "the most obvious conclusion is that such a strange relationship is due to a selective bias" (p. 14). He suggests that it is due to selective reporting of significant small studies. "This is understandable," Hyman suggests (p. 14), "in that a significant outcome is likely to be accepted for publication even if the sample size is small. But a nonsignificant study with only 5 to 19 trials is easy to dismiss as having inadequate power."

Using the figures Hyman cites for the observed and expected number of significant studies (pp. 13–14) and performing a standard chi-square calculation yields a chi-square of 24.56, not 31.42 as reported by Hyman. The chi-square test is not really appropriate here, however, because of the extremely small expected frequency (< 1) in the cell representing studies with less than 20 trials, which is the cell responsible for the significant chi-square value. Cochran (1954) is widely cited in this context and cautions that for chi-square tests with df > 1, no cell should have an expected frequency < 1. Therefore, I used an exact binomial test instead of the chi-square test used by Hyman. This confirmed the apparent clustering of significant studies in the cell with < 20 trials (p = .0006).

[†]*For the benefit of readers who may want to conduct their own analyses of the data, it should be noted that there appear to be a number of errors in the specific figures Hyman cites. I find slightly different numbers of studies and significant studies in the four classes of sample size that Hyman used. For the class with 6 to 19 trials, Hyman reports 5 of 7 studies significant; I find 6 out of 8 studies significant. For the class with 20 to 29 trials, Hyman reports 6/12 rather than 5/11. For classes 30 to 44 and 45 to 180, Hyman reports 7/14 and 5/9, respectively, whereas I find 6/12 and 6/11. Since Hyman does not document his assignment of studies to classes, it is not possible to resolve these discrepancies with the information provided in his paper. Another discrepancy occurs in the number of direct-hits studies and trials: Hyman uses the direct-hits studies with p(hit) = .25 to estimate the "true" hit rate for use in his power analysis. He says (p. 13) that there are 22 studies, comprising 746 trials, As the table in Appendix A shows, of the 28 direct-hits studies, there are actually 24 with p(hit) = .25, comprising 722 trials. The proportion of hits in these 722 trials, however, is .38, the figure Hyman reports. I also disagree with Hyman's treatment of studies that used the binary coding index. He appears to treat each binary coding trial as a single trial. This seems inappropriate for power analysis because each binary coding trial actually comprises 10 independent binary trials and the significance tests whose power is being evaluated were based on 10 binary trials per session.*

[‡]*Hyman does not document the precise method by which he calculated the expected number of successful studies obtained in each class, but it appears that the assumed "true" hit rate of .38, the obtained hit rate for each class, and the median sample size for the class are used to obtain the power for each class, and the expected number of successful studies is obtained by multiplying the power by the median sample size. He appears to have used this estimate of the "true" hit rate even when analyzing the 18 studies that have hit probabilities other than .25 (i.e., studies in which the chance probability of a hit was .5, .2, and .167). No rationale or justification is given for doing this, and none is apparent to me.*

This argument, however, ignores the fact that free-response psi experiments (both significant and nonsignificant) typically have small sample sizes. The Maimonides ESP-dream studies, from which the ganzfeld work developed, generally involved seven or eight trials per series (Ullman, Krippner, & Vaughan, 1973). Sample sizes under 20 trials also characterize psi relaxation studies (Braud & Braud, 1973, 1974a, 1974b) and remote-viewing studies (Puthoff, Targ, & May, 1981). Studies failing to replicate free-response psi effects are also characterized by small sample sizes. For example, three reported failures to replicate the Maimonides dream ESP studies (Belvedere & Foulkes, 1971; Foulkes et al., 1972, and Globus, Knapp, Skinner, & Healy, 1968) involved, respectively, 8, 8, and 17 trials. Nine of 13 reported failures to replicate remote-viewing effects involved 12 or fewer trials (Allen, Green, Rucker, Goolsby, & Morris, 1976; Marks & Kammann, 1980; Rauscher, Weissman, Sarfatti, & Sirag, 1976; Solfvin, Roll, & Kreiger, 1978).

Although a selective bias of the type suggested by Hyman is a possibility, it is not the only interpretation possible nor is it strongly supported by the examples he cites. Hyman describes his retroactive-study hypothesis as follows:

> This proposed bias toward reporting small studies only if they succeed is related to what I refer to as the "retrospective study." This is the tendency to decide to treat a pilot or exploratory series of trials as a study if it turns out that the outcome happens to be significant or noteworthy [p. 14].

He says that "two studies in the data base are clearly retrospective" (p. 14). One (Study 4) is described by its authors as a "class demonstration," and the other (Study 7) is my seven-session demonstration series with TV film crews. "If the demonstrations had not resulted in significant psi-hitting," he says, "we probably would never have heard of them" (p. 14). I disagree, but it is a moot point, and my only comment is that the TV sessions could be conducted only when a TV film crew was present and, as Hyman himself notes (p. 14), it took 16 months to collect just seven trials.

"Strong circumstantial evidence exists," Hyman continues (p. 15), "to suggest that four others of the 'significant' studies were also retrospective: Studies 2, 33, 34, 37." One of these (Study 2), as we will see later, was a small but systematic and thoughtfully conceived study which seems to have aroused Hyman's suspicions because it was published "almost 3 years after it was conducted" and "a single individual served as the experimenter and agent" (p. 15). "In the other three," Hyman says, "the authors referred to their studies as 'preliminary,' 'exploratory,' or 'pilot.' This again suggests that the only reason we are reading about them is because they gave significant results" (p. 15). But one of these (Study 37) was in fact a *nonsignificant* study and the remaining two (Studies 33 and 34) were complex and elaborate experiments with large sample sizes. Study 33, with 100 trials has the *largest* sample size of all the direct-hits studies and Study 34 has 40 trials. Both were exploratory in the sense that they introduced and attempted to assess the effects of novel conditions or experimental manipulations on psi ganzfeld performance, but neither fits Hyman's description of a "retrospective" study.

Nor does the retrospective bias hypothesis receive encouragement from Blackmore's (1980) survey of reporting practices. In addition to the 19 studies that had not (at the time of her inquiry) been published, she also found 12 studies that had not been completed. "In no case," she said, "was 'results not significant' given as the sole reason for failing to complete [the study] and therefore no selection at this stage was apparent" (p. 216). Thus, neither the examples cited nor what is known about reporting practices in this area strongly support a reporting bias interpretation of Hyman's finding.

As Hyman says, *all other things being equal,* statistical power should increase with the square root of the sample size. That all things cannot be assumed to be equal across the psi ganzfeld studies is evident by the fact that these studies varied greatly in specific instructions given, use of naïve or experienced subjects, ganzfeld duration, sender conditions (lab sender, friend of subject, no sender), use of preparatory relaxation exercises, type and orthogonality of target sets used, and so on. Indeed, we cannot assume that all things are equal within a single study.

Consider two studies in the psi ganzfeld data base that provided information on the number of sessions run per day by an individual experimenter. Habel (Study 6), with 90 sessions, found a drop in subjects' performance as the number of sessions run per day was doubled to expedite completion of the study. Habel used a partial-hits index with $p(\text{hit}) = 1/2$. She reported a decline in scoring rate from 55% in the period with 1 to 3 sessions per day, to 41% in the later period with 5 to 8 sessions per day. Sondow [33], with 100 sessions, also found a decline in performance as the number of sessions per day increased. With a chance expectation for each session of 25%, a 51% hit rate occurred on days when she ran only one session ($n = 41$), compared to 39% on days when she ran two sessions ($n = 38$) and 24% when she ran 3 sessions per day ($n = 21$).

The Habel and Sondow studies are among the largest studies in the data base, and in both cases, a single individual served as primary experimenter. It is not implausible that an experimenter's enthusiasm and interest might change over the course of a long workday and that such changes might be communicated to subjects and reflected in their subsequent performance. Like Hyman's selective-bias interpretation, this possibility must remain conjecture until it has been explicitly studied, though it is hoped that it will be taken into consideration by future experimenters in the design of new ganzfeld studies. Even as conjecture, however, it does illustrate the danger of assuming "all things are equal" in situations involving repeated interactions among human participants and experimenters.

Regardless of the interpretation of the excess of significant outcomes in studies with small sample sizes, this finding does not materially affect the overall significance of the ganzfeld data base. Even if we use only studies with 20 or more trials, the success rate of the larger sample size studies is not substantially diminished. Using the original classification (used in Hyman's analysis) we find that 17 of the studies with 20 or more trials are significant and 17 are nonsignificant, a success rate of 50%. Using the revised classification, which corrects for multiple analysis, the result is 14 significant and 20 nonsignificant experiments (41%). Of the 18 direct-hits studies, 22 have 20 or more trials, and the cumulative results for these is nearly the same as for all 28 studies. The mean Z score is 1.24 (SD = 1.48) and the Stouffer Z = 5.83 (p = 2.8 × 10^{-9}). Ten of the 22 studies, or 45%, are independently significant (p = 3.62 × 10^{-8}). (See table in Appendix A.)

SUMMARY

Although selective reporting bias can never be conclusively refuted, a number of considerations strongly mitigate against the likelihood of a serious reporting problem in this area: (a) the publication policies and practices in parapsychology show that reporting of null results is commonplace; (b) a large number of the existing ganzfeld studies report null results; (c) the file-drawer estimate of the number of fugitive null studies required to wash out the known results requires 15 such fugitive studies for each one known; and (d) Hyman's hypothesis that there may be a tendency to report small studies only if they are significant is not strongly supported by the examples he cites and is inconsistent with the literature on free-response psi research, which shows that both significant and nonsignificant free-response studies typically have small sample sizes.

Study Quality

We have seen that the cumulative psi ganzfeld effects remains highly significant when evaluated by a single uniform test and index, that the effect is not dependent on the studies of one or two investigators, and that the cumulative effect cannot be attributed to selective reporting bias without assuming the existence of a large number of unreported studies averaging null outcomes. The second stage of our meta-analysis attempts to account for some of the variability in study outcomes by examining their relationship to procedural variations across studies. Specifically, we will be concerned with the relationship between study outcome and procedural variations related to study quality. One of the principal advantages of meta-analysis over traditional narrative reviews is that it seeks empirical assessment of methodological issues rather than relying on a priori judgments of research quality. Glass, McGaw, & Smith (1981) express the attitude of meta-analysis as follows:

> An important part of every meta-analysis with which we have been associated has been the recording of methodological weaknesses in the original studies and the examination of their covariance of study findings. Thus, the influence of "study quality" on findings has been regarded consistently as an empirical a posteriori question, not an a priori matter of opinion or judgement used in excluding large numbers of studies from consideration [pp. 221–222].

The general procedure is to define and encode relevant study features, then use statistical analysis to evaluate the impact of variations across studies on their outcomes. A number of problems arise in the course of this process. Some are due to ambiguous specification of features to be encoded and inconsistencies in encoding them. In meta-analysis of controversial research domains such as psi research, it is especially important that the study variables to be encoded be defined as unambiguously as possible to allow independent reexamination by other reviewers. The criteria used by a meta-analytic reviewer should be specified (and documented) in such a way that others can, by going to the original research reports, reconstruct the analysis and satisfy themselves as to the appropriateness of the original coding and analysis. As Cooper (1984) advises, reviewers should "open their rules of inference to public inspection" (p. 111).

For the purpose of my own meta-analysis of study quality, I have defined variables to be encoded in terms of procedural descriptions (or their absence) in the research reports, and I have avoided as much as possible, making inferences that go beyond what is given in the reports. As in the preceding section, my analysis is limited to studies that used a uniform test and index, which will eliminate concern over multiple-analysis options. After presenting my own meta-analysis, I shall describe what I believe are serious problems in Hyman's approach and document specific instances to illustrate the problems.

Sensory Cues

Since the ganzfeld is a perceptual isolation procedure, it eliminates potential sensory contact between percipient and target during the session. The percipient's auditory and visual input typically consists of white noise and an unpatterned visual field. Sender and target are isolated in a different room. Except for the possibility of deliberate electronic sabotage, these procedures prohibit conventional information exchange between sender and receiver during the psi ganzfeld session.

A channel for potential sensory cues does exist, however, in the judging phase of blind-judging studies in which the same target set used by the sender (or by an experimenter in clairvoyance studies) during the session is then used by the percipient for blind-judging at the end of the session. In these cases, a sender or experimenter may have physically handled the target, enabling transmission of potential cues concerning target identity in the form of fingerprints, smudges, or other markings that might differentiate target from decoys. Though it might be argued that the likelihood of handling cues would be diminished in clairvoyance studies where there was no sender, there is no way to eliminate the possibility of such cues in studies that used single target-sets, and I have made no attempt to differentiate studies within that class.

CUE RATINGS

For the purpose of the present analysis, a cue rating (CUE) was assigned to each study on the basis of procedural descriptions in the reports. A CUE rating of 2 was assigned to studies reporting the use of duplicate target-sets, which eliminate possible handling cues. Studies using single target-sets were given a CUE rating of 1. A CUE rating of 0 was assigned to one study (Study 10) that, in addition to the use of a single target pack, provided two other opportunities for sensory cues: (a) During the sending period, the experimenter-sender rolled a clay ball over the target, increasing the possibility of handling cues; and (b) after the sending period, the experimenter-sender had sensory contact with a second experimenter who later supervised the percipient's judging. (The outcome of the study was nonsignificant, $Z = -.57$.)

EFFECT OF CUE CONTROL PROCEDURES ON STUDY OUTCOME

CUE ratings for all 28 direct-hits studies are given in column 2 of Table 4. Although studies with better controls against sensory cues (CUE = 2) were slightly more successful than those permitting handling cues (CUE < 2) ($t[26] = .318$; $p = .687$), this finding is limited because all but one of the studies with a CUE of 2 come from one laboratory. The correlation between cue control and study outcome is nonsignificant ($r[26]$ = .134).

STUDIES ELIMINATING POTENTIAL HANDLING CUES

Ten studies used duplicate target-sets for sender and percipient judging (CUE = 2). The mean Z score was 1.38, and the combined (Stouffer) Z was 4.35 ($p = 6.8 \times 10^{-6}$). Half the studies in this group (5/10) were independently significant (p = .000064, exact binomial test with p = .05 and q = .95).

BINARY CODING STUDIES

From the standpoint of cue control, studies using the binary coding index deserve special attention because the procedure does not involve exposing the subject to a judging pool, so no opportunity for transmission of handling cues exists. This index was used in five studies that do not overlap with the direct-hits studies described above (Studies 3, 20, 32, 37, 40) and was the only index possible for all but one of these studies (Study 3). In Study 3, a blind-judging partial-hits index was also used, with the judging taking place *after* the binary coding (p. 415). The combined (Stouffer) Z score for the binary coding studies* was 2.84 (p = .0023). Three of the five studies (by two of the three contributing investigators) were independently significant (p = .0012, exact binomial test with p = .05 and q = .95).

Randomization

Psi ganzfeld studies have used a number of methods for target selection. For the direct-hits studies, tables of random numbers or random number generators were reported in 16, or 57%, of the studies; handshuffling and related methods (die-casting and coin-flipping) were used in 7, or 25%, of the studies. Numbered poker chips were shaken together and selected by hand in 2 of the remaining 5 studies (Studies 16, 17). Randomization was not described in the other three reports.

What would constitute a randomization problem in these studies is not entirely clear. In 20 studies, 71% of the total, subjects contributed only one trial each (for study documentation, see the table in Appendix

---

*I have not accumulated Z scores for binary coding and direct-hits blind-judging studies because the number of trials going into the two cases differ so much. The direct-hits studies have sample sizes ranging from 7 to 100 trials, and the binary coding studies have sample sizes ranging from 150 to 1800 trials.

326 Basic Research in Parapsychology

A). For each subject, then, this amounts to one random selection with, usually, $p = 1/4$. It is not clear that random number tables provide better randomization than shuffling techniques when a separate randomization is used for each trial. The single-trial-per-subject studies are independently quite significant (Stouffer $Z = 4.61$; $p = .000002$), with 8 of the 20 studies, or 40%, individually significant at the 5% level (exact $p = .000003$, with $p = .05$ and $q = .95$), and the mean Z score for this group does not differ significantly from that for studies with multiple trials per subject ($t[26] = 1.17$; $p = .126$, one-tailed). Further, I suspect that if all the studies under consideration had used random number generators, critics pursuing alternative explanations of putative psi effects might reasonably request specifications of generator characteristics and performance. As it is, it might be best that a variety of methods have been used, *if* it can be shown that study outcomes are independent of the method of randomization. For the purpose of analysis, however, I have adopted what is surely the most popular opinion, that use of random number tables or generators is superior to hand-shuffling and related methods.

RAND RATINGS

Studies reporting the use of random number tables or random number generators for target selection were assigned a RAND rating of 2. Studies in which target selection was based on card-shuffling, coin-flipping or die-casting were given RAND ratings of 1. RAND ratings of 0 were assigned for any other method of target selection or when the method of randomization was not specified.

EFFECT OF RANDOMIZATION PROCEDURES ON STUDY OUTCOME

RAND ratings are given for each study in column 3 of Table 4. The correlation between RAND ratings and study outcome (Z scores) is non-significant ($r[26] = -.095$). The outcome of studies using random number tables or generators (RAND = 2) does not differ significantly from that of studies using other randomization methods or studies not specifying the method of randomization (RAND < 2) ($t[26] = -.824, p = .422$).

STUDIES USING RANDOM NUMBER TABLES OR GENERATORS

Of the 28 direct-hits studies, 16 reported target-selection procedures based on random number tables or random number generators* (RAND = 2). The mean Z score for these studies was 1.04, and the combined

---

*The reports of 7 of the 16 studies in this group provided specific descriptions of how the random number table or generator was used in target selection (Studies 2, 11, 12, 24, 30, 31, 34), whereas the reports of the remaining 9 studies simply stated that such methods were used (Studies 1, 10, 23, 25–28, 41, 42). This difference was not related to study outcome (Z score) (t[14] = -.3, p = .77).

Table 4

Methodology Ratings and Study Outcome

Study	CUE[a]	RAND[b]	Z score
Studies with Z > median			
16	1	0	4.02
33	1	1	3.41
39	1	1	3.24
26	2	2	3.15
31	1	2	3.11
7	1	1	3.00
42	1	2	2.89
30	2	2	2.16
1	2	2	2.15
8	1	1	2.02
24	2	2	1.74
25	2	2	1.74
38	1	1	1.62
27	2	2	.97
Means	1.43	1.50	
Studies with Z < median			
34	2	2	.92
21	1	1	.79
2	1	2	.76
17	1	0	.76
19	1	0	.76
23	2	2	.48
18	1	0	.25
28	2	2	.24
29	2	0	.21
11	1	2	− .39
10	0	2	− .57
41	1	2	− .82
4	1	1	−1.71
12	1	2	−1.97
Means	1.21	1.28	

[a]*CUE ratings are as follows: 2 = use of duplicate target-sets documented in report; 1 = single target-set described; 0 = other potential sources of cues evident in report.*
[b]*RAND ratings are as follows: 2 = report describes target selection using random number tables or generators; 1 = target selection involving shuffling techniques described; 0 = any other randomization technique, or method not described.*

(Stouffer) Z was 4.14 (p = .000017). Seven of the 16 studies, or approximately 44%, were independently significant at the %5 level ($p = 5.98 \times 10^{-6}$). The studies in this group were contributed by six different investigators.

Covariation of Study Quality and Outcome

The joint effects of cue control and randomization method on study outcome were evaluated through a multiple regression analysis, with CUE and RAND ratings as the independent variables and study Z score as the dependent variable. The resulting multiple correlation of .195 is nonsignificant ($F[2, 25]$ = .493, p = .613). Thus, there appears to be no systematic relationship between these indices of study quality and study outcomes.

Hyman's Flaw Classification

Hyman's Initial Tally of Flaws

Hyman first reported an analysis of flaws in his earlier review of psi ganzfeld research (Hyman, 1983, p. 23). "In the data base of 42 studies," he said, "the three most common flaws were multiple tests of significance (64%), possibilities of sensory leakage (60%), and inadequate randomization (45%)." He obtained an overall flaw count by tallying the number of flaws he found in the reports of each study, and then he compared the average number of flaws in the significant versus the nonsignificant studies. He reported a significant difference in the average number of flaws for the two groups ($t[40]$ = 2.85; p < .01) and concluded, "There is a strong tendency for the rate of success to increase with the number of obvious defects."

This analysis was straightforward and easy to interpret. If the classification of flaws was correct, Hyman would have clearly demonstrated a link between successful outcomes and procedural flaws in the studies. Because my own analysis of the covariation of study quality and outcome differed so markedly from Hyman's, I requested study-by-study documentation of his flaw classification prior to the cojoint SPR and PA meeting in Cambridge. The document I received (personal communication from Ray Hyman, July 29, 1982) contained a large number of errors in the assignment of flaws to studies, which, I was later informed (personal communication from Ray Hyman, November 29, 1982), were typing errors rather than errors in classification.

Hyman's Second Classification of Flaws

The November 1982 communication was accompanied by a revised classification and analysis based on five categories of flaws: the three just described, plus inadequate documentation (defined the same way as in his current analysis) and feedback (assigned when "no precautions had been taken to insure that the target reported by the agent at feedback had, indeed, been the target actually used"). Hyman's flaw assignments again led to a significant difference, with more flaws assigned to significant than to nonsignificant studies ($t[40] = 2.89$; $p = .006$), and I again seriously objected to many of his classifications, such as the assignment of a feedback flaw to a clairvoyance study in which there were no senders (agents).

Hyman's Current Classification of Flaws

Hyman's present classification of flaws is thus the third iteration, and it is appropriate that our differences in the assessment of the quality of psi ganzfeld research be made available for evaluation by the research community.

In his present paper, Hyman has six categories of procedural flaws. As described in the previous section, I have dealt with multiple analysis through the use of a uniform index and test and am therefore omitting consideration of Hyman's six multiple analysis flaws (three of which he also discards from his analysis, and none of which, as we have seen, correlates with study outcome). Hyman's procedural flaw categories now include sensory cues, randomization, feedback (with a revised definition), security, documentation, and statistical errors. I have serious objections to Hyman's definition and coding of some of these flaws. In what follows, I shall briefly discuss his categories and provide examples illustrating problems in flaw definition and attribution. I shall then examine in some detail Hyman's flaw ratings of a single study to show how his count greatly inflates the number of flaws in the study. Finally, I shall consider his current analysis.

I begin by noting two areas in which Hyman and I are in agreement.

SINGLE TARGET (ST)

The definition of ST is very similar to my CUE criteria, and the two indices are highly correlated ($r[26] = .94$). Hyman says, "My analysis agrees with Honorton in showing no correlation between the use of single targets and significance" (p. 30). For the direct-hits studies, the correlation between ST and study outcome (Z score) is close to zero ($r[26] = -.062$).

STATISTICAL ERRORS (STAT)

I agree with Hyman that six of the direct-hits studies contain statistical errors (Studies 4, 16, 17, 31, 33, 34).

FEEDBACK (FB)

Hyman claims that although ST does not correlate with study outcome, the FB flaw that can only occur with ST does correlate with success. He assigned the FB flaw to ST studies that "typically did not use an adequate procedure to insure that the target was properly randomized among the other candidates in the pool before being presented for judging" (p. 28). His appendix definition, however, adds a second condition for the assignment of FB: "Inadequate randomization of target and foils at judging, *or* inadequate precautions against communication from percipient *to* agent at feedback" (p. 44, emphasis added). Hyman provides no elaboration or commentary on this second condition, how it was evaluated from the research reports, or why he included it under FB rather than under security (SEC), for which he has another flaw category. It should be noted that this second definition is the same definition of feedback given in Hyman's second classification (November 1982) and that the assignment of FB in the second classification was not limited to studies using single target-sets. The formulation given implies deliberate fraud: The sender, having received feedback of the percipient's choice, substitutes the target chosen by the percipient for the actual target, thereby creating a spurious hit. (The first condition for FB, which is the judging order, may also imply cheating, with the sender [-experimenter] in single-target experiments placing the actual target in a constant location in the judging pack.) I shall use the designations FB-1 and FB-2 to identify the two parts of Hyman's definition of this flaw.

Hyman is not consistent in his flaw assignments. He assigned FB to 10 of the 18 direct-hits studies using single target-sets (Studies 2, 4, 7, 8, 16, 17, 21, 33, 38, 39). The reports of all but three of these (Studies 16, 17, 21) describe procedures for ordering targets at judging. And he did not charge an FB flaw against two studies that failed to describe the method of ordering targets at judging (Studies 18, 19).

ASSESSMENT OF FB-1

To evaluate the effects of these procedures, I coded each of the 18 direct-hits studies as follows: A rating of 2 was given for each study that described the arrangement of targets in numerical (or alphabetical) order; a rating of 1 was given to studies describing the reordering of targets by hand-shuffling, and studies that did not report the method of ordering targets for judging were given a rating of zero. These ratings are listed in Table 5. There is no significant relationship between target-ordering procedures and study outcome (Z score): The correlation (with 16 df) is −.138.

Except for two cases (Studies 7, 21), the studies to which Hyman has

Table 5
Ordering of Targets in Direct-Hits Studies with Single Target-Sets

Study	JORD rating[a]	Z score
16	0	4.02
33	2	3.41
39	1	3.24
31	2	3.11
7	1	3.00
42	2	2.89
8	1	2.02
38	1	1.62
21	0	.79
2	2	.76
17	0	.76
19	0	.76
18	0	.25
11	2	− .39
10	2	− .57
41	2	− .82
4	1	−1.71
12	2	−1.97

[a]*JORD refers to the method of ordering the targets for judging. The JORD ratings are as follows: 2=report describes target and decoys presented in numerical or alphabetical order; 1 = report describes judging order via hand-shuffling; 0 = order of targets at judging not described.*

assigned FB flaws explicitly report experimenter monitoring of feedback. Examination of some of the studies assigned FB flaws makes it clear that if the study is to be faulted for FB, it is FB-2 that is operative and that the experimenter would have to be implicated in any cheating scenario. In Study 33, for instance, significance was contributed primarily by subjects in one of the two experimental groups, who received feedback only after completing four of their five trials. The report also indicates that the targets were displayed in numerical order at judging:

> Subjects in the Association group were asked to read a set of instructions before looking at the four pictures, *which were laid out on the desk in numerical order.* Their associations to each of the pictures were then recorded by the experimenter on a separate sheet of paper. Subjects were allowed to read through their complete records while making these associations, and were encouraged to use them in making their ranking decisions. After the experimenter recorded these decisions, the subject left the building. *The experimenter then opened the envelope containing the number of the target picture and recorded it* [Sondow, 1979, p. 132, emphasis added].

RANDOMIZATION (R)

Hyman defines a randomization flaw (p. 44) as "inadequate randomization" or "inadequately described" randomization. He says that he considered studies to have adequate randomization when the authors describe "using a table of random numbers or a random number generator to select the specific target from a pool" (p. 27). He now finds that 74% of the studies failed these criteria and were guilty of "suboptimal" randomization—up from 45% in his first and 52% in his second evaluations of the same studies. For the direct-hits studies, Hyman considers that only 5 studies or 18% used "adequate" randomization (Studies 10–12, 31, 34). A typical example is Study 10: "J.P. selected both the set and the picture within the set that was to be the target by referring to a random number table" (p. 50).

Again, Hyman has not consistently applied his own criteria in coding the studies; many of those he cites as having "inadequate" or "suboptimal" randomization contain descriptions that satisfy his stated criteria (e.g., Studies 1, 2, 23, 41, 42). The authors of Study 41, for instance, report that "the [experimenter-]agent used card cuts and random number tables to choose one slide out of 1,024" (p. 84). Similarly, the randomization procedure in Study 42 describes "individual targets ... selected using a random number generator from each mini-target pool by an otherwise uninvolved assistant" (pp. 48–49).

SECURITY (SEC)

Hyman's definition of a security flaw is "inadequate security, usually in monitoring crucial phases of the study or in having only one experimenter" (p. 44). SEC was also assigned for "failing to monitor the agent" (p. 28). I will discuss the single-experimenter issue below in regard to a study (Study 2) that illustrates a valid one-experimenter design. It is unclear both from Hyman's definition and his assignments just what other "crucial phases" of an experiment he has in mind that are not already covered by his flaw categories for sensory cues, "feedback," and randomization problems.

DOCUMENTATION (DOC)

Concern over possibilities of sender-receiver cheating appears to supply the impetus for another Hyman flaw category, documentation (DOC), which we are told was usually assigned for "failure to report the number of times the agent was a friend of the percipient or to provide data on whether this made a difference in those studies in which subjects were encouraged to bring their own agents" (p. 28). Since Hyman's interest is whether there is a psi effect, not with its relationship to psychological variables, his focus on sender-receiver relations appears to be motivated by security concerns. As we have seen, security is a separate category of flaw that already covers monitoring the sender. One of the studies faulted was a clairvoyance study in which there were no senders (Study 17), and Hyman does not specify what other conditions prompted his assignment of DOC flaws.

ASSESSMENT OF SENDER-RECEIVER DOCUMENTATION
To evaluate study outcomes in relation to the one positive condition that Hyman specifies for the DOC flaw, I performed a sender-receiver DOC (SR-DOC) rating on each of the direct-hits studies. Ratings of 1 were given to studies that satisfied one of three conditions: (a) The report specified that the sender was always the experimenter; (b) sender-receiver breakdowns were provided; or (c) the study used clairvoyance procedures and there were no senders. The correlation between SR-DOC and study outcome is nonsignificant (point-biserial $r[26] = -.165$). My SR-DOC ratings are given in Table 6.

Why There Are So Many Flaws: A Detailed Example

I have described several examples of what I consider inappropriate flaw coding. To illustrate how these problems can grossly overestimate the flaw count for an individual study, I will use one of Hyman's frequently used examples, the study by Braud, Wood, & Braud (1974). This is Study 2 in the present data base and is one that Hyman suggested was a "retrospective" study. Hyman charges this study with four different procedural flaws: ST, R, FB, and SEC. As with all of the early ganzfeld studies, a single target-set was used by the experimenter-sender and by the subject for judging, so there is no question that this study should be faulted for ST. The remaining three flaws Hyman assigns to this study are, I believe, inappropriate. The study is charged with "suboptimal" randomization. Yet, ironically, it has one of the most complete descriptions of randomization using random number tables in the data base, one that is as complete as any that Hyman has acquitted of randomization flaws:

> Target preparation and selection techniques were identical to those described in Braud and Braud (1974b). The [experimenter-]agent randomly selected (using card cuts, coin tosses, and a table of random numbers) one out of a pool of 20 packs, then one of the six pictures within that chosen pack as the actual target [Braud, Wood, & Braud, 1975, p. 108].

Table 6
Sender/Receiver Documentation in Direct-Hits Studies

Study	SR-DOC rating[a]	Z score
16	1	4.02
33	1	3.41
39	0	3.24
26	1	3.15
31	1	3.11
7	0	3.00
42	1	2.89
30	1	2.16
1	1	2.15
8	0	2.02
24	1	1.74
25	1	1.74
38	0	1.62
27	1	.97
34	0	.92
21	0	.79
2	1	.76
17	1	.76
19	1	.76
23	1	.48
18	1	.25
28	1	.24
29	0	.21
11	1	− .39
10	1	− .57
41	1	− .82
4	1	−1.71
12	1	−1.97

[a]The rating for sender-receiver documentation (SR-DOC) is as follows: 1 = experimenter always sender, or no sender (clairvoyance), or sender/receiver pairing specified; 0 = sender/receiver pairing not specified.

The auxiliary citation (Braud & Braud, 1974b) provides details of the method used to obtain an entry point in the random number table and how the entry point was used to select a specific target and decoys for each session:

> After leaving the subject, [the experimenter-agent] randomly selected first a pack and then an envelope within that pack through the use of a 40-row × 40-column table of random numbers in which the entry point was determined by two cuts of a well-shuffled deck of cards bearing the numbers 1 through 40 and a coin toss to determine row vs. column. The chosen envelope contained the target for that session and the others were the controls [p. 232].

Compare this description with that for Study 10 which Hyman approved of (see the paragraph entitled *Randomization* in the preceding section).

Hyman's assignment of FB and SEC flaws to Study 2 appears to be due to the use of a single experimenter or agent but is clearly inappropriate given the protocol described in the report. Following Hyman's definition, FB should not be charged against this study because the report states that the target and decoys were replaced in their original numerical order and because there was no opportunity for communication between subject and experimenter-agent until after the subject completed judging:

> At the termination of the psi impression period, the subject self-terminated his hypnagogic state (signaled by five thumping sounds recorded at the end of a continuously playing tape], recorded his impressions on paper, and read the instructions inside an envelope which had been placed in his room before the session began. At the same time, the [experimenter-] agent recorded the code number of the correct target on his data sheet, replaced all six pictures in their individual envelopes (in their original numerical order) back into their larger envelope. He then placed the packet of six pictures on a stool outside the still-closed door of the subject's room and returned to his room without sensorially encountering the subject [Braud, Wood, & Braud, 1975, p. 108].

It is clear from this description that considerable care was taken by the investigators to eliminate security problems. Elsewhere, the authors describe the one-way signaling system used to mark the beginning and end of the 5-min sending–psi-impression period. It seems excessive to charge this experiment with a security lapse only because there was a single experimenter. If anything, the design of this experiment illustrates how an isolated investigator working alone might conduct an adequately controlled psi ganzfeld experiment. If a duplicate target-set had been included in the subject's postsession judging packet, I believe the Braud-Wood-Braud protocol would be completely adequate.

In summary, whereas Hyman has charged this study with four procedural flaws, consistent application of his flaw criteria suggests that it should be charged only with one.

Summary on Hyman's Flaw Classification

It is clear that Hyman's assignment of flaws is itself seriously flawed. There are problems in the definition of several of his flaw categories, largely owing to vagueness in specifying codable characteristics of the flaw (e.g., "inadequate security, usually in monitoring crucial phases of the study…"), and to the use of disjunctive definitions (FB-1 *or* FB-2). In addition, Hyman has been inconsistent in his assignment of flaws, with the effect of spuriously increasing the flaw count in some studies that appear to satisfy his stated criteria and decreasing the flaw count in other studies that fail his criteria. Interested readers who are willing to consult the research reports can verify this for themselves.

HYMAN'S CURRENT ANALYSIS OF FLAWS

Given these problems, any statistical analysis involving Hyman's flaw ratings would be uninterpretable. My response, however, would be incomplete without a brief comment on Hyman's current analysis. Unlike his two earlier evaluations, which involved a straightforward *t* test of the relationship between flaws and study outcome, Hyman now performs a factor analysis to demonstrate such a relationship. In view of his earlier statement about "being startled by investigators routinely doing factor analyses on sample sizes of 30 or less" (p. 6), it comes as somewhat of a surprise to find him now basing his own evaluation on a factor analysis involving 36 cases! His analysis is sufficiently complex that it seemed advisable to me to have it evaluated by someone well versed in factor analysis, and I have asked a psychological statistician, David R. Saunders, to examine it. Saunders's (1985) conclusion is that both the factor analysis and Hyman's interpretation of it are faulty.

Discussion

Is there a significant psi ganzfeld effect? I believe my evaluation of direct-hits studies justifies an affirmative answer to this question. When multiple analysis problems are eliminated through use of a uniform test and index, the effect remains highly significant. And though selective reporting bias cannot be conclusively ruled out, consideration of reporting practices in this area and the file-drawer estimate of the extent of selective reporting necessary to jeopardize the known data base indicate that selective reporting bias does not pose a serious problem.

Does the ganzfeld paradigm represent a step toward replicability of psi effects? Significant direct-hits studies have been reported by 6 of the 10 contributing investigators. Even though the number of investigators may be too small to allow a firm conclusion to be reached, this result is certainly encouraging. New replication efforts are, however, clearly needed and, ideally, by as many new replicators as possible.

On the evaluation of study quality, many readers will find it disconcerting that two reviewers should come to such divergent conclusions in evaluating the same set of studies. Neither Hyman nor I conducted our evaluations of study quality on a blind basis, and it would not be unreasonable for readers to suppose that the disagreement mainly reflects our respective a priori views. This is a matter that the reader will have to decide. I am hopeful that at least a few readers will want to consult the original studies and make their own determination.

If we are to be more successful in achieving consensus over future studies, we must be able to agree in advance on the criteria that will be used to assess them. This is crucial, and the absence of such agreement in the past has, in my opinion, contributed heavily to the perennial standoff between psi researchers and critics. Hyman and I are in substantial agreement on the need to improve study documentation. Clearly there is work to be done both in improving the level of procedural description and in specifying the potentially important moderators. The psi ganzfeld research has been underway now for a decade, and it is reasonable to expect some degree of standardization in reporting work in this area. For this reason, the Council of the Parapsychological Association has commissioned a study group to develop specific guidelines for reporting psi ganzfeld studies and research in other areas that have been ongoing over a substantial period of time. The study group will consist of researchers with varied outcome histories, critics, and editors of PA-affiliated journals. I am pleased that Hyman has agreed to participate in the development of guidelines for future ganzfeld studies.

Appendix A

The Data Base

Study numbers in this data base are the same as those used by Hyman. References preceded by an asterisk represent the ones for which longer unpublished reports were provided to Hyman.

I. STUDIES USING DIRECT-HITS INDEX

1. Ashton, H.T., Dear, P.R., Harley, T.A., & Sargent, C.L. (1981). A four-subject study of psi in the ganzfeld. *Journal of the Society for Psychical Research*, **51**, 12–21.

2. Braud, W.G., Wood, R., & Braud, L.W. (1975). Free-response GESP performance during an experimental hypnagogic state induced by

visual and acoustic ganzfeld techniques: A replication and extension. *Journal of the American Society for Psychical Research*, 69, 105–113.

4.   Child, I.L., & Levi, A. (1979). Psi-missing in free-response settings. *Journal of the American Society for Psychical Research*, 73, 273–289.

7.   Honorton, C. (1976). Length of isolation and degree of arousal as probable factors influencing information retrieval in the ganzfeld. In J.D. Morris, W.G. Roll, & R.L. Morris (Eds.), *Research in parapsychology, 1975* (pp. 184–186). Metuchen, NJ: Scarecrow Press.

8.   Honorton, C., & Harper, S. (1974). Psi-meditated imagery and ideation in an experimental procedure for regulating perceptual input. *Journal of the American Society for Psychical Research*, 68, 156–168.

10.   Palmer, J., & Aued, I. (1975). An ESP test with psychometric objects and the ganzfeld: negative findings. In J.D. Morris, W.G. Roll, & R.L. Morris (Eds.), *Research in parapsychology, 1974* (pp. 50–53). Metuchen, NJ: Scarecrow Press.

11.   Palmer, J., Bogart, D.N., Jones, S.M., & Tart, C.T. (1977). Scoring patterns in an ESP ganzfeld experiment. *Journal of the American Society for Psychical Research*, 71, 121–145.

12.   Palmer, J., Khamashta, K., & Israelson, K. (1979). An ESP ganzfeld experiment with Transcendental Meditators. *Journal of the American Society for Psychical Research*, 73, 333–348.

16.   Raburn, L. (1975). *Expectation and transmission factors in psychic functioning.* Unpublished honors thesis, Tulane University, New Orleans, LA. [GESP cell]

17.   Ibid. [Clairvoyance cell]

18.   Rogo, D.S. (1976). ESP in the ganzfeld: An exploration of parameters. In J.D. Morris, W.G. Roll, & R.L. Morris (Eds.), *Research in parapsychology, 1975* (pp. 174–176). Metuchen, NJ: Scarecrow Press. [Experiment 1]

19.   Ibid. [Experiment 2]

21.   Rogo, D.S., Smith, M., & Terry, J. (1976). The use of short-duration ganzfeld stimulation to facilitate psi-mediated imagery. *European Journal of Parapsychology*, 1, 72–77.

23.   Sargent, C.L. (1980). Exploring psi in the ganzfeld. *Parapsychological Monographs* (No. 17). [Experiment 1]

24.   Ibid. [Experiment 2]

25.   Ibid. [Experiment 3]

26.   Ibid. [Experiment 5]

27.   Ibid. [Experiment 6]

*28.   Sargent, C.L., Bartlett, H.J., & Moss, S.P. (1982). Response structure and temporal incline in ganzfeld free-response GESP testing.

In W.G. Roll, R.L. Morris, & R. White (Eds.), *Research in parapsychology, 1981* (pp. 79–81). Metuchen, NJ: Scarecrow Press.

29. Sargent, C.L., Harley, T.A., Lane, J., & Radcliffe, K. (1981). Ganzfeld psi-optimization in relation to session duration. In W.G. Roll & J. Beloff (Eds.), *Research in parapsychology 1980* (pp. 82–84). Metuchen, NJ: Scarecrow Press.

*30. Sargent, C.L., & Matthews, G. (1982). Ganzfeld GESP performance with variable duration testing. In W.G. Roll, R.L. Morris, & R. White (Eds.), *Research in parapsychology, 1981* (pp. 159–160). Metuchen, NJ: Scarecrow Press.

31. Schmitt, M., & Stanford, R.G. (1978). Free-response ESP during ganzfeld stimulation: The possible influence of menstrual cycle phase. *Journal of the American Society for Psychical Research*, **72**, 177–182.

33. Sondow, N. (1979). Effects of associations and feedback on psi in the ganzfeld: Is there more than meets the judge's eye? *Journal of the American Society for Psychical Research*, **73**, 123–150.

*34. Sondow, N., Braud, L., & Barker, P. (1981). Target qualities and affect measures in an exploratory psi ganzfeld. In W.G. Roll, R.L. Morris, & R. White (Eds.), *Research in parapsychology 1981* (pp. 82–85). Metuchen, NJ: Scarecrow Press.

38. Terry, J.C., & Honorton, C. (1976). Psi information retrieval in the ganzfeld: Two confirmatory studies. *Journal of the American Society for Psychical Research*, **70**, 207–217. [Experiment 1]

39. Ibid. [Experiment 2]

41. Wood, R., Kirk, J., & Braud, W. (1977). Free response GESP performance following ganzfeld stimulation vs. induced relaxation, with verbalized vs. nonverbalized mentation: A failure to replicate. *European Journal of Parapsychology*, **1**, 80–93.

*42. York, M. (1977). The defense mechanism test (DMT) as indicator of psychic performance as measured by a free-response clairvoyance test using a ganzfeld technique. In W.G. Roll & R.L. Morris (Eds.), *Research in parapsychology, 1975* (pp. 48–49). Metuchen, NJ: Scarecrow Press.

II. STUDIES USING BINARY-CODING INDEX

3. Braud, W.G., & Wood, R. (1977). The influence of immediate feedback on free-response GESP performance during ganzfeld stimulation. *Journal of the American Society for Psychical Research*, **71**, 409–427.

20. Rogo, D.S. (1977). A preliminary study of precognition in the ganzfeld. *European Journal of Parapsychology*, **2** (1), 60–67.

*32. Smith, M., Tremmel, L., & Honorton, C. (1976). A comparison

Table A1
The Direct-Hits Studies

Study	No. of subjects	No. of trials	Direct hits	p(hit)	Proportion of hits	Zscore	Effect size
1	4	32	14	.25	.44	2.15	.37
2	10	10	3	.167	.30	.76	.31
4	14	14	0	.20	.00	−1.71	− .93
7	4	7	6	.25	.86	3.00	1.33
8	30	30	13	.25	.43	2.02	.38
10	40	40	6.5[a]	.20	.16	− .57	− .32
11	30	30	7	.25	.23	− .39	− .05
12	20	20	2	.25	.10	−1.97	− .40
16	10	10	9	.25	.90	4.02	1.44
17	10	10	4	.25	.40	.76	.32
18	28	28	8	.25	.29	.25	.09
19	1	10	4	.25	.40	.76	.32
21	20	20	7	.25	.35	.79	.22
23	26	26	8	.25	.31	.48	.13
24	20	20	9	.25	.45	1.74	.42
25	20	20	9	.25	.45	1.74	.42
26	30	30	16	.25	.53	3.15	.58
27	3	36	12	.25	.33	.97	.18
28	32	32	9	.25	.28	.24	.07
29	40	40	11	.25	.28	.21	.07
30	26	26	12	.25	.46	2.16	.44
31	20	20	12	.25	.60	3.11	.73
33	20	100	41	.25	.41	3.41	.34
34	40	40	13	.25	.33	.92	.18
38	12	27	11	.25	.41	1.62	.34
39	6	60	27	.25	.45	3.24	.42
41	24	48	10	.25	.21	− .82	− .10
42	49	49	18.5[a]	.20	.38	2.89	.40

Note. Effect size index is Cohen's h. See Cohen (1977), pp. 179–213.
[a] *Ranks derived from tied ratings.*

of psi and weak sensory influences on ganzfeld mentation. In J.D. Morris, W.G. Roll, & R.L. Morris (Eds.), *Research in parapsychology, 1975* (pp. 191–194). Metuchen, NJ: Scarecrow Press.

37. Terry, J.C. (1976). Comparison of stimulus duration in sensory and psi conditions. In J.D. Morris, W.G. Roll, & R.L. Morris (Eds.), *Research in parapsychology, 1975*. Metuchen, NJ: Scarecrow Press.

40. Terry, J.C., Tremmel, L., Kelly, M., Harper, S., & Barker, P. (1976). Psi information rate in guessing and receiver optimization. In J.D. Morris, W.G. Roll, & R.L. Morris (Eds.), *Research in parapsychology, 1975* (pp. 195–198). Metuchen, NJ: Scarecrow Press.

III. STUDIES USING OTHER INDICES

5. Dunne, B.J., Warnock, E., & Bisaha, J.P. (1977). Ganzfeld techniques with independent rating for measuring GESP and precognition. In J.D. Morris, W.G. Roll, & R.L. Morris (Eds.), *Research in parapsychology, 1976* (pp. 41–43). Metuchen, NJ: Scarecrow Press.

6. Habel, M.M. (1976). Varying auditory stimuli in the ganzfeld: The influence of sex and overcrowding on psi performance. In J.D. Morris, W.G. Roll, & R.L. Morris (Eds.), *Research in parapsychology, 1975* (pp. 181–184). Metuchen, NJ: Scarecrow Press.

*9. Keane, P., & Wells, R. (1979). An examination of the menstrual cycle as a hormone related physiological concomitant of psi performance. In W.G. Roll (Ed.), *Research in parapsychology, 1978* (pp. 72–74). Metuchen, NJ: Scarecrow Press.

13. Palmer, J., Whitson, T., & Bogart, D.N. (1980). Ganzfeld and remote viewing: A systematic comparison. In W.G. Roll (Ed.), *Research in parapsychology, 1979* (pp. 169–171). Metuchen, NJ: Scarecrow Press.

14. Parker, A. (1975). Some findings relevant to the change in state hypothesis. In J.D. Morris, W.G. Roll, & R.L. Morris (Eds.), *Research in parapsychology, 1974* (pp. 40–42). Metuchen, NJ: Scarecrow Press.

15. Parker, A., Millar, B., & Beloff, J. (1977). A three-experimenter ganzfeld: An attempt to use the ganzfeld technique to study the experimenter effect. In J.D. Morris, W.G. Roll, & R.L. Morris (Eds.), *Research in parapsychology, 1976* (pp. 52–54). Metuchen, NJ: Scarecrow Press.

22. Roney-Dougal, S.M. (1982). A comparison of psi and subliminal perception: A confirmatory study. In W.G. Roll, R.L. Morris, & R. White (Eds.), *Research in parapsychology, 1981* (pp. 96–99). Metuchen, NJ: Scarecrow Press.

35. Stanford, R.G. (1979). The influence of auditory ganzfeld characteristics upon free-response ESP performance. *Journal of the American Society for Psychical Research*, **73**, 253–272.

*36. Stanford, R.G., & Neylon, A. (1975). Experiential factors related to free-response clairvoyance performance in a sensory uniformity setting (ganzfeld). In J.D. Morris, W.G. Roll, & R.L. Morris (Eds.), *Research in parapsychology, 1974* (pp. 89–93). Metuchen, NJ: Scarecrow Press.

References

Allen, S., Green, P., Rucker, K., Goolsby, C., & Morris. R.L. (1976). A remote viewing study using a modified version of the SRI procedure. In J.D. Morris, W.G.

Roll, & R.L. Morris (Eds.), *Research in parapsychology, 1975.* Metuchen, NJ: Scarecrow Press.

Bartlett, M.S. (1950). Tests of significance in factor analysis. *British Journal of Psychology, Statistical Section,* **3**, 77–85.

Belvedere, E., & Foulkes, D. (1971). Telepathy and dreams: A failure to replicate. *Perceptual and Motor Skills,* **33**, 783–789.

Bozarth, J.D., & Roberts, R.R. (1972). Signifying significant significance. *American Psychologist,* **27**, 774–775.

Blackmore, S. (1980). The extent of selective reporting of ESP ganzfeld studies. *European Journal of Parapsychology,* **3**, 213–219.

Braud, W.G. (1978). Psi conducive conditions: Explorations and interpretations. In B. Shapin & L. Coly (Eds.), *Psi and states of awareness* (pp. 1–34). New York: Parapsychology Foundation, Inc.

Braud, L.W., & Braud, W.G. (1974a). The influence of relaxation and tension on the psi process. In W.G. Roll, R.L. Morris, & J.D. Morris (Eds.), *Research in parapsychology, 1973* (pp. 11–13). Metuchen, NJ: Scarecrow Press.

Braud, L.W., & Braud, W.G. (1974b). Further studies of relaxation as a psi-conducive state. *Journal of the American Society for Psychical Research,* **68**, 229–245.

Braud, W.G., & Braud, L.W. (1973). Preliminary explorations of psi-conducive states: Progressive muscular relaxation. *Journal of the American Society for Psychical Research,* **67**, 26–46.

Braud, W.G., Wood, R., & Braud, L.W. (1975). Free-response GESP performance during an experimental hypnagogic state induced by visual and acoustic ganzfeld techniques. A replication and extension. *Journal of the American Society for Psychical Research,* **69**, 105–113.

Carroll, J.B. (1961). The nature of the data, or how to choose a correlation coefficient [Presidential address]. *Psychometrika,* **26**, 347–372.

Cochran, W.G. (1954). Some methods for strengthening the common X^2 tests. *Biometrics,* **10**, 417–451.

Cohen, J. (1977). *Statistical power analysis for the behavioral sciences.* New York: Academic Press.

Cooper, H. (1984). *The integrative research review: A social science approach.* Beverly Hills, CA: Sage Publications.

Dunn, A.J. (1980). Neurochemistry of learning and memory: An evaluation of recent data. *Annual Review of Psychology,* **31**, 343–390.

Foulkes, D., Belvedere, E., Masters, R., Houston, J., Krippner, S., Honorton, C., & Ullman, M. (1972). Long-distance, "sensory bombardment" ESP in dreams: A failure to replicate. *Perceptual and Motor Skills,* **35**, 731–734.

Freeman, M.F., & Tukey, J.W. (1950). Transformations related to the angular and the square root. *Annals of Mathematical Statistics,* **21**, 607–611.

Glass, G.V., McGaw, B., & Smith, M.L. (1981). *Meta-analysis in social research.* Beverly Hills, CA: Sage Publications.

Globus, G.G., Knapp, P.H., Skinner, J.C., & Healy, G. (1968). An appraisal of telepathic communication in dreams. *Psychophysiology,* **4**, 365. (Abstract)

Harris, R.J. (1976). The invalidity of partitioned-U tests in canonical correlation and multivariate analysis of variance. *Multivariate Behavioral Research,* **11**, 353–365.

Honorton, C. (1975). Objective determination of information rate in psi tasks with pictorial stimuli. *Journal of the American Society for Psychical Research,* **69**, 353–359.

Honorton, C. (1977). Psi and internal attention states. In B.B. Wolman (Ed.), *Handbook of parapsychology* (pp. 435–472). New York: Van Nostrand Reinhold.

Honorton, C. (1978. Psi and internal attention states: Information retrieval in the ganzfeld. In B. Shapin & L. Coly (Eds.). *Psi and states of awareness* (pp. 79–90). New York: Parapsychology Foundation, Inc.

Honorton, C. (1983). Response to Hyman's critique of psi ganzfeld studies. In W.G. Roll, J. Beloff, & R.A. White (Eds.), *Research in parapsychology, 1982* (pp. 23–26). Metuchen, NJ: Scarecrow Press.

Honorton, C., & Harper, S. (1974). Psi-mediated imagery and ideation in an experimental procedure for regulating perceptual input. *Journal of the American Society for Psychical Research*, **68**, 156–168.

Honorton, C., & Krippner, S. (1969). Hypnosis and ESP performance: A review of the experimental literature. *Journal of the American Society for Psychical Research*, **63**, 214–252.

Hyman, R. (1983). Does the ganzfeld experiment answer the critics' objections? In W.G. Roll, J. Beloff, & R.A. White (Eds.), *Research in parapsychology, 1982* (pp. 21–23). Metuchen, NJ: Scarecrow Press.

Hyman, R. (1985). The ganzfeld psi experiment: A critical appraisal. *Journal of Parapsychology*, **49**, 3–49.

Kirk, R.E. (1982). *Experimental design: Procedures for the behavioral sciences* (2nd ed.). Belmont, CA: Brooks/Cole Publishing Company.

Marks, D., & Kammann, R. (1980). *The psychology of the psychic.* Buffalo, NY: Prometheus.

Parker, A. (1975). Some findings relevant to the change in state hypothesis. In J.D. Morris, W.G. Roll, & R.L. Morris (Eds.). *Research in parapsychology, 1974* (00. 40–42). Metuchen, NJ: Scarecrow Press.

Parker, A. (1978). A holistic methodology in psi research. *Parapsychology Review*, **9**, 1–6.

Puthoff, H.E., & Targ, R. (1976). A perceptual channel for information transfer over kilometer distances: Historical perspective and recent research. *Proceedings of the IEEE*, **64**, 329–354.

Puthoff, H.E., Targ, R., & May, E.C. (1981). Experimental psi research: Implications for physics: In R.G. Jahn (Ed.), *The role of consciousness in the physical world.* Boulder, CO: Westview Press.

Raburn, L. (1975). *Expectation and transmission factors in psychic functioning.* Unpublished honors thesis, Tulane University, New Orleans, LA.

Rauscher, E., Weissman, G., Sarfatti, J., & Sirag, S.-P. (1976). Remote perception of natural scenes, shielded against ordinary perception. In J.D. Morris, W.G. Roll, & R.L. Morris (Eds.), *Research in parapsychology, 1975.* Metuchen, NJ: Scarecrow Press.

Rosenthal, R. (1979). The "file drawer problem" and tolerance for null results. *Psychological Bulletin*, **86**, 638–641.

Rosenthal, R. (1984). *Meta-analytic procedures for social research.* Beverly Hills, CA: Sage Publications.

Rosenthal, R., & Rubin, D. (1984). Multiple contrasts and ordered Bonferroni procedures. *Journal of Educational Psychology*, 1028–1034.

Saunders, D.R. (1985). On Hyman's factor and analysis. *Journal of Parapsychology*, 49, 86–88.

Solfvin, G.F., Kelly, E.F., & Burdick, D.S. (1978). Some new methods of analysis for preferential-ranking data. *Journal of the American Society for Psychical Research*, 72, 93–110.

Solfvin, G.F., Roll, W.G., & Krieger, J. (1978). Meditation and ESP: Remote viewing. In W.G. Roll (Ed.), *Research in parapsychology, 1977*. Metuchen, NJ: Scarecrow Press.

Sommer, R., & Sommer, B. (1983). Mystery in Milwaukee. *American Psychologist*, 38, 982–985.

Spencer Brown, G. (1953). Statistical significance in psychical research. *Nature*, 172, 154–156.

Spencer Brown, G. (1957). *Probability and scientific inference*. New York: Longmans, Green.

Stanford, R.G., & Sargent, C.L. (1983). Z scores in free-response methodology: Comments on their utility and correction of an error. *Journal of the American Society for Psychical Research*, 77, 319–326.

Sterling, T.C. (1959). Publication decisions and their possible effects on inferences drawn from tests of significance—or vice versa. *Journal of the American Statistical Association*, 54, 30–34.

Ullman, M., Krippner, S., & Vaughan, A. (1973). *Dream telepathy*. New York: Macmillan.

CHAPTER 19

Does Psi Exist? Replicable Evidence for an Anomalous Process of Information Transfer

Daryl J. Bem *and* Charles Honorton

The term *psi* denotes anomalous processes of information or energy transfer, processes such as telepathy or other forms of extrasensory perception that are currently unexplained in terms of known physical or biological mechanisms. The term is purely descriptive: It neither implies that such anomalous phenomena are paranormal nor connotes anything about their underlying mechanisms.

Does psi exist? Most academic psychologists don't think so. A survey of more than 1,100 college professors in the United States found that 55% of natural scientists, 66% of social scientists (excluding psychologists), and 77% of academics in the arts, humanities, and education believed that ESP is either an established fact or a likely possibility. The comparable figure for psychologists was only 34%. Moreover, an equal number of psychologists declared ESP to be an impossibility, a view expressed by only 2% of all other respondents (Wagner & Monnet, 1979).

We psychologists are probably more skeptical about psi for several reasons. First, we believe that extraordinary claims require extraordinary proof. And although our colleagues from other disciplines would probably agree with this dictum, we are more likely to be familiar with the methodological and statistical requirements for sustaining such claims,

Reprinted with permission from *Psychological Bulletin*, 1994, **115**, 4–18.

as well as with previous claims that failed either to meet those requirements or to survive the test of successful replication. Even for ordinary claims, our conventional statistical criteria are conservative. The sacred p = .05 threshold is a constant reminder that it is far more sinful to assert that an effect exists when it does not (the Type 1 error) than to assert that an effect does not exist when it does (the Type II error).

Second, most of us distinguish sharply between phenomena whose explanations are merely obscure or controversial (e.g., hypnosis) and phenomena such as psi that appear to fall outside our current explanatory framework altogether. (Some would characterize this as the difference between the unexplained and the inexplicable.) In contrast, many laypersons treat all exotic psychological phenomena as epistemologically equivalent; many even consider déjà vu to be a psychic phenomenon. The blurring of this critical distinction is aided and abetted by the mass media, "new age" books and mind-power courses, and "psychic" entertainers who present both genuine hypnosis and fake "mind reading" in the course of a single performance. Accordingly, most laypersons would not have to revise their conceptual model of reality as radically as we would in order to assimilate the existence of psi. For us, psi is simply more extraordinary.

Finally, research in cognitive and social psychology has sensitized us to the errors and biases that plague intuitive attempts to draw valid inferences from the data of everyday experience (Gilovich, 1991; Nisbett & Ross, 1980; Tversky & Kahneman, 1971) . This leads us to give virtually no probative weight to anecdotal or journalistic reports of psi, the main source cited by our academic colleagues as evidence for their beliefs about psi (Wagner & Monnet, 1979).

Ironically, however, psychologists are probably not more familiar than others with recent experimental research on psi. Like most psychological research, parapsychological research is reported primarily in specialized journals; unlike most psychological research, however, contemporary parapsychological research is not usually reviewed or summarized in psychology's textbooks, handbooks, or mainstream journals. For example, only 1 of 64 introductory psychology textbooks recently surveyed even mentions the experimental procedure reviewed in this article, a procedure that has been in widespread use since the early 1970s (Roig, Icochea, & Cuzzucoli, 1991). Other secondary sources for nonspecialists are frequently inaccurate in their descriptions of parapsychological research. (For discussions of this problem, see Child, 1985, and Palmer, Honorton, & Utts, 1989.)

This situation may be changing. Discussions of modern psi research have recently appeared in a widely used introductory textbook (Atkinson,

Atkinson, Smith, & Bem, 1990, 1993), two mainstream psychology journals (Child, 1985; Rao & Palmer, 1987), and a scholarly but accessible book for nonspecialists (Broughton, 1991). The purpose of the present article is to supplement these broader treatments with a more detailed, meta-analytic presentation of evidence issuing from a single experimental method: the *ganzfeld* procedure. We believe that the replication rates and effect sizes achieved with this procedure are now sufficient to warrant bringing this body of data to the attention of the wider psychological community.

The Ganzfeld Procedure

By the 1960s, a number of parapsychologists had become dissatisfied with the familiar ESP testing methods pioneered by J. B. Rhine at Duke University in the 1930s. In particular, they believed that the repetitive forced-choice procedure in which a subject repeatedly attempts to select the correct "target" symbol from a set of fixed alternatives failed to capture the circumstances that characterize reported instances of psi in everyday life.

Historically, psi has often been associated with meditation, hypnosis, dreaming, and other naturally occurring or deliberately induced altered states of consciousness. For example, the view that psi phenomena can occur during meditation is expressed in most classical texts on meditative techniques; the belief that hypnosis is a psi-conducive state dates all the way back to the days of early mesmerism (Dingwall, 1968); and cross-cultural surveys indicate that most reported "real-life" psi experiences are mediated through dreams (Green, 1960; Prasad & Stevenson, 1968; L. E. Rhine, 1962; Sannwald, 1959).

There are now reports of experimental evidence consistent with these anecdotal observations. For example, several laboratory investigators have reported that meditation facilitates psi performance (Honorton, 1977). A meta-analysis of 25 experiments on hypnosis and psi conducted between 1945 and 1981 in 10 different laboratories suggests that hypnotic induction may also facilitate psi performance (Schechter, 1984). And dream-mediated psi was reported in a series of experiments conducted at Maimonides Medical Center in New York and published between 1966 and 1972 (Child, 1985; Ullman, Krippner, & Vaughan, 1973).

In the Maimonides dream studies, two subjects—a "receiver" and a "sender"—spent the night in a sleep laboratory. The receiver's brain waves and eye movements were monitored as he or she slept in an isolated room.

When the receiver entered a period of REM sleep, the experimenter pressed a buzzer that signaled the sender—under the supervision of a second experimenter—to begin a sending period. The sender would then concentrate on a randomly chosen picture (the "target") with the goal of influencing the content of the receiver's dream.

Toward the end of the REM period, the receiver was awakened and asked to describe any dream just experienced. This procedure was repeated throughout the night with the same target. A transcription of the receiver's dream reports was given to outside judges who blindly rated the similarity of the night's dreams to several pictures, including the target. In some studies, similarity ratings were also obtained from the receivers themselves. Across several variations of the procedure, dreams were judged to be significantly more similar to the target pictures than to the control pictures in the judging sets (failures to replicate the Maimonides results were also reviewed by Child, 1985).

These several lines of evidence suggested a working model of psi in which psi-mediated information is conceptualized as a weak signal that is normally masked by internal somatic and external sensory "noise." By reducing ordinary sensory input, these diverse psi-conducive states are presumed to raise the signal-to-noise ratio, thereby enhancing a person's ability to detect the psi-mediated information (Honorton, 1969, 1977). To test the hypothesis that a reduction of sensory input itself facilitates psi performance, investigators turned to the ganzfeld procedure (Braud, Wood, & Braud, 1975; Honorton & Harper, 1974; Parker, 1975), a procedure originally introduced into experimental psychology during the 1930s to test propositions derived from gestalt theory (Avant, 1965; Metzger, 1930).

Like the dream studies, the psi ganzfeld procedure has most often been used to test for telepathic communication between a sender and a receiver. The receiver is placed in a reclining chair in an acoustically isolated room. Translucent Ping-Pong ball halves are taped over the eyes and headphones are placed over the ears; a red floodlight directed toward the eyes produces an undifferentiated visual field, and white noise played through the headphones produces an analogous auditory field. It is this homogeneous perceptual environment that is called the *Ganzfeld* ("total field"). To reduce internal somatic "noise," the receiver typically also undergoes a series of progressive relaxation exercises at the beginning of the ganzfeld period.

The sender is sequestered in a separate acoustically isolated room, and a visual stimulus (art print, photograph, or brief videotaped sequence) is randomly selected from a large pool of such stimuli to serve as the target for the session. While the sender concentrates on the target, the receiver provides a continuous verbal report of his or her ongoing imagery and mentation, usually for about 30 minutes. At the completion of the ganzfeld period, the receiver is presented with several stimuli (usually four) and, without knowing which stimulus was the target, is asked to rate the degree to which each matches the imagery and mentation experienced during the ganzfeld period. If the receiver assigns the highest rating to the target stimulus, it is scored as a "hit." Thus, if the experiment uses judging sets containing four stimuli (the target and three decoys or control stimuli), the hit rate expected by chance is .25. The ratings can also be analyzed in other ways; for example, they can be converted to ranks or standardized scores within each set and analyzed parametrically across sessions. And, as with the dream studies, the similarity ratings can also be made by outside judges using transcripts of the receiver's mentation report.

Meta-Analyses of the Ganzfeld Database

In 1985 and 1986, the *Journal of Parapsychology* devoted two entire issues to a critical examination of the ganzfeld database. The 1985 issue comprised two contributions: (a) a meta-analysis and critique by Ray Hyman (1985), a cognitive psychologist and skeptical critic of parapsychological research, and (b) a competing meta-analysis and rejoinder by Charles Honorton (1985), a parapsychologist and major contributor to the ganzfeld database. The 1986 issue contained four commentaries on the Hyman-Honorton exchange, a joint communiqué by Hyman and Honorton, and six additional commentaries on the joint communiqué itself. We summarize the major issues and conclusions here.

Replication Rates

RATES BY STUDY

Hyman's meta-analysis covered 42 psi ganzfeld studies reported in 34 separate reports written or published from 1974 through 1981. One of the first problems he discovered in the database was multiple analysis. As noted earlier, it is possible to calculate several indexes of psi performance in a ganzfeld experiment and, furthermore, to subject those indexes to several kinds of statistical treatment. Many investigators reported multiple indexes or applied multiple statistical tests without adjusting the criterion significance level for the number of tests conducted. Worse, some may have "shopped" among the alternatives until finding one that yielded a significantly successful outcome. Honorton agreed that this was a problem.

Accordingly, Honorton applied a uniform test on a common index across all studies from which the pertinent datum could be extracted, regardless of how the investigators had analyzed the data in the original reports. He selected the proportion of hits as the common index because it could be calculated for the largest subset of studies: 28 of the 42 studies. The hit rate is also a conservative index because it discards most of the rating information; a second place ranking—a "near miss"—receives no more credit than a last place ranking. Honorton then calculated the exact binomial probability and its associated z score for each study.

Of the 28 studies, 23 (82%) had positive z scores ($p = 4.6 \times 10^{-4}$, exact binomial test with $p = q = .5$). Twelve of the studies (43%) had z scores that were independently significant at the 5% level ($p = 3.5 \times 10^{-9}$, binomial test with 28 studies, $p = .05$, and $q = .95$), and 7 of the studies (25%) were independently significant at the 1% level ($p = 9.8 \times 10^{-9}$). The composite Stouffer z score across the 28 studies was 6.60 ($p = 2.1 \times 10^{-11}$).* A more conservative estimate of significance can be obtained by including 10 additional studies that also used the relevant judging procedure but did not report hit rates. If these studies are assigned a mean z score of zero, the Stouffer z across all 38 studies becomes 5.67 ($p = 7.3 \times 10^{-9}$).

Thus, whether one considers only the studies for which the relevant information is available or includes a null estimate for the additional studies for which the information is not available, the aggregate results cannot reasonably be attributed to chance. And, by design, the cumulative outcome reported here cannot be attributed to the inflation of significance levels through multiple analysis.

RATES BY LABORATORY

One objection to estimates such as those just described is that studies from a common laboratory are not independent of one another (Parker, 1978). Thus, it is possible for one or two investigators to be disproportionately responsible for a high replication rate, whereas other, independent investigators are unable to obtain the effect.

The ganzfeld database is vulnerable to this possibility. The 28 studies providing hit rate information were conducted by investigators in 10 different laboratories. One laboratory contributed 9 of the studies.

---

*Stouffer's z is computed by dividing the sum of the z scores for the individual studies by the square root of the number of studies (Rosenthal, 1978).

Honorton's own laboratory contributed 5, 2 other laboratories contributed 3 each, 2 contributed 2 each, and the remaining 4 laboratories each contributed 1. Thus, half of the studies were conducted by only 2 laboratories, 1 of them Honorton's own.

Accordingly, Honorton calculated a separate Stouffer z score for each laboratory. Significantly positive outcomes were reported by 6 of the 10 laboratories, and the combined z score across laboratories was 6.16 ($p = 3.6 \times 10^{-10}$). Even if all of the studies conducted by the 2 most prolific laboratories are discarded from the analysis, the Stouffer z across the 8 other laboratories remains significant ($z = 3.67, p = 1.2 \times 10^{-4}$). Four of these studies are significant at the 1% level ($p = 9.2 \times 10^{-6}$), binomial test with 14 studies, $p = .01$, and $q = .99$), and each was contributed by a different laboratory. Thus, even though the total number of laboratories in this database is small, most of them have reported significant studies, and the significance of the overall effect does not depend on just one or two of them.

Selective Reporting

In recent years, behavioral scientists have become increasingly aware of the "file-drawer" problem: the likelihood that successful studies are more likely to be published than unsuccessful studies, which are more likely to be consigned to the file drawers of their disappointed investigators (Bozarth & Roberts, 1972; Sterling, 1959). Parapsychologists were among the first to become sensitive to the problem, and, in 1975, the Parapsychological Association Council adopted a policy opposing the selective reporting of positive outcomes. As a consequence, negative findings have been routinely reported at the association's meetings and in its affiliated publications for almost two decades. As has already been shown, more than half of the ganzfeld studies included in the meta-analysis yielded outcomes whose significance falls short of the conventional .05 level.

A variant of the selective reporting problem arises from what Hyman (1985) has termed the "retrospective study." An investigator conducts a small set of exploratory trials. If they yield null results, they remain exploratory and never become part of the official record; if they yield positive results, they are defined as a study after the fact and are submitted for publication. In support of this possibility, Hyman noted that there are more significant studies in the database with fewer than 20 trials than one would expect under the assumption that, all other things being equal, statistical power should increase with the square root of the sample size.

Although Honorton questioned the assumption that "all other things" are in fact equal across the studies and disagreed with Hyman's particular statistical analysis, he agreed that there is an apparent clustering of significant studies with fewer than 20 trials. (Of the complete ganzfeld database of 42 studies, 8 involved fewer than 20 trials, and 6 of those studies reported statistically significant results.)

Because it is impossible, by definition, to know how many unknown studies—exploratory or otherwise—are languishing in file drawers, the major tool for estimating the seriousness of selective reporting problems has become some variant of Rosenthal's file-drawer statistic, an estimate of how many unreported studies with z scores of zero would be required to exactly cancel out the significance of the known database (Rosenthal, 1979). For the 28 direct-hit ganzfeld studies alone, this estimate is 423 fugitive studies, a ratio of unreported-to-reported studies of approximately 15:1. When it is recalled that a single ganzfeld session takes over an hour to conduct, it is not surprising that—despite his concern with the retrospective study problem—Hyman concurred with Honorton and other participants in the published debate that selective reporting cannot plausibly account for the overall statistical significance of the psi ganzfeld database (Hyman & Honorton, 1986).*

Methodological Flaws

If the most frequent criticism of parapsychology is that it has not produced a replicable psi effect, the second most frequent criticism is that many, if not most, psi experiments have inadequate controls and procedural safeguards. A frequent charge is that positive results emerge primarily from initial, poorly controlled studies and then vanish as better controls and safeguards are introduced.

Fortunately, meta-analysis provides a vehicle for empirically evaluating the extent to which methodological flaws may have contributed to artifactual positive outcomes across a set of studies. First, ratings are assigned to each study that index the degree to which particular methodological flaws are or are not present; these ratings are then correlated with the studies' outcomes. Large positive correlations constitute evidence that the observed effect may be artifactual.

In psi research, the most fatal flaws are those that might permit a

*A 1980 survey of parapsychologists uncovered only 19 completed but unreported ganzfeld studies. Seven of these had achieved significantly positive results, a proportion (.37) very similar to the proportion of independently significant studies in the meta-analysis (.43) (Blackmore, 1980).

subject to obtain the target information in normal sensory fashion, either inadvertently or through deliberate cheating. This is called the problem of *sensory leakage*. Another potentially serious flaw is inadequate randomization of target selection.

SENSORY LEAKAGE

Because the ganzfeld is itself a perceptual isolation procedure, it goes a long way toward eliminating potential sensory leakage during the ganzfeld portion of the session. There are, however, potential channels of sensory leakage after the ganzfeld period. For example, if the experimenter who interacts with the receiver knows the identity of the target, he or she could bias the receiver's similarity ratings in favor of correct identification. Only one study in the database contained this flaw, a study in which subjects actually performed slightly below chance expectation. Second, if the stimulus set given to the receiver for judging contains the actual physical target handled by the sender during the sending period, there might be cues (e.g., fingerprints, smudges, or temperature differences) that could differentiate the target from the decoys. Moreover, the process of transferring the stimulus materials to the receiver's room itself opens up other potential channels of sensory leakage. Although contemporary ganzfeld studies have eliminated both of these possibilities by using duplicate stimulus sets, some of the earlier studies did not.

Independent analyses by Hyman and Honorton agreed that there was no correlation between inadequacies of security against sensory leakage and study outcome. Honorton further reported that if studies that failed to use duplicate stimulus sets were discarded from the analysis, the remaining studies are still highly significant (Stouffer $z = 4.35$, $p = 6.8 \times 10^{-6}$).

RANDOMIZATION

In many psi experiments, the issue of target randomization is critical because systematic patterns in inadequately randomized target sequences might be detected by subjects during a session or might match subjects' preexisting response biases. In a ganzfeld study, however, randomization is a much less critical issue because only one target is selected during the session and most subjects serve in only one session. The primary concern is simply that all the stimuli within each judging set be sampled uniformly over the course of the study. Similar considerations govern the second randomization, which takes place after the ganzfeld period and determines the sequences in which the target and decoys are presented to the receiver (or external judge) for judging.

Nevertheless, Hyman and Honorton disagreed over the findings here. Hyman claimed there was a correlation between flaws of randomization and study outcome; Honorton claimed there was not. The sources of this disagreement were in conflicting definitions of flaw categories, in the coding and assignment of flaw ratings to individual studies, and in the subsequent statistical treatment of those ratings.

Unfortunately, there have been no ratings of flaws by independent raters who were unaware of the studies' outcomes (Morris, 1991). Nevertheless, none of the contributors to the subsequent debate concurred with Hyman's conclusion, whereas four nonparapsychologists—two statisticians and two psychologists—explicitly concurred with Honorton's conclusion (Harris & Rosenthal, 1988b; Saunders, 1985; Utts, 1991a). For example, Harris and Rosenthal (one of the pioneers in the use of meta-analysis in psychology) used Hyman's own flaw ratings and failed to find any significant relationships between flaws and study outcomes in each of two separate analyses: "Our analysis of the effects of flaws on study outcome lends no support to the hypothesis that Ganzfeld research results are a significant function of the set of flaw variables" (1988b, p. 3; for a more recent exchange regarding Hyman's analysis, see Hyman, 1991; Utts, 1991a, 1991b).

Effect Size

Some critics of parapsychology have argued that even if current laboratory-produced psi effects turn out to be replicable and nonartifactual, they are too small to be of theoretical interest or practical importance. We do not believe this to be the case for the psi ganzfeld effect.

In psi ganzfeld studies, the hit rate itself provides a straight-forward descriptive measure of effect size, but this measure cannot be compared directly across studies because they do not all use a four-stimulus judging set and, hence, do not all have a chance baseline of .25. The next most obvious candidate, the difference in each study between the hit rate observed and the hit rate expected under the null hypothesis, is also intuitively descriptive but is not appropriate for statistical analysis because not all differences between proportions that are equal are equally detectable (e.g., the power to detect the difference between .55 and .25 is different from the power to detect the difference between .50 and .20).

To provide a scale of equal detectability, Cohen (1988) devised the effect size index h, which involves an arcsine transformation on the proportions before calculation of their difference. Cohen's h is quite general and can assess the difference between any two proportions drawn from independent samples or between a single proportion and any specified hypothetical value. For the 28 studies examined in the meta-analyses, h was .28, with a 95% confidence interval from .11 to .45.

But because values of h do not provide an intuitively descriptive scale, Rosenthal and Rubin (1989; Rosenthal, 1991) have recently suggested a new index, π, which applies specifically to one-sample, multiple-choice data of the kind obtained in ganzfeld experiments. In particular, π expresses all hit rates as the proportion of hits that would have been obtained if there had been only two equally likely alternatives—essentially a coin flip. Thus, π ranges from 0 to 1, with .5 expected under the null hypothesis. The formula is

$$\pi = \frac{P(k-1)}{P(k-2)+1},$$

Where P is the raw proportion of hits and k is the number of alternative choices available. Because π has such a straightforward intuitive interpretation, we use it (or its conversion back to an equivalent four-alternative hit rate) throughout this article whenever it is applicable.

For the 28 studies examined in the meta-analyses, the mean value of π was .62, with a 95% confidence interval from .55 to .69. This corresponds to a four-alternative hit rate of 35%, with a 95% confidence interval from 28% to 43%.

Cohen (1988, 1992) has also categorized effect sizes into small, medium, and large, with medium denoting an effect size that should be apparent to the naked eye of a careful observer. For a statistic such as π, which indexes the deviation of a proportion from .5, Cohen considers .65 to be a medium effect size. A statistically unaided observer should be able to detect the bias of a coin that comes up heads on 65% of the trials. Thus, at .62, the psi ganzfeld effect size falls just short of Cohen's naked-eye criterion. From the phenomenology of the ganzfeld experimenter, the corresponding hit rate of 35% implies that he or she will see a subject obtain a hit approximately every third session rather than every fourth.

It is also instructive to compare the psi ganzfeld effect with the results of a recent medical study that sought to determine whether aspirin can prevent heart attacks (Steering Committee of the Physician's Health Study Research Group, 1988). The study was discontinued after 6 years because it was already clear that the aspirin treatment was effective ($p < .00001$) and it was considered unethical to keep the control group on placebo medication. The study was widely publicized as a major medical breakthrough. But despite its undisputed reality and practical importance, the size of the aspirin effect is quite small: Taking aspirin reduces the probability of suffering a heart attack by only .008. The corresponding effect size (h) is .068, about one third to one fourth the size of the psi ganzfeld effect (Atkinson et al., 1993, p. 236; Utts, 1991b).

In sum, we believe that the psi ganzfeld effect is large enough to be of both theoretical interest and potential practical importance.

Experimental Correlates of the Psi Ganzfeld Effect

We showed earlier that the technique of correlating variables with effect sizes across studies can help to assess whether methodological flaws might have produced artifactual positive outcomes. The same technique can be used more affirmatively to explore whether an effect varies systematically with conceptually relevant variations in experimental procedure. The discovery of such correlates can help to establish an effect as genuine, suggest ways of increasing replication rates and effect sizes, and enhance the chances of moving beyond the simple demonstration of an effect to its explanation. This strategy is only heuristic, however. Any correlates discovered must be considered quite tentative, both because they emerge from post hoc exploration and because they necessarily involve comparisons across heterogeneous studies that differ simultaneously on many interrelated variables, known and unknown. Two such correlates emerged from the meta-analyses of the psi ganzfeld effect.

Single-Versus Multiple-Image Targets

Although most of the 28 studies in the meta-analysis used single pictures as targets, 9 (conducted by three different investigators) used View Master stereoscopic slide reels that presented multiple images focused on a central theme. Studies using the View Master reels produced significantly higher hit rates than did studies using the single-image targets (50% vs. 34%), $t(26) = 2.22$, $p = .035$, two-tailed.

SENDER-RECEIVER PAIRING

In 17 of the 28 studies, participants were free to bring in friends to serve as senders. In 8 studies, only laboratory-assigned senders were used. (Three studies used no sender.) Unfortunately, there is no record of how many participants in the former studies actually brought in friends. Nevertheless, those 17 studies (conducted by six different investigators) had significantly higher hit rates than did the studies that used only laboratory-assigned senders (44% vs. 26%), $t(23) = 2.39$, $p = .025$, two-tailed.

The Joint Communiqué

After their published exchange in 1985, Hyman and Honorton agreed to contribute a joint communiqué to the subsequent discussion that was published in 1986. First, they set forth their areas of agreement and disagreement:

> We agree that there is an overall significant effect in this data base that cannot reasonably be explained by selective reporting or multiple analysis. We continue to differ over the degree to which the effect constitutes evidence for psi, but we agree that the final verdict awaits the outcome of future experiments conducted by a broader range of investigators and according to more stringent standards [Hyman & Honorton, 1986, p. 351].

They then spelled out in detail the "more stringent standards" they believed should govern future experiments. These standards included strict security precautions against sensory leakage, testing and documentation of randomization methods for selecting targets and sequencing the judging pool, statistical correction for multiple analyses, advance specification of the status of the experiment (e.g., pilot study or confirmatory experiment), and full documentation in the published report of the experimental procedures and the status of statistical tests (e.g., planned or post hoc).

The National Research Council Report

In 1988, the National Research Council (NRC) of the National Academy of Sciences released a widely publicized report commissioned by the U.S. Army that assessed several controversial technologies for enhancing human performance, including accelerated learning, neurolinguistic programming, mental practice, biofeedback, and parapsychology (Druckman & Swets, 1988; summarized in Swets & Bjork, 1990). The report's conclusion concerning parapsychology was quite negative: "The Committee finds no scientific justification from research conducted over a period of 130 years for the existence of parapsychological phenomena" (Druckman & Swets, 1988, p. 22).

An extended refutation strongly protesting the committee's treatment of parapsychology has been published elsewhere (Palmer et al., 1989). The pertinent point here is simply that the NRC's evaluation of the ganzfeld studies does not reflect an additional, independent examination of the ganzfeld database but is based on the same meta-analysis conducted by Hyman that we have discussed in this article.

Hyman chaired the NRC's Subcommittee on Parapsychology, and, although he had concurred with Honorton 2 years earlier in their joint communiqué that "there is an overall significant effect in this data base that cannot reasonably be explained by selective reporting or multiple analysis" (p. 351) and that "significant outcomes have been produced by a number of different investigators" (p. 352), neither of these points is acknowledged in the committee's report.

The NRC also solicited a background report from Harris and Rosenthal (1988a), which provided the committee with a comparative methodological analysis of the five controversial areas just listed. Harris and Rosenthal noted that, of these areas, "only the Ganzfeld ESP studies [the only psi studies they evaluated] regularly meet the basic requirements of sound experimental design" (p. 53), and they concluded that

> it would be implausible to entertain the null given the combined p from these 28 studies. Given the various problems or flaws pointed out by Hyman and Honorton ... we might estimate the obtained accuracy rate to be about ⅓ ... when the accuracy rate expected under the null is ¼ [p. 51].*

The Autoganzfeld Studies

In 1983, Honorton and his colleagues initiated a new series of ganzfeld studies designed to avoid the methodological problems he and others had identified in earlier studies (Honorton, 1979; Kennedy, 1979). These studies compiled with all of the detailed guidelines that he and Hyman were to publish later in their joint communiqué. The program continued until September 1989, when a loss of funding forced the laboratory to close. The major innovations of the new studies were computer control of the experimental protocol—hence the name *autoganzfeld*—and the introduction of videotaped film clips as target stimuli.

Method

The basic design of the autoganzfeld studies was the same as that

---

*In a troubling development, the chair of the NRC Committee phoned Rosenthal and asked him to delete the parapsychology section of the paper (R. Rosenthal, personal communication, September 15, 1992). Although Rosenthal refused to do so, that section of the Harris-Rosenthal paper is nowhere cited in the NRC report.

described earlier*: A receiver and sender were sequestered in separate, acoustically isolated chambers. After a 14-min. period of progressive relaxation, the receiver underwent ganzfeld stimulation while describing his or her thoughts and images aloud for 30 min. Meanwhile, the sender concentrated on a randomly selected target. At the end of the ganzfeld period, the receiver was shown four stimuli and, without knowing which of the four had been the target, rated each stimulus for its similarity to his or her mentation during the ganzfeld.

The targets consisted of 80 still pictures (static targets) and 80 short video segments complete with soundtracks (dynamic targets), all recorded on videocassette. The static targets included art prints, photographs, and magazine advertisements; the dynamic targets included excerpts of approximately 1-min. duration from motion pictures, TV shows, and cartoons. The 160 targets were arranged in judging sets of four static or four dynamic targets each, constructed to minimize similarities among targets within a set.

TARGET SELECTION AND PRESENTATION

The VCR containing the taped targets was interfaced to the controlling computer, which selected the target and controlled its repeated presentation to the sender during the ganzfeld period, thus eliminating the need for a second experimenter to accompany the sender. After the ganzfeld period, the computer randomly sequenced the four-clip judging set and presented it to the receiver on a TV monitor for judging. The receiver used a computer game paddle to make his or her ratings on a 40-point scale that appeared on the TV monitor after each clip was shown. The receiver was permitted to see each clip and to change the ratings repeatedly until he or she was satisfied. The computer then wrote these and other data from the session into a file on a floppy disk. At that point, the sender moved to the receiver's chamber and revealed the identity of the target to both the receiver and the experimenter. Note that the experimenter did not even know the identity of the four-clip judging set until it was displayed to the receiver for judging.

RANDOMIZATION

The random selection of the target and sequencing of the judging

*Because Honorton and his colleagues have complied with the Hyman-Honorton specification that experimental reports be sufficiently complete to permit others to reconstruct the investigator's procedures, readers who wish to know more detail than we provide here are likely to find whatever they need in the archival publication of these studies in the Journal of Parapsychology (Honorton et al., 1990).

set were controlled by a noise-based random number generator interfaced to the computer. Extensive testing confirmed that the generator was providing a uniform distribution of values throughout the full target range (1-160). Tests on the actual frequencies observed during the experiments confirmed that targets were, on average, selected uniformly from among the 4 clips within each judging set and that the 4 judging sequences used were uniformly distributed across sessions.

ADDITIONAL CONTROL FEATURES

The receiver's and sender's rooms were sound-isolated, electrically shielded chambers with single-door access that could be continuously monitored by the experimenter. There was two-way intercom communication between the experimenter and the receiver but only one-way communication into the sender's room; thus, neither the experimenter nor the receiver could monitor events inside the sender's room. The archival record for each session includes an audiotape containing the receiver's mentation during the ganzfeld period and all verbal exchanges between the experimenter and the receiver throughout the experiment.

The automated ganzfeld protocol has been examined by several dozen parapsychologists and behavioral researchers from other fields, including well-known critics or parapsychology. Many have participated as subjects or observers. All have expressed satisfaction with the handling of security issues and controls.

Parapsychologists have often been urged to employ magicians as consultants to ensure that the experimental protocols are not vulnerable either to inadvertent sensory leakage or to deliberate cheating. Two "mentalists," magicians who specialize in the simulation of psi, have examined the autoganzfeld system and protocol. Ford Kross, a professional mentalist and officer of the mentalist's professional organization, the Psychic Entertainers Association, provided the following written statement "In my professional capacity as a mentalist, I have reviewed Psychophysical Research Laboratories' automated ganzfeld system and found it to provide excellent security against deception by subjects" (personal communication, May, 1989).

Darryl J. Bem has also performed as a mentalist for many years and is a member of the Psychic Entertainers Association. This article had its origins in a 1983 visit he made to Honorton's laboratory, where he was asked to critically examine the research protocol from the perspective of a mentalist, a research psychologist, and a subject. Needless to say, this article would not exist if he did not concur with Ford Kross's assessment of the security procedures.

Experimental Studies

Altogether, 100 men and 140 women participated as receivers in 354 sessions during the research program.* The participants ranged in age from 17 to 74 years (M = 37.3, SD = 11.8), with a mean formal education of 15.6 years (SD = 2.0). Eight separate experimenters, including Honorton, conducted the studies.

The experimental program included three pilot and eight formal studies. Five of the formal studies used novice (first-time) participants who served as the receiver in one session each. The remaining three formal studies used experienced participants.

PILOT STUDIES

Sample sizes were not preset in the three pilot studies. Study 1 comprised 22 sessions and was conducted during the initial development and testing of the autoganzfeld system. Study 2 comprised 9 sessions testing a procedure in which the experimenter, rather than the receiver, served as the judge at the end of the session. Study 3 comprised 35 sessions and served as practice for participants who had completed the allotted number of sessions in the ongoing formal studies but who wanted additional ganzfeld experience. This study also included several demonstration sessions when TV film crews were present.

NOVICE STUDIES

Studies 101-104 were each designed to test 50 participants who had no prior ganzfeld experience; each participant served as the receiver in a single ganzfeld session. Study 104 included 16 of 20 students recruited from the Juilliard School in New York City to test an artistically gifted sample. Study 105 was initiated to accommodate the overflow of participants who had been recruited for Study 104, including the 4 remaining Juilliard students. The sample size for this study was set to 25, but only 6 sessions had been completed when the laboratory closed. For purposes of exposition, we divided the 56 sessions from Studies 104 and 105 into two parts: Study 104/105(a) comprises the 36 non-Juilliard participants, and Study 104/105(b) comprises the 20 Juilliard students.

STUDY 201

This study was designed to retest the most promising participants

*A recent review of the original computer files uncovered a duplicate record in the autoganzfeld database. This has now been eliminated, reducing by one the number of subjects and sessions. As a result, some of the numbers presented in this article differed slightly from those in Honorton et al. (1990).

from the previous studies. The number of trials was set to 20, but only 7 sessions with 3 participants had been completed when the laboratory closed.

STUDY 301

This study was designed to compare static and dynamic targets. The sample size was set to 50 sessions. Twenty-five experienced participants each served as the receiver in 2 sessions. Unknown to the participants, the computer control program was modified to ensure that they would each have 1 session with a static target and 1 session with a dynamic target.

STUDY 302

This study was designed to examine a dynamic target set that had yielded a particularly high hit rate in the previous studies. The study involved experienced participants who had no prior experience with this particular target set and who were unaware that only one target set was being sampled. Each served as the receiver in a single session. The design called for the study to continue until 15 sessions were completed with each of the targets, but only 25 sessions had been completed when the laboratory closed.

The 11 studies just described comprise all sessions conducted during the 6.5 years of the program. There is no "file drawer" of unreported sessions.

Results

OVERALL HIT RATE

As in the earlier meta-analysis, receivers' ratings were analyzed by tallying the proportion of hits achieved and calculating the exact binomial probability for the observed number of hits compared with the chance expectation of .25. As noted earlier, 240 participants contributed 354 sessions. For reasons discussed later, Study 302 is analyzed separately, reducing the number of sessions in the primary analysis to 329.

As Table 1 shows, there were 106 hits in the 329 sessions, a hit rate of 32% ($z = 2.89$, $p = .002$, one-tailed), with a 95% confidence interval from 30% to 35%. This corresponds to an effect size (π) of .59, with a 95% confidence interval from .53 to .64.

Table 1 also shows that when Studies 104 and 105 are combined and re-divided into Studies 104/105(a) and 104/105(b), 9 of the 10 studies yield positive effect sizes, with a mean effect size (π) of .61, $t(9) = 4.44$, $p = .0008$,

Table 1
Outcome by Study

Study	Study/subject description	N subjects	N trials	N hits	% hits	Effect size π	z
1	Pilot	19	22	8	36	.62	0.99
2	Pilot	4	9	3	33	.60	0.25
3	Pilot	24	35	10	29	.55	0.32
101	Novice	50	50	12	24	.47	- 0.30
102	Novice	50	50	18	36	.63	1.60
103	Novice	50	50	15	30	.55	0.67
104/105(a)	Novice	36	36	12	33	.60	0.97
104/105(b)	Juilliard sample	20	20	10	50	.75	2.20
201	Experienced	3	7	3	43	.69	0.69
301	Experienced	25	50	15	30	.56	0.67
302	Experienced	25	25	16	54*	.78a	3.04a
Overall (Studies 1–301)		240	329	106	32	.59	2.89

Note. All z scores are based on the exact binomial probability, with p = .25 and q = .75. ªAdjusted for response bias; the hit rate actually observed was 64%.

one-tailed. This effect size is equivalent to a four-alternative hit rate of 34%. Alternatively, if Studies 104 and 105 are retained as separate studies, 9 of the 10 studies again yield positive effect sizes, with a mean effect size (π) of .62, $t(9) = 3.73$, $p = .002$, one-tailed. This effect size is equivalent to a four-alternative hit rate of 35% and is identical to that found across the 28 studies of the earlier meta-analysis.*

Considered together, sessions with novice participants (Studies 101-105) yielded a statistically significant hit rate of 32.5% ($p = .009$), which is not significantly different from the 31.6% hit rate achieved by experienced participants in Studies 201 and 301. And, finally, each of the eight experimenters also achieved a positive effect size, with a mean π of .60, $t(7) = 3.44$, $p = .005$, one-tailed.

THE JUILLIARD SAMPLE

There are several reports in the literature of a relationship between creativity or artistic ability and psi performance (Schmeidler, 1988). To explore this possibility in the ganzfeld setting, 10 male and 10 female

As noted above, the laboratory was forced to close before three of the formal studies could be completed. If we assume that the remaining trials in Studies 105 and 201 would have yielded only chance results, this would reduce the overall z for the first 10 autoganzfeld studies from 2.89 to 2.76 ($p = .003$). Thus, inclusion of the two incomplete studies does not pose an optional stopping problem. The third incomplete study, Study 302, is discussed below.

undergraduates were recruited from the Juilliard School. Of these, 8 were music students, 10 were drama students, and 2 were dance students. Each served as the receiver in a single session in study 104 or 105. As shown in Table 1, these students achieved a hit rate of 50% (p = .014), one of the five highest hit rates ever reported for a single sample in a ganzfeld study. The musicians were particularly successful: 6 of the 8 (75%) successfully identified their targets (p = .004; further details about this sample and their ganzfeld performance were reported in Schlitz & Honorton, 1992).

STUDY SIZE AND EFFECT SIZE

There is a significant negative correlation across the 10 studies listed in Table 1 between the number of sessions included in a study and the study's effect size (π), r = -.64, $t(8)$ = 2.36, p < .05, two-tailed. This is reminiscent of Hyman's discovery that the smaller studies in the original ganzfeld database were disproportionately likely to report statistically significant results. He interpreted this finding as evidence for a bias against the reporting of small studies that fail to achieve significant results. A similar interpretation cannot be applied to the autoganzfeld studies, however, because there are no unreported sessions.

One reviewer of this article suggested that the negative correlation might reflect a decline effect in which earlier sessions of a study are more successful than later sessions. If there were such an effect, then studies with fewer sessions would show larger effect sizes because they would end before the decline could set in. To check this possibility, we computed point-biserial correlations between hits (1) or misses (0) and the session number within each of the 10 studies. All of the correlations hovered around zero; six were positive, four were negative, and the overall mean was .01.

An inspection of Table 1 reveals that the negative correlation derives primarily from the two studies with the largest effect sizes: the 20 sessions with the Juilliard students and the 7 sessions of Study 201, the study specifically designed to retest the most promising participants from the previous studies. Accordingly, it seems likely that the larger effect sizes of these two studies—and hence the significant negative correlation between the number of sessions and the effect size—reflect genuine performance differences between these two small, highly selected samples and other autoganzfeld participants.

STUDY 302

All of the studies except Study 302 randomly sampled from a pool of 160 static and dynamic targets. Study 302 sampled from a single, dynamic target set that had yielded a particularly high hit rate in the previous studies. The four film clips in this set consisted of a scene of a tidal wave from the movie *Clash of the Titans*, a high-speed sex scene from *A Clockwork Orange*, a scene of crawling snakes from a TV documentary, and a scene from a Bugs Bunny cartoon.

The experimental design called for this study to continue until each of the clips had served as the target 15 times. Unfortunately, the premature termination of this study at 25 sessions left an imbalance in the frequency with which each clip had served as the target. This means that the high hit rate observed (64%) could well be inflated by response biases.

As an illustration, water imagery is frequently reported by receivers in ganzfeld sessions, whereas sexual imagery is rarely reported. (Some participants probably are reluctant both to report sexual imagery and to give the highest rating to the sex-related clip.) If a video clip containing popular imagery (such as water) happens to appear as a target more frequently than a clip containing unpopular imagery (such as sex), a high hit rate might simply reflect the coincidence of those frequencies of occurrence with participants' response biases. And, as the second column of Table 2 reveals, the tidal wave clip was ranked first closely matches the frequency with which each appeared as the target.

One can adjust for this problem by using the observed frequencies in these two columns to compute the hit rate expected if there were no psi effect. In particular, one can multiply each proportion in the second column by the corresponding proportion in the third column—yielding the joint probability that the clip was the target and that it was ranked first—and then sum across the four clips. As shown in the fourth column of Table 2, this computation yields an overall expected hit rate of 34.08%. When the observed hit rate of 64% is compared with this baseline, the effect size (h) is .61. As shown in Table 1, this is equivalent to a four-alternative hit rate of 54%, or a π value of .78, and is statistically significant ($z = 3.04$, $p = .0012$).

The psi effect can be seen even more clearly in the remaining columns of Table 2, which control for the differential popularity of the imagery in the clips by displaying how frequently each was ranked first when it was the target and how frequently it was ranked first when it was one of the control clips (decoys). As can be seen, each of the four clips was selected as the target relatively more frequently when it was the target than when it was a decoy, a difference that is significant for three of the four clips. On average, a clip was identified as the target 58% of the time when it was the target and only 14% of the time when it was a decoy.

Table 2
Study 302: Expected Hit Rate and Proportion of Sessions in Which Each Video Clip Was Ranked First When It Was a Target and When It Was a Decoy

Video clip	Relative frequency as target	Relative frequency of first place ranking	Expected hit rate (%)	Ranked first when target	Ranked first when decoy	Difference	Fisher's exact p
Tidal wave	.28 (7/25)	.24 (6/25)	6.72	.57 (4/7)	.11 (2/18)	.46	.032
Snakes	.12 (3/25)	.12 (3/25)	1.44	.67 (2/3)	.05 (1/22)	.62	.029
Sex scene	.16 (4/25)	.08 (2/25)	1.28	.25 (1/4)	.05 (1/21)	.20	.300
Bugs Bunny	.44 (11/25)	.56 (14/25)	24.64	.82 (9/11)	.36 (5/14)	.46	.027
Overall			34.08	.58	.14	.44	

DYNAMIC VERSUS STATIC TARGETS

The success of Study 302 raises the question of whether dynamic targets are, in general, more effective than static targets. This possibility was also suggested by the earlier meta-analysis, which revealed that studies using multiple-image targets (View Master stereoscopic slide reels) obtained significantly higher hit rates than did studies using single-image targets. By adding motion and sound, the video clips might be thought of as high-tech versions of the View Master reels.

The 10 autoganzfeld studies that randomly sampled from both dynamic and static target pools yielded 164 sessions with dynamic targets and 165 sessions with static targets. As predicted, sessions using dynamic targets yielded significantly more hits than did sessions using static targets (37% vs. 27%; Fisher's exact $p < .04$).

SENDER-RECEIVER PAIRING

The earlier meta-analysis revealed that studies in which participants were free to bring in friends to serve as senders produced significantly higher hit rates than studies that used only laboratory-assigned senders. As noted, however, there is no record of how many of the participants in the former studies actually did bring in friends. Whatever the case, sender-receiver pairing was not a significant correlate of psi performance in the autoganzfeld studies: The 197 sessions in which the sender and receiver were friends did not yield a significantly higher proportion of hits than did the 132 sessions in which they were not (35% vs. 29%; Fisher's exact $p = .28$).

CORRELATIONS BETWEEN RECEIVER
CHARACTERISTICS AND PSI PERFORMANCE

Most of the autoganzfeld participants were strong believers in psi: On a 7-point scale ranging from *strong disbelief in psi* (1) to *strong belief in psi* (7), the mean was 6.2 (SD = 1.03); only 2 participants rated their belief in psi below the midpoint of the scale. In addition, 88% of the participants reported personal experiences suggestive of psi, and 80% had some training in meditation or other techniques involving internal focus of attention.

All of these appear to be important variables. The correlation between belief in psi and psi performance is one of the most consistent findings in the parapsychological literature (Palmer, 1978). And, within the autoganzfeld studies, successful performance of novice (first-time) participants was significantly predicted by reported personal psi experiences, involvement with meditation or other mental disciplines, and high scores on the Feeling and Perception factors of the Myers-Briggs Type Inventory (Honorton, 1992; Honorton & Schechter, 1987; Myers & McCaulley, 1985). This recipe for success has now been independently replicated in another laboratory (Broughton, Kanthamani, & Khilji, 1990).

The personality trait of extraversion is also associated with better psi performance. A meta-analysis of 60 independent studies with nearly 3,000 subjects revealed a small but reliable positive correlation between extraversion and psi performance, especially in studies that used free-response methods of the kind used in the ganzfeld experiments (Honorton, Ferrari, & Bem, 1992). Across 14 free-response studies conducted by four independent investigators, the correlation for 612 subjects was .20 (z = 4.82, p = 1.5 × 10^{-6}). This correlation was replicated in the autoganzfeld studies, in which extraversion scores were available for 218 of the 240 subjects, r = .18, $t(216)$ = 2.67, p = .004, one-tailed.

Finally, there is the strong psi performance of the Juilliard students, discussed earlier, which is consistent with other studies in the parapsychological literature suggesting a relationship between successful psi performance and creativity or artistic ability.

Discussion

Earlier in this article, we quoted from the abstract of the Hyman-Honorton (1986) communiqué: "We agree that the final verdict awaits the outcome of future experiments conducted by a broader range of investigators and according to more stringent standards" (p. 351). We believe that the "stringent standards" requirement has been met by the autoganzfeld studies. The results are statistically significant and consistent with those in the earlier database. The mean effect size is quite respectable in comparison with other controversial research areas of human performance (Harris & Rosenthal, 1988a). And there are reliable relationships between successful psi performance and conceptually relevant experimental and subject variables, relationships that also replicate previous findings. Hyman (1991) has also commented on the autoganzfeld studies: "Honorton's experiments have produced intriguing results. If ... independent laboratories can produce similar results with the same relationships and with the same attention to rigorous methodology, then parapsychology may indeed have finally captured its elusive quarry" (p. 392).

Issues of Replication

As Hyman's comment implies, the autoganzfeld studies by themselves cannot satisfy the requirement that replications be conducted by a "broader ranger of investigators." Accordingly, we hope the findings reported here will be sufficiently provocative to prompt others to try replicating the psi ganzfeld effect.

We believe that it is essential, however, that future studies comply with the methodological, statistical, and reporting standards set forth in the joint communiqué and achieved by the autoganzfeld studies. It is not necessary for studies to be as automated or as heavily instrumented as the autoganzfeld studies to satisfy the methodological guidelines, but they are still likely to be labor intensive and potentially expensive.*

Statistical Power and Replication

Would-be replicators also need to be reminded of the power requirements for replicating small effects. Although many academic psychologists do not believe in psi, many apparently do believe in miracles when it comes to replication. Tversky and Kahneman (1971) posed the following problem to their colleagues at meetings of the Mathematical Psychology Group and the American Psychological Association:

> Suppose you have run an experiment on 20 subjects and have obtained a significant result which confirms your theory ($z = 2.23$, $p < .05$, two-tailed). You now have cause to run an additional group of 10 subjects. What do you think the probability is that the results will be significant, by a one-tailed test, separately for this group? [p. 105].

The median estimate was .85, with 9 of 10 respondents providing an estimate greater than .60. The correct answer is approximately .48.

As Rosenthal (1990) has warned: "Given the levels of statistical power at which we normally operate, we have no right to expect the proportion of significant results that we typically do expect, even if in nature there is a very real and very important effect" (p. 16). In this regard, it is again instructive to consider the medical study that revealed a highly significant effect of aspirin on the incidence of heart attacks. The study monitored

*As the closing of the autoganzfeld laboratory exemplifies, it is also difficult to obtain funding for psi research. The traditional, peer-refereed sources of funding familiar to psychologists have almost never funded proposals for psi research. The widespread skepticism of psychologists toward psi is almost certainly a contributing factor.

more than 22,000 subjects. Had the investigation monitored 3,000 subjects, they would have had less than an even chance of finding a conventionally significant effect. Such is life with small effect sizes.

Given its larger effect size, the prospects for successfully replicating the psi ganzfeld effect are not quite so daunting, but they are probably still grimmer than intuition would suggest. If the true hit rate is in fact about 34% when 25% is expected by chance, then an experiment with 30 trials (the mean for the 28 studies in the original meta-analysis) has only about 1 chance in 6 of finding an effect significant at the .05 level with a one-tailed test. A 50-trial experiment boosts that chance to about 1 in 3. One must escalate to 100 trials to come close to the break-even point, at which one has a 50-50 chance of finding a statistically significant effect (Utts, 1986). (Recall that only 2 of the 11 autoganzfeld studies yielded results that were individually significant at the conventional .05 level.) Those who require that a psi effect be statistically significant every time before they will seriously entertain the possibility that an effect really exists know not what they ask.

Significant Versus Effect Size

The preceding discussion is unduly pessimistic, however, because it perpetuates the tradition of worshipping the significance level. Regular readers of this journal are likely to be familiar with recent arguments imploring behavioral scientists to overcome their slavish dependence on the significance level as the ultimate measure of virtue and instead to focus more of their attention on effect sizes: "Surely, God loves the .06 nearly as much as the .05" (Rosnow & Rosenthal, 1989, p. 1277). Accordingly, we suggest that achieving a respectable effect size with a methodologically tight ganzfeld study would be a perfectly welcome contribution to the replication effort, no matter how untenurable the p level renders the investigator.

Career consequences aside, this suggestion may seem quite counterintuitive. Again, Tversky and Kahneman (1971) have provided an elegant demonstration. They asked several of their colleagues to consider an investigator who runs 15 subjects and obtains a significant t value of 2.46. Another investigator attempts to duplicate the procedure with the same number of subjects and obtains a result in the same direction but with a nonsignificant value of t. Tversky and Kahneman then asked their colleagues to indicate the highest level of t in the replication study they would describe as a failure to replicate. The majority of their colleagues regarded $t = 1.70$ as a failure to replicate. But if the data from two such studies (t = 2.46 and t = 1.70) were pooled, the t for the combined data would be about 3.00 (assuming equal variances):

> Thus, we are faced with a paradoxical state of affairs, in which the same data that would increase our confidence in the finding when viewed as part of the original study, shake our confidence when viewed as an independent study [Tversky & Kahneman, 1971, p. 108].

Such is the iron grip of the arbitrary .05. Pooling the data, of course, is what meta-analysis is all about. Accordingly, we suggest that two or more laboratories could collaborate in a ganzfeld replication effort by conducting independent studies and then pooling them in meta-analytic fashion, what one might call real-time meta-analysis. (Each investigator could then claim the pooled p level for his or her own curriculum vitae.)

Maximizing Effect Size

Rather than buying or borrowing larger sample sizes, those who seek to replicate the psi ganzfeld effect might find it more intellectually satisfying to attempt to maximize the effect size by attending to the variables associated with successful outcomes. Thus, researchers who wish to enhance the chances of successful replication should use dynamic rather than static targets. Similarly, we advise using participants with the characteristics we have reported to be correlated with successful psi performance. Random college sophomores enrolled in introductory psychology do not constitute the optimal subject pool.

Finally, we urge ganzfeld researchers to read carefully the detailed description of the warm social ambiance that Honorton et al. (1990) sought to create in the autoganzfeld laboratory. We believe that the social climate created in psi experiments is a critical determinant of their success or failure.

The Problem of "Other" Variables

This caveat about the social climate of the ganzfeld experiment prompted one reviewer of this article to worry that this provided "an escape clause" that weakens the falsifiability of the psi hypothesis: "Until Bem and Honorton can provide operational criteria for creating a warm social ambiance, the failure of an experiment with otherwise adequate power can always be dismissed as due to a lack of warmth."

Alas, it is true; we devoutly wish it were otherwise. But the operation of unknown variables in moderating the success of replications is a fact of life in all of the sciences. Consider, for example, an earlier article in this journal by Spence (1964). He reviewed studies testing the straightforward derivation from Hullian learning theory that high-anxiety subjects should condition more strongly than low-anxiety subjects. This hypothesis was confirmed 94% of the time in Spence's own laboratory at the University of Iowa but only 63% of the time in laboratories at other universities. In fact, Kimble and his associates at Duke University and the University of North Carolina obtained results in the opposite direction in two of three experiments.

In searching for a post hoc explanation, Spence (1964) noted that "a deliberate attempt was made in the Iowa studies to provide conditions in the laboratory that might elicit some degree of emotionality. Thus, the experimenter was instructed to be impersonal and quite formal ... and did not try to put [subjects] at ease or allay any expressed fears" (pp. 135–136). Moreover, he pointed out, his subjects sat in a dental chair, whereas Kimble's subjects sat in a secretarial chair. Spence even considered "the possibility that cultural backgrounds of southern and northern students may lead to a difference in the manner in which they respond to the different items in the [Manifest Anxiety] scale" (p. 136). If this was the state of affairs in an area of research as well established as classical conditioning, then the suggestion that the social climate of the psi laboratory might affect the outcome of ganzfeld experiments in ways not yet completely understood should not be dismissed as a devious attempt to provide an escape clause in case of replication failure.

The best the original researchers can do is to communicate as complete a knowledge of the experimental conditions as possible in an attempt to anticipate some of the relevant moderating variables. Ideally, this might include direct training by the original researchers or videotapes of actual sessions. Lacking these, however, the detailed description of the auto-ganzfeld procedures provided by Honorton et al. (1990) comes as close as current knowledge permits in providing for other researchers the "operational criteria for creating a warm social ambiance."

Theoretical Considerations

Up to this point, we have confined our discussion to strictly empirical matters. We are sympathetic to the view that one should establish the existence of a phenomenon, anomalous or not, before attempting to explain it. So let us suppose for the moment that we have a genuine anomaly of information transfer here. How can it be understood or explained?

The Psychology of Psi

In attempting to understand psi, parapsychologists have typically begun with the working assumption that, whatever its underlying mechanisms, it should behave like other, more familiar psychological phenomena. In particular, they typically assume that target information behaves like an external sensory stimulus that is encoded, processed, and experienced in familiar information-processing ways. Similarly, individual psi performances should covary with experimental and subject variables in psychologically sensible ways. These assumptions are embodied in the model of psi that motivated the ganzfeld studies in the first place.

THE GANZFELD PROCEDURE

As noted in the introduction, the ganzfeld procedure was designed to test a model in which psi-mediated information is conceptualized as a weak signal that is normally masked by internal somatic and external sensory "noise." Accordingly, any technique that raises the signal-to-noise ratio should enhance a person's ability to detect psi-mediated information. This noise-reduction model of psi organizes a large and diverse body of experimental results, particularly those demonstrating the psi-conducive properties of altered states of consciousness such as meditation, hypnosis, dreaming, and, of course, the ganzfeld itself (Rao & Palmer, 1987).

Alternative theories propose that the ganzfeld (and altered states) may be psi conducive because it lowers resistance to accepting alien imagery, diminishes rational or contextual constraints on the encoding or reporting of information, stimulates more divergent thinking, or even just serves as a placebo-like ritual that participants perceive as being psi conducive (Stanford, 1987). At this point, there are no data that would permit one to choose among these alternatives, and the noise-reduction model remains the most widely accepted.

THE TARGET

There are also a number of plausible hypotheses that attempt to account for the superiority of dynamic targets over static targets: Dynamic targets contain more information, involve more sensory modalities, evoke more of the receiver's internal schemata, are more lifelike, have a narrative structure, are more emotionally evocative, and are ""richer" in other, unspecified ways. Several psi researchers have attempted to go beyond the simple dynamic-static dichotomy to more refined or theory-based definitions of a good target. Although these efforts have involved examining both psychological and physical properties of targets, there is as yet not much progress to report (Delanoy, 1990).

THE RECEIVER

Some of the subject characteristics associated with good psi performance also appear to have psychologically straightforward explanations. For example, garden-variety motivational explanations seem sufficient to account for the relatively consistent finding that those who believe in psi perform significantly better than those who do not. (Less straightforward, however, would be an explanation for the frequent finding that nonbelievers actually perform significantly worse than chance [Broughton, 1991, p. 109].)

The superior psi performance of creative or artistically gifted individuals—such as the Juilliard students—may reflect individual differences that parallel some of the hypothesized effects of the ganzfeld mentioned earlier: Artistically gifted individuals may be more receptive to alien imagery, be better able to transcend rational or contextual constraints on the encoding or reporting of information, or be more divergent in their thinking. It has also been suggested that both artistic and psi abilities might be rooted in superior right-brain functioning.

The observed relationship between extraversion and psi performance has been of theoretical interest for many years. Eysenck (1966) reasoned that extraverts should perform well in psi tasks because they are easily bored and respond favorably to novel stimuli. In a setting such as the ganzfeld, extraverts may become "stimulus starved" and thus may be highly sensitive to any stimulation, including weak incoming psi information. In contrast, introverts would be more inclined to entertain themselves with their own thoughts and thus continue to mask psi information despite the diminished sensory input. Eysenck also speculated that psi might be a primitive form of perception antedating cortical developments in the course of evolution, and, hence, cortical arousal might suppress psi functioning. Because extraverts have a lower level of cortical arousal than introverts, they should perform better in psi tasks (the evolutionary biology of psi has also been discussed by Broughton, 1991, pp. 347–352).

But there are more mundane possibilities. Extraverts might perform better than introverts simply because they are more relaxed and comfortable in the social setting of the typical psi experiment (e.g., the "warm social ambiance" of the autoganzfeld studies). This interpretation is strengthened by the observation that introverts outperformed extraverts in a study in which subjects had no contact with an experimenter but worked alone at home with materials they received in the mail (Schmidt & Schlitz, 1989). To help decide among these interpretations, ganzfeld experimenters have begun to use the extraversion scale of the NEO Personality Inventory (Costa & McCrae, 1992), which assesses six different facets of the extraversion-introversion factor.

THE SENDER

In contrast to this information about the receiver in psi experiments, virtually nothing is known about the characteristics of a good sender or about the effects of the sender's relationship with the receiver. As has been shown, the initial suggestion from the meta-analysis of the original ganzfeld database that psi performance might be enhanced when the sender and receiver are friends was not replicated at a statistically significant level in the autoganzfeld studies.

A number of parapsychologists have entertained the more radical hypothesis that the sender may not even be a necessary element in the psi process. In the terminology of parapsychology, the sender-receiver procedure tests for the existence of *telepathy*, anomalous communication between two individuals; however, if the receiver is somehow picking up the information from the target itself, it would be termed clairvoyance, and the presence of the sender would be irrelevant (except for possible psychological reasons, such as expectation effects).

At the time of his death, Honorton was planning a series of auto-ganzfeld studies that would systematically compare sender and no-sender conditions while keeping both the receiver and the experimenter blind to the condition of the ongoing session. In preparation, he conducted a meta-analytic review of ganzfeld studies that used no sender. He found 12 studies, with a median of 33.5 sessions, conducted by seven investigators. The overall effect size (π) was .56, which corresponds to a four-alternative hit rate of 29%. But this effect size does not reach statistical significance (Stouffer $z = 1.31$, $p = .095$). So far, then, there is no firm evidence for psi in the ganzfeld in the absence of a sender. (There are, however, non-ganzfeld studies in the literature that do report significant evidence for clairvoyance, including a classic card-guessing experiment conducted by J.B. Rhine and Pratt [1954].)

The Physics of Psi

The psychological level of theorizing just discussed does not, of course, address the conundrum that makes psi phenomena anomalous in the first place: their presumed incompatibility with our current conceptual model of physical reality. Parapsychologists differ widely from one another in their taste for theorizing at this level, but several whose training lies in physics or engineering have proposed physical (or biophysical) theories of psi phenomena (an extensive review of theoretical parapsychology was provided by Stokes, 1987). Only some of these theories would force a radical revision in our current conception of physical reality.

Those who follow contemporary debates in modern physics, however, will be aware that several phenomena predicted by quantum theory and confirmed by experiment are themselves incompatible with our current conceptual model of physical reality. Of these, it is the 1982 empirical confirmation of Bell's theorem that has created the most excitement and controversy among philosophers and the few physicists who are willing to speculate on such matters (Cushing & McMullin, 1989; Herbert, 1987). In brief, Bell's theorem states that any model of reality that is compatible with quantum mechanisms must be *nonlocal*: It must allow for the possibility that the results of observations at two arbitrarily distant locations can be correlated in ways that are incompatible with any physically permissible causal mechanism.

Several possible methods of reality that incorporate nonlocality have been proposed by both philosophers and physicists. Some of these models clearly rule out psi-like information transfer, others permit it, and some actually require it. Thus, at a grander level of theorizing, some parapsychologists believe that one of the more radical models of reality compatible with both quantum mechanics and psi will eventually come to be accepted. If and when that occurs, psi phenomena would cease to be anomalous.

But we have learned that all such talk provokes most of our colleagues in psychology and in physics to roll their eyes and gnash their teeth. So let's just leave it at that.

Skepticism Revisited

More generally, we have learned that our colleagues' tolerance for *any* kind of theorizing about psi is strongly determined by the degree to which they have been convinced by the data that psi has been demonstrated. We have further learned that their diverse reactions to the data themselves are strongly determined by their a priori beliefs about and attitudes toward a number of quite general issues, some scientific, some not. In fact, several statisticians believe that the traditional hypothesis-testing methods used in the behavioral sciences should be abandoned in favor of Bayesian analysis, which taken into account a person's a priori beliefs about the phenomenon under investigation (e.g., Bayarri & Berger, 1991; Dawson, 1991).

In the final analysis, however, we suspect that both one's Bayesian a prioris and one's reactions to the data are ultimately determined by whether one was more severely punished in childhood for Type I or Type II errors.

References

Atkinson, R., Atkinson, R.C., Smith, E.E., & Bem, D.J. (1990). *Introduction to psychology* (10th ed.). San Diego, CA: Harcourt Brace Jovanovich.

Atkinson, R., Atkinson, R.C., Smith, E.E., & Bem, D.J. (1993). *Introduction to psychology* (11th ed.). San Diego, CA: Harcourt Brace Jovanovich.

Avant, L.L. (1965). Vision in the ganzfeld. *Psychological Bulletin, 64*, 246–258.

Bayarri, M.J., & Berger, J. (1991). Comment. *Statistical Science, 6*, 379–382.

Blackmore, S. (1980). The extent of selective reporting of ESP ganzfeld studies. *European Journal of Parapsychology, 3*, 213–219.

Bozarth, J.D., & Roberts, R.R. (1972). Signifying significant significance. *American Psychologist, 27*, 774–775.

Braud, W.G., Wood, R., & Braud, L.W. (1975). Free-response GESP performance during an experimental hypnagogic state induced by visual and acoustic ganzfeld techniques. A replication and extension. *Journal of the American Society for Psychical Research, 69*, 105–113.

Broughton, R.S. (1991). *Parapsychology: The controversial science.* New York: Ballantine Books.

Broughton, R.S., Kanthamani, H., & Khilji, A. (1990). Assessing the PRL success model on an independent ganzfeld data base. In L. Henkel & J. Palmer (Eds.), *Research in parapsychology 1989* (pp. 32–35). Metuchen, NJ: Scarecrow Press.

Child, I.L. (1985). Psychology and anomalous observations: The question of ESP in dreams. *American Psychologist, 40*, 1219–1230.

Cohen, J. (1988). *Statistical power analysis for the behavioral sciences* (2nd ed.). Hillsdale, NJ: Erlbaum.

Cohen, J. (1992). Statistical power analysis. *Current Directions in Psychological Science, 1*, 98–101.

Costa, P.T. Jr., & McCrae, R.R. (1992). *Revised NEO Personality Inventory (NEO-PI-R) and NEO Five-Factor Inventory (NEO-FFI): Professional manual.* Odessa, FL: Psychological Assessment Resources.

Cushing, J.T., & McMullin, E. (Eds.) (1989). *Philosophical consequences of quantum theory: Reflections on Bell's theorem.* Notre Dame, IN: University of Notre Dame Press.

Dawson, R. (1991). Comment. *Statistical Science, 6*, 382–385.

Delanoy, D.L. (1990). Approaches to the target: A time for reevaluation. In L.A.

Henkel & J. Palmer (Eds.), *Research in parapsychology 1989* (pp. 89–92). Metuchen, NJ: Scarecrow Press.

Dingwall, E.J. (Ed.). (1968). *Abnormal hypnotic phenomena* (4 vols.). London: Churchill.

Druckman, D., & Swets, J.A. (Eds.). (1988). *Enhancing human performance: Issues, theories, and techniques*. Washington, DC: National Academy Press.

Eysenck, H.J. (1966). Personality and extra-sensory perception. *Journal of the Society for Psychical Research, 44*, 55–71.

Gilovich, T. (1991). *How we know what isn't so: The fallibility of human reason in everyday life*. New York: Free Press.

Green, C.E. (1960). Analysis of spontaneous cases. *Proceedings of the Society for Psychical Research, 53*, 97–161.

Harris, M.J., & Rosenthal, R. (1988a). *Human performance research: An overview*. Washington, DC: National Academy Press.

Harris, M.J., & Rosenthal, R. (1988b). *Postscript to "Human performance research: An overview."* Washington, DC: National Academy Press.

Herbert, N. (1987). *Quantum reality: Beyond the new physics*. Garden City, NY: Anchor Books.

Honorton, C. (1977). Psi and internal attention states. In B.B. Wolman (Ed.), *Handbook of parapsychology* (pp. 435–472). New York: Van Nostrand Reinhold.

Honorton, C. (1979). Methodological issues in free-response experiments. *Journal of the American Society for Psychical Research, 73*, 381–394.

Honorton, C. (1985). Meta-analysis of psi ganzfeld research: A response to Hyman. *Journal of Parapsychology, 49*, 51–91.

Honorton, C. (1992, August). *The ganzfeld novice: Four predictors of initial ESP performance*. Paper presented at the 35th annual convention of the Parapsychological Association, Las Vegas, NV.

Honorton, C., Berger, R.E., Varvoglis, M.P., Quant, M., Derr, P., Schechter, E.I., & Ferrari, D.C. (1990). Psi communication in the ganzfeld: Experiments with an automated testing system and a comparison with a meta-analysis of earlier studies. *Journal of Parapsychology, 54*, 99–139.

Honorton, C., Ferrari, D.C., & Bem, D.J. (1992). Extraversion and ESP performance: Meta-analysis and a new confirmation. In L.A. Henkel & G.R. Schmeidler (Eds.), *Research in parapsychology 1990* (pp. 35–38). Metuchen, NJ: Scarecrow Press.

Honorton, C., & Harper, S. (1974). Psi-mediated imagery and ideation in an experimental procedure for regulating perceptual input. *Journal of the American Society for Psychical Research, 68*, 156–168.

Honorton, C., & Schechter, E.I. (1987). Ganzfeld target retrieval with an automated testing system: A model for initial ganzfeld success. In D.B. Weiner & R.D. Nelson (Eds.), *Research in parapsychology 1986* (pp. 36–39). Metuchen, NJ: Scarecrow Press.

Hyman, R. (1985). The ganzfeld psi experiment: A critical appraisal. *Journal of Parapsychology, 49*, 3–49.

Hyman, R. (1991). Comment. *Statistical Science. 6*, 389–392.

Hyman, R., & Honorton, C. (1986). A joint communiqué: The psi ganzfeld controversy. *Journal of Parapsychology, 50*, 351–364.

Kennedy, J.E. (1979). Methodological problems in free-response ESP experiments. *Journal of the American Society for Psychical Research, 73*, 1–15.

Metzger, W. (1930). Optische Untersuchungen am Ganzfeld: II. Zur phänome-nologie des homogenen Ganzfelds [Optical investigation of the Ganzfeld: II Toward the phenomenology of the homogeneous Ganzfeld]. *Psychologis-che Forschung*, 13, 6–29.

Morris, R.L. (1991). Comment. *Statistical Science*, 6, 393–395.

Myers, I.B. & McCaulley, M.H. (1985). *Manual: A guide to the development and use of the Myers-Briggs Type Indicator*. Palo Alto, CA: Consulting Psychologists Press.

Nisbett, R.E., & Ross, L. (1980). *Human inference: Strategies and shortcomings of social judgment*. Englewood Cliffs, NJ: Prentice Hall.

Palmer, J. (1978). Extrasensory perception: Research findings. In S. Krippner (Ed.), *Advances in parapsychological research* (Vol. 2, pp. 59–243). New York: Plenum Press.

Palmer, J.A., Honorton, C., & Utts, J. (1989). Reply to the National Research Council Study on Parapsychology. *Journal of the American Society for Psychical Research*, 83, 31–49.

Parker, A. (1975). Some findings relevant to the change in state hypothesis. In J.D. Morris, W.G. Roll, & R.L. Morris (Eds.), *Research in parapsychology*, 1974 (pp. 40–42). Metuchen, NJ: Scarecrow Press.

Parker, A. (1978). A holistic methodology in psi research. *Parapsychology Review*, 9, 1–6.

Prasad, J., & Stevenson, I. (1968). A survey of spontaneous psychical experiences in school children of Uttar Pradesh, India. *International Journal of Parapsychology*, 10, 241–261.

Rao, K.R., & Palmer, J. (1987). The anomaly called psi: Recent research and criticism. *Behavioral and Brain Sciences*, 10, 539–551.

Rhine, J.B., & Pratt, J.G. (1954). A review of the Pearce-Pratt distance series of ESP tests. *Journal of Parapsychology*, 18, 165–177.

Rhine, L.E. (1962). Psychological processes in ESP experiences. I. Waking experiences. *Journal of Parapsychology*, 26, 88–111.

Roig, M., Icochea, H., & Cuzzucoli, A. (1991). Coverage of parapsychology in introductory psychology textbooks. *Teaching of Psychology*, 18, 157–160.

Rosenthal, R. (1978). Combining results of independent studies. *Psychological Bulletin*, 86, 638–641.

Rosenthal, R. (1979). The "file-drawer problem" and tolerance for null results. *Psychological Bulletin*, 86, 638–641.

Rosenthal, R. (1990). Replication in behavioral research. *Journal of Social Behavior and Personality*, 5, 1–30.

Rosenthal, R. (1991). *Meta-analytic procedures for social research* (Rev. ed.). Newbury Park, CA: Sage.

Rosenthal, R., & Rubin, D.B. (1989). Effect size estimation for one-sample multiple-choice-type data: Design, analysis, and meta-analysis. *Psychological Bulletin*, 106, 332–337.

Rosnow, R.L., & Rosenthal, R. (1989). Statistical procedures and the justification of knowledge in psychological science. *American Psychologist*, 44, 1276–1284.

Sannwald, G. (1959). Statistische untersuchungen an Spontanphänomene [Statistical investigation of spontaneous phenomena]. *Zeitschrift fur Parapsychologie and Grenzgebiete der Psychologie*, 3, 59–71.

Saunders, D.R. (1985). On Hyman's factor analyses. *Journal of Parapsychology*, 49, 86–88.

Schecter, E.I. (1984). Hypnotic induction vs. control conditions: Illustrating an approach to the evaluation of replicability in parapsychology. *Journal of the American Society for Psychical Research*, 78, 1–27.

Schlitz, M.J., & Honorton, C. (1992). Ganzfeld psi performance within an artistically gifted population. *Journal of the American Society for Psychical Research*, 86, 83–98.

Schmeidler, G.R. (1988). *Parapsychology and psychology: Matches and mismatches.* Jefferson, NC: McFarland.

Schmidt, H., & Schlitz, M.J. (1989). A large scale pilot PK experiment with pre-recorded random events. In L.A. Henkel & R.E. Berger (Eds.). *Research in parapsychology 1988* (pp. 6–10). Metuchen, NJ: Scarecrow Press.

Spence, K.W. (1964). Anxiety (drive) level and performance in eyelid conditioning. *Psychological Bulletin*, 61, 129–139.

Stanford, R.G. (1987). Ganzfeld and hypnotic-induction procedures in ESP research: Toward understanding their success. In S. Krippner (Ed.), *Advances in parapsychological research* (Vol. 5, pp. 39–76). Jefferson, NC: McFarland.

Steering Committee of the Physicians' Health Study Research Group. (1988). Preliminary report: Findings from the aspirin component of the ongoing Physicians' Health Study. *New England Journal of Medicine*, 318, 262–264.

Sterling, T.C. (1959). Publication decisions and their possible effects on inferences drawn from tests of significance—or vice versa. *Journal of the American Statistical Association*, 54, 30–34.

Stokes, D.M. (1987). Theoretical parapsychology. In S. Krippner (Ed.), *Advances in parapsychological research* (Vol. 5, pp. 77–189). Jefferson, NC: McFarland.

Swets, J.A., & Bjork, R.A. (1990). Enhancing human performance: An evaluation of "new age" techniques considered by the U.S. Army. *Psychological Science*, 1, 85–96.

Tversky, A., & Kahneman, D. (1971). Belief in the law of small numbers. *Psychological Bulletin*, 2, 105–110.

Ullman, M., Krippner, S., & Vaughan, A. (1973). *Dream telepathy.* New York: Macmillan.

Utts, J. (1986). The ganzfeld debate: A statistician's perspective. *Journal of Parapsychology*, 50, 393–402.

Utts, J. (1991a). Rejoinder. *Statistical Science*, 6, 396–403.

Utts, J. (1991b). Replication and meta-analysis in parapsychology. *Statistical Science*, 6, 363–378.

Wagner, M.W., & Monnet, M. (1979). Attitudes of college professors toward extrasensory perception. *Zetetic Scholar*, 5, 7–17.

Contributors

Daryl J. Bem, Professor of Psychology at Cornell University, obtained his B.A. degree in physics from Reed College and his Ph.D. in social psychology from the University of Michigan. He has taught at Carnegie-Mellon University, Stanford, Harvard, and Cornell, where he has been since 1978. Professor Bem published on several diverse topics in psychology, including psi phenomena, group decision making, self-perception, personality theory, and sexual orientation. He is co-author of an introductory textbook in psychology and the author of *Beliefs, Attitudes, and Human Affairs* (1970) and *Exotic Becomes Erotic: Explaining the Enigma of Sexual Orientation* (forthcoming).

John Bradish holds an M.S. degree in electrical engineering from Columbia University. He is currently at the Princeton Engineering Anomalies Research Laboratories, Princeton University. He acts there as Technical Facilitator and has the responsibility for the design, construction and maintenance of the experimental hardware. He is also involved in planning sessions for future experimental designs and technical support to other investigators.

Lendell W. Braud is a licensed psychologist and full-time Professor of Psychology at Texas Southern University in Houston, Texas. Her current research is in the area of abused and delinquent youth with learning disabilities and behavior problems. She is investigating alternative methods of dealing with behavior problems and aggression, including relaxation therapy. She has presented papers on this subject in several forums, including international conferences.

William Braud received his Ph.D. degree in experimental psychology from the University of Iowa. He taught at the University of Houston. After conducting full-time research in parapsychology for a number of years at the Mind Science Foundation in San Antonio, Texas, William Braud joined the Institute of Transpersonal Psychology (Palo Alto, CA) as Professor and Research Director. His current research is on alternative ways of knowing and exceptional human experiences. He has published numerous research articles. He is co-author of *Transpersonal Research Methods for the Social Sciences: Honoring Human Experience* (Sage, 1998) with Rosemarie Anderson.

Remi J. Cadoret is a physiologist who taught at the University of Manitoba Medical College, Winnipeg, Canada. He worked with J.B Rhine at the Parapsychology Laboratory of Duke University in the early Fifties and investigated certain physiological aspects of parapsychological phenomena, including EEG and GSR.

James C. Carpenter is a practicing clinical psychologist in Chapel Hill, NC. He did his undergraduate work at Duke University and received his Ph.D. in clinical psychology from Ohio State University, Columbus, Ohio. A student of J. B. Rhine, Dr. Carpenter has been involved in research and teaching of parapsychology since his undergraduate days at Duke. He serves on the Board of Directors of the Rhine Research Center in Durham, NC. Earlier he was on the psychology faculty of the University of North Carolina at Chapel Hill.

Irvin L. Child is Professor Emeritus at Yale University. He received his B.A. degree from the University of California at Los Angeles and Ph.D. from Yale University. He taught at Harvard University and Radcliffe College before joining the psychology faculty at Yale University in 1942 from where he retired in 1985. Dr. Child's main interest has been in the interaction between individual and society. His extensive research on psychological esthetics is also characterized by the interaction between psychological and social processes. His publications include *Humanistic Psychology and the Research Traditions: Their Several Virtues* (Wiley, 1973).

York. H. Dobyns is a physicist who received his Ph.D. from Princeton University. He has worked at the Princeton Engineering Anomalies Research laboratory at Princeton University from 1987. His responsibilities there include programming support, data management and analysis, and theoretical modeling.

Hamlyn Dukhan was a psychologist from the West Indies. He worked in the Education Department of Government of Trinidad and Tobago.

He was a research fellow in the Department of Psychology and Parapsychology, Andhra University, during 1974–76. His research in parapsychology is focussed on the effect of meditation on ESP scoring.

Brenda J. Dunne holds degrees in psychology and the humanities from Mundelein College in Chicago and a M.S. in human development from the University of Chicago. She has been the Manager of the Princeton Engineering Anomalies Research (PEAR) laboratory since 1979. Her responsibilities include the supervision of the full spectrum of PEAR activities, overseeing the research projects of visiting scholars and student interns. She is on the Council of the Society for Scientific Exploration. She is also Vice President and Treasurer of the International Consciousness Research Laboratories.

Jarl Ingmar Fahler is a psychologist and hypnotherapist in Finland. He graduated from the University of Helsinki and was on the staff of the Finnish Ministry of Home Affairs. He was William Bentley Fellow at the Parapsychology Laboratory at Duke University, where he continued his research on the effects of hypnosis on ESP. Dr. Fahler was also on the research staff of the Parapsychology Foundation in New York.

Dianne Ferrari studied psychology at Rider University. She worked with Charles Honorton as Research Associate at the Psychophysical Research Laboratories in Princeton, NJ. She also worked for some time assisting Dean Radin at Princeton University.

Elmar Gruber is a German parapsychologist. He studied and worked with Hans Bender who pioneered parapsychological research in Germany. He is affiliated with the Institut fur Grenzgebiete der Psychologie und Psychohygiene in Freiburg, Germany.

Charles Honorton (1946–1992) studied with J. B. Rhine and joined him to work for the Institute for Parapsychology in 1965. He later worked at the Dream Laboratory of the Maimonides Medical Center in New York with Montague Ullman and Stanley Krippner. He then moved to Princeton, NJ, where he established the Psychophysical Research Laboratories in 1979. At the time of his premature death in 1992, he was a Fellow at the University of Edinburgh in Scotland. Mr. Honorton served as the President of the Parapsychological Association

Robert G. Jahn is Professor of Aerospace Sciences and Dean Emeritus of the School of Engineering and Applied Science at Princeton University.

He obtained B.S.E., M.A., and Ph.D. degrees from Princeton University. He held faculty positions at Lehigh University and the California Institute of Technology. He has been the Director of the Princeton Engineering Anomalies Research laboratory since its inception in 1979. He is the President of the International Consciousness Research Laboratories and Vice President of the Society for Scientific Exploration. His publications in the area of parapsychology include *Margins of Reality* (1987) with Brenda Dunne.

Huggahalli Kanthamani (B.K. Kanthamani) is a licensed clinical psychologist with a Ph.D. degree from Andhra University, India. She was a research associate at the Parapsychology Laboratory of Duke University and later at the Institute for Parapsychology in Durham, NC. She worked as a lecturer in the Department of Psychology and Parapsychology at Andhra University and as the Director of Education at the Foundation for Research on the Nature of Man. Currently she is a psychologist in the Mental Health Center of the city of Durham, NC.

Stanley Krippner who received his Ph.D. degree from Northwestern University is currently Professor of Psychology at Saybrook Graduate School, San Francisco, CA. He is the past president of the Parapsychological Association, the Association for the Study of Dreams, the Association for Humanistic Psychology, and two divisions of the American Psychological Association. He worked as the Director of the Dream Laboratory at the Maimonides Medical Center and co-authored *Dream Studies and Telepathy: An Experimental Approach (1970)*. Dr. Krippner is the co-editor of *Varieties of Anomalous Experience*, published in 2000 by the American Psychological Association.

Roger D. Nelson is an experimental psychologist. Dr. Nelson is currently the Coordinator of Research at the Princeton Engineering Anomalies Research laboratory and the Director of the Global Consciousness Project. His main research focus has been on the role of consciousness and intention in anomalous information transfer and interactions with physical systems. His recent work has concentrated on "Field REG" studies using random event generator technology to study group consciousness.

John A. Palmer obtained his B.A. degree from Duke University and Ph.D. from the University of Texas in psychology. He has been actively involved in parapsychology for 28 years, serving twice as the President of the Parapsychological Association. He has written numerous professional articles and is co-author of *Foundations of Parapsychology*. He is currently acting Director of the Institute for Parapsychology in Durham, NC and editor of the *Journal of Parapsychology*.

Joseph Gaither Pratt (1910–1979), a psychologist with a Ph.D. degree from Duke University was a long time associate of J.B. Rhine. He co-authored with Rhine *Parapsychology: Frontier Science of the Mind*. Pratt's other books include *ESP Research Today: A Study of Developments in Parapsychology since 1960 (1973)*. After leaving Duke University in 1965, Pratt joined University of Virginia as Professor in the Division of Personality.

Dean I. Radin is a psychologist currently at the University of Nevada in Los Vegas. His previous appointments include Director of Human Information Processing Group at Princeton University, and visiting fellow at the University of Edinburg, Scotland. Dr. Radin was a past president of the Parapsychological Association. His publications include *The Conscious Universe* (1997).

P.V. Krishna Rao obtained his M.A. and Ph.D. degrees in psychology from Andhra University. He is currently Professor of Psychology and the Director of the Institute for Yoga and Consciousness at Andhra University, India. He was earlier a visiting research fellow at Psychical Research Foundation and the Institute for Parapsychology in Durham, NC and the Institute for Religious Psychology, Tokyo, Japan.

Koneru Ramakrishna Rao obtained his M.A. from the University of Chicago and Ph.D. and D.Litt. degrees from Andhra University, India. Professor Rao held various academic and administrative positions in India and the US. They include: Professor and Head of the Department of Psychology and Parapsychology, Dean Faculty of Arts and Social Sciences, and Vice-Chancellor at Andhra University; Director, Institute for Parapsychology and Executive Director, Foundation for Research on the Nature of Man, Durham, NC; Advisor on Higher Education and Vice-Chairman, State Planning Board, Government of Andhra Pradesh, India. Dr. Rao's publications include *Experimental Parapsychology: A Review and Interpretation* and *Gandhi and Pragmatism*.

Joseph Banks Rhine (1895–1980), a biologist with a Ph.D. degree from the University of Chicago, is considered the father of experimental parapsychology. Along with William McDougall, Dr. Rhine founded the Parapsychology Laboratory at Duke University and the *Journal of Parapsychology*, which he edited for a number of years. After his retirement from Duke in 1965, he established the Institute for Parapsychology and the Foundation for Research on the Nature of Man in Durham, NC. Dr. Rhine published extensively. Among his widely circulated books are *Extra-Sensory Perception* (1934), *The Reach of the Mind* (1947) and *The New World of the Mind* (1953).

Ephraim Schechter is an experimental psychologist with a Ph.D. degree from the University of Pittsburgh. Dr. Schechter, who began his parapsychological research in the mid–1970s, was a Senior Researcher at Psychophysical Research Laboratories in Princeton, NJ, where he worked with Charles Honorton.

Marilyn Schlitz, past president of the Parapsychological Association, is currently the Director of Research at the Institute of Noetic Sciences in Sausalito, CA. Dr. Schlitz obtained her Ph.D. in anthropology. She worked earlier as Research Fellow at the Institute for Parapsychology in Durham, NC and as Research Associate of the Mind Science Foundation in San Antonio, Texas.

Helmut Schmidt studied mathematics and physics. He taught theoretical physics at universities in Germany, Canada, and USA. He worked for the Boeing Company, where he also began conducting precognition and psychokinesis experiments with electronic equipment. He later joined Rhine's Institute for Parapsychology and then the Mind Science Foundation in San Antonio, Texas. A pioneer in micro–PK experiments, Dr. Schmidt is currently engaged in developing psi tests for use over the internet.

Montague Ullman is Clinical Professor of Psychiatry Emeritus at Albert Einstein College of Medicine. He retired as Director of Psychiatry at the Maimonides Medical Center in New York, where he established a dream laboratory to study ESP in dreams. Dr. Ullman taught at New York Medical College, New York University College of Medicine, and Downstate Medical Center of State University of New York. He was President of the American Society for Psychical Research (1971–1980) and a past president of the Parapsychological Association. He is the co-author of *Dream Studies and Telepathy: An Experimental Approach* (1970) and *Dream Telepathy* (1973) with Stanley Krippner.

Jessica Utts is Professor of Statistics at the University of California at Davis. Her research includes application of statistics to a variety of disciplines, most notably to parapsychology. She is an award winning teacher and author of *Seeing Through Statistics* (2nd Ed., 1999). She is a Fellow of the American Association for the Advancement of Science, the American Statistical Association and the Institute of Mathematical Statistics.

Richard Wiseman works in the Department of Psychology of the University of Hertfordshire in Hatfield, England. He is a parapsychologist of skeptical persuasion. He published several critical reviews pointing out possible flaws in some of the published parapsychological reports.

Bibliography

Allison, P.D. (1973). *Sociological Aspects of Innovations: The Case of Parapsychology.* Unpublished Master of Science dissertation, University of Wisconsin.

Altom, K., & Braud, W.G. (1976). Clairvoyant and telepathic impressions of musical targets. In J.D. Morris, W.G. Roll, & R.L. Morris (Eds.), *Research in parapsychology 1975* (pp. 171–174). Metuchen, NJ: Scarecrow Press.

Anand, B.K., Chhina, G.S., & Singh, B. (1961). Some aspects of electroencephalographic studies in yogis. *Electroencephalography and Clinical Neurophysiology*, 13, 452–456.

Bartlett, F.C. (1932). *Remembering.* Cambridge: Cambridge University Press.

Becker, R.O. (1992). Electromagnetism and psi phenomena. *Journal of the American Society for Psychical Research*, 86, 1–17.

Beloff, J. (1974). ESP: The search for a physiological index. *Journal of the Society for Psychical Research*, 47, 403–420.

Beloff, J. (1980). Seven evidential experiments. *Zetetic Scholar*, 6, 91–94.

Belvedere, E., & Foulkes, D. (1971). Telepathy and dreams: A failure to replicate. *Perceptual and Motor Skills*, 33, 783–789.

Bem, D.J., & Honorton, C. (1994). Does Psi exist? Replicable evidence for an anomalous process of information transfer. *Psychological Bulletin*, 115, 4–18.

Bem, D.J., Palmer, J. and Broughton, R.S. (2001). Updating the ganzfeld database: A victim of its own success. *Journal of Parapsychology*, 65.

Berger, R.E., & Persinger, M.A. (1991). Geophysical variables and behavior: LXVII. Quieter annual geomagnetic activity and larger effect size for experimental psi (ESP) studies over six decades. *Perceptual and Motor Skills, 73*, 1219–1223.

Bergson, H. (1921). *Mind-energy.* London: Macmillan.

Bhadra, B.J. (1966). The relationship of test scores to belief in ESP. *Journal of Parapsychology*, 30, 1–17.

Bisaha, J., & Dunne, B.J. (1979). Multiple subject and long-distance precognitive remote viewing of geographical locations. In C.T. Tart, H.E. Puthoff, & R. Targ (Eds.), *Mind at Large* (pp. 107–124). New York: Praeger.

Braud, W., Shafer, D., & Andrews, S. (1990). Electrodermal correlates of remote attention: Autonomic reactions to an unseen gaze. *Proceedings of the Parapsychological Association 33rd Annual Convention*, 14–28.

Braud, W.G. (1975). Psi-conducive states. *Journal of Communication*, 25, 142–152.

Braud, W.G., & Braud, L.W. (1973). Preliminary explorations of psi-conducive states: Progressive muscular relaxation. *Journal of the American Society for Psychical Research*, 67, 26–46.

Brown, B.B. (1970). Recognition of aspects of consciousness through association with EEG alpha activity represented by a light signal. *Psychophysiology*, 6, 442–452.

Brugmans, H.J.F.W. (1922). Une communication sur des experiences telepathiques au laboratoire de psychologie a Groningue faites par M. Heymans, Docteur Weinberg et Docteur H.I.F.W. Brugmans, *Le Compte Renda Officiel du Premier Congres Internaional des Recherches Psychiques* (pp. 396–408). (For a free translation from the French into English see G. Murphy (1961) *Challenge of psychical research*, New York: Harper.)

Carpenter, J.C. (1971). The differential effect and hidden target differences consisting of erotic and neutral stimuli. *Journal of the American Society for Psychical Research*, 65, 204–214.

Carpenter, J.C. (1977). Intrasubject and subject-agent effects in ESP experiments. In B.B. Wolman (Ed.), *Handbook of parapsychology*, New York: Van Nostrand Reinhold.

Casler, L. (1962). The improvement of clairvoyance scores by means of hypnotic suggestion. *Journal of Parapsychology*, 26, 77–87.

Casler, L. (1964). The effects of hypnosis on GESP. *Journal of Parapsychology*, 28, 126–134.

Child, I.L. (1985). Psychology and anamalous observations. The question of ESP in dreams. *American Psychologist*, 40, 1219–1230.

Coover, J. E. (1975). *Experiments in psychical research*. New York: Arno Press (first published in 1917).

Davis, J. W. (1979). Psi in animals: A review of laboratory research. *Parapsychology Review*,10, 1–9.

Dean, E.D. (1962). The Plethysmograph as an indicator of ESP. *Journal of the Society for Psychical Research*, 41, 351–353.

Devereux, G. (Ed.). (1953). *Psychoanalysis and the occult*. New York: International Universities Press.

Dixon, N.F. (1979). Subliminal perception and parapsychology: Points of contact. *Parapsychology Review*, 10 (No. 3), 1–6.

Dobyns, Y., Dunne, B., Jahn, R., & Nelson, R. (1994). Reply to Hansen, Utts, and Markwick's "Statistical and methodological problems of the PEAR remote viewing [sic] experiments." In E.W. Cook and D.L.Delanoy (Eds.), *Research in parapsychology 1991* (pp. 108–111). Metuchen, NJ: Scarecrow Press.

Dodds, E.R. (1971). Supernormal phenomena in classical antiquity. *Proceedings of the Society for Psychical Research*, 55, 189–237.

Don, N.S., McDonough, B.E., & Warren, C.A. (1998). Event-related brain potential (ERP) indicators of unconscious psi: A replication using subjects unselected for psi. *Journal of Parapsychology*, 62, 127–145.

Duval, P., & Montredon, E. (1968a). ESP experiments with mice. *Journal of Parapsychology*, 32, 153–166.

Duval, P., & Montredon, E. (1968b). Further psi experiments with mice. *Journal of Parapsychology*, 32, 260. (Abstract).

Ebbinghaus, H. (1964). *Memory*. New York: Dover. (Originally published in 1885).

Eisenbud, J. (1965). Perceptin of subliminal visual stimuli in relation to ESP. *International Journal of Parapsychology, 7,* 161–181.

Estabrooks, G. (1961). A contribution to experimental telepathy. *Journal of Parapsychology, 25,* 190–213. (Originally published in 1927).

Eysenck, H.J. (1967). Personality and extra-sensory perception. *Journal of the Society for Psychical Research, 44,* 55–71.

Fahler, J. (1957). ESP card tests with and without hypnosis. *Journal of Parapsychology, 21,* 179–185.

Feather, S.R. (1967). A quantitative comparison of memory and psi. *Journal of Parapsychology, 31,* 93–98.

Figar, S. (1959). The application of plethysmography to the objective study of so-called extrasensory perception. *Journal of the Society for Psychical Research, 40,* 162–172.

Freeman, J. A., & Nielsen, W. (1964). Precognition score deviation as related to anxiety levels. *Journal of Parapsychology, 28,* 239–249.

Freeman, J.A. (1969). Decline of variance in school precognition tests. *Journal of Parapsychology, 33,* 72–73.

Grela, J.J. (1945). Effect on ESP scoring of hypnotically induced attitudes. *Journal of Parapsychology, 9,* 194–202.

Hansel, C.E.M. (1961).A critical analysis of the Pearce-Pratt experiment: A controversy over charges of fraud in ESP. *Journal of Parapsychology, 25,* 86–91.

Hansel, C.E.M. (1966). *ESP: A scientific evaluation.* New York: Scribners.

Hansel, C.E.M. (1980). *ESP and parapsychology: A critical re-evaluation.* Buffalo, NY: Prometheus Books.

Hansel, C.E.M. (1981). A critical analysis of H. Schmidt's psychokinesis experiments. *Skeptical Inquirer, 5*(3), 26–33.

Hansel, C.E.M. (1989). *The search for psychic power: ESP & parapsychology revisited.* Buffalo, NY: Prometheus Books.

Hansen, G.P., Utts, J., & Markwick, B. (1994). Statistical and methodological problems of the PEAR remote viewing experiments. In E.W. Cook and D.L. Delanoy (Eds.), *Research in parapsychology 1991* (pp. 103–107). Metuchen, NJ: Scarecrow Press.

Haraldsson, E. (1978). ESP and the defense mechanism test (DMT): A further validation. *European Journal of Parapsychology, 2,* 104–114.

Honorton, C. (1965). The relationship between ESP and manifest anxiety level. *Journal of Parapsychology, 29,* 291–292. (Abstract).

Honorton, C. (1969). Relationship between EEG alpha activity and ESP card-guessing performance. *Journal of the American Society for Psychical Research, 63,* 365–374.

Honorton, C. (1976). Has science developed the competence to confront claims of the paranormal? In J.D. Morris, W.G. Roll, & R.L. Morris (Eds.), *Research in parapsychology, 1975* (199–223). Methuchen, NJ: Scarecrow Press.

Honorton, C. (1977). Psi and internal attention states. In B.B. Wolman (Ed.), *Handbook of parapsychology.* New York: Van Nostrand Reinhold.

Honorton, C., & Harper, S. (1974). Psi-mediated imagery and ideation in an experimental procedure for regulating perceptual input. *Journal of the American Society for Psychical Research, 68,* 156–168.

Honorton, C., Davidson, R., & Bindler, P. (1971). Feedback-augmented EEG alpha, shifts in subjective state, and ESP card-guessing performance. *Journal of the American Society for Psychical Research*, 65, 308–323.

Honorton, C., Ferrari, D.C., & Bem, D.J. (1998). Extroversion and ESP performance: A meta-analysis and new confirmation. *Journal of Parapsychology*, 62, 255–276.

Honorton, C., Ramsey, M., & Cabibbo, C. (1975). Experimenter effects in extrasensory perception. *Journal of the American Society for Psychical Research*, 69, 135–149.

Humphrey, B.M. (1946a). Success in ESP as related to form of response drawings. I. Clairvoyance experiments. *Journal of Parapsychology*, 10, 78–106.

Humphrey, B.M. (1946b). Success in ESP as related to form of response drawings. II. GESP experiments. *Journal of Parapsychology*, 10, 181–196.

Hyman, R. (1985). The ganzfeld ESP experiment: A critical appraisal. *Journal of Parapsychology*, 49, 3–49.

Hyman, R. (1986). Outracing the evidence: The muddled mind race. In K. Frazier (Ed.), *Science confronts the paranormal* (pp. 91–108). Buffalo, NY: Prometheus Books.

Hyman, R. (1994). Anomaly or artifact? Comments on Bem and Honorton. *Psychological Bulletin*, 115, 19–24.

Hyman, R. (1996). Evaluation of a program on anomalous mental phenomena. *Journal of Scientific Exploration*, 10, 31–58.

Hyman, R., & Honorton, C. (1986). A joint communiqué: The psi ganzfeld controversy. *Journal of Parapsychology*, 50, 351–364.

Inglis, B. (1977). *Natural and supernatural: A history of the paranormal from earliest times to 1914*. London: Hodder and Stoughton.

Jahn, R.G. (1982). The persistent paradox of psychic phenomena: An engineering perspective. *Proceedings of the IEEE*, 70, 136–170.

Jahn, R.G., & Dunne, B.J. (1987). *Margins of reality: The role of consciousness in the physical world*. New York: Harcourt Brace Jovanovich.

James, W. (1890). *The principles of psychology*. New York: Henry Holt & Co.

Johnson, M., & Haraldsson, E. (1984). Icelandic experiments IV and V with the defense mechanism test. *Journal of Parapsychology*, 48, 185–200.

Johnson, M., & Kanthamani, B.K. (1967). The defense mechanism test as a predictor of ESP scoring direction. *Journal of Parapsychology*, 31, 99–100.

Jung, C.G., & Pauli, W. (1955). *The interpretation of nature and the psyche: Synchronicity and the influence of archetypal ideas on the scientific theories of Kepler*. New York: Pantheon.

Kamiya, J. (1969). Operant control of the EEG alpha rhythm and some of its reported effects on consciousness. In C.T. Tart (Ed.). *Altered States of Consciousness*. New York: Wiley.

Kanthamani, B.K. (1965). A study of differential response in language ESP tests. *Journal of Parapsychology*, 29, 27–34.

Kanthamani, B.K., & Rao, H. H. (1974). A study of memory ESP relationships using linguistic forms. *Journal of Parapsychology*, 38, 286–300.

Kanthamani, B.K., & Rao, K.R. (1973a). Personality characteristics of ESP subjects: IV. Neuroticism and ESP. *Journal of Parapsychology*, 37, 37–50.

Kasamatsu, A., & Hirai, T. (1969). An electroencephalographic study of the Zen meditation (zazen). *Psychologia*, 12, 205–225.

Kennedy, J.E., & Taddonio, J.L. (1976). Experimenter effects in parapsychological research. *Journal of Parapsychology*, 40, 1–33.

Kragh, U., & Smith, G. (1970). *Percept-genetic analysis.* Lund: Gleerups.

Kramer, J.K., & Terry, R.L. (1973). GESP and personality factors: A search for correlates. *Journal of Parapsychology*, 37, 74–75. (Abstract).

Kreitler, H., & Kreitler, S. (1972). Does extrasensory perception affect psychological experiments? *Journal of Parapsychology*, 36, 1–45.

Kreitler, H., & Kreitler, S. (1973). Subliminal perception and extrasensory perception. *Journal of Parapsychology*, 37,163–188.

Kreitler, H., & Kreitler, S. (1974a). ESP and cognition. *Journal of Parapsychology*, 38, 267–285.

Kreitler, H., & Kreitler, S. (1974b). Optimization of experimental ESP results. *Journal of Parapsychology*, 38, 383–392.

Krippner, S. (1969). Investigations of extrasensory phenomena in dreams and other altered states of consciousness. *Journal of the American Society of Psychosomatic Dentistry and Medicine*, 16, 7–14.

Krippner, S., Honorton, C., & Ullman, M. (1972). A second precognitive dream study with Malcolm Bessent. *Journal of the American Society for Psychical Research*, 66, 269–279.

Krippner, S., Honorton, C., & Ullman, M. (1973). A long-distance ESP dream study with "Grateful Dead." *Journal of the American Society for Psychosomatic Dentistry and Medicine*, 20, 9–17.

Krippner, S., Honorton, C., Ullman, M., Masters, R., & Houston, J. (1971). A long distance "sensory bombardment" study of ESP in dreams. *Journal of the American Society for Psychical Research*, 65, 468–475.

Krishna, S.R., & Rao, K.R. (1991). Effect of ESP feedback on subjects' responses to a personality questionnaire. *Journal of Parapsychology*, 55, 147–158.

Lantz, N.D., Luke, W.L., & May, E.C. (1994). Target and sender dependencies in anomalous cognition experiments. *Journal of Parapsychology*, 58, 285–302.

Lawrence, T. (1993). Gathering in the sheep and goats: A meta-analysis of forced-choice sheep-goat ESP studies, 1947–1993. *Proceedings of the Parapsychological Association 36th Annual Convention* (pp. 75–86).

Lovitts, B. (1981). The sheep-goat effect turned upside down. *Journal of Parapsychology*, 45, 293–310.

Lubke, C., & Rohr, W. (1975). Psi and subliminal perception: A replication of the Kreitler and Kreitler study. In J.D. Morris, W.G. Roll, & R.L. Morris (Eds.), *Research in parapsychology 1974* (161–164). Metuchen, NJ: Scarecrow Press.

Mackenzie, B. (1977). Three stages in the history of parapsychology. Paper presented at the Quadrennial Congress on History of Science, Edinburgh, Scotland.

Marks, D.F. & Kammann, R. (1978). Information transmission in remote viewing experiments. *Nature*, 274, 680–681.

Marks, D.F. & Kammann, R. (1980). *The psychology of the psychic.* Buffalo, NY: Prometheus Books.

Marks, D.F. (1986). Remote viewing revisited. In K. Frazier (Ed.), *Science confronts the paranormal* (pp. 110–121). Buffalo, NY: Prometheus Books.

Marks, D.F., & Scott, C. (1986). Remote viewing exposed. *Nature*, 319, 444.

May, E.C. (1998). Response to "Experiment one of the SAIC remote viewing program: A critical re-evaluation." *Journal of Parapsychology*, 62, 309–318.

McMahan, E. (1946). Success in ESP as related to form of response drawings. II. GESP experiments. *Journal of Parapsychology*, 10, 169–180.

McVaugh, M.R., & Mauskopf, S.H. (1976). J.B.Rhine's extra-sensory perception and its background in psychical research. *Isis*, 67, 161–189.

Milton, J., and Wiseman, R. (1999). Does psi exist? Lack of replication of an anomalous process of information transfer. *Psychological Bulletin*, 125, 387–391.

Miller, N.E., Barber, T.X., Dicara, L.V., Kamiya, J., Shapiro, D., & Stoyva, J. (Eds.). (1974). *Biofeedback and self-control 1973: An Aldine annual on the regulation of bodily processes and consciousness.* Chicago: Aldine.

Morris, R.L. (1970). Psi and animal behavior: A survey. *Journal of the Society for Psychical Research*, 64, 242–260.

Morris, R.L., Roll, W.G., Klein, J., & Wheeler, G. (1972). EEG patterns and ESP results in forced-choice experiments with Lalsingh Harribance. *Journal of the American Society for Psychical Research*, 66, 253– 268.

Myers, F.W.H. (1915). *Human personality and its survival of death* (2 vols.). New York: Longmans, Green & Co. (Original work published 1903).

Nelson, R.D., & Radin, D.I. (1989). Statistically robust anomalous effects: Replication in random event generator experiments. In L.A. Henkel and R.E. Berger (Eds.), *Research in parapsychology 1988* (23–27). Metuchen, NJ: Scarecrow Press.

Nelson, R.D., Dunne, B.J., & Jahn, R.G. (1984). *An REG experiment with large data base capability. 3: Operator related anomalies.* (Technical Note PEAR 83002). School of Engineering/ Applied Science, Princeton University.

Osis, K. (1952). A test of the occurrence of a psi effect between man and the cat. *Journal of Parapsychology*, 16, 233–256.

Osis, K., & Bokert, E. (1971). ESP and changed states of consciousness induced by meditation. *Journal of the American Society for Psychical Research*, 65, 17–65.

Osis, K., & Dean, D. (1964). The effect of experimenter differences and subject's belief level upon ESP scores. *Journal of the American Society for Psychical Research*, 58, 158–185.

Osis, K., & Foster, E.B. (1953). A test of ESP in cats. *Journal of Parapsychology*, 17, 168–186.

Otani, S. (1965). Some relations of ESP scores to change in skin resistance. In *Parapsychology: From Duke to FRNM.* Durham, NC: Parapsychology Press.

Palmer, J. (1971). Scoring in ESP tests as a function of belief in ESP. Part I: The sheep-goal effect. *Journal of the American Society for Psychical Research*, 65, 373–408.

Palmer, J. (1972). Scoring in ESP tests as a function of belief in ESP. Part II. Beyond the Sheep-goat effect. *Journal of the American Society for Psychical Research*, 66, 1–26.

Palmer, J. (1978). Extrasensory perception: Research findings. In S. Krippner (Ed.), *Advances in Parapsychological Research II: Extrasensory Perception.* New York: Plenum Press.

Palmer, J. (1979). A community mail survey of psychic experiences. *Journal of the American Society for Psychical Research*, 73, 221–251.

Palmer, J., & Carpenter, J.C. (1998). Comments on the extroversion-ESP meta-analysis by Honorton, Ferrari and Bem. *Journal of Parapsychology*, 62, 277–282

Parapsychological Association (1989). Terms and methods in parapsychological research. *Journal of Humanistic Psychology*, 29, 394–399.

Pekala, R.J., Kumar, V.K., & Marcano, G. (1995). Anomalous/paranormal experiences, hypnotic susceptibility, and dissociation. *Journal of the American Society for Psychical Research*, 89, 313–332.

Persinger, M.A. (1985). Subjective telepathic experiences, geomagnetic activity and the ELF hypothesis: Part II. Stimulus features and neural detection. *Psi Research*, 4(2), 4–23.

Persinger, M.A. (1989). Psi phenomena and temporal lobe activity: The geomagnetic factor. In L.A. Henkel & R.E. Berger (Eds.), *Research in parapsychology 1988* (pp. 121–156). Metuchen, NJ: Scarecrow Press.

Persinger, M.A. & Krippner, S. (1989). Dream ESP experiments and geomagnetic activity. *Journal of the American Society for Psychical Research*, 83, 101–116.

Peterson, D.M. (1978). *Through the looking glass: An investigation of the faculty of extra-sensory detection of being stared at.* Unpublished master's thesis, University of Edinburgh.

Podmore, F. (1894). *Apparitions and thought-transference.* London: Scott.

Polanyi, M. (1958). *Personal knowledge.* Chicago: University of Chicago Press.

Poortman, J.J. (1959). The feeling of being started at. *Journal of the Society for Psychical Research*, 40, 4–12.

Pratt, J.G., & Price, M.M. (1938). The experimenter-subject relationship in tests for ESP. *Journal of Parapsychology*, 2, 84–94.

Pratt, J.G., Rhine, J.B., Smith, B.M., Stuart, C.E., & Greenwood, J.A. (1966). *Extrasensory Perception After Sixty Years.* Boston: Bruce Humphries (originally published in 1940

Puthoff, H.E., & Targ, R. (1976). A perceptual channel for information transfer over kilometer distances: Historical perspective and recent research. *Proceedings of the IEEE*, 64(3), 329–354.

Radin, D.I., May, E.C., & Thomas, M.J. (1986) Psi experiments with random number generators: Meta-analysis, Part-I. In D.H. Weiner & D.I Radin (Eds.), *Research in parapsychology 1985* (pp. 14–17), Methuchen, NJ: Scarecrow Press.

Rao, K.R. (1962). The preferential effect in ESP. *Journal of Parapsychology*, 26, 252–259.

Rao, K.R. (1963a). Studies in the preferential effect I: Target preference with types of targets unknown. *Journal of Parapsychology*, 27, 23–32.

Rao, K.R. (1963b). Studies in the preferential effect II: A language ESP test involving precognition and "intervention." *Journal of Parapsychology*, 27, 147–160.

Rao, K.R. (1963c). Studies in the preferential effect III: The reversal effect in psi preference. *Journal of Parapsychology*, 27, 242–251.

Rao, K.R. (1964a). The differential response in three new situations. *Journal of Parapsychology*, 28, 82–92.

Rao, K.R. (1965a). ESP and the Manifest Anxiety Scale. *Journal of Parapsychology*, 29, 12–18.

Rao, K.R. (1965b). The bidirectionality of psi. *Journal of Parapsychology*, 29, 230–250.

Rao, K.R. (1981). Correspondence. *Journal of the Society for Psychical Research*, 51, 191–194.

Rao, K.R. (1982). J.B. Rhine and his critics. In K.R. Rao (Ed.), *J.B. Rhine: On the frontiers of science* (192–212). Jefferson, NC: McFarland & Co.

Rao, K.R. (1992). On the other hand: The two sides of the psi debate. *Contemporary Psychology*, 37, 1106–1108.

Rao, K.R., Morrison, M., Davis, J.W., & Freeman, J. (1977). The role of association in memory-recall and ESP. *Journal of Parapsychology*, 41, 190–197.

Rao, K.R., & Feola, J. (1979). Electrical activity of the brain and ESP: An exploratory study of alpha rhythm and ESP scoring. *Journal of Indian Psychology*, 1979, 2, 118–133.

Rao, K.R., & Palmer, J. (1987). The anomaly called psi: Recent research and criticism. *Behavioral and Brain Sciences*, 10, 539–555.

Rao, K.R., & Puri, I. (1978). Subsensory perception (SSP), extrasensory perception (ESP) and transcendental meditation, *Journal of Indian Psychology*, 1, 69–74.

Rao, K.R., Dukhan, H., & Rao, P.V.K. (1978). Yogic meditation and psi scoring in forced-choice and free-response tests. *Journal of Indian Psychology*, 1, 160–175.

Rao, P.V.K., & Rao, K.R. (1982). Two studies of ESP and subliminal perception, *Journal of Parapsychology*, 46, 185–207.

Rhine, J.B. (1936). Some selected experiments in extrasensory perception. *Journal of Abnormal and Social Psychology*, 31, 216–228.

Rhine, J.B. (1938). Experiments bearing on the precognition hypothesis. *Journal of Parapsychology*, 2, 38–54.

Rhine, J.B. (1952). The problem of psi-missing. *Journal of Parapsychology*, 16, 90–129.

Rhine, J.B. (1969). Psi-missing re-examined. *Journal of Parapsychology*, 33, 1–38.

Rhine, J.B. (1973/1934). *Extra-sensory perception*. Brookline Village, Mass.: Branden Press. (Originally published in 1934).

Rhine, J.B. (1974). A new case of experimenter unreliability. *Journal of Parapsychology*, 38, 215–225.

Rhine, J.B. (1977). Extrasensory perception. In B.B. Wolman (Ed), *Handbook of parapsychology*. New York: Van Nostrand Reinhold.

Rhine, J.B., & Feather, S.R. (1957). The study of psi-trailing in animals. *Journal of Parapsychology*, 21, 245–258.

Rhine, J.B., & Pratt, J.G. (1954). A review of the Pearce-Pratt distance series of ESP tests. *Journal of Parapsychology*, 18, 165–177.

Rhine, J.B., & Pratt, J.G. (1961). A reply to the Hansel critique of the Pearce-Pratt series. *Journal of Parapsychology*, 25, 92–98.

Rhine, L.E. (1962). Psychological processing in ESP experiences. Part II. Dreams. *Journal of Parapsychology*, 26, 172–199.

Rhine, L.E. (1965). Toward understanding psi-missing. *Journal of Parapsychology*, 29, 259–274.

Rhine, L.E. (1967). *ESP in life and lab: Tracing hidden channels*. New York: Macmillan.

Richet, C. (1975). *Thirty years of psychical research*. New York: Arno Press, (originally published in 1923).

Rosenthal, R. (1966). *Experimenter effects in behavioral research*. New York: Appleton-Century-Crofts.

Rosenthal, R., & Rubin, D.B. (1978). Interpersonal expectancy effects: The first 345 studies. *Behavioral and Brain Sciences*, 3, 377–386.

Ryzl, M. (1962). Training the psi faculty by hypnosis. *Journal of the Society for Psychical Research*, 41, 234–252.

Ryzl, M., & Ryzlova, J. (1962). A case of high-scoring ESP performance in the hypnotic state. *Journal of Parapsychology*, 26, 153–171.

Sailaja, P., & Rao, K.R. (1973). *Experimental studies of the differential effect in life setting*. (Parapsychological Monographs No.13). New York: Parapsychology Foundation.

Sanders, M.S. (1962). A comparison of verbal and written responses in a precognition experiment. *Journal of Parapsychology*, 26, 23–24.

Sargent, C.L. (1981). Extraversion and performance in "extra-sensory perception" tasks. *Personality and Individual Differences*, 2, 137–143.

Schechter, E.I. (1984). Hypnotic induction vs. control conditions. Illustrating an approach to the evaluation of replicability in parapsychological data. *Journal of the American Society for Psychical Research*, 78, 1–27.

Schlitz, M.J., & LaBerge, S. (1997). Covert observation increases skin conductance in subjects unaware of when they are being observed: A replication. *Journal of Parapsychology*, 61, 185–196.

Schmeidler, G.R. (1970). High ESP scores after a swami's brief instruction in meditation and breathing. *Journal of the Society for Psychical Research*, 64, 100–103.

Schmeidler, G.R. (1971). Respice, adspice, prospice. *Proceedings of the Parapsychological Association*, 8, 117–143.

Schmeidler, G.R., & McConnell, R.A. (1958). *ESP and personality patterns*. New Haven, CN: Yale University Press.

Schmidt, H. (1973). PK tests with a high-speed random number generator. *Journal of Parapsychology*, 37, 105–118.

Schmidt, H., Morris, R.L., & Rudolph, L. (1986). Channeling evidence for PK effects to independent observers. *Journal of Parapsychology*, 50, 1–16.

Schouten, S. (1972). Psi in mice: Positive reinforcement. *Journal of Parapsychology*, 36, 261–282.

Sharp, V. & Clark, C.C. (1937). Group tests for extrasensory perception. *Journal of Parapsychology*, 1, 123–142.

Sheldrake, R. (1994). *Seven experiments that could change the world*. London: Fourth Estate.

Sidgwick, H., Sidgwick, E.M., & Smith, G.A. (1889). Experiments in thought transference. *Proceedings of the Society for Psychical Research*, 6, 128–170.

Sinclair, U. (1930). *Mental Radio*. Monrovia, CA: Sinclair.

Smith, W.R., et al. (1963). *Testing for extrasensory perception with a machine*. Bedford: Air Force Cambridge Research Laboratories.

Stanford, R.G. (1970). Extrasensory effects upon "memory." *Journal of the American Society for Psychical Research*, 64, 161–186.

Stanford, R.G. (1971). EEG alpha activity and ESP performance: A replicative study. *Journal of the American Society for Psychical Research*, 65, 144–154.

Stanford, R.G. (1973). Extrasensory effects upon associative processes in a directed free-response task. *Journal of the American Society for Psychical Research*, 67, 147–190.

Stanford, R.G. (1974). An experimentally testable model for spontaneous psi events. I Extrasensory events. *Journal of the American Society for Psychical Research*, 68, 34–57

Stanford, R.G. (1977). Experimental psychokinesis: A review from diverse perspectives. In B.B. Wolman (Ed.), *Handbook of parapsychology* (pp. 324–381). New York: Van Nostrand Reinhold.

Stanford, R.G., & Mayer, B. (1974). Relaxation as a psi-conducive state: A replication and exploration of parameters. *Journal of the American Society for Psychical Research*, 68, 182–191.

Stanford, R.G., & Palmer, J. (1973). Meditation prior to the ESP task: An EEG study with an outstanding ESP subject. In W.G. Roll, R.L. Morris, and J.D. Morris (Eds.), *Research in parapsychology 1972*, Methuchen, NJ: Scarecrow Press.

Stanford, R.G., & Stanford, B.E. (1969). Shifts in EEG alpha rhythm as related to calling patterns and ESP run-score variance. *Journal of Parapsychology*, 33, 39–47.

Stanford, R.G., & Stein, A.G. (1994). A meta-analysis of ESP studies contrasting hypnosis and a comparison condition. *Journal of Parapsychology*, 58, 235–269.

Stanford, R.G., & Stevenson, I. (1972). EEG correlates of free-response GESP in an individual subject. *Journal of the American Society for Psychical Research*, 66, 357–368.

Steinkamp, F., Milton, J., & Morris, R.L. (1998). A meta-analysis of forced-choice experiments comparing clairvoyance and precognition. *Journal of Parapsychology*, 62, 193–218.

Stevenson, I. (1967). An antagonist's view of parapsychology. A review of Professor Hansel's "ESP: A scientific evaluation." *Journal of the American Society for Psychical Research*, 61, 254–267.

Stokes, D.M. (1998). Book Review: K. Frazier (Ed.). *Encounters with the paranormal: Science, knowledge and belief. Journal of Parapsychology*, 62, 158–170.

Stuart, C.E. (1946). An interest inventory relation to ESP scores. *Journal of Parapsychology*, 10, 154–161.

Targ, R., & Puthoff, H.E. (1977). *Mind reach*. New York: Delacorte Press/ Eleanor Friede.

Tart, C.T., Puthoff, H.E., & Targ, R. (1980). Information transmission in remote viewing experiments. *Nature*, 204, 191.

Tenny, K. (1962). Physiological responses during an ESP test. Abstract. *Journal of Parapsychology*, 13, 138.

Toddonio, J.L. (1976). The relationship of experimenter expectancy to performance on ESP tasks. *Journal of Parapsychology*, 40, 107–115.

Troland, L.T. (1976). A technique for the experimental study of telepathy and other alleged clairvoyant processes. *Journal of Parapsychology*, 40, 194–216. (Original work published 1917).

Ullman, M., & Krippner, S. (1970). *Dream studies and telepathy: An experimental approach.* (Parapsychological Monographs No.12). New York: Parapsychology Foundation.

Ullman, M., Krippner, S., & Feldstein, S. (1966). Experimentally induced telepathic dreams: Two studies using EEG-REM monitoring techniques. *International Journal of Neuropsychiatry*, 2, 420–437.

Ullman, M., Krippner, S., & Vaughan, A. (1973). *Dream telepathy.* New York: Macmillan.

Underwood, B. (1969). Attributes of memory. *Psychological Review*, 76, 559–573.

Van de Castle, R. (1977). Sleep and dreams. In B.B. Wolman (Ed.), *Handbook of parapsychology* (pp. 473–499). New York: Van Nostrand Reinhold.

Vasiliev, L.L. (1963). *Experiments in mental suggestion*. Church Crookham: Institute for the Study of Mental Images.

Warren, C.A., McDonough, B.E., & Don, N.S.(1992a). Event-related brain potential changes in a psi task. *Journal of Parapsychology*, 56, 1–30.

Warren, C.A., McDonough, B.E., & Don, N.S. (1992b). Partial replication of single subject event-related potential effects in a psi task. *Proceedings of the Parapsychological Association 35th Annual Convention*, 169–181.

West, D.J., & Fisk, G.W. (1953). A dual ESP experiment with clock cards. *Journal of the Society for Psychical Research*, 37, 185–197.

White, R.A. (1964). A comparison of old and new methods of response to targets in ESP experiments. *Journal of the American Society for Psychical Research* 58, 21–56.

White, R.A. (1976). The limits of experimenter influence on psi test results: Can any be set? *Journal of the American Society for Psychical Research*, 70, 333–369.

White, R.A. (1977). The influence of experimenter motivation, attitudes, and methods of handling subjects in psi test results. In B.B. Wolman (Ed.), *Handbook of parapsychology* (pp. 273–301). New York: Van Nostrand Reinhold.

Wiseman, R., & Milton, J. (1998). Experiment one of the SAIC remote viewing program: A critical re-evaluation. *Journal of Parapsychology*, 62, 297–308.

Wiseman, R., & Smith, M.D. (1994). A further look at the detection of unseen gaze. *Proceedings of the Parapsychological Association 37th Annual convention*, 480–492.

Wiseman, R., Smith, M.D., Freedman, D., & Hurst, C. (1995). Two further experiments concerning the remote detection of an unseen gaze. *Proceedings of the Parapsychological Association 38th Annual Convention*, 480–492.

Woods, J.H. (1927). *The Yoga system of Patanjali*. Cambridge: Harvard University Press.

Index